A Journey Through Economics

Detlef Pietsch

A Journey Through Economics

On Prosperity, Digitalization, and Justice

Detlef Pietsch
München, Germany

ISBN 978-3-658-47092-0   ISBN 978-3-658-47093-7   (eBook)
https://doi.org/10.1007/978-3-658-47093-7

Translation from the German language edition: "Eine Reise durch die Ökonomie" by Detlef Pietsch, © Springer Fachmedien Wiesbaden GmbH, ein Teil von Springer Nature 2022. Published by Springer Fachmedien Wiesbaden. All Rights Reserved.

This book is a translation of the original German edition "Eine Reise durch die Ökonomie," 2nd edition, by Detlef Pietsch, published by Springer Fachmedien Wiesbaden GmbH in 2022. The translation was done with the help of an artificial intelligence machine translation tool. A subsequent human revision was done primarily in terms of content, so that the book will read stylistically differently from a conventional translation. Springer Nature works continuously to further the development of tools for the production of books and on the related technologies to support the authors.

© The Editor(s) (if applicable) and The Author(s), under exclusive license to Springer Fachmedien Wiesbaden GmbH, part of Springer Nature 2025

This work is subject to copyright. All rights are solely and exclusively licensed by the Publisher, whether the whole or part of the material is concerned, specifically the rights of translation, reprinting, reuse of illustrations, recitation, broadcasting, reproduction on microfilms or in any other physical way, and transmission or information storage and retrieval, electronic adaptation, computer software, or by similar or dissimilar methodology now known or hereafter developed.

The use of general descriptive names, registered names, trademarks, service marks, etc. in this publication does not imply, even in the absence of a specific statement, that such names are exempt from the relevant protective laws and regulations and therefore free for general use.

The publisher, the authors and the editors are safe to assume that the advice and information in this book are believed to be true and accurate at the date of publication. Neither the publisher nor the authors or the editors give a warranty, expressed or implied, with respect to the material contained herein or for any errors or omissions that may have been made. The publisher remains neutral with regard to jurisdictional claims in published maps and institutional affiliations.

Cover picture: How to stop time passing? by panjj (stock.adobe.com)

This Springer imprint is published by the registered company Springer Fachmedien Wiesbaden GmbH, part of Springer Nature.
The registered company address is: Abraham-Lincoln-Str. 46, 65189 Wiesbaden, Germany

If disposing of this product, please recycle the paper.

Dedicated to my son Alexander and all those interested in economics

Preface to the Second Edition

Since the release of the first edition at the end of 2019, the world has dramatically changed. At the beginning of 2020, a global pandemic developed, reaching an unprecedented scale in its consequences and intrusions into human life. Hundreds of millions of people worldwide have fallen ill with the Covid-19 virus, with several million also dying from it. The pandemic has brought infinite suffering to the world's population, not to mention the economic consequences. Entire industries, such as the tourism, aviation, or trade fair sectors, were on the brink of extinction in the short term. Others, like the restaurant industry or the hotel business, were sustainably threatened in their existence. The same applied to culture, sports, many retail stores, and companies worldwide. The pandemic had temporarily brought the economy almost to a standstill. People were also temporarily not allowed to meet, children were taught from home, and hospital and nursing staff worked to the edge of their physical and psychological abilities. Social isolation, mental depression, and exhaustion spread worldwide. People are already talking about a "Corona Generation". The images of the numerous infected people who had to be ventilated in intensive care units and were struggling with death will not be forgotten. Every day, we were shaken by new reports of the number of new infections and deaths. New Corona variants continuously clouded the daily news picture.

As if that wasn't bad enough, the flood disaster of summer 2021 was added, which took away the homes and possessions of thousands of people in parts of Germany, and despite the immediate relief efforts by volunteers, left countless desperate people behind. By now, it is clear to everyone that climate change has struck with force and is leaving its mark. While the past years of the Corona pandemic with their dramatic events will go down in history books, the year 2022 seems to be a veritable *annus horribilis,* a year of horror: War has reached the world again. More than 76 years after the last world war, Ukraine, a free and independent state, was attacked by Russian forces and forced into a war. The international community is resisting not only with extensive aid deliveries to Ukraine, but also with arms deliveries and severe economic sanctions. Economic measures are being used as legitimate weapons of defense and are also intended to help the suffering Ukrainian population in the form of donations. All three disasters, the Corona pandemic, the flood, and the war in Ukraine, made it necessary to add another subchapter in this second edition. For understandable reasons, it is called: *Economics in Uncertain Times*. In this, I have tried to trace the essential developments of the past months mainly from an economic perspective and thus bring the "journey through economics" up to date. How the dramatic events surrounding the war in Ukraine and the pandemic will continue, we will all follow with great concern and sympathy.

I would also like to express my sincere thanks to Dr. Isabella Hanser and her team at Springer Verlag for their, as always, very professional and valuable collaboration in the context of this second edition. Furthermore, my personal thanks, as always, go to my family.

Munich
in the spring of 2022

Detlef Pietsch

Preface

I want to take you on a journey. A journey through the economy of yesterday, today, and tomorrow. Do you also feel that you dare not pick up a specialist book on economic topics? A lot of technical jargon, often too difficult and from the perspective of an interested layperson, usually very hard to understand. What a pity! After all, economics as the science of business is one of the most exciting topics in the world. I have thought about how I could explain the economy to my son, who is 19 years old and not too long ago completed his high school diploma, and make the subject "tasty" to him. He is studying business administration. So I thought, I'll try to take him on a journey through the exciting world of business.

I would like to invite you, dear reader, to join us on this journey. In doing so, I deliberately choose the path "via the back stairs" (cf. Weischedel, 2005): A path that does not go through the main entrance over the arduous path of the complex theoretical edifices of economics, but rather presents the essential core thoughts and ideas of the greatest economic thinkers of all time and aims to entertain its readers. Although this path is less glamorous than the path through the main entrance, it nevertheless leads to its goal, to explore the lofty heights of economic thinking and to divide the journey into manageable steps and stair levels.

You are probably wondering how I dare to presume to explain the economy to my son and you. Primarily, I do not want to explain it, but rather take a look at the economy together with you, identify its core issues, and think together about how the economy can continue to develop in the right direction. A brief introduction to myself: I studied business administration at the University of Mannheim over 30 years ago and subsequently received my doctorate in this field. Afterwards, I worked in various management positions in a large international company, where I am still active. So, after studying economic theory for many years, I was able to apply it in practice for over 25 years and closely follow economic development.

I have noticed that critical voices about the economy have increasingly grown (among others Küng, 2010). The system of capitalism is under heavy fire and suspected of going off course and exacerbating economic injustice and inequality (see Atkinson, 2015; Piketty, 2014). Numerous are the debates about the high salaries of, for example, hedge fund managers amidst increasing unemployment in parts of the world and the accompanying old-age poverty. The pursuit of happiness seems to have been largely replaced by the pursuit of wealth. But was the wealth of a few ever the original goal of the economy?

I do not wish to lecture in this book. I too have not found the philosopher's stone. I cannot and do not wish to inundate you, dear reader, with theories and interpretations, but rather invite you to take exciting steps into the realm of economics. Together, we want to discuss pressing issues of today's economy such as justice, the goal of "prosperity for all" (Erhard, 1964), which Ludwig Erhard issued in the young Federal Republic, and try to sketch possible solutions. Perhaps we can manage to design an economy that "creates value". An economy that allows everyone a decent and self-determined life, that keeps inequalities within narrow limits and that provides the "greatest happiness for the greatest number of people", as the English philosopher Jeremy Bentham (Bentham, 1776, p. 393) put it. What the best goal of the economy is, we will develop together in the course of reading this book. The path from the first "real" economist, the moral philosopher Adam Smith, who was mainly concerned with how nations can achieve prosperity (Smith, 2009), was very long and rocky. Today, the question is rather how prosperity can reach everyone in times of digitization and globalization. It's about the question of justice. Therefore, I have given our journey through economic history the subtitle "About Prosperity, Digitization and Justice". Three terms that reflect the economic issues of yesterday, today and tomorrow like no other.

The book is primarily aimed at all those interested in economics and does not require any prior knowledge. Those who wish to engage more deeply with the theoretical questions of economic science or understand the connection between economics and other areas of human life, I refer to the relevant textbooks and recommend reading my more recent work "Limits of Economic Thinking—where does the human being stand in economics?" (Pietsch, 2017). I now invite you to join our shared journey through the history of economic ideas (Part I) and to a subsequent discussion about the pressing issues of the present and future (Part II) and wish you much enjoyment in reading.

Munich, Germany　　　　　　　　　　　　　　　Detlef Pietsch

Contents

Part I A Journey Through the History
of Economics

1 **Stone Age, Antiquity, and Pre-Classical Era**   3
    1.1   Stone Age   3
    1.2   Ancient Times   8
    1.3   Middle Ages   19
    1.4   Preclassical   27
    References   35

2 **Classical Era**   39
    2.1   Adam Smith   39
    2.2   The Classics   68
    2.3   Karl Marx   92
    References   120

xvi Contents

3 Neoclassical and Recent Past — 125
- 3.1 The Neoclassicists — 125
- 3.2 The Austrian School — 144
- 3.3 Thorstein Veblen — 161
- 3.4 John Maynard Keynes — 167
- 3.5 Milton Friedman — 190
- 3.6 The Ordoliberals — 207
- References — 227

4 Present — 233
- 4.1 The Ethicists — 236
- 4.2 The Behavioral Economists — 246
- References — 254

Part II Current and Future Challenges of the Economy

5 The Quintessence of Economic Thinking — 259
- 5.1 Essential Ideas of Economics — 259
- 5.2 The Logic of Economic Research — 273
- 5.3 Contributions From Other Disciplines — 276
- 5.4 Mathematics in Economic Theory — 281
- 5.5 Limits of Economic Theory — 285
- References — 297

6 The Most Pressing Issues of Tomorrow's Economy — 301
- 6.1 Justice — 301
- 6.2 Capitalism as a Model on the Way Out? — 311
- 6.3 Economy and Ethics — 316
- 6.4 Limits of Growth — 334
- 6.5 Globalization and Digitization — 341
- 6.6 Economy and Ecology — 351

6.7	The Working Society of Tomorrow	357
6.8	The Economy of the Good Life	361
6.9	Outlook: Economy in Uncertain Times	372
References		394

Acknowledgements 403

References 405

Part I

A Journey Through the History of Economics

In Part I of this book, we want to delve deeply into the history of economics. In doing so, we go far back into the Stone Age (Chap. I. 1.1), we will encounter both the ancient Greeks Plato and Aristotle (Chap. I. 1.2), the most educated people of their time, as well as thinkers of the Middle Ages like Thomas Aquinas (Chap. I. 1.3) or pre-classical thinkers like Jean-Baptiste Colbert and François Quesnay (Chap. I. 1.4). When thinking about the history of economic ideas, one cannot avoid the classics of this subject, foremost among them the moral philosopher and first modern economist Adam Smith (Chap. I. 2.1). The classics of economic theory expanded Smith's ideas (Chap. I. 2.2): David Ricardo extended the horizon in foreign trade theory, among other things, with his principle of comparative cost advantages; Jean-Baptiste Say focused on market supply and claimed, "every supply creates its demand" (cf. Stehle 2014). Socialist thinkers like Karl Marx (Chap. I. 2.3) focused on the increasing class difference between rich and poor, between owners ("capitalists") and poor wage earners ("proletarians") and their life and work at the subsistence level.

While the neoclassicists (Chap. I. 3.1) forced the introduction of mathematics into optimization considerations and prepared the ground for the formalization of economics, the "Austrian School" (Chap. I. 3.2), formed by renowned economists, propagated the advantages of the free market economy and a restraint of the state in economics (Chap. I. 3.3 via Thorstein Veblen). This was taken up again by the monetarist Milton Friedman (Chap. I. 3.5), who was a radical advocate of the free, almost state-uninfluenced market economy. The most influential economist of the 20th century, the Englishman John Maynard Keynes (Chap. I. 3.4), was primarily concerned with how to avoid a future global economic crisis (after the one just experienced). The ordoliberals (Chap. I. 3.6) in Germany, especially after the Second World War, tried to combine the best of two worlds: The state should only set the framework and otherwise let the economy develop freely. Recent developments in the history of economic ideas show an increased focus on different topics: Joseph Stiglitz, among others, denounces the misdevelopments of globalization and growing inequality. Amartya Sen advocates for a more humane economy (Chap. I. 4.1), Daniel Kahneman and Richard Thaler (Chap. I. 4.2) finally introduce the idea of a more realistic human image with behavioral economics, supplemented by psychological components.

1

Stone Age, Antiquity, and Pre-Classical Era

1.1 Stone Age

I deliberately do not want to start here with textbook formulas such as "scarcity" or "optimization" or the economic principle. On the contrary, I would like to invite you to penetrate the essence of economics with me through simple questions. Where does man's preoccupation with economics come from? What constitutes economics? Why do we need economics? As in many topics of life, the backgrounds of economics are revealed by looking into history. Let's go back many, many years in human history, to be precise, about 600,000 years: to the Old Stone Age. The beginnings of humanity as we know it today go back to about 500,000 BC. After a long pre-ice age, human life could develop in a period of warmth due to climatic changes—a so-called interglacial period. In the period of the first of these interglacial periods around 500,000 BC, remains of the "Heidelberg Man", Homo heidelbergensis, were found in Europe (cf. Bick, 2012; Bortis n.d.; Kaier, 1974, p. 2 ff.).

How did people live together back then? First, the people of the Old Stone Age learned to handle fire and were relatively early able to produce tools such as the hand axe. They lived together in small, village-like communities and were primarily hunters and gatherers. The caught fish or the hunted game, as well as the collected berries and fruits, were gathered together and shared in the village community. The tools were made from raw materials such as stones from the immediate surroundings. The production of the tools was carried out in the group. The community provided for itself: food, clothing, and other goods of daily need of the group were produced by the community for its own use.

As a result, there was neither the necessity nor the desire for an exchange of goods. As a group of self-sufficient people, each community was content with what nature offered around them. The hunting of elephants, bears, giant deer, etc. was mainly reserved for the naturally stronger and faster men, while the women were more gatherers of plants, fruits, and berries and supervised the children. Thus, each member of the community had certain tasks to perform and contributed to the survival of the community according to their abilities. This led to the still important division of labor in a then predominant family economic unit.

This changed with the warmer climate of the Middle Stone Age between 10,000 and about 2,500 BC. The glaciers slowly melted, the cold-loving animals followed the ice limit to the north, and the people followed these animals. Large lakes were formed from the meltwater, which offered the people rich food through their fish stocks. With the onset of warmth, the forests grew. The people of the Middle Stone Age increasingly began not only to harvest plant tubers but also to plant them specifically and to store larger reserves for the winter. At that time, they laid the foundations for agriculture. They domesticated wild animals such as wild boars and wolves and invented pottery. They used hollowed-out dugout canoes as a boat and constructed axes from flint splinters, which they attached to a handle. They also bred sheep, goats, cattle, and horses. At the end of the Middle Stone Age around 2,500 BC, people became sedentary.

In the New Stone Age from about 2,500 to 1,500 BC, people had already evolved from the former hunters and gatherers to shepherds and farmers, who built fortified settlements and stable house facilities with increasing skill, replacing the light dwellings of the hunters and gatherers. Cultivated grain was harvested and stored. Wild plant species were cultivated and animals were kept, grain and legumes were grown and harvested on fields and farmland. The keeping and breeding of domestic animals built up a meat reserve, and hunting lost its importance. As tasks such as cultivation, harvest, animal husbandry, and the construction of house facilities brought an ever-increasing number of specialized activities, the division of labor among people in the community became more pronounced. Each member focused on what they could do best. Products not used by themselves were exchanged. For example, a talented toolmaker focused on the production of tools and exchanged them for the food needed by him and his family. New functions of the Stone Age economy required new devices and tools: In the New Stone Age, the spindle and loom were invented, hoe and later plow and wagon wheel facilitated cultivation on larger areas and the transport of goods.

As the people of the Neolithic period began to accumulate or breed more and more supplies and store them in fireproof clay vessels, the surplus was exchanged for other objects and food, eventually even domestic animals such as sheep and goats. This led to a barter economy, the core idea of which was to eliminate scarcity and deficiencies of certain goods. The prerequisite for bartering was the fact that the person willing to barter finds a partner who has a surplus of a good and can spare it and in return can exchange his need for the abundant good of the other. Thus, the owner of several cattle can exchange part of his possessions for tools or seeds for growing grain. The essential point was now reached at the end of the Neolithic period: Man produced more than he himself needed, stored in reserve, and exchanged for other goods of his individual needs. Thus, the barter economy *goods for goods* emerged with pronounced specialization of the people of a sedentary community.

After the Neolithic period, a new era was ushered in by metal processing: the Iron and Bronze Age. Coming from the Middle East, bronze casting became known in Europe around 1800 BC. Metal extraction was promoted by the invention of the furnace. The craft industry further specialized, new professions in metal processing were added, and the division of labor in the economy grew. The increasing specialization of professions and activities in a community intensified cooperation and exchange between increasingly distant communities. Metal extraction and processing further strengthened trade relations. Raw materials for tools and weapons were obtained and exchanged from ever more distant sources. Over time, trade routes for copper, bronze, and tin, among others, were established. Copper, gold, and amber were traded as well as jewelry. Commodities served as means of payment. High-quality animal furs such as beaver pelts were used as a basis of measurement and reference value for barter.

So what do we conclude for our topic of economics based on this brief historical excursion into human

1 Stone Age, Antiquity, and Pre-Classical Era

history? If a community can organize the necessities of life such as food, clothing, shelter, etc. itself, there is no need to exchange with other communities. However, each member must be used according to his abilities and contribute to the common good: men, for example, hunting, women gathering. Only when the activities and professions become increasingly specialized and not everyone can live from his activity alone, does barter become interesting. Especially when the amount of goods available for daily needs, such as food, is limited, barter becomes necessary. This results primarily from the fact that each member, due to the division of labor specialization, focuses on his activity (e.g., toolmaker) and trades goods that another member of the community has specialized in. Another reason for barter and trade are existing resources: If I have more raw materials in the form of metals available for extraction in one region, I can trade with someone who has more furs available because more animals live in his area. Barter then serves, along with the trade of goods for goods, to balance scarcity. If you now visualize the Stone Age community outlined, we will quickly realize what the essence of economics is:

Through division of labor and specialization of activities, a community maximizes the use of existing, scarce resources. These are then distributed to individual members of the community to ensure survival, "welfare". In barter trade with other communities, only what one can most easily do without or rather has in abundance is offered and therefore can be exchanged for the good that one lacks. A decisive role for trade or barter of goods is that I can exchange a necessary good like food or a desired good like jewelry for something that I own but consider less valuable than the item to be bartered. This creates the economic *incentive*.

Through trade, everyone is better off, as, for example, the Stone Age toolmaker can trade for the coveted food that he cannot procure while working on his tools. Trade usually takes place in a location where several people meet to exchange their goods and evaluate the value of the exchange based on the traded good. Thus, the woman with the top-quality beaver pelt considers what she can exchange for this beaver pelt for her family in the best case. She has in mind exactly how much effort her community put into hunting and professionally skinning the beaver. You see, even then people were already thinking about their "productivity" in the economy. Legal frameworks did not explicitly exist in the Stone Age. However, it can be assumed that the animals killed for trade belonged to the community and the barters were subject to certain rules. One thing has also become clear in this depiction of early economic activity: The more goods and items of daily life were produced and traded, the higher was the standard of living of the people in a community. In antiquity, which we will look at next, the conceptual and "scientific" examination of economics took place for the first time.

1.2 Ancient Times

Western science, as we know it, famously began with the ancient Greeks. Thanks to their ability to marvel, "thaumázein" (Plato 1991a), the Greek thinkers of antiquity developed essential insights into the principles of the world and the interaction of people in general. However, while the "Presocratics"—who preceded Plato and Aristotle in time—were primarily concerned with the primal basis of the world, Plato and Aristotle also focused on questions where man is at the forefront. Thus, Plato described in his work "The Republic" (orig. *Politeia*) his version of an ideal state in which people lived virtuously (Plato, 1991b). Of course, this also included economic issues such as money or the form of economy in general. However, it is essential that the economy per se did not enjoy a particularly high status in the philosophical framework of the ancient philosophers. This topic was naturally considered in the context of the discussion about state and society. So let's start with Plato, one of the most influential philosophers of antiquity alongside Aristotle.

Plato (cf. Schefold, 1989, p. 23 ff.; Hoffmann, 2009, p. 23 ff.; Höffe, 2015, p. 129 ff.; Hülser, 1991) was born in 427 BC at the height of Attic democracy and 2 years after the death of Pericles in Athens. He came from an aristocratic family and was connected due to his kinship with the political and social leaders. Originally, Plato wanted to become a politician, but then at the age of 20, he joined Socrates as a student, one of the leading thinkers—today one would say, one of the leading intellectuals. When Plato met Socrates, the latter was already 62 years old. Socrates resisted the unreflective adoption of knowledge, as he believed was primarily practiced by the "universal scholars" sophists of his time. Socrates' philosophy was mainly based on questioning everything existing due to his assumption that he "knew, knew nothing". The focus of his questioning was the dialogue with his fellow citizens, whom he engaged in conversations in which he pursued questions of virtue and much more. Socrates left no written records. Most of what was handed down from him was written down by Plato in his numerous dialogically written books.

After the forced death of his teacher—Socrates had to drink the hemlock cup with poison in 399 BC because, from the perspective of the Athenian authorities, he led the youth to godlessness, "Eusebia"—Plato fled to the port city of Megara. After that, he undertook various journeys that took him, among other places, to Egypt and the then Greek cities of southern Italy and Sicily. In 387 BC—when Plato was already 40 years old—he founded his own school in Athens, the Academy. In this school, the students mainly devoted themselves to the study of sciences. The Academy continued for another 900 years. Plato's research and teaching at his Academy was only briefly interrupted when he became an advisor to the King of Syracuse, Dionysius II. After his stay in Syracuse, he returned to his Academy, where he died at the age of 80 in 347 BC.

Approaches to economic thinking can be found primarily in Plato's main political work *Politeia*. There he describes that people live together in a community because they have different needs, need different things, which are best produced through division of labor. Each citizen is naturally different and suited to a different business. The result of the division of labor are the individual goods, which are exchanged for coin on the market according to needs between the individual members of the state. In his late work "Laws" (orig. *Nomoi;* subsequently quoted from the edition by Hülser, 1991), Plato demands that goods are to be sold according to their value and not two prices for the same commodity may be given. Wealth corrupts the soul of man. Poverty is likewise a "misery" and to be avoided (cf. Plato, 1991c). Plato's state of estates with the philosophers as kings, a class of guardians who must do without private property and live together, is particularly well known. Marriage and family do not exist for the guardians, but everything is common to them. However, this does not apply to the other estates. Plato's state has been described as "proto-communist" and its design as a "social utopia" (cf. Kurz, 2013, p.14).

In Plato's view, the "intellectuals", the philosophers who are constantly in search of knowledge, have the highest value. Typical economic activities such as trade, commerce, and production are the tasks of the "lower" classes. The pursuit of gain and the search for ultimate profit should be kept out of the ideal state of Platonic imprint. With Plato, we find the first ideas for social justice. Using the example of the potter, Plato describes how wealth causes him to neglect his art and become increasingly lazy. On the other hand, a poor potter will no longer be able to afford his necessary tools and will therefore inevitably do his work worse. At the same time, he can no longer pass on the craft quality to his sons and other students. Plato presents another argument against wealth: if the guards themselves had assets, they would only be concerned with managing their assets and could no longer focus on their actual task of guarding and defending the state.

In his work "Laws", *Nomoi,* Plato explicitly demands that citizens should neither suffer from oppressive poverty nor be excessively rich. The legislator must set fixed limits for poverty and wealth. Plato arbitrarily sets this limit at a maximum of four times: anyone who owns more than four times the amount of a poor citizen should give the surplus—no matter how it was acquired, whether from a gift, find, business conduct, or simply luck—to the "treasury of the state". Otherwise, he must be punished or lose his good name (Plato, 1991c, 744e and 745a). The entire property of all citizens should be publicly listed at an authority that has the task of monitoring the wealth conditions.

Plato expressly forbids taking interest (Plato, 1991c, 742c), "since it is up to the debtor not to pay it, or even not to repay the capital." Interest payment is only allowed if the wage for work done is not paid on time. In this case, the debtor owes "double", and if the payment is outstanding for over a year, an additional sixth should be paid monthly for each owed drachma as interest. Otherwise, money should only be lent without interest in the "state" (Plato, 1991c, 921c, d).

Plato's main concern in his ideal state is ethical regulations. He particularly criticizes the economic causes of injustice. He becomes very clear in the following passage from the Laws, in which he demands to "redistribute" unjustified profits in order to do justice and not to reward excessive profit-seeking: "But if someone has sold more or bought more expensive than the law allows, which prescribes at what degree of increase of wealth no further growth and at which decrease no decrease of the same […] is permitted, the resulting surplus should immediately be noted by the law administrators in their records, but the missing amount should be deleted in the same" (Plato, 1991c, 850a).

It should be noted that Plato was primarily concerned with the ideal state. In this, the economy plays only a subordinate role. If at all, it is used to secure nutrition and sufficient wealth only to supply the population with the things of daily need. Only the lower, but not the educated classes and certainly not the philosophers may deal with these "lower" topics. If Plato addresses the topic at all in his writings, he is primarily concerned with the ethical dimensions of economic action: neither calculating interest nor building up excessive wealth are allowed, poverty is also to be avoided. The mundane pursuit of profit and a society of excess and consumption are as suspect to Plato as materialistic values, which play no role compared to the actual virtues such as wisdom, justice, courage, and prudence. Nevertheless, we have found some modern topics in Plato, especially on the points of the general conception of the state and the focus on topics such as social justice.

On these, Plato's student, Aristotle, builds and deepens the insights in an unparalleled way.

Hardly any philosopher has shaped the intellectual development of antiquity and the West more than Aristotle (cf. Schefold, 1989, p. 33 ff.; Dettling, 1996, p. 3 ff.; Hoffmann, 2009, p. 46 ff.; Flashar, 2013 especially p. 9 ff.). He can rightly be called a universal scholar. Today, there is hardly any significant science that Aristotle did not co-found or at least lay the intellectual foundations for. Aristotle also deserves the credit for giving the subject of economics its name: *oikonomiké*, i.e., roughly the art of household management, from *oikos* = house and *nomos* = law. Of course, the subject in antiquity only had limited to do with today's topics of economics. But back then, the first foundations were laid.

Aristotle was born in 384 BC in the small town of Stageira on the border between Thrace and Macedonia. He was the son of the personal physician of King Amyntas III of Macedonia, the father of Philip II and the grandfather of Alexander the Great. Philip II initiated the rise of Macedonia from a backward agrarian state to the leading power of Greece. His son Alexander the Great expanded the empire eastward to the Indian border. Aristotle's parents died early, and his guardian Proxenos sent Aristotle to Plato's Academy at the age of 17, which was then considered the best educational institution in Greece, where he stayed for about 20 years until Plato's death. According to recent research, such as that by Flashar (2013), Aristotle returned to Macedonia in 343 BC, mainly due to the anti-Macedonian sentiment in Athens at the time, via Assos and Lesbos, where he became the teacher of Alexander the Great. In 339 BC, he returned to Stageira and founded his own school, the Lyceum, in Athens four years later, in 335 BC. During these years, Aristotle laid the foundations for extensive scientific studies in almost every known field of knowledge, including economics. Due to anti-Macedonian unrest, Aristotle had to leave Athens 12 years later, in 323 BC, and spent another year in Chalcis, where he died in 322 BC at the age of 62.

Like his teacher Plato, the city, the *Polis,* was at the forefront of Aristotle's considerations. From his work, like his teacher Plato's "The State", *Politeia* (quoted from Aristotle, 1995, 1253a 2 f.), comes the famous sentence "Man is by nature a state-forming being" *(ho anthropos physei zoon politikón).* The house, *oikos,* and the household community were the germ cells of economic action in ancient Greece. The art of household management, *oikonomiké,* includes the house, the agricultural farm, the family, and everything that encompasses their livelihood. Each member of the house, father, mother, children, and slaves (!), each take on different economic roles. Unlike his teacher Plato, Aristotle differentiates between the tasks of household management and state administration. This results in a separation of two areas of knowledge that still exists today, political science and economics.

From Aristotle's perspective, the goal of economics is to provide Greek citizens with the necessary material means for a good life. In this context, moderate material prosperity is a goal that should play only a subordinate role in human life. Unlike Plato, Aristotle is a strong advocate of private property. The self-interest of the individual is better served and helps with economic progress (Aristotle, 1995, 1263 a 27). Ownership should remain private, but its use should be communal (Politics 1263 a 38). Aristotle mentions different types of acquisition art: On the one hand, shepherds, hunters, fishermen, and farmers produce or procure economic goods, and on the other hand, everyday items are exchanged to ensure the natural self-sufficiency of the house. For Aristotle, wealth and the acquisition of material goods serve only as a means to the end of a good life for the household community. The highest goal in life is the pursuit of higher insight through philosophy.

The exchange of everyday goods between neighboring households and later across countries led to trade, which was facilitated by the introduction of money in the form of iron, silver, or coins minted from them. Aristotle criticized the misdevelopments that the introduction of money inevitably caused: Money became an end in itself and served to enrich. He rejected this senseless multiplication of money in the hands of a few individuals as unethical. Natural wealth, *plutos kata physin,* is something different from the "art of enrichment", *chrematistiké,* which he categorically rejected. The pursuit of wealth is unworthy of a philosophical thinker, says Aristotle, and underscores this with an example: the "original philosopher" Thales of Miletus, one of the pre-Socratics, was initially mocked for his poverty. Philosophy is therefore a breadless art. However, using astronomical considerations, Thales was able to correctly predict the expected sparse olive harvest, he speculated and earned a fortune with the timely purchase and later sale of scarce olives. For philosophers, it is therefore easy, according to Aristotle, to become rich if they wanted to, but they do not value it (Aristotle, 1995, 1259 a 17 ff.).

For Aristotle, money was only created for the exchange of goods. He rejected interest for the creation of money from money without the exchange of goods, just like his teacher Plato. This form of money acquisition is against nature (Aristotle, 1995, 1258 b 5 ff.). Similarly, Aristotle unsurprisingly rejected usury for ethical reasons. Aristotle provided an interesting insight into the world of state revenues and ways to increase them in his second book, the *Oeconomica.* Some measures are mentioned here as examples (cf. Brodersen, 2006): levies on the sale of salt, on stands of miracle workers and magicians, taxes on long hair or on front doors that open onto the street. Furthermore, Aristotle considered, for example, postponing payment dates for state expenditures by one month, or introducing a currency reform, minting money with cheaper metal like tin instead of gold or silver, cancelling a public holiday including a state-funded festival, granting citizenship only for cash (!) or prescribing unpaid vacation days.

However, like Plato, Aristotle focuses his economic considerations primarily on the ethical aspects, as illustrated by the example of the "just exchange", which he describes in his "Nicomachean Ethics" (Aristotle, 2007). For Aristotle, justice, *dikaiosyne,* is the most noble of all virtues. He distinguishes between distributive and corrective justice:

According to *distributive justice,* for material goods such as money and possessions, it should apply that equals are due equal and unequals are due unequal. Specifically, for Aristotle, this means that each person is entitled to "his own" according to merit, "dignity" and status. A citizen active in state affairs must therefore generally be considered disproportionately in the distribution of wealth or material things compared to someone who has not made a contribution to the state. Aristotle leaves open whether the individual's position in the state is based on his own merit, such as special talent or performance, or on the merit of his ancestors. The essential point is: The distribution is just when the positions of individual citizens to each other are proportionally considered in the distribution of material goods. This serves only as an ethical guideline and of course does not specify a concrete value.

In the case of *corrective justice,* the circumstances of the persons involved in relation to their different social status do not matter. Here, Aristotle is primarily concerned with compensating for the damage caused, for example,

1 Stone Age, Antiquity, and Pre-Classical Era 17

by fraud, robbery, theft, but also by loans, guarantees, etc. In this case, all citizens are equal before the law. The damage caused by fraud or theft, for example, must be fully compensated, regardless of the person of the victim. Loans must then also be repaid in full, as must the price for a purchased item. For Aristotle, a just exchange is primarily based on reciprocity, *antipeponthós*. The status and worthiness of the persons involved in the exchange significantly determine the reciprocity. Aristotle gives a concrete example in his Nicomachean Ethics of how to imagine this just exchange (Aristotle, 2007, 1133 a 9 ff.):

Person A is a builder, *oikodomos,* person B is a shoemaker, *skytotómos,* C is a house and D are shoes. If A and B exchange their products, "the builder must now receive the work of the shoemaker and give him some of his own in return. If first the proportional equality is established and then the retribution, i.e., the reciprocity, *antipeponthós,* occurs, then what we mean, the just exchange, happens. If not, then we have no equality and no connection" (Aristotle, 2007, 1133 a 11–13). In this just exchange from Aristotle's perspective, the things are adjusted according to their proportional exchange value, not the persons. For Aristotle, money provides a standard to make the goods to be exchanged comparable. The just exchange demonstrated by Aristotle using the practical example is difficult to transfer to today's economic reality. From today's perspective, it would most likely mean that the value created by the house builder, measured in units of money, corresponds to the amount of shoes with the same value, measured by the price. The principle of "proportionality of persons" is difficult to understand from today's perspective and is related to the person's status in the community. Aristotle's main concern is to illustrate the highest virtue of justice using this economic example. The economic action itself was secondary for Aristotle.

As the quintessence of Aristotle's economic considerations, we can conclude that although he was the namesake of economics, he was less interested in the fundamental questions, such as market prices, profit-making, or even economic efficiency. However, it is noticeable that economic activities naturally had their place in the community and were part of human life. Although Aristotle gave some suggestions, for example, on generating and increasing state revenues, his economic descriptions are to be seen as part of his overall theory on the design of the community, the *politeia,* and the shaping of practical coexistence, ethics. His goal and that of his academic teacher Plato was the pursuit of happiness, the happy life, the *eudaimonia.* All other thoughts and considerations had to be subordinated to this goal. Aristotle's considerations were built upon in the Middle Ages, especially by a man whose life and work we want to discuss in section 1.3: Thomas Aquinas.

With this, we take a big leap of about 1500 years on our journey through time. However, this is not the place to present the various economic ideas that matured already in antiquity and at the beginning of the Middle Ages. To cushion this leap somewhat and bridge it conceptually, I sketch here without claim to completeness some of the core ideas of economic thinking and action from the long time between Aristotle and Thomas Aquinas (cf. among others Hoffmann, 2009, p. 64–89). For example, there is the influential philosophical school of the **Stoics,** which emphasizes the individual's indifference to external possessions as a norm. Thus, the Stoic **Seneca** writes in his famous letters to Lucilius: "Nemo alius est deo dignus quam qui opes contempsit" ("No one else is worthy of God than he who despises treasures") (Rosenbach 2011, vol. 3, p. 144–145). In the first book and his second letter to Lucilius (5,6), Seneca even emphasizes: "Honesta, inquit, res est laeta paupertas. Illa vero non est paupertas, si laeta est: non qui parum habt, sed qui plus cupit, pauper est" (An honorable thing, he says, is joyful poverty. But that is not poverty, if it is joyful: not he who has too little, but he who desires more, is poor) (Rosenbach, 2011, vol. 3, p. 8–11). Seneca writes particularly clearly in his 87th letter that some wealth only arises from greed and leads to evil (Rosenbach, 2011, vol. 4, p. 272–275). Wealth does not provide for greatness of soul or freedom from worry, but mainly for presumption. Stoics like Seneca, Epictetus, a freed slave, and later Marcus Aurelius, the philosophizing Roman emperor, emphasized that wealth is fleeting, in stark contrast to the imperishable possession of truth. Economic thinking was clearly dominated by moral and ethical considerations.

1.3 Middle Ages

The Middle Ages were characterized by the reception of Christian ethics. Jesus had cared for the poor, weak, sick, and disenfranchised, rejected wealth, and proclaimed the kingdom of God. In the New Testament of the Bible, especially in the Gospels, there are various places where Jesus has set clear messages on monetary topics. For example, in Luke 6:20, "Blessed are the poor, for theirs is the kingdom of heaven." Or in the text Mark 10:21, where Jesus instructs a rich young man to sell his wealth and follow him, Jesus. This thought is anchored in the Christian belief that in view of the return of Christ and the imminent end of the world, material things lose their value. The maxim of personal needlessness was considered the core maxim of medieval monastic life in poverty. The maxim of the disdain for wealth and money in particular was furthered by **Augustine of Hippo** (354–430), the significant philosopher, church father, and bishop of Hippo Regius. Augustine also warns: "The wicked have money in a bad way, the good, however, in a much better way, the less they love it" (Letter No. 153 to Macedonius, quoted after Hoffmann, 2009, p. 80).

The medieval economy was for a long time characterized primarily by a barter economy, in which the farmers gave a certain part of their harvest to the feudal lord. Only with the emergence of city-states and active trade was the barter economy gradually replaced by the money economy. Since the 12th century, craft guilds have emerged in the commercial sector, which strongly regulated the individual's life course, but economically secured him and gave him political influence. Christian value orientation was still shaping economic activities. Thus, *usury and loan interest were frowned upon* and rejected as unethical. The issue of justice remained strongly in focus. Therefore, it is not surprising that in economic actions the question of the just price, the "iustum pretium", was intensively discussed. This question was later taken up again by Thomas Aquinas.

Thomas Aquinas (cf. Beutter, 1989, p. 56 ff.; Sander, 1996, p. 8 ff.; Hoffmann, 2009, p. 90 ff.) was born on New Year's Day 1225 at Roccasecca Castle above the then city of Aquino, not far from Naples. Thomas' parents were Count Landulf of Aquino and Donna Theodora, Countess of Teate, both of whom belonged to the lower nobility. At the age of only 5 years, they sent their seventh child for education to the Benedictine monastery of Montecassino. The family thus followed the tradition of having the youngest son pursue a religious career. In 1239, Thomas went to study generale in Naples, where he came into intensive contact with the writings of Aristotle and Averroes, another significant philosopher. In 1244, against his parents' wishes, he joined the Dominican Order,

1 Stone Age, Antiquity, and Pre-Classical Era   21

founded as a mendicant order in 1215. To keep him away from his parents, his order first sent him to Rome and later to Bologna. However, on the way there, he was attacked by his brothers on behalf of his mother in 1244, taken to Monte San Giovanni Campano Castle, and then held at Roccasecca. But all efforts of his family to persuade Thomas to leave the mendicant order of the Dominicans failed, and so they finally had to let him move to Naples.

From 1245 to 1248, Thomas studied theology with Albertus Magnus (Albert of Lauingen), one of the most significant scholars of the time, whom he followed to the University of Cologne. From 1248 to 1252, he was a student and later assistant to Albertus Magnus. In 1250/51, Thomas was ordained a priest in Cologne. From 1252, he taught in Paris, initially on the Sentences (doctrines) of the theologian Peter Lombard, from 1256 to 1259 as a Master of Theology on a chair of the Dominicans. From 1259 to 1269, Thomas served as a Master first in Naples, then in Orvieto, Rome, and Viterbo. After the death of Pope Urban, he was entrusted with the management of the Santa Sabina study in Rome. Subsequently, Thomas spent another year at the papal court in Viterbo. In Viterbo, he began writing his main work, the three-part treatise "Summa Theologiae" (The Sum of Theology), in which he systematically attempted to create an overview of the theology of the time. After completing the first volume, Thomas was sent to Paris for a second time from 1269 to 1272. During this intellectually productive period, he completed the second part of his "Summa Theologiae", began the third part, and wrote numerous commentaries on all of Aristotle's main works.

During this time, Thomas worked very efficiently, dictating his theological thoughts to three or four secretaries at the same time with high concentration from his excellent memory. He read a lot and quickly, memorized the reading precisely, and wrote just as quickly in his famous, rather illegible handwriting of the "Scriptura inintelligibilis". In 1272, his order commissioned him to establish a new study generale at a location of his choice. Thomas chose Naples. Since he had a smaller teaching load there, he could devote himself to the third part of the completion of his "Summa Theologiae". He also wrote further commentaries on Aristotle and selected Psalms. On December 6, 1273, Thomas was struck by an unspecified object during a morning mass, suddenly felt weak, and doubted everything he had written so far. From then on, he changed and only prayed. Despite this, he complied with the request of his supportive King of Sicily, Charles of Anjou, to come to the 2nd Council in Florence. On the journey there, he unfortunately hit his head on a tree lying across the path. Severely weakened by this fall, he asked to be taken to his niece in the nearby Cistercian Abbey of Fossanova. There, Thomas Aquinas died on February 7, 1274, at not even 50 years old.

The backgrounds of the sudden exhaustion, the psychological change of mind, and his death have never been clarified. In addition to the tragic fall, psychosomatic reasons probably played a role: Reports have been made of psychological and physical exhaustion in the sense of a "burn-out". Other causes of exhaustion could have been a cerebral hemorrhage, accompanied by a speech disorder and movement restriction. The great Italian poet Dante suggested that the physician of King Charles of Anjou had murdered Thomas with a poisoned confection. The background was probably a power struggle between the Counts of Aquino and King Charles. The physician may have wanted to do the king a "favor" and eliminate Thomas Aquinas before he became too powerful and was elevated to the rank of cardinal as a member of the Counts of Aquino's lineage. However, there was never any confirmation of the rumor ("si dice") that Thomas Aquinas had been murdered. Thomas was canonized "saint" by Pope John XXII in 1323. His mortal remains have been kept in the Church of the Dominican Monastery Les Jacobins in Toulouse since 1974.

Thomas Aquinas sees economic action as part of human reality, driven by the idea that everything comes from God and leads back to him as the ultimate goal. The task of economics is to ensure the physical and psychological basic needs of humans for food, clothing, housing, etc. In the Christian tradition, the handling of material goods should be within the limits of prudence, *prudentia,* and wisdom, *sapientia*. However, Thomas admits that such external goods are important for human happiness, *beatitudo*. Entirely in the logic of Aristotle, who developed the Greek term *zoon politikón* for the human living and acting in the community (section 1.2), for Thomas, the economy is a social and communal action ("communicatio oeconomica"). The ultimate goal of economics is the well-being in a community ("ad bene vivere totum") (Thomas Aquinas, 2012, Secunda Pars Secundae Partis q. 50 a. 3 arg. 1).

It is essential to act economically wisely and reasonably. Thomas equates this action with justice. In the exchange of goods, there should be exchange justice ("iustitia commutativa", literally a mutual justice). At the same time, a *just distribution* ("iustitia distributiva") should be made. According to Thomas, the function of economics is primarily to supply the citizens of a state with goods of daily need and not the accumulation of wealth. The public good ("bonum commune") is clearly in the foreground in his considerations. Thomas considers work to be a natural task of man assigned by God. In line with the theological orientation of his economic reflections, work should contribute to the glory of God and the completion of creation. Work pursues four goals: livelihood, avoidance of idleness, moderation of desire, and hardening of the body. Finally, work should also contribute to providing the needy with the necessary for survival ("necessarium vitae"). However, Thomas leaves no doubt that he prefers intellectual work, such as philosophizing, to physical work.

Like Aristotle, Thomas advocates private property. He justifies this primarily by the fact that man cares more about his own goods ("propria") than about the common good ("commune omnium"). Furthermore, human relations would be more orderly through private property, as everyone takes care of his earthly possessions. Finally, the internal peace of a community is better secured when everyone has his share of earthly goods with which he is satisfied and can lead a decent life. However, Thomas restricts private property insofar as everyone may participate in the use of individual possessions, especially when they are in need ("urgens necessitas"). After all, the goods of the earth are there for all people.

For Thomas, money is a means to measure the price of individual goods and to carry out a fair exchange. Money is a human-made institution for the purpose of payment and as a unit of account. A fair exchange only takes place for Thomas if the money is stable in value over time. Here he anticipates important considerations on inflation (devaluation of money). Money should ensure that a fair price ("pretium iustum") is achieved. A price is fair for Thomas if it is truthful and thus there is a healthy relationship between the human needs for a good and its properties that fulfill these needs. As an example, Thomas mentions a simple calculation: If a house has a value of five units of money and a bed has a value of one unit of money, then the house must have the value of five beds at a fair price. If this is the case, which had to come about intuitively through trading in the case of pure barter, then the equality of value is ensured, and the prices for the house and bed are fair. Thomas already recognized the value of supply and demand back then. Goods that are available in larger quantities achieve a lower price than those that are only very limitedly available ("propter diversitatem copiae et inopiae rerum") (Thomas Aquinas, 2012, Secunda Pars Secundae Partis q. 77 a. 2 ad 2).

Determinants of the price are not only the quality but also the work involved, the costs associated with the production of a good. Different prices in different places are therefore allowed. Profit may only accrue to the extent that it is a fair remuneration for the work or the good, but should not be specifically sought. Here one can also read out the influence of Aristotle, to achieve everything in "measure", i.e., in the "middle" between too much and too little. According to Thomas, a trader may sell a good more expensively than he bought it if he has changed and improved it qualitatively—today we would call this "value creation"—transported it somewhere or the price has changed in the meantime.

Thomas rejects loan interest in the best Aristotelian and Christian tradition on the grounds that something is being sold that does not exist at all. For only the borrowed amount of money exists, not the amount of money increased by the interest. Thomas only allows an exception if the money lender suffers an economic loss or if the loan recipient gives the loan provider a gift in thanks. Thomas already thinks very modernly in entrepreneurial questions. Thus, it is allowed for a partner of a company to receive a corresponding share of the profit in return for the capital invested in the company.

In essence, it can be stated: Thomas Aquinas combines in his works, from an economic perspective, the ideas of Aristotle with Christian thought and "translates" them into the context of his time. The main goal of the economy should be to enable all people to live a life in a dignified form. It is interesting to note the position that economics is a part of daily human life. He integrates this into his philosophical-theological considerations as a matter of course, which means that Thomas represents some quite modern views. As with almost all philosophers discussed so far, his focus is also on ethical considerations. Nevertheless, Thomas Aquinas has influenced and inspired the economic ideas of other thinkers.

I would now like to take a detour to the economic thought world of **Martin Luther** (1483–1546; cf. among others Hoffmann, 2009, p. 99 ff.). Luther also primarily addresses ethical issues within the framework of economics. Thus, he rejects the poverty ideal of his time: While man should not strive for money and work towards maximum possible prosperity, Luther on the other hand grants man the right to have money and goods; he does not have to discard it in the sense of a higher goal. However, one should not strive for it as the only goal in life, but maintain an "inner distance" to the external good: "The good should be in the hands, not in the heart." Luther values work as such positively, as it is necessary to secure the well-being of people on earth and to "subdue the earth." He also sees the merchant's profession as necessary to ensure the supply of the citizens of a state with the things of daily need. However, Luther rejects long-distance trade, as "in itself strong economies are weakened without apparent benefit" (Hoffmann, 2009, p. 105).

The merchant should set the selling price fairly so that the neighbor is not harmed by it. Ideally, the price setting of the free market is controlled by a state authority. Luther is rather reserved towards credit transactions. He advises cash transactions or the exchange of goods for goods. He opposes usury and criticizes the formation of monopolies, which leads to unfair prices. In essence, Luther's main concern is that no one should enrich themselves at the expense of their neighbor in economic action, as this would harm the common good. Here the maxim of the Sermon on the Mount clearly comes to the fore, which is oriented towards mercy and not towards utility maximization. In his well-known treatise "To the Christian Nobility of the German Nation," Martin Luther speaks of putting a "bridle in the mouth of the Fuggers and similar societies." The state, in Luther's time these are rather small state units, should ensure that the coexistence of people is not harmed by excessive profit maximization.

1.4 Preclassical

Jean-Baptiste Colbert was strictly speaking (cf. especially Born, 1989, p. 96 ff.; Hoffmann, 2009, p. 139 ff.) not an economic theorist. Rather, he was a politician and practitioner in French economic and financial policy of his time. Nevertheless, he has left in his numerous writings essential thoughts on economic policy in the time of mercantilism, which should be taken into account in the context of economic thinking. Therefore, we want to take a closer look at the life and work of Jean-Baptiste Colbert.

Born on August 29, 1619 in Reims as the son of a cloth merchant family and bankers, Colbert received early education at a Jesuit college. Living in Paris since 1629, he underwent a broad education with a banker, a notary, the royal court of the city of Paris, and an army supplier. Later, he was called to the military administration, and then worked with his cousin, the Secretary of State for War. His cousin later helped him get a job as a property manager for Cardinal and Minister Mazarin, the most powerful politician of his time. While Colbert skillfully increased the private wealth of the Cardinal, he enjoyed firsthand a good insight into his political activities and thus learned the craft of politics. After Mazarin's death, Colbert succeeded Nicholas Foucquet, the deposed head of state finances. His range of tasks grew in the following years. In 1665, Colbert was appointed Finance Minister of France under Louis XIV, the "Sun King" ("Contrôleur général des finances").

During his time as Finance Minister, the increase in state revenues through the increase of direct and indirect taxes was particularly notable. He standardized civil and criminal procedural law, as well as the system of measurement and weight in France. To stimulate foreign trade, Colbert invested in road and transport infrastructure, brought foreign skilled workers into the country, standardized products, and improved their quality for export. Thus, textile producers who manufactured various types of cloth received precise instructions regarding the required quality and essential dimensions. Colbert specifically promoted the manufactures, but also large enterprises, by offering state transfer payments for their establishment or allowing temporary production or sales monopolies. Colbert "rewarded" families with ten or more children financially, provided none of the children pursued a "celibate" profession such as priest, nun, etc., by exempting them from taxes. He also pursued an intensive colonial policy, founded five trading companies similar to the English East India Companies, among others in India, and invested in the French merchant fleet. Colbert understood foreign trade policy as power politics to enhance the prestige and importance of France, based on economic strength. The state should finance its investments solidly and avoid debt as much as possible. Colbert renewed the state accounting system and simplified financial administration. Jean-Baptiste Colbert died on 06.09.1683.

Colbert reports on his numerous activities as Finance Minister primarily in his ten-volume writings "Lettres, instructions et mémoires de Colbert". In them, his essential ideas on financial policy can be read. Colbert's financial-economic actions, his economic thinking, were always subject to the primacy of politics: Only what benefits the state, in his case France, is implemented economically. What is coming back into fashion in Germany today, ensuring a balanced state budget of revenues and expenditures, was for Colbert a self-evident objective of financial policy at the time. He foresaw early on that the increased state expenditures for military, representation, magnificent buildings, etc., could not be compensated indefinitely by increased taxes. If the majority of the working population does not earn enough, increased taxes will only lead to more unemployment and impoverishment of the population, thereby counteracting the effect of tax increases. Colbert assumed a numerical relationship (1:3) between tax revenue and the amount of money circulating in the country, which allowed him to better plan tax revenue.

Colbert also paid attention to the even and fair distribution of the tax burden among the individual provinces of France. Thus, disproportionately higher flows of state money went to those provinces that were particularly burdened by the tax sums. To achieve his primary goal of increasing state revenues, Colbert turned various financial policy screws. He encouraged citizens to work hard daily—he himself set an example with a 16-hour workday and passed this work ethic on to his sons—and tried to direct the working population into those professions that brought the state the most revenue. From Colbert's point of view, these were primarily agriculture, trade, especially foreign trade, industrial production, and military service at sea and on land. He did not consider religious professions such as priest, nun, but also administrative jobs in the large bureaucratic organizations of justice and finance, to be useful in achieving his goals. State revenues could also be increased by increasing the number of taxpayers. Thus, Colbert promoted early marriages, reduced the dowry for women in marriage, and protected the highly successful Jewish merchants in trade, who were under attack under Louis XIV.

In industrial policy, Colbert's primary goal was to make France as independent as possible from imports from other countries. To this end, he promoted the entrepreneurs he saw as hardworking and capable and tried to prevent the formation of monopolies and privileges of all kinds. He subsidized large manufactures and businesses because he expected them to produce the most efficient production and improvement of domestic quality products. Colbert envisaged tax relief for these businesses as well as (interest-free) state loans and even the provision of state-subsidized, cost-effective, but high-quality raw materials. Temporary protective tariffs for domestic productions were intended to strengthen the French economy, as was the advertising-effective wearing of domestic fabrics by the French king.

Since Colbert considered both the amount of money and the quantity of goods on the world market to be more or less constant, in his opinion, growth of the French economy could only occur at the expense of other countries ("zero-sum game"). To achieve this, exports had to be increased—which increased the amount of money in France—and imports had to be reduced. Colbert aimed to increase exports primarily through the expansion of domestic large enterprises and manufactures already described, but also through the targeted promotion of trading companies overseas. Imports, on the other hand, were heavily taxed or subject to high import duties. Furthermore, Colbert urged his compatriots to buy domestic products to keep the money in the country and support domestic industry. Similar protectionist tendencies can currently be observed again in individual countries of the western world.

International trade was primarily based on a developed and secure transport system. Therefore, Colbert invested not only in road and traffic systems, but also heavily in the trade and war fleet. In his aim to strengthen foreign trade for France, he did not shy away from a war, among others, against the Dutch trade and fleet power, which he did not win, but which more or less ended in a draw (Peace of Nijmegen, 1678).

Essential for the economic ideas of interest to us here is above all Colbert's policy of systematic and sustainable promotion of the French economy. The economy was strategically used for the first time to expand power against other states. Colbert's economic system ("Colbertism") became a model for some state leaders of his time. Above all, Frederick the Great in Prussia saw himself in this sense as a "Colbertist". The example of Colbert can primarily show how the state can increase the prosperity and living conditions of the population through targeted economic and financial policy. This form of economy to increase the wealth of a state was named "Mercantilism" after the Latin term "mercantia" (trade or goods). Colbert was one of its most famous representatives. However, this was at the expense of state dirigisme. No serious politician today would think of influencing family policy in the sense of rewarding a high number of children or favoring certain "value-creating" professions. That import tariffs have a negative effect on the prosperity of a population is now common economic knowledge, especially since the counter-reaction of other countries does not take long. Nevertheless, we can learn from Colbert's economic activities how to systematically increase state revenues per saldo. No other statesman of his time was as successful in his economic efforts. A compatriot built on Colbert's preliminary considerations and practical approaches a little later: François Quesnay.

François Quesnay (cf. Gilibert, 1989, p. 114 ff.; Zank, 1996, p. 20 ff.; Hoffmann, 2009, p. 144 ff.), born in 1694 as the son of a farming family in a village near Île de France, was a doctor and surgeon by training. In 1749, he became the personal physician of the famous Marquise de Pompadour, later also of King Louis XVI, and worked in Versailles. Unlike his more theoretical-philosophizing medical colleagues, Quesnay was a man of experiments: He tried to gain medical knowledge through experiments. He wrote a series of medical textbooks, for example, on fever. Only at the age of about 60 did Quesnay first deal intensively with economic issues, which he addressed in selected articles in the *Encyclopédie*. He was primarily interested in economic aspects of agriculture, which had occupied him since his childhood days on the farm. In 1758, he published his most important model of the economy, the *"Tableau économique",* the first schematic representation of the economic cycle, with the help of which Quesnay comprehensively depicted the economy. From 1768 until his death in 1774, Quesnay dealt with selected problems of geometry such as the trisection of the angle and the quadrature of the circle. However, his most important achievement in the field of economics remains the "Tableau économique", a schematic representation of the economic cycle, which I would like to discuss in the following.

Quesnay understood the system of agricultural production and consumption as a circular process. Goods are produced solely for human consumption, the quantity of which is oriented towards consumption. On the other hand, the consumption of goods defines the quantity of goods to be produced in the future. From Quesnay's point of view, the essential task and challenge of economics is to research the technical and social conditions of this circular process between production and consumption. The monetary surplus of production measured at the consumption of an economy is called "net product" and is considered an indicator of the economic wealth of a country. The society of a country is divided into individual classes, depending on the contribution they make to production and consumption.

According to Quesnay, the Tableau comprises three classes: the class of landowners, the "sterile" class of craftsmen, and the "productive" class of tenants, who organize agricultural production. This "productive" class also includes agricultural day laborers, who, however, are passive compared to the tenants because they are subject to the instructions of the tenants. Since production takes an average of one year, the tenant must advance and make annual "advances": For example, seeds must be purchased, the farm workers must receive their daily wages regardless of the time of harvest. These advances are consumed during the production process—unlike the initial capital for the purchase of machines and equipment, which are not consumed, but whose acquisition costs are supposed to amortize, i.e., pay off, during the production process. Therefore, the latter are so-called "primary advances".

The ongoing production year is financed with the advances from the previous year: The "productive" class of farmers possesses the food and raw materials such as seeds, among other things, to feed their families and simultaneously invest in the new production year. Furthermore, they have sufficient capital to gradually replace non-functioning agricultural production equipment. The situation is similar for the "sterile" class of craftsmen, who are also supplied from the previous year with enough food and raw materials or replacement equipment to adequately support the production process. The farmers set aside the monetary equivalent of their harvest each year as advances for the following year. In return for selling a portion of the harvest to the craftsmen, the farmers purchase replacement equipment for production in the next year from them. The landowners receive an annual rent from the farmers as tenants of their property. In return, the landowners spend a portion of their rental income on purchasing food from the farmers and another portion on purchasing artisanally crafted goods. The craftsmen thus sell their products to landowners and farmers and thus have the means to purchase the necessary food and raw materials for themselves and their families.

Quesnay depicted this relationship between the three classes in his famous "Tableau économique". He assumes that the sum of the outgoing monetary flows is equal to the sum of the incoming ones. In this model, farmers, "tenants", and craftsmen make no profit. Only the landowners receive a rent for leasing the land to the tenants. This "profit" is completely consumed by the purchase of food and artisanal goods. Quesnay's evaluative view of the craftsmen was already critically seen at that time: He saw them from the perspective of the landowners as a "sterile" class, as they "only" supplied artisanal products and in return bought food from the farmers. According to Quesnay's argument, only the farmers created actual productive added value with their products on the one hand and with their rent paid to the landowners on the other. According to Quesnay's tableau, the rent represents the only profit, the "net income".

The impact of Quesnay on subsequent economic thinkers is not to be underestimated. For example, Karl Marx adopted the idea and structure of the tableau and applied it to his contemporary economic conditions. While Quesnay and his followers emphasized the special importance of nature for the economic process—indicative of this is the focus on agricultural, natural production, Quesnay and his movement were called *the Physiocrats*—from ancient Greek *physis* (= nature) and *kratéo* (= I rule)—Marx adapted the tableau to the time of the industrial revolution. In Marx's view, the landowners became capitalists and the craftsmen and farmers became two different industries. Adam Smith also incorporated the core ideas of the Physiocrats, namely Quesnay, in his groundbreaking work "The Wealth of Nations". Even if one can no longer agree with the basic assumption of the Physiocrats from today's perspective, that there is only *one* productive force with nature and only *one* productive class with the farmers, Quesnay's ideas with the "Tableau économique" have left their mark on economic history. They were further developed by Jacques Turgot, Victor de Mirabeau and in Germany by August Schlettwein. These and all other thinkers described in this chapter from antiquity through the Middle Ages to the pre-classical period laid the intellectual foundations for a man who in the true sense of the word became the founder of modern national economics: the *Scottish moral philosopher Adam Smith* (1723–1790). He will be discussed in detail at the beginning of Chapter 2.

References

Aristoteles. (1995). *Philosophische Schriften in sechs Bänden* (Politik, Bd. 4). Übersetzt von Rolfes E. Felix Meiner. Meiner.

Aristoteles. (2007). *Nikomachische Ethik* (2. Aufl.). Tusculum.

Atkinson, A. B. (2015). *Inequality—What can be done?*. Harvard University Press.

Bentham, J. (1776). A fragment on government. In J. H. Burns, & H. L. A. Hart (Hrsg.), *A comment on the commentaries and a fragment on government* (S. 391–551). (The collected works of Jeremy Bentham) London 1977.

Beutter, F. (1989). Thomas von Aquin. In J. Starbatty (Hrsg.), *Klassiker des ökonomischen Denkens* (2 Bände, S. 56–75). Beck.

Bick, A. (2012). *Die Steinzeit* (2., korr. u. akt. Aufl.). Theiss in Wissenschaftliche Buchgesellschaft (WBG).

Born, K. E. (1989). Jean Baptiste Colbert. In J. Starbatty (Hrsg.), *Klassiker des ökonomischen Denkens* (2 Bände, S. 96–113). Beck.

Bortis, H. (o. J.). Anfänge der Wirtschaft und Wirtschaft der Antike. https://www.unifr.ch/withe/assets/files/Bachelor/Wirtschaftsgeschichte/Anfaenge_der_Wirtschaft_Wige.pdf. Zugegriffen: 19. März 2019.

Brodersen, K. (Hrsg.). (2006). *Aristoteles—77 Tricks zur Steigerung der Staatseinnahmen, Oikonomika II*. Reclam.

Dettling, W. (1996). Wie modern ist die Antike? In N. Piper (Hrsg.), *Die großen Ökonomen. Leben und Werk der wirtschaftswissenschaftlichen Vordenker* (2., überarb. Aufl., S. 3–7). Schäffer-Poeschel.

Erhard, L. (1964). *Wohlstand für alle* (8. Aufl,, bearbeitet von Wolfram Langer). Ludwig-Erhard-Stiftung e. V. https://www.ludwig-erhard.de/wp-content/uploads/wohlstand_fuer_alle1.pdf. Zugegriffen: 17. Juni 2018.

Flashar, H. (2013). *Aristoteles—Lehrer des Abendlandes*. Beck.

Gilibert, G. (1989). François Quesnay. In J. Starbatty (Hrsg.), *Klassiker des ökonomischen Denkens* (2 Bände, S. 114–133). Beck.

Höffe, O. (2015). Platon. Griechenlands bester Ökonom. In L. Nienhaus (Hrsg.), *Die Weltverbesserer—66 große Denker, die unser Leben verändern* (S. 129–131). Hanser.

Hoffmann, T. S. (2009). *Wirtschaftsphilosophie—Ansätze und Perspektiven von der Antike bis heute*. Marix.

Hülser, K. H. (Hrsg.). (1991). *Platon. Sämtliche Werke griechisch und deutsch* (10 Bände). Insel.

Kaier, E. (Hrsg.). (1974). *Grundzüge der Geschichte: Band 1 Von der Urgeschichte bis zum Ende der Völkerwanderungszeit* (12. Aufl.). Moritz Diesterweg.

Küng, H. (2010). *Anständig wirtschaften—Warum Ökonomie Moral braucht.* Piper.

Kurz, H. D. (2013). *Geschichte des ökonomischen Denkens.* Beck, S. 14

Pietsch, D. (2017). *Grenzen des ökonomischen Denkens—Wo bleibt der Mensch in der Wirtschaft?* Eul/Lohmar.

Piketty, T. (2014). *Das Kapital im 21. Jahrhundert.* Beck.

Platon. (1991a). Theaitetos. Sämtliche Werke IV. In K. H. Hülser (Hrsg.), *Sämtliche Werke griechisch und deutsch* (Bd. 10). Insel.

Platon (1991b). Politeia. Sämtliche Werke V. In K. H. Hülser (Hrsg.), *Sämtliche Werke griechisch und deutsch* (Bd. 10). Insel.

Platon (1991c). Nomoi. Sämtliche Werke IX. In K. H. Hülser (Hrsg.), *Sämtliche Werke griechisch und deutsch* (Bd. 10). Insel.

Rosenbach, M. (Hrsg.). (2011). *Seneca. Philosophische Schriften lateinisch und deutsch* (2. Aufl., Bd. 5). Wissenschaftliche Buchgesellschaft.

Sander, O. (1996). Die Zeit gehört Gott. In N. Piper (Hrsg.), *Die großen Ökonomen. Leben und Werk der wirtschaftswissenschaftlichen Vordenker* (2., überarb. Aufl., S. 8–13). Schäffer-Poeschel.

Schefold, B. (1989). Platon und Aristoteles. In J. Starbatty (Hrsg.), *Klassiker des ökonomischen Denkens* (2 Bände, S. 19–55). Beck.

Smith, A. (2009). *Wohlstand der Nationen.* Nach der Übersetzung von Max Stirner, hrsg. von Heinrich Schmidt. Anaconda.

Stehle, A. (2014). Jedes Angebot schafft sich seine Nachfrage. *Wirtschaftswoche* 06.02.2014. https://www.wiwo.de/politik/konjunktur/geistesblitze-der-oekonomie-xiv-jedes-angebot-schafft-sich-seine-nachfrage/9412150.html. Zugegriffen: 29. Mai 2019.

Thomas von Aquin. (2012). Summa Theologiae. http://www.unifr.ch/bkv/summa/inhalt1.htm. Zugegriffen: 6. Juni 2019.

Weischedel, W. (2005). *Die philosophische Hintertreppe. Die großen Philosophen im Alltag und Denken* (Ungekürzte Ausgabe). dtv.

Zank, W. (1996). Reiche Bauern, reiches Land. In N. Piper (Hrsg.), *Die großen Ökonomen. Leben und Werk der wirtschaftswissenschaftlichen Vordenker* (2., überarb. Aufl., S. 20–25). Schäffer-Poeschel.

2

Classical Era

2.1 Adam Smith

Every science has its "classics", every field something like a "founder". In sociology, Auguste Comte is generally considered the father of modern social theory, and in economics, it is the Scottish moral philosopher Adam Smith (cf. Recktenwald, 1989, p. 134 ff.; Bofinger, 2015, p. 31 ff.; Kurz, 1996a, p. 29 ff.; Hoffmann, 2009, p. 154 ff.; Thornton, 2015, p. 13 ff.; Herrmann, 2016, p. 15 ff.; Streminger, 2017). Hardly any other economist has been written about as much, hardly any book has been discussed and interpreted as often as Smith's main work "The Wealth of Nations" (orig. "The Wealth of Nations"). However, he was not a classical economist by nature—this field did not yet exist as an independent science in his lifetime. Rather, he saw himself as a philosopher, who primarily dealt with the topics of morality and ethics. When Adam Smith is mentioned, the most famous quote from his main work is usually also cited, which appears only once in the opus magnum: "the invisible hand of the market", "the invisible hand of the market". Often characterized as a market liberal, Smith was more of a fighter for social reforms in the society of his time and wanted to curtail the privileges of the rich. But one thing at a time.

Adam Smith was born on 16.06.1723 in the small Scottish port town of Kirkcaldy, about 18 kilometers from Edinburgh, as the son of Adam Smith senior, who was a lawyer and became private secretary to Hugh Campbell, the Earl of Loudoun, at the age of 26. Unfortunately, his father died very early: He was only 44 years old when he died in early 1723, about half a year before the birth of his second son Adam. Smith's parents both came from the Scottish upper class. His father belonged to an influential family. His mother, Margaret Douglas, was the second wife of Adam Smith senior. The first wife Lilias was the daughter of the mayor of Edinburgh, who died early. Margaret Douglas, Adam Smith's mother, was the daughter of a wealthy landowner and the granddaughter of the 3rd Lord Balfour of Burleigh. She became a widow at 29 and did not remarry. She focused on her only child Adam, with whom she lived almost continuously until she died at the age of 90.

Adam Smith was a frail and sickly child at birth, lovingly cared for by his mother. Therefore, it is not surprising that Adam Smith had a very close relationship with his mother throughout his life, also in the absence of a paternal parent. The Smith family was a religious family. This is evidenced not only by the approximately 80 books of predominantly religious content from the father's estate, but also by numerous pictures in the Smith house, which among other things portrayed the Virgin Mary and the Three Wise Men. Going to church on Sundays was one of the family's obligatory duties. The sermons seem to have aroused more interest in ethical questions than in religious rites per se in young Adam. Due to his rather weak physical constitution, Adam did not go to school until he was 9 years old, although he could have started school much earlier due to his intellectual abilities and his keen interest in books. It was noticed early on that Adam Smith was occasionally absent-minded and even talked to himself. Apparently, he was mentally very busy with many topics, which he tried to explain to himself.

Adam Smith attended the highly renowned Burgh School of Kirkcaldy, where children of different classes learned Latin together and performed plays. At the age of 14, Smith left the school in Kirkcaldy to study in Glasgow. The young age was not unusual at the time, as the curriculum was not as extensive as it is today and above all life expectancy was much lower. Due to his already good knowledge of Latin, Smith was able to skip the preparatory year and studied diligently logic, natural philosophy, mathematics, geometry, and metaphysics, with the exception of geometry and mathematics, classical subjects of philosophy. The teacher who made the most impression on Adam Smith at the time was the Scottish moral philosopher Francis Hutcheson. He taught, among other things, that morality could be recognized independently of the knowledge of God. Human nature tends to be more altruistic, benevolent behavior towards fellow human beings. In the spring of 1740, at just under 17 years of age, Adam Smith completed his studies at the University of Glasgow with a "Master of Arts" and received one of the highly renowned and coveted "Snell" scholarships, which enabled him to study at the elite university in Oxford. However, it was expected of the scholarship holders that they would pursue the career of an Anglican clergyman at the end of their studies. It is likely that his deeply religious mother also sent him to Oxford for this reason.

In July 1740, Adam Smith had just turned 17 years old, he enrolled at the University of Oxford and studied for 6 years at the prestigious Balliol College. Smith was very diligent and immersed himself primarily in the study of ancient and English classics in their original language. However, he was disappointed with the philosophical studies: Adam Smith criticized the one-sided fixation on Aristotelian doctrine, regular prayer, and high tuition fees. In addition to university reading, Smith worked meticulously through the first volumes of David Hume's "Treatise on Human Nature" in self-study—his old teacher and promoter Hutcheson seemed to have drawn his attention to this work. In contrast to his spiritual teachers in Oxford, who were primarily concerned with eschatology (the doctrine of the last things in life) and the afterlife, Smith endeavored to understand the events on earth and humans in this life.

In general, he thought little of his teachers in Oxford, criticizing their turn to outdated dogmas and their authoritarian, mentally inflexible teaching. After 6 years of study, Smith returned to Kirkcaldy in 1746. Since he did not want to become an Anglican priest under any circumstances, he supported himself as a private tutor and freelance lecturer. Smith gave lectures on law, especially natural law, in Edinburgh and was thus able to achieve financial independence. Particularly revealing are a series of essays he wrote between 1748 and 1750, which reveal his intellectual range at that time: Smith developed a theory of "intellectual sensations" and determined the role and task of philosophy and science. He outlined his ideas on ancient physics, logic, and metaphysics, especially Plato's, and attempted an essay on the external senses, especially sight. Epistemology also captivated him. Smith was an extraordinarily broad-minded and profound thinker who did not want to deal with just one specialty.

In 1751, Smith was appointed to a chair of logic in Glasgow. He gave his inaugural lecture on the topic "De origine idearum" (On the Origin of Ideas). In it, he primarily dealt with the question of the origin of human impressions and ideas. In April 1752, Smith moved to the chair of moral philosophy. From that point on, his lectures increasingly revolved around natural religion, ethics, law, and political economy. To understand the breadth of topics, one must realize that the English term "moral philosophy" is not only focused on morality and ethics, but is more generally conceived and refers to "human behavior in sum". Transferred to the present day, one could speak of "humanities and social sciences" with Gerhard Streminger (2017, p. 46). In my opinion, this is also the key point of Adam Smith's scientific approach: Economics is not seen in isolation from other humanities and social science areas, but as an integral part to explain human behavior. At the same time, Smith founded the "Literary Society" in 1752, in which he gave lectures on such diverse topics as aesthetics, literary criticism, and the history of philosophy. In addition, like many merchants, he was a member of the "Political Economy Club", whose main goal was to analyze trade in all its facets. Finally, Smith was also active in a club of Scottish Enlightenment thinkers, the "Select Society Club", which aimed to promote Scotland's economic development.

Theory of Ethical Feelings

Smith's extensive intellectual work, but especially his years of lectures and talks on "moral philosophy", culminated in 1759 in his first book with the telling title "Theory of Moral Sentiments". In it, Smith shows how ethical action works in practice. Smith's starting point was the task of moral philosophers, who since antiquity had to show the ways to earthly happiness. Smith criticizes that theologians and religious people believe that they can recommend themselves for the afterlife by slavishly following empty religious rites and actions. But according to Smith, it is not about happiness in the afterlife, but about happiness here and now on earth. Smith was driven by the question under what conditions people behave morally and virtuously. He postulated that both ethical behavior and morality are naturally inherent in humans. Ethical behavior is therefore a natural behavior of humans. Ethical behavior is not exclusively justifiable rationally, i.e., according to reason, but arises as an expression of various human emotions. Thus, we humans share in the fate of other people, we suffer with them. We show "sympathy" from ancient Greek "*syn/m* = with" and "*pathos* = suffering". We put ourselves in the position of the other person and can thus empathize with the feelings of other people. So we can feel their loss of a loved one, of a spouse, of a child, of parents. However, this empathy also has a cognitive, intellectual component: We evaluate the feelings in terms of their appropriateness: Thus, excessive grief through high intensity and long duration is considered as inappropriate as no or only few emotional reactions at the death of a loved one. However, this again depends on the external circumstances and the cultural context.

In "Theory of Moral Sentiments," Adam Smith also deals with human emotions. In the second section of the first part of his treatise, he distinguishes between physical and psychological emotions, particularly antisocial, social, and self-related emotions (Smith, 2010, p. 38 ff.). For instance, Smith mentions the various facets of hunger, which on one hand can be repulsive when one eats too greedily; on the other hand, hunger can be seen positively by others when the meal is enjoyed with a good appetite. However, physical emotions are generally seen as negative: "Such is our aversion to all desires that originate from the body: any strong expression of them is disgusting and unpleasant. According to some ancient philosophers, these are the passions that we share with animals, and since they are not related to the characteristic features of human nature, they are therefore beneath its dignity." (Smith, 2010, p. 39). Physical pain, like hunger, is seen ambivalently: loud screaming due to physical pain is perceived as unmanly and ill-mannered. At the same time, people empathize with the pain of those close to them. Smith explains the moral assessment of behavior when suffering physical pain with the little sympathy we show these people.

In the case of emotions caused by emotions, the sympathy we feel for our fellow human beings is also differentiated: "When our friend has been insulted, we easily sympathize with his desire for revenge and become angry at the person he is also angry at. If he has received a favor, we gladly share his gratitude and have a great understanding of the merit of his benefactor. But if he is in love—even if we consider his passion to be just as reasonable as any other of this kind—we never consider ourselves obliged to feel a passion of the same kind and especially for the same person he has developed it for." (Smith, 2010, p. 45). So, we can empathize with certain situations that we can generally understand, e.g., insults, favors. Concrete feelings of love for certain people, however, not so much, but in the form of a generalizing feeling of love as such. In this way, Smith repeatedly draws on ancient or modern literature, e.g., Ovid and Horace or Thomas Otway.

In the third chapter of the second section, Smith deals with antisocial emotions. These include hatred and the desire for revenge "with all their various offshoots" (Smith, 2010, p. 49). The desire for revenge against an offender is experienced more intensely the more patient, gentle, and humane the offended person is perceived to be. This person, however, must not act too passively, as a "sufferer," as he quickly appears as a coward and is therefore despised. Even with antisocial emotions, there are rules and measures that can reverse their negative effects: "In short, our entire behavior must clearly show—without us trying to display this in an artificial way—that passion has not stifled our humanity and that, if we give in to the commands of revenge, we do so with reluctance, under the compulsion of necessity and as a result of great and repeated challenges. If the desire for revenge is guarded and limited in this way, it can even be recognized as noble and distinguished." (Smith, 2010, p. 57).

Regarding social effects, Smith says in the fourth chapter of the second section: "Generosity, humanity, kindness, compassion, mutual friendship and respect, all the social and benevolent inclinations, when they express themselves in our demeanor and behavior even towards those who are not particularly close to us, almost always arouse the approval of the impartial observer." (Smith, 2010, p. 58). Smith also has understanding for the human weakness of parents who are too gentle or indulgent towards their children or love them too much. This weakness would be perceived by others with sympathy and kindness and rather classified in the category of pity for parental weaknesses.

Finally, Adam Smith outlines one last category of emotions: the selfish emotions. He defines these as the "middle ground" between social and antisocial emotions and characterizes them as "sorrow and joy, insofar as we feel them for the sake of our own personal happiness or unhappiness …" (Smith, 2010, p. 61). We humans tend to sympathize with the "small joys and great sufferings" (Smith, 2010, p. 61). If a man suddenly comes into wealth, even his best friends will only be limitedly pleased, as they are seized by envy and from a selfish point of view would rather be as rich as their friend. On the other hand, the friend who has become rich can counteract this feeling of envy and feigned sympathy through his explicit modesty. The line between the sympathy and pity of friends in the case of severe illness or a minor mishap, such as being left by a loved one, is also thin.

In "Theory of Moral Sentiments," Smith not only discusses various types and causes of sympathy and human affections, but also deals with a whole range of other human characteristics. For example, he deals with the origin of human ambition and social distinctions. Furthermore, he discusses the fact that we tend to admire the rich and great, while we despise the poor and members of the lower strata of society (3rd section of the first part). In the second part of his work, Smith deals with human merit and guilt, contrasting these with reward and punishment. He outlines human justice and benevolence and describes the influence of chance on human sensations. The third part is entirely devoted to the basis for people's judgments about their behavior and feelings. Thus, Smith vividly describes the human desire for praise and the fear of blame, the influence of conscience in this regard, and the general rules of morality and duty. The fourth and fifth parts focus on the influence of utility, custom, and fashion on the feeling of moral approval and disapproval. The sixth part deals exclusively with answering the question of what we call virtuous. In the seventh and final part, Smith describes some systems of moral philosophy and explores how humans form their judgments about ethical behavior.

This is not the place to describe the complete work of "Theory of Moral Sentiments" in detail. However, it should have become clear from the previous explanations that Smith, in his description, wants to get as close as possible to the feelings and actions of the real people of his time. He describes both the human weaknesses of envy and disapproval as well as positive characteristics such as sympathy and altruism. This creates a very differentiated picture of human behavior individually and collectively, which has nothing in common with the Homo oeconomicus of neoclassical imprint. Smith is primarily concerned with the question that has already preoccupied ancient philosophers: How can man act virtuously? For him, self-control, "self-command," is the most difficult but necessary condition for virtuous action. Self-control helps to successfully implement virtues such as prudence, justice, and benevolence, to control affections, and to achieve inner and outer balance. The systems of moral philosophy described in the last chapter of his work "Theory of Moral Sentiments" each contain only parts of the truth, which Smith combines into a homogeneous system.

With his debut work of 1759, which received great international attention and was positively received, Adam Smith laid the foundation for his main work published in 1776, which made him the founder of modern economics: "The Wealth of Nations". Often, in view of the fact that Smith sketches the human facets of sympathy and altruism in "Theory of Moral Sentiments" and selfish action in "Wealth of Nations", the contentual opposition of both works is emphasized. To the argument (by Charles Gide) that human sympathy belongs to the world of morality, while in the economic world the consideration of utility dominates, the translator of the German edition of "Theory of Moral Sentiments", Walter Eckstein, counters in his introduction as follows: "Against both attempts at solution it must be objected …, that the two main works of Smith, according to the report of his biographers, were parts of a course on moral philosophy, so it must seem unlikely from the outset that Smith wanted to express such a fundamentally different attitude in the two works. It would also be hard to see how the economic world could be separated from the world of morality, since the latter cannot be thought of as anything other than encompassing all of life." (Smith, 2010, p. XLV).

Before Smith could tackle his groundbreaking main work, however, the professor at the University of Glasgow was involved in numerous offices and tasks: He was the quaestor of the university library, dean, and finally president of the university administration and prorector. In addition to his immense lecture load—he gave lectures on such diverse topics as rhetoric, the origin of language and language types, law, stages of social development, different forms of government and political economy—Smith was busy with his research, writing major works and administrative tasks at the university: He procured funds, allocated lecture halls, or took care of the construction of a chemistry laboratory and an observatory. Essential for Smith's theory of economics was that he dealt with a multitude of different humanities and social science topics, but at the same time did not lose touch with practice.

In 1764, Smith received an offer to come to France as a private tutor to Henry Scott, the Duke of Buccleugh. This provided him with the opportunity to devote more time to his main work, "The Wealth of Nations". At the same time, he received a significantly higher salary than in Oxford, including a generous pension, and was able to engage with the *Encyclopédie* in France and enjoy the milder climate. Shortly thereafter, Smith completely gave up his professorship in Glasgow. During his 3 years as a tutor to the Duke of Buccleugh, he traveled to Toulouse, visited Voltaire in Paris, and personally met the significant French national economists and physiocrats Turgot and Quesnay. At the end of 1766, Smith returned to London, his protege with whom he had gotten along excellently during his tutoring time, got married and no longer needed a private tutor. After a six-month stay in

London, during which he was one of the advisors to the British finance minister, Smith retired to his relatives and old acquaintances in his Scottish hometown of Kirkcaldy, where he worked intensively on his main work, "The Wealth of Nations". From 1773 to 1776, he then lived again in London and gave his book the final touch. On 09.03.1776, it was published with the original title: "An Inquiry into the Nature and the Causes of the Wealth of Nations".

Wealth of Nations
The crux of Smith's main work (Smith, 2009) is the search for the cause and nature of the wealth of nations and its distribution. From today's perspective, this is a very obvious question, especially when striving for a deeper understanding of economics. Unlike the thinkers of antiquity and the Middle Ages, who sought happiness in spiritual matters or referred to the kingdom of heaven, Smith, in line with Goethe's Faust, wanted to understand "what holds the economy together at its core". Smith reaches the absolute origin of economic thinking: such as how to explain the progress in productive labor forces and how the labor yield is distributed, about the nature of capital, how nations achieve wealth, different economic systems, and public finances. Smith also structures his extensive main work into five volumes based on these subject areas (Smith, 2009).

In the first volume, Smith describes the nature of the division of labor, how it comes about, and how the division of labor relates to the extent of the market (Chap. 1–3, first volume). Then he tackles money, introducing the origin and use of money (4th chapter, first volume). The 5th to 7th chapter of the first volume focuses on determining the value of goods measured by labor and money value, the price of goods and its composition, the natural and market price. In the 8th chapter of the first volume, Smith explains the concept of wages, in the 9th the capital gain, and in the 10th volume the returns of labor and capital, namely wages and profits, as well as the inequalities that come with different returns. In the 11th and final chapter of the first volume, Smith devotes himself to the ground rent of the land.

The second volume, with its five chapters, is entirely dedicated to capital, its nature, how capital accumulation occurs, and how it is applied. In the third volume, Smith explains in four chapters how the progress of wealth varies among different nations. At the same time, Smith shows how large and small cities have developed after the fall of the Roman Empire and what economic growth results from. In the fourth volume, Smith tackles the various economic systems of his time, especially mercantilism and physiocracy (Chap. 1). In Chap. 2–4, Smith explains the different import restrictions and their effects. He further describes such diverse topics as export premiums (Chap. 5), trade agreements (Chap. 6), reasons for founding new colonies, their economic development, and the benefits for the mother countries (Chap. 7). The final chapters 8 and 9 then again deal with mercantilism and physiocracy. In the concluding fifth volume, Smith devotes three chapters to the finances of the state, logically starting with state expenditures (Chap. 1) and revenues (Chap. 2). The concluding 3rd chapter of the fifth and final volume deals with state debts.

Classified into modern economic theory, Smith thus touches on essential parts of trade theory, fiscal science, economic policy, and macroeconomics. He explains all of this against the background of real historical developments and concrete practical examples. After the brief presentation of the structure of his main work, let us now delve into the core topics of Adam Smith's economic considerations.

Division of Labor

"The greatest progress in productive forces and the increase in skill, agility, and insight with which work is directed or performed anywhere seems to have been an effect of the division of labor." (Smith, 2009, p. 11). With these words, Smith introduces his main work and emphasizes the statement made earlier in our explanations about the importance of the division of labor for economic progress. While in the Stone Age hunters and gatherers still provided for themselves, work is increasingly specialized and divided into various sub-activities. Using the example of a pin maker, Smith explains the advantage of specialization: "One draws the wire, another stretches it, a third cuts it off, a fourth sharpens it, a fifth grinds it at the top end where the head is attached …" (Smith, 2009, p. 12). Through these specializations of work and division into small, comparable subunits, which two centuries later became known as "Taylorism"—Frederick Winslow Taylor was an American engineer and founder of work science, he also coined the term "Scientific Management"—the output quantity of production can be multiplied.

Smith on this: "These ten people [of a pin factory, note by the author] could therefore produce over forty-eight thousand pins daily. Since each made one-tenth of forty-eight thousand pins, each can be calculated to make four thousand eight hundred pins daily. If, on the other hand, they had all worked individually and independently, and none had been trained for this particular activity, certainly none could have made twenty, perhaps not a single pin daily …" (Smith, 2009, p. 12 f.). The cause of this enormous increase in productivity is the greater specialization ("greater skill") in learned, repeatedly performed activities—modernly one would speak of an experience curve effect—and the introduction of machines that facilitate work. In addition, the time loss associated with constant changes in work activity is saved—today one would speak of "set-up time" in industrial production.

The cause of the division of labor is man's inclination to trade. "This division of labor, from which so many advantages arise, is originally not the work of human wisdom, which would have foreseen and intended the general prosperity to which it leads. It is the necessary, albeit very slow and gradual consequence of a certain inclination of human nature, which does not have such extensive benefit in mind: the inclination to exchange, to barter and to exchange one thing for another." (Smith, 2009, p. 20). It is noteworthy that Smith, analogous to his first work "Theory of Moral Sentiments", deals very clearly with the feelings and thoughts of his actors: "It is not from the benevolence of the butcher, brewer, or baker that we expect our meal, but from their regard to their own interest. We address not their humanity but their self-love, and never talk to them of our needs, but of their advantages." (Smith, 2009, p. 21).

However, the market size limits the advantages of the division of labor: "If the market is very limited, no one can be encouraged to devote himself entirely to a single occupation, because there is a lack of the possibility to exchange that whole surplus product of his work, which goes far beyond his own consumption, for such products of the work of others that he needs." (Smith, 2009, p. 24). The limits of the division of labor are, however, limited by the size of the city: A large city can afford to have a butcher, baker, and brewer each. A small village, on the other hand, must combine various crafts such as carpentry, blacksmithing, or masonry in one person, as the number of requests for individual craft activities in a small village in the Scottish Highlands, for example, is far too low to justify specialization. Often the geographical conditions of a region are decisive for the type and extent of trade and division of labor. In his considerations on the division of labor, Smith takes a wide historical arc and usually uses concrete examples to explain his theories: "It is remarkable that neither the ancient Egyptians, Indians, nor Chinese encouraged foreign trade, but all owe their great wealth to this inland navigation." (Smith, 2009, p. 27).

Value Theory
As we have seen in earlier chapters, the exchange came about in antiquity because the surplus of a commodity that was not consumed itself was exchanged for other goods that were needed for daily life but were not produced themselves (or could not be produced). Since mutual exchange was not always sensible and could involve various trading partners—e.g., the baker wants to exchange surplus baked goods for the butcher's meat, but the butcher has no use for it (or not to the same extent)—money or coins made of metal were developed as a means of payment and exchange. "In this way, money has become the general means of trade among all civilized peoples, through whose mediation goods of all kinds are bought and sold or exchanged for each other." (Smith, 2009, p. 33). Essential for Smith is a question that still preoccupies economists and even modern marketing researchers today—the one about the exchange value and the composition of the price of a commodity: "To investigate the principles that regulate the exchange value of goods, I will try to explain, first: What is the true measure of exchange value, or what constitutes the real price of all goods. Second: What different parts this real price is composed of or becomes a whole." (Smith, 2009, p. 34).

Thus, Smith distinguishes between the exchange value and the use value of a commodity. Water, for example, has a relatively low exchange value because it is usually common and has only a low exchange value. The opposite is the case with diamonds, which have a low use value but, due to their rarity, have a high exchange value. The fair measure of the exchange value of a commodity for Smith is the amount of labor that must be expended for its production: "That money or those goods actually save us this labor. They contain the value of a certain quantity of labor, which one exchanges for something, believing at the time that it contains the value of an equal quantity." (Smith, 2009, p. 35). However, in the economic reality depicted by Smith, the workers do not receive the amount of labor invested in the commodity: Since the commodity is exchanged for money after the introduction of money, the money value of a commodity will be determined by the law of supply and demand. If the demand for a commodity increases, its price, measured in money value, also increases. If, on the other hand, demand decreases, the price, i.e., the money value of this commodity, usually also decreases. The money value then no longer represents, or only partially represents, the amount of labor used to produce the commodity.

However, in the economy there are not only workers, but also entrepreneurs and landowners. The entrepreneurs, who have accumulated the capital, employ workers, just as the landowners lease their land. While the entrepreneurs want to make a profit on the one hand and have to pay their workers wages, the landowners want to earn a rent from their tenants that will allow them a sufficient profit or rent. Without this prospect of profit, no entrepreneur will want to take the entrepreneurial risk. Therefore, the value of the raw material increased by labor is divided into two parts: into a part of the wage and into the other part of the entrepreneur's profit or the landowner's rent. To put it in Smith's words: "Under these circumstances, the entire product of labor does not always belong to the worker. In most cases, he must share it with the capitalist who employs him." (Smith, 2009, p. 55).

Smith was convinced that people's self-interests must be channeled in meaningful ways if human society is to function. On the one hand, he spoke out against the formation of monopolies and the enforcement of individual interests. On the other hand, he was concerned with promoting competition, which stimulates innovation and drives the entire economy. Every worker should be able to live on his wage and support a family. "A man must absolutely live from his work, and the wage must at least be sufficient to provide him with maintenance." (Smith, 2009, p. 74). Entrepreneurs' profits depend on the level of credit interest and the amount of capital invested. The rent or lease of the rented farmland, in turn, depends on the quality in terms of yield richness and the size of the farmland.

In the third volume of his main work, Smith comes to the essential question of how prosperity comes about in individual nations. The development proceeds in different steps. Initially, trade takes place within a country between the cities and the rural part. The surplus of agricultural production, especially food, clothing, housing, etc., is exchanged or traded for money. Consequently, capital is mainly invested in agriculture. Smith explained the rise of agriculture and the increase in the wealth of the rural population mainly with the abolition of serfdom for farmers. These became tenants who increasingly acted entrepreneurially and invested their own capital. Since at the same time the demand for agricultural products increased due to the increased population growth, the farmers or owners of larger farms were able to accumulate an ever greater wealth.

The cities and their populations acquired wealth in other ways. Primarily through the trade of luxury goods such as jewelry for the nobility, individual urban entrepreneurs were able to amass considerable wealth, which they lent to the landowners, thereby gaining interest and influence. The increasing accumulation of wealth in the cities further stimulated demand for agricultural products, so that the benefiting farmers and their workers also became wealthier. At the same time, urban merchants invested their money in agricultural land according to return on investment considerations, thus creating additional jobs and agricultural supply. Craftsmen and traders were now no longer dependent on a large landowner as in the old feudal system, but—quite modern—on many customers and buyers of their products. Thus, Smith formulated a law that is still valid today: Once the needs for basic foodstuffs and everyday goods were met, the demand for luxury items began, which are not necessary for daily survival, but make life more beautiful and pleasant.

In the fourth volume of "The Wealth of Nations", Smith deals with the systems of political economy, which he defines at the very beginning as follows: "Political economy, considered as a field of science of a statesman or legislator, has two different objectives: Firstly, it has to provide the people with ample income or sustenance, or rather, to enable them to provide themselves with such income or sustenance; secondly, it has to provide the state or the community with an income sufficient to cover public services. Its purpose is to enrich both the people and the head of state." (Smith, 2009, p. 423). According to the then prevailing economic system of mercantilism, a country's gold quantity should be maximized to promote the wealth of a nation. To this end, exports were boosted and imports curtailed, as these led to a gold outflow. Smith considered this economic maxim to be completely wrong: The prevented imports would have to be compensated to the same extent by a partly much more expensive production in one's own country. At the same time, this would interfere with the economy and hinder free trade.

Smith has a number of arguments in favor of free trade. Each country can focus on the products it can produce best due to climatic and geographical conditions. For example, Scotland is a country naturally predestined for sheep farming, while high-quality wine matures in southern countries with more sun. The goods not produced in one's own country can then be exchanged for goods from the other country with its respective product specialization. This is of course only possible with free trade without tariffs and other import restrictions. Furthermore, free trade prevents famines, as the necessary foodstuffs, which can be produced much cheaper in another country due to climatic conditions, can be obtained cheaper from abroad. Some products also do not grow in sufficient quantities in one's own country. Since each country focuses on the good that the other countries depend on due to international trade relations, the probability of a (trade) war is also reduced.

In sum, Smith says: "We can rely with complete certainty that the freedom of trade will always supply us with as much wine as we need, and with equal certainty we can expect that it will always supply us with all the gold and silver we are able to buy and apply either for the circulation of our goods or for other purposes." (Smith, 2009, p. 430). However, Smith was a realist in every respect. Having familiarized himself with the nature of his fellow men in his first work "Theory of Moral Sentiments", he saw very clearly the limits of free trade: "To hope, however, that the freedom of trade will ever be fully established in Great Britain is as foolish as to expect that an Oceana or a Utopia will ever come about here. Not only the prejudices of the public, but, what is even more insurmountable, the private interests of many individuals stand directly in the way." (Smith, 2009, p. 468).

In his relatively extensive chapter on the colonies, their origin and economic development, Smith explains the cultural influence on economic development. He soberly states that no colony has made as great economic progress as the English in North America. The main reason for the outstanding development of the English colonies in North America were the legal framework conditions: The purchase of undeveloped land was more restricted than in other colonies. Furthermore, buyers were obliged to use the land productively, i.e. to cultivate it, within a certain period of time. If they failed to do so, the land could be passed on to other interested parties. In addition, for example in Pennsylvania, there was no primogeniture. The land was distributed evenly among the offspring. "Since the work of the English colonies is more devoted to the cultivation and culture of the land, it also produces a larger and more valuable product than that of the colonists of the three other nations, which is directed more or less to other industries by the accumulation of land." (Smith, 2009, p. 581). Finally, the relatively low taxes and levies prevailing in the English colonies led to more profits being made and the inhabitants being able to invest more in their economic activities.

The chapter on the colonies is very interesting and testifies to the author's extensive reading. In it, Adam Smith effortlessly draws historical comparisons of ancient colonization among the ancient Greeks, Romans, writes about the explorers Marco Polo, Columbus, as well as about the individual colonies. Like a true moral philosopher, he harshly criticizes the approach of the colonialists towards the indigenous population: The greed for gold and silver, for fertile land drove the Europeans. Land and mineral resources, which they took from the natives, even though these, the colonialists, met them with good heart and hospitality. Nevertheless, at the end of his remarks on the colonies, Smith must note that European culture and politics ultimately educated and shaped the people in the colonies in such a way that they were only then capable of such economic achievements. Smith primarily means the immigrants. However, the indigenous people also participate in the economic achievements. Thus, both groups are affected and are meant by "people in the colonies".

In his concluding remarks of Chapter 8 of the fourth volume, Smith describes why he rejects the mercantile system. In his opinion, the monopoly laws are more likely to support the traders and merchants than the welfare of the consumer. The physiocrats around François Quesnay, on the other hand, would have clearly recognized that the capital stock of a country is lower due to artificial interventions—Smith describes a series of measures for import restrictions, monopolies and state export promotion measures—than in a state of complete freedom. To quote a very famous passage by Adam Smith: "If one therefore completely removes all systems of favoritism and restriction, the clear and simple system of natural freedom establishes itself. Every man has, as long as he does not violate the laws of justice, complete freedom to pursue his interest in his own way and to bring his industry as well as his capital into competition with the industry and capital of other people or other classes of people." (Smith, 2009, p. 703).

Subsequently, Smith formulates the essential tasks of the state within the given natural freedom: "According to the system of natural freedom, the state government only has three duties to observe, (…): The first is the duty to protect the nation against the violence and attacks of independent nations; the second is the duty to protect each individual member of the nation against the injustice or oppression of any other member of the same as much as possible, i.e. the duty to maintain exact justice; the third duty finally is to establish and maintain certain public works and institutions, the establishment and maintenance of which can never be in the interest of a private man or a small number of private men, because the profit from it would never compensate a private man or a small number of private men, although it often more than indemnifies a great nation." (Smith, 2009, p. 703). Today, these requirements of the state could be formulated in such a way that the state should ensure the security of its citizens both externally and internally, provide a clear legal order and ensure the provision of public goods such as museums, parks, roads, etc. However, it is essential that Smith was not only concerned with the freedom of the economy and citizens, but also with ensuring that justice prevails in an economy and that oppression is avoided.

With the duties of the state come tasks and expenses that must be counter-financed through the corresponding state revenues. Therefore, Smith devotes his fifth and final volume to the finances of the state. First, he explains in the very exciting chapter on defense spending the expenses that result from the various types of establishing a war power i.e. an army in times of peace as well as in times of war. In doing so, Smith draws on a rich fund of practical comparisons from the ancient Greeks to the Romans, the Germans, up to the Russian army in the 18th century.

In the next chapter, Smith presents the judiciary with its essential tasks and expenses, among others, for courts, parliaments and their members. It is again very interesting to observe that Smith does not only deal with the economic aspects in his explanations, such as today in the comparable field of financial science, which deals with the state's revenues and expenses. On the contrary, he describes, for example, four different reasons why individual members of society "rise above others", i.e. why there is a natural hierarchy and subordination of people: On the one hand, it is due to personal characteristics such as strength and beauty, intelligence, wisdom, virtue, bravery etc., mostly classical ancient virtues, as Plato demanded from his "philosopher kings" in his work The State. On the other hand, there is age, the higher the better, as it is more experienced and wise, the greater wealth and the associated higher reputation of the wealthy. (Smith does not evaluate, but describes the facts given in his view in his time.) Finally, he gives preference to birth. As an example, Smith mentions rich, influential and/or noble families.

Other necessary expenses of the state are investments in a country's infrastructure, which are intended to facilitate trade, such as roads, bridges, canals, ports, etc. These not only need to be built, but also regularly modernized and maintained. Smith deals with both institutions, like the East India Company, which are supposed to promote trade in the colonies, and with corporations.

A significant aspect of state expenditure, according to Smith—and here he is again a very modern economist and state theorist—are investments in education. By this, he does not only mean the education of the youth, but, as he writes in another chapter, also "educational institutions for people of all ages". It is fascinating again how detailed Smith deals with the contents of education and presents them, e.g. the linguistic education of philosophers and theologians in the ancient languages Latin, Greek and Hebrew.

As the last block of expenditure, Smith outlines the "expenditure for maintaining the dignity of the head of state". As a justification for this type of state task, Smith writes: "In a rich and flourishing society, where the various classes of a people spend more and more each day on their houses, their equipment, their table, their clothing and their carriage, one can hardly expect the prince alone to lag behind fashion. He too will therefore naturally—or rather necessarily—spend more on all these items. And even his dignity seems to require it to be so." (Smith, 2009, p. 838).

In terms of state revenue, Smith distinguishes between "sources of income that belong directly to the head of state or the state". These are returns on the capital of the head of state. The capital can be invested and generates a profit, today one would rather speak of return. Or the capital can be lent and then generates interest according to the market situation. Lands generate a ground rent, modernly one would say: a property tax. Smith also includes the state's revenue from leasing the lands to farmers or large landowners who pay the rent from the proceeds of their agricultural products. The second category of state revenue is taxes. The following basic rules for taxes must be observed:

1. Taxes must be paid "according to the proportion of the income that each enjoys under the protection of the state" (Smith, 2009, p. 848): high income, high taxes, large wealth, high taxes.
2. The tax must be precisely determined and must not be arbitrary. The method and manner of payment must be as clear as the exact, traceable sum and the time of payment.
3. Every tax must be levied at a time and in a manner that is easiest for the taxpayer.
4. The tax should also reach the state and be as low as possible for the purposes of the state.

Smith sees the tax on ground rent, i.e. the yield of the ground and the (arable) soil (property tax), as necessary taxes. Furthermore, taxes that are based on the soil yield, i.e., not the land ownership itself is taxed, but what is "extracted" from the soil. House and land ownership are separately used for taxation by the state. Other taxes are those on profit and capital income (dividends), the capital value of lands, houses and movable goods, on wages. In addition, *head taxes* are essentially discussed on wealth, although wealth, from Smith's point of view, is subject to very large fluctuations and is difficult to measure individually, and *consumption taxes,* comparable to our value-added tax. In his final chapter, Smith describes the nature and cause of public debt, which arises, among other things, from the temporal discrepancy between state expenditure and revenue: The state must go into debt in times of war, but has the proceeds of a "war tax" only after a few months. Often, bankruptcy is the only way for over-indebted states to get rid of public debt.

So how was Smith's work received by the public, and what remained at the end of the day? Even today, the founder of national economics is mistakenly equated with the founder of liberalism: The egoisms of the acting individuals lead in a free, untamed market through the action of "the invisible hand" to the fact that everyone enjoys an economic advantage. This false notion resulted from the (one-time) mention of the invisible hand in the following passage in The Wealth of Nations in the fourth volume on the systems of political economy (Chap. 2): "By preferring the support of domestic to that of foreign industry, he [the individual, note by the author] intends only his own security; and by directing that industry in such a manner as its produce may be of the greatest value, he intends only his own gain, and he is in this, as in many other cases, led by an invisible hand to promote an end which was no part of his intention… By pursuing his own interest he frequently promotes that of the society more effectually than when he really intends to promote it." (Smith, 2009, p. 451).

This is, as already mentioned at the beginning of this chapter, the most famous passage of Adam Smith's approximately 1000-page work. It is always quoted indiscriminately when it comes to using Adam Smith as a guarantor of a liberal economic order. Since man in his economic actions unintentionally achieves the right result, prosperity for all, in his self-interest, the state should stay out of the economy as much as possible. Smith merely describes human behaviors that—then as now—are predominantly profit-oriented and selfish, but in sum advance the economy. In continuity with his primarily moral-philosophical work "The Theory of Moral Sentiments", Smith is primarily concerned with a realistic image of man: Each individual should be able to develop economically against the background of a stable, liberal commonwealth protected by law and order. This should take place against the background of clear moral rules and be protected by laws from injustices. The state, insofar as this is indeed a liberal and enlightened understanding of the state, should at most set the basic rules, sanction non-compliance, and protect the state and citizens from harm from outside and inside. The essential aspect of Adam Smith's theory about man is that human selfishness or self-interest and personal greed must be balanced by empathy, striving for justice, and strict legislation for the overall well-being of all people. In this respect, Smith remains in the continuity of "The Theory of Moral Sentiments".

In sum, it can be said about the main work "The Wealth of Nations": Adam Smith wrote a classic of national economics, not despite, but precisely because he meticulously analyzed human behavior in economic situations and let his moral-philosophical considerations flow into reality. It is a magnificent overall work that above all reveals the immense erudition of Adam Smith, who substantiates every economic description with comprehensive current examples and at the same time draws parallels to other peoples and nations. His comparative historical representations reach back to antiquity, in which he was also excellently versed—linguistically as well. This work is still groundbreaking today for all those who have dedicated themselves to the study of economics and should be read at least once in a lifetime, possibly for ease in the German translation.

Let us now return to the biography of Adam Smith, whose life story is far from over with the publication of his main work. Although financially independent, Smith accepted the offer in 1778 to become one of five customs commissioners in Edinburgh. There he dealt with such diverse topics as the plan for the construction of a lighthouse, rigorously enforced the use of the military against smugglers, supervised salary assignments or the construction of a coal mine. Smith managed to reform the monetary system in Scotland. His frail constitution, which had characterized him since childhood, also burdened him in old age. On July 17, 1790, at the age of 67, he died of clear mind, after having suffered from stomach pains and constipation for a long time. The lack of food utilization was too much for the weakened body. The drawers of his desk were still full of documents, including a script of dialogues on natural religion, which he had destroyed by his closest friends after his death.

Thank God, in addition to the two main works, numerous transcripts of his lectures have been preserved. The destroyed estate would probably have filled about 16 manuscript volumes, estimates his biographer Gerhard Streminger. Streminger even goes so far as to claim: "If the 16 manuscript volumes had been published as Smith's estate, no one would probably consider him anything other than the founder of the free trade doctrine. Probably there would be no other modern philosopher who would have deserved the honorary title "modern Aristotle" as much as the scholar from the small town of Kirkcaldy on the Scottish Firth of Forth." (Streminger, 2017, p. 219). Like hardly any other scholar of the West, Aristotle, among other things with his metaphysics and physics, built an extensive knowledge building and thus laid the foundations for almost all later sciences and at the same time created a timeless terminology (section 1.2).

Thus, Adam Smith is remembered not only as the founder of economics, but also as an outstanding philosopher who, coming from moral philosophy, taught and researched various disciplines, although unfortunately his writings were not preserved in all subject areas. Adam Smith is and remains a comprehensively educated scholar and scientist who had a great admiration for the *Encyclopédie*. His long life as a perpetual bachelor by his mother's side and his physically weak constitution from birth make his creative power shine all the more and deserve our admiration. Often he is portrayed as a "scatterbrained professor" who was always lost in thought, talked to himself, and occasionally seemed detached from the world. However, this cannot be entirely true, as Smith performed numerous practical tasks in his life, including as a proctor, customs commissioner, advisor to the finance minister, and never lost sight of reality. Rather, his two main works show that he was firmly grounded in life and developed his theoretical considerations based on the precise observation of his fellow human beings' behavior. Only the reflection of his empirically gained knowledge on Smith's extensive theoretical knowledge made these groundbreaking works possible. It is no coincidence that Smith is considered the founder of modern economics today: because he perfectly combined practice with theory and thought far beyond the pure boundaries of his subject. Smith composed the (philosophical) knowledge of his time in such a way that it served him as an explanatory approach to the economy of his time. In doing so, he did not only do a favor to economists, but to all people interested in science.

2.2 The Classics

Thomas Robert Malthus (cf. Steinmann, 1989, p. 156 ff.; Petersdorff, 2015, p. 115 ff.; Zank, 1996a, p. 44 ff.; Hoffmann, 2009, p. 162 ff.) was born on 13.02.1766 in Guilford, England. Due to a congenital cleft lip, which hindered his speech, he believed he could not pursue his calling as a preacher. Educated by two private tutors, Malthus entered Jesus College at the University of Cambridge in 1784, where he studied mathematics and theology. He received a prize there for outstanding mathematical skills. Ordained a priest in 1788, he became a parish priest in Albury (Surrey) in 1798 after several years as a fellow at Jesus College. Malthus' first work on the principles of population development ("An Essay on the Principle of Population, as it affects the future of society …") was published anonymously in 1798 and became a bestseller. In it, he polemically addressed the thesis that humanity was growing faster than food production. Arguing strictly mathematically, Malthus pointed out the different growth rates of population and food production: while the population grew in a geometric series (e.g., 1, 2, 4, 8, 16 etc.), food production only increased in an arithmetic series (e.g., 1, 2, 3, 4 etc.). These diverging development hypotheses inevitably led to famines, social unrest, impoverishment, and finally a war for food, according to Malthus. As a response, Malthus recommended a simple but relatively unrealistic measure: people should practice sexual abstinence, marry late, and have only a manageable number of children that they can feed themselves. Malthus himself set a good example and only married at the age of 38 when he had been appointed to a chair of political economy in Haileybury, and had—rather unusually for that time—"only" three children.

A key economic point in Malthus' considerations was that population growth per se was the necessary driving force of economic growth. Because firstly, an increasing number of children per family leads to an increase in family working hours and thus family income—with less being saved and more being invested—and secondly, the old, inefficient method of agricultural production must give way to an innovative and more efficient method to increase food production.

Malthus only laid the core of his economic theory in his third main work on the principles of political economy ("Principles of Political Economy"), published in 1820. His second work was a completely new and expanded version of population development, 2nd edition or "second essay" called, with the number of pages increased from 396 to 610 compared to the 1st edition and supplemented with numerous empirical numbers, data, and facts on population growth from Scandinavia, Russia, France, and Switzerland.

In contrast to his friend David Ricardo, who worked more theoretically and abstractly, Malthus believed that the lack of demand for essential and non-essential goods, such as luxury goods, would lead to the decline of the economy. Workers would have to use almost all their income and wealth to purchase essential products, thereby maintaining high demand. However, this does not apply to luxury goods, which only the wealthy landowners and entrepreneurs bought in limited quantities, saving the rest of their money. This lack of demand is necessary to stimulate the economy and create enough jobs for workers. Consequently, Malthus proposed public investments and employment measures to promote economic demand, which we will find again later in Keynes' theory.

Malthus not only faced criticism for indirectly promoting social Darwinism with his theory of "overpopulation". His view on the devastating consequences of population explosion has been very controversially discussed and has not come true in large parts of the world (although one can still think about Malthus' thesis today due to the famines in some parts of Africa). A major point of criticism was Malthus' fixation on the lack of demand—John Maynard Keynes, the most important economist of the 20th century, not without reason called Malthus his intellectual predecessor. Thus, Malthus not only opposed John Stewart Mill, but also his friend David Ricardo and Jean-Baptiste Say, who had claimed: "Every supply creates its own demand." i.e., the production of goods creates supply and thus (work) income, which is needed for a corresponding demand for goods. Therefore, we will now deal with Jean-Baptiste Say and, subsequently, with the ideas of David Ricardo. For the sake of completeness, it should be mentioned that Thomas Robert Malthus died at the age of 68 from a heart condition.

Jean-Baptiste Say (cf. Krelle, 1989, p. 172 ff.; Hoffmann, 1992, 2009, p. 165 ff.; Brost, 1999) was born in Lyon in 1767 as the son of a Protestant merchant. His father was a cloth maker. After a commercial education in London, Say was, among other things, the editor of a magazine and published minor scientific papers of non-economic content. In 1799, Say was briefly in the Tribunate under Napoleon's consulate, but left in 1804 due to differences with Napoleon over free trade. As a result, Napoleon banned the 2nd edition of Say's main work "Traité d'economie politique", Treatise on Political Economy. This work was published in 1803 and made Say famous in Europe overnight. In 1815, after the fall of Napoleon, Say traveled to England for study purposes, met with David Ricardo, and was able to analyze the

English economic system on site. He continued to earn his living as a co-entrepreneur of a cotton spinning mill, but also gave lectures on industrial economy, "Economie industrielle", at the Conservatoire des Arts et Métiers. In 1830, he was appointed to the Collège de France in Paris, where he died in 1832 at the age of 65.

Say had not only spread his core ideas in "Traité d'economie politique", but also in "Catéchisme d'economie politique", Catechism of Political Economy—a question-and-answer script—as well as a collection of his lectures and numerous letters to Robert Malthus on political economy, "Lettres à M. Malthus sur différents sujets d'economie politique". Jean-Baptiste Say was very much influenced by Adam Smith's "Wealth of Nations". However, the assessment that Say was merely a commentator on Smith's work is completely wrong. Say, who *rejected the use of mathematics in economics*, because in economics one can only do more or less, but no exact calculations, illustrated his statements with practical examples from economic policy.

The key point of Say's theoretical structure is the thesis that the individually responsible person is at the center of economic action. Say was skeptical about the state and its ability to influence the economy. This again reflected the merchant in Say. According to Say, there are three factors of production: labor, capital, and land. The entrepreneur combines the factors of production, new production methods and products increase labor productivity. The value that is created is not measured by the labor used, but by the benefit it provides to the buyer or customer. The selling price of the product should cover the costs of the materials used and the necessary production costs and help the entrepreneur make a reasonable profit. Say divided scientific economics into three parts. This division also follows the structure of the individual books in

"Traité d'economie politique": Production, Distribution, Consumption.

Production is divided into agriculture, manufacturing, and trade including transport and traffic. Technological progress in production arises more from improving knowledge about various production methods—modernly one would probably speak of an "experience curve effect"—than from division of labor and specialization. Foreign trade and capital accumulation bring great advantages to the nation. Particularly interesting in this book "Traité d'economie politique" is the theory of distribution channels: *Every product offer creates a demand among the population,* by creating certain needs and paving the way for other products of a similar kind. The problem is not the demand for certain products, but the lack of supply. (One inevitably thinks here of the triumph of smartphones in the last decade.) However, this assumes that every economic actor is interested in the well-being of others. Ultimately, according to Say's approach, it is less about consumption than about the production of goods and services. Consequently, in this theorem, the social product is limited less by total economic demand than by production. An approach that was heavily criticized in the following decades or in the next century by Karl Marx and John Maynard Keynes. According to them, it is exactly the opposite: The lack of total economic demand causes the social product to shrink.

Say joins the ranks of economists who, like Adam Smith, oppose state intervention in production. For Say, the money supply itself plays only a subordinate role. Contrary to the mercantilist view, money has no major influence on a state's economic policy. Otherwise, Say advocates for free, unlimited trade. He vehemently opposes the Napoleonic Continental Blockade. He sees monopolies as an economic evil and strictly opposes any kind of privileges, whether they are those of craft guilds or trading companies. The state should rather focus on providing public goods such as parks, roads, security, and infrastructures that are useful to the citizen.

Also interesting are Say's comments on the various factors influencing the profit of a company, but also the factors of production labor, capital, and land. For example, the wage for labor is higher the more dangerous, strenuous, and unpleasant a job is. For capital, the profit comes from the interest income. The interest rate, in turn, depends on supply and demand. Therefore, the highest relative interest profit can be achieved in times of capital shortage. The income from land and soil is ultimately a question of the productivity of the soil, i.e., what yield per square meter of seed is achieved in a year.

In terms of consumption, Say distinguishes between reproductive and unproductive consumption: This becomes clearer using the example of a car: An automobile manufacturer needs the preliminary services of various suppliers such as raw car bodies, transmissions, or steering columns to produce a car. In the production of the car, these supplier components are "consumed" i.e., used up, to create the final product, the finished car. According to Say, this is reproductive consumption, because supplier services and goods are consumed for the actual consumer product, the car. The unproductive or pleasure-generating consumption is performed by the buyers of the car, who "consume" the services of the car until it is eventually taken out of service. Furthermore, Say distinguishes between private and public consumption, viewing public consumption rather critically. This is only to be approved if it results in an advantage for the nation. Say is very critical of the state and the civil servants working in it, especially in terms of their productivity and contribution to the whole.

Parallel to his critical view of state activity, Say criticizes the state's tax policy: Taxes should be as low as possible, as this would increase the incentive to do business and tax revenues would rise. The increasing economic activity would overcompensate for the tax cuts and thus lead to a net increase in tax revenues. The costs of tax collection should also be very low, so that more money is available net for state expenditure. Inheritance taxes are paid out of the substance, i.e., since the inheritance is already made up of taxed income or profit, a further tax on it like the inheritance tax is to be rejected. Say, on the other hand, sees tax progression, i.e., the increase in the tax rate from certain income thresholds, as fair. However, too high taxes rather choke off production and worsen a country's competitive position.

In summary, Jean-Baptiste Say was a market-affirming, liberal economist, whose ideas were fed by Adam Smith and who also became a thought supplier for the liberal thinkers of the 20th century.

David Ricardo (cf. Eltis, 1989, p. 188 ff.; Kurz, 1996b, p. 37 ff.; Hoffmann, 2009, p. 159 ff.; Thornton, 2015, p. 41 ff.) was born in 1772 in London as the son of a Jewish stockbroker. The family originated from Portugal, moved to London via Amsterdam, and all members became British citizens. At the age of 14, Ricardo was introduced to the stock exchange business by his father, who was a committee member at the London Stock Exchange. A scandal with his family occurred in 1793 when Ricardo married a Christian, renounced his Jewish faith, and was subsequently kept very short of money by his family. Ricardo then started his own brokerage business based on loans and was soon so successful that he was able to retire from the stock exchange business with a comparatively large fortune. He invested his money mainly in real estate, including Gatcombe Park in Gloucestershire, which appointed him as the county's chief officer in 1818. A year later, he became a member of the House of Commons by "buying" into the Irish constituency of Portarlington: Ricardo lent a considerable sum of money to the landowner who had the most influence on the election of the regional representative, and was thus able to be nominated and eventually elected. After leaving the stock exchange, Ricardo used his time to intensively study mathematics and natural sciences. Reading Adam Smith's main work "Wealth of Nations" inspired him to engage with economics. Thus, he was able to draw attention to himself in Parliament with competent economic speeches and discussions. Politically, he advocated, among other things, for free and secret elections, an urgently needed reform of criminal law, and—biographically motivated—for religious tolerance. The father of eight children died in 1823 at the age of 51 from a middle ear infection.

Ricardo was not concerned with developing a comprehensive theory of economics, but rather focused on individual core areas. However, he wanted to investigate more precisely how wealth is created and distributed in the economy. Using the example of an agriculturally dominated economy, he worked out the basic mechanisms of economic activities. Thus, Ricardo found that the population was constantly growing and, consequently, the demand for agricultural food. Therefore, farmers had to cultivate more or less fertile land to satisfy the increased demand. Now the farmers, who had mostly only leased the land, were forced to invest more to cultivate the less fertile soil. At the same time, wages also increased as they had to keep up with the food prices, which had also risen due to the increased demand. The farmers and their families depended on the food to maintain their labor power and to lead a decent life. The tenants with the capital power, in turn, increased the rent for the fertile farmland—they too had to brace themselves against the rising prices. This in turn increased the costs of the farmers as tenants of the land, and profits fell—not least because wages were rising.

From this, Ricardo derived—in contrast to Adam Smith—the law that the increasing value of labor, i.e., the rising wages, leads to a reduction in profit, i.e., to a *falling profit rate*. (Adam Smith was famously of the opposite opinion, that higher wages lead to more profit and lower rents.) Furthermore, Ricardo found that goods that are labor-intensive to produce are less in demand due to the wage increase compared to products that are capital-intensive to produce. The capital-intensive goods become cheaper relative to the labor-intensive goods. Conversely, companies replace machines with people when the wage falls compared to capital costs and the use of people instead of machines becomes more attractive. This is the core of Ricardo's *labor theory of value*.

Ricardo also dealt with currency issues. He followed the development of the exchange value of the pound sterling into an ounce of gold, the gold standard. The Bank of England committed itself to exchange an ounce of gold for a clearly specified amount of sterling. During the turmoil of the Napoleonic wars, the gold value of the pound fell, and the British price level rose sharply. The Bank of England was forced to abandon the gold standard with the fixed exchange ratio of sterling to gold. Contrary to his colleagues in national economics, Ricardo explained the rise in prices not with the demand for goods, but with the fact that Britain had left the gold standard with the fixed currency relation, now had to spend more sterling for an ounce of gold, and therefore prices rose. Prices also rose because other countries stuck to the gold standard and Britain had to compensate accordingly. Therefore, the Bank of England must return to the gold standard.

Ricardo already envisaged—very foresightful and modern from today's perspective—to subject the circulation of money to the control of an independent supervisory authority. In his writing "Plan for the Establishment of a Central Bank", published posthumously in 1824, he anticipated the role of today's central banks and the European Central Bank.

In his "Essay on the Influence of a low Price of Corn on the Profits of Stock," Ricardo fought against the Corn Law of his time. Due to the Napoleonic Wars, the increased demand and scarcity of fertile farmland led to a sharp rise in grain prices. At the same time, the tenants increased the price for the rental of farmland by the farmers. Along with the patriotic efforts to protect domestic agriculture, the British Parliament demanded a ban on foreign grain imports ("Corn Law") in 1813. Two years later, in 1815, when peace was restored, the demand for corn fell dramatically, and grain prices plummeted. According to Ricardo, the Corn Law, with its factual trade barriers, was the main cause of high grain prices and high rent that farmers had to pay.

The lack of foreign grain imports reduced the amount of grain offered on the market, leading to an artificially high price level. Furthermore, entrepreneurs were motivated by the prospect of lucrative profits to invest in agriculture. Profits that would not normally arise to such an extent if grain imports were not hindered by high tariffs. As a result, Ricardo argued, society's funds would be redirected to areas of the economy where they did not belong according to regular market laws. This would result in a fatal and incorrect redistribution of money flows against market demand. At the same time, the state effectively created a grain monopoly, which also drove up prices for all affected products, such as bread, beer. This, in turn, increased the prices of basic foodstuffs for workers, who then needed higher wages to compensate, thereby reducing entrepreneurs' profits. Therefore, Ricardo called for the admission of grain imports and the use of capital in those areas of production that Britain understood better than grain cultivation. With this demand, Ricardo promoted his most famous theorem, the "theory of comparative costs."

With the theory of comparative costs, Ricardo excellently demonstrated that foreign trade is profitable for two countries even if one country is inferior in the production of both goods to another country. One might immediately object that a country that is superior in all aspects of the production of both goods—Ricardo talks about cloth in England and wine in Portugal—should produce both. However, Ricardo argued that it would be more economically sensible if the "superior" country focused on the production of the good in which it is "even more superior" to the other country than the other good. As a modern example, consider the USA with tablet computers and Germany with cars. Even if it were the case—let's assume this for a moment—that Germany had advantages in the production of both cars and tablet computers because the labor and material costs in both cases would be cheaper than in the USA, then according to Ricardo's theory of comparative costs, Germany would focus on car production and import tablet computers, as the profit margins in the car business are significantly higher than in tablet computers. The full concentration on the more profitable car production is worth it. With the additional profit, the tablet computer imports from the USA can be easily paid for. Conversely, the USA can focus on the production of one good and does not have to be active in two industries. In essence, according to Ricardo, foreign trade is therefore worthwhile for both countries.

Ricardo also dealt with the effects of a tax cut on citizens' saving behavior. Normally, one would assume that citizens would spend at least part of their saved money on more consumption due to lower taxes (as John Maynard Keynes described in his multiplier theory; section 3.4). However, Ricardo took into account the expectations of his fellow citizens in the event of a tax cut: The state has a lower budget volume due to lower tax revenues. If one assumes that state expenditures remain the same due to citizens' expectations and laws, the state's budget deficit increases. However, from Ricardo's point of view, citizens assume that they will have to pay the same amount in taxes at a later date according to the equivalence principle as their previous savings to be able to offset the state's budget deficit, they will save the money in full and not consume anything. This core statement describes the "equivalence theorem" named after Ricardo. The truth is probably somewhere in the middle: at least part of the savings will be allocated to consumption and investments. We will see this later when describing the Keynesian multiplier effect (section 3.4).

Although Ricardo did not leave behind a closed theoretical structure, we can at least note for our purposes that he

- advocated for free trade and the focus on goods with comparative cost advantages, thereby theoretically paving the way for international trade,
- was the first to analyze the value of labor and differentiated between labor-intensive and capital-intensive production,
- observed citizens' behavior in response to tax cuts and found that instead of increased consumption, the money gained is more likely to be saved in anticipation of a future higher tax that taxes away the savings,

- early on demanded the independence of a regulatory authority in the form of a kind of central bank in his currency writings, thus providing suggestions for modern times.

Even though he stood in the shadow of Adam Smith, Ricardo made a significant contribution to the development of economic ideas.

Friedrich List (cf. Häuser, 1989, p. 225 ff.; Daniels, 1996, p. 127 ff.; Braunberger, 2015, p. 23 ff.; Hoffmann, 2009, p. 251 ff.) was born in 1789 as the eighth of eleven children in Reutlingen. His father was a respected member of the bourgeois society of the time and belonged to the city council. His mother lovingly raised the children and took care of the household, which was comparatively well equipped financially. After an apprenticeship as a clerk, he was trained as an actuary in 1814. In addition, he attended legal and political science lectures at the University of Tübingen, which fascinated him. There he met the university curator von Wangenheim, who recognized List's talent and promoted him accordingly after he became a minister in the cabinet of the King of Württemberg. Two years after his actuary exam, List was promoted to accountant. After his promoter von Wangenheim switched from the Ministry of the Interior to the Ministry of Church and School, List was appointed professor of political economy. Previously, he had written a corresponding expert opinion on the establishment of a faculty of political science for his minister.

At the beginning of his teaching career, List had a hard time with his fellow professors. He himself had never studied at a university, let alone the subject he was now supposed to represent in research and teaching. Rather, he had acquired his knowledge through avid reading of Montesquieu, Smith, Say, etc. He tried to compensate for these prejudices, among other things, by frequently publishing articles in the quarterly journal *Württembergisches Archiv*, which he himself edited. During a visit to Frankfurt, List was asked to draft a petition to the Federal Assembly, demanding the abolition of internal tariffs and an external tariff for Germany. This was then accused of him at home in Württemberg as interference in the political affairs of the (Hessian) foreign country. As a result, List resigned from his professorship and became the managing director of the Association of German Merchants and Manufacturers. Even then, he was driven by the idea of merging the then still existing 39 sovereign states in Germany into a customs union. Today, one would probably speak of a trade union. But his efforts were not successful at that time—also due to a lack of political influence. Therefore, List decided to accept the Württemberg parliamentary mandate offered to him by the city of Reutlingen. A "Reutlingen Petition" he wrote, which was supposed to strengthen the citizens' basic rights and the self-administration of the municipality, was distributed to the citizens in an aggressive manner via leaflets, which was seen by the royal government as a call to incite the citizens. List was then sentenced to 10 months of fortress imprisonment, which gnawed at List for a long time and barred him from holding a public office in Germany in the future.

List fled to Strasbourg without having served his sentence. After stops in Paris and Switzerland, he then returned remorsefully to Württemberg and served 5 months of fortress imprisonment. The rest was waived on the condition that he leave Württemberg forever. With his wife and children, List emigrated to the USA. He finally settled in Reading, Pennsylvania, and returned to journalism in German: He published the newspaper *Readinger Adler*, in which he could bring his economic and political ideas closer to the German-speaking population. Through his travels in America, he developed his ideas for a protective tariff: List clearly saw that the emerging American iron and steel industry could only be protected from cheaper imports from England in this way.

Since his editorial work did not generate enough income for him and his family, List, together with a partner, bought a large piece of undeveloped land in the Little Schuylkill region. There, he developed the urban infrastructure with roads, houses, schools, etc., had railway tracks laid, and founded a railway company. This made List a wealthy entrepreneur and eventually a US citizen. In 1832, he was first offered the US consulate in the Grand Duchy of Baden and then in the Kingdom of Saxony. Equipped with the associated political immunity, List then moved with his family to Karlsruhe and later to Leipzig. Armed with the experience of railway construction in the United States, he actively participated in the discussion about railway construction in Germany. Thus, he pushed for the construction of a railway line from Leipzig to Dresden. A section was successfully implemented in 1837. However, after he had only moderate success in Germany with his ideas for promoting further railway construction—above all, his initiatives did not pay off sufficiently for him financially -, he went to Paris and designed a national railway system including a financing plan for the French King Louis Philippe I. Through this successful conception of railway construction in France, List became more sought after in Germany and therefore returned to Thuringia. But even here, his commitment did not pay off further.

For a long time, List had been dealing with national economics, as economics was called at the time. He now set out to write a multi-volume work on national economics. However, this resulted in only one volume titled

"International Trade, Trade Policy and the German Customs Union," which was published in four editions in 1842. The work made List famous in Germany overnight. Despite his high reputation as an entrepreneur and scientist, he could never regain a professional foothold in Württemberg due to his political past and prison sentence. In poor health, he declined the position of editor-in-chief of the *Rheinische Zeitung* in Cologne. This position was taken over by an up-and-coming man from Trier, Karl Marx (Section 2.3). Instead, List founded his own newspaper, the *Zollvereinsblatt,* in which he wrote several hundred articles and which helped him to make ends meet. His accumulated wealth from the USA was largely depleted.

In Germany, the customs union sought by List had meanwhile been realized. In his talks with the Austrian statesman Metternich, he even tried to promote a customs union with Austria-Hungary, which later, under the mediation of England, Hanover, Bremen, and Hamburg were to join. Further weakened in health—List suffered from depression -, he was very worried about his future and that of his family. His fortune was depleted, that of his wife (she was the widow of a wealthy Bremen merchant when he married her) he did not want to use up completely. He was so desperate that, as he wrote in his farewell letter to his friend Dr. Kolb, he saw no way out of this difficult financial situation. On his return journey from a cure in Merano, List ended his life in Kufstein on November 30, 1846.

List's best-known thesis was the positive evaluation of restricted free trade: "Free trade yes, but ..." was one of his most frequent formulations. List advocated the removal of all trade barriers throughout his life. He did this primarily against the historical background that Germany during his lifetime consisted of 39 sovereign states, all of which traded with each other. From today's perspective, Friedrich

List can be called a liberal with certain restrictions: He not only advocated free trade, but also freedom of trade, a lean state, and a simple, manageable tax system. The essential point for List, however, was that both countries should have a comparable level of economic development in trade. Thus, while he advocated the abolition of internal tariffs in Germany between the individual states, he believed that predominantly agricultural Germany needed to be protected against highly industrialized England. He had already had these experiences in America, which in his opinion had to protect itself, at least temporarily, from English imports through trade restrictions, protective tariffs.

The idea of the protective tariff as an educational tariff—only when the economy to be protected has caught up with or at least caught up with the trading partner, can the trade barriers be slowly dismantled again. Behind this was also List's political idea that economic interests represent national interests at the same time. List's ideas have been taken up again and again by emerging or developing countries to this day in order to protect the domestic economy. It is difficult to assess the true significance of the economist and human List for science. List, as can be seen from the extensive biographical narrative, was more of a pragmatist and politician, entrepreneur and journalist than a scientist, let alone a national economist. Through his extensive publications—mostly newspaper articles, also in English—he influenced the economic and political thinking of his contemporaries in the USA and in Germany. Based on his experience with the establishment of a railway system, List saw the outstanding importance of a transport infrastructure for the flourishing of a country's economy. In doing so, he did not overlook the geopolitical advantages of trading nations, which, for example, enjoyed natural advantages in their economic activity due to their proximity to waterways, such as England and Italy. Therefore, in Germany, especially inland transport by rail was a crucial element of economic activity.

List, as a politician and former civil servant, primarily criticized Smith's view, whom he otherwise greatly appreciated, that a distinction should be made between the individual economic interests of individuals and entire nations. For example, free trade for an economy as developed as England's at the time should be assessed differently than Germany's, with its strong agricultural character and fragmentation into territorial states, or the USA's, a young, emerging industry that should be protected if in doubt. The national interests of a country should be included in the economic equation: National economy is not just the sum of all individuals of a country and their economic interests. Private economy is not the same as national economy. Therefore, in his main work "The National System of Political Economy" (cf. List, 2008), List devoted about a third to the economic history of the most important nations. In addition, which is particularly important for our time travel through the history of the economy, he developed a stage theory of economic development: Accordingly, an economy develops from primitive culture in the Stone Age (self-sufficiency) via a pastoral and agricultural culture to a manufacture and finally to a trading state. Even though List was not an outstanding economic theorist, his thoughts on free trade and protective tariffs remain alive in the international community of economists. His impact was nevertheless not to be underestimated, especially since he, as a politician and entrepreneur, also left traces in his temporary place of activity, the USA.

John Stuart Mill (cf. Marchi, 1989, p. 266 ff.; Zank, 1996b, p. 55 ff.; Schipper, 2015, p. 106 ff.; Hoffmann, 2009, p. 244 ff.) was born in 1806 as the oldest of nine children in London into an intellectually stimulating environment: His father James Mill was a pioneer of liberalism, whose best friend was David Ricardo. The philosopher and utilitarian Jeremy Bentham was also a friend of the Mills. All of them shared a belief in freedom and free markets. From this, they believed that society consisted primarily of rational individuals who pursue their personal interests and for whom the moral concepts of their time, especially those of the church, are outdated and should no longer play a role in society.

The eldest son John Stuart is the ideal study object to put the theories of his father into reality. Analogous to the philosopher kings of the Platonic ideal state, who surpass their fellow citizens through comprehensive philosophical knowledge and virtue, young John Stuart is introduced to the ancient Greek language at the age of 3 (!). As a seven-year-old, he begins reading Plato in the original, at 10 years old he masters Latin at university level and at 13 years old he ventures into the political economy of David Ricardo and Adam Smith. Mill reads all the ancient classics from Xenophon to Herodotus and Diogenes Laertius. In Montpellier, Mill then studies a broad range of subjects at the age of 14: chemistry, zoology, mathematics, logic, and metaphysics. Only after this does he come into contact with peers, when he learns to ride, swim, fence, and dance near Toulouse. Mill quickly becomes enthusiastic about the ideals of the French Revolution, especially supports the end of the estate society, and welcomes the development towards a freer society. He founds and participates in the Utilitarian Society for the discussion of ethical and socio-political questions and the London Debating Society with a similar intention. At just 17 years old, John Stuart Mill joins the East India Trading Company and quickly takes on a leadership role due to his commitment and outstanding intellectual abilities.

Devoured by his father's educational ambition, John Stuart Mill suffers the first of several depressive breakdowns in his early 20s—today one would speak of "burnout". These childhood years were so formative for Mill that he decided to focus his research interest, among other things, on the personal happiness of the individual. In addition, he was interested in the economic and social conditions that must be given so that the individual can freely develop his personality. His concept of freedom was characteristic: The freedom of the individual may only be restricted if harm to other people is averted.

One can summarize Mill's childhood in such a way that his father raised him to be a "thinking machine". Rationality was paramount. His intellectual sparring partners were the Stoics and their competing school of Epicureans, even the ascetic Cynics. In this rational school, coupled with the utilitarian doctrines of Jeremy Bentham—in short: maximum utility or maximum well-being for the greatest possible number of people—intellectual striving and professional advancement are always coupled with pleasure. Only useless and harmful activities cause pain and suffering. These were the core theses of the rationalism represented by his father. John Stuart Mill experienced firsthand that this could not be true, through his depression despite his constant professional and intellectual striving. Therefore, it was understandable that Mill focused on the free development of personality in his theory development. Thus, he fought against too strong an influence of the state on individual development, such as in a collective socialism, and emphasized a moderate liberalism. Specifically, Mill believed that the state, with all its authority, was necessary to uphold the laws and order and to protect individuals in the state against injustice. It was only consistent that he advocated for a social minimum security for citizens, but also emphasized the individual's responsibility in society, e.g., to provide for themselves and their family and not to rely solely on state subsidies.

In addition to his father James, who died in 1836, causing Mill to fall into another depressive crisis so that he could not work for months, his later wife Harriet had the greatest influence on him. Although he found an intellectual counterpart in the married Harriet Taylor early on, he did not marry her until 2 years after her husband's death, over 20 years after their first meeting in 1830. Harriet was a very committed, left-wing intellectual and combative woman who was very committed to women's rights. She died of tuberculosis in France in 1859. Mill had already retired a few months earlier at the age of 52 as the former president of the Examination Office of the East India Company to devote himself to his studies.

In 1866, Mill entered the English Parliament for the liberal Whig party. In memory of his wife, he advocated, among other things, for women's suffrage, supported social reforms, and campaigned for a more liberal society. However, he was voted out in 1868 because his constituency was not satisfied with his political work. He was granted five more years after his departure from Parliament, which he spent mainly writing his autobiography and editing his father's works. He then died shortly before his 67th birthday of erysipelas in Avignon.

Shaped by his restrictive childhood, Mill's economic ideas were characterized by the idea of individual self-realization. He was particularly bothered by the fact that wealth and life chances were extremely unevenly distributed in his then world. Unlike his intellectual comrades, Mill did not believe that this phenomenon was caused by capitalism and thus God-given. A condition that one must come to terms with. The theories of his time, on the contrary, were designed to see man as a selfish profit maximizer and unsocial economic actor. While Mill did not demonize capitalism across the board, he criticized its negative side effects. Of course, capitalism could increase wealth, albeit only for a short time. In the long run, this development would reverse: Unbroken population growth, increasing competition among workers for coveted jobs and entrepreneurs for the greatest profit would lower the general wage level to a survival minimum and shrink corporate profits. Mill believed that in the long run, the supply in the labor market would increase so much that the general wage level would fall and not enough jobs would be left for everyone. But this would make things worse for the workers, who would consume less and thus demand less. Corporate profits would fall.

Therefore, Mill recommended not to abolish the capitalist system, but to intervene in a regulatory manner. For example, he called for higher taxation of inheritances, because they had not been earned by the heirs and therefore there was no right to the full inheritance. The same applies to raw materials such as oil found on a property. The owner is not responsible for this either, and his profit must therefore be taxed disproportionately in order to involve the general public more in the benefits of the raw materials. Since the wealth of a society is limited, the state must actively intervene in birth planning and limit population development. This way, wealth would be distributed among fewer heads and would be enough for everyone. Workers should also be more involved in the profits of companies. While many of these points—with the exception of birth control—could still be signed by any socially (democratic) thinking person today, Mill thought more aristocratically in terms of education: Education, especially the classical one, which he had "enjoyed" extensively at a very young age, was a decisive factor in society for him. Mill even went so far as to demand that the educated and wealthy (the intellectual and financial elite) should receive additional votes in elections.

Mill's understanding of the state differed from the prevailing laissez-faire attitude of his time: The state should not only be responsible for the framework conditions, i.e., through a differentiated legal system, security and defense institutions such as police and military, the currency, etc., but should also show responsibility for its citizens. Mill saw the state primarily as a competition guardian, preventing monopolies in gas and water supply or railway construction, and supporting the poor with care and financial subsidies. While comprehensive education should be the goal of the personal development of each individual citizen, the state should, however, stay out of the content design of education, e.g., through curricula. As already mentioned, Mill also advocated for a multi-class voting right based on education: The higher the education, the more votes the citizen should have, or he should be assigned to another voting class. And only persons with the highest possible education should be eligible as political office holders. Here, Mill's elitist understanding of education, influenced by the reading of Plato's "Philosopher Kings," becomes clear.

Mill was particularly concerned with the concept of freedom. Fundamental rights such as freedom of expression and freedom of the press and assembly were for Mill the greatest good in the state, which had to be protected under all circumstances. Each individual citizen is master over his own body and mind and should not be forced to do anything. Essential prerequisites for this are the freedom of thought and feeling and conviction, as well as the free choice of lifestyle, including education. The only legitimate intervention of the state is to ward off damage or dangers to the state or the citizens as a whole. However, this only applies to mature, i.e., mentally healthy, adult people.

In his main (political-)economic work "Principles of Political Economy," Mill defined the most important goals of the economy for him: The freedom of the individual and a "good living" for all (Mill, 2004). One could also speak of "prosperity for all" in the more modern words of Ludwig Erhard. In this sense, Mill equated the greatest possible prosperity with the greatest possible happiness. He advocated for an optimal population number, saw the elite of idlers with superior education as the moral guiding instance of society. Mill's goal of his ideal society was a society with socially secured citizens—today one speaks of minimum wage and/or minimum pension. Mill tried to achieve this goal, among other things, by partially redistributing land ownership: It is not in the interest of prosperity for all if land ownership is in the hands of a few large landowners. The state must therefore initially carry out a redistribution. The state could buy the land at fair prices and sell it again with corresponding subsidies. As already mentioned, Mill recommended taxing inheritances more heavily and involving workers more in company profits.

Many of these positions are relevant again today, such as the lofty goal of achieving prosperity for all, not letting any citizen suffer, and distributing too large fortunes for the common good. Admittedly, this is not feasible and desired in its pure form. However, Mill provides suggestions on what a society should look like from an economic point of view, in which all people live more or less happily together. Mill also clearly described the role of the state for the economy against the background of the pronounced freedom of thought of the individual. He did not develop any significant new economic ideas and concepts. But Mill already put his finger on the wound in 19th century England. He saw the capitalist system of his time quite critically, but did not want to abolish it, but to reform it as best as possible.

Mill's ideal was a society in which "no one is poor, no one wishes to be richer, and no one has reason to fear that he will be pushed back by the efforts of others who push themselves forward." Mill was already critical of the economic pursuit of (permanent) growth. His lofty claim to society was that man should renounce this addiction to limitless growth. Then the highest possible societal and cultural progress would be achieved. In addition, industrial improvements in the sense of productivity increases would be more sensibly used in shortening working hours with the same prosperity for all than in an even greater profit for the entrepreneur. One might see these positions as very idealistic and contrary to human nature. However, one will never achieve that all people are satisfied with what they have achieved, accept a reduction of their profit or wealth, and work less for it. In not too few cases, this is actually the case, keyword "work-life balance". Mill thus brought surprisingly modern approaches into the economic discussion.

2.3 Karl Marx

Karl Marx (see Ott, 1989, p. 7 ff., Oertzen, 1991, p. 139 ff.; Starbatty, 1989, p. 211 ff.; Thornton, 2015, p. 63 ff.; Kurz, 2015, p. 78 ff.; Herrmann, 2016, p. 75 ff.; Hoffmann, 2009, p. 219 ff.) led such a tumultuous life that it probably provides material for further exciting film adaptations (see, among others, the film by Raoul Peck about the young Marx from 2017). He was born in 1818 as the third of nine children in Trier. His father Heinrich was a lawyer and came from a Trier rabbinical family. His mother Henriette was the daughter of the textile merchant and Jew Isaak Heyman Pressburg. Raised as a Jew, Father Heinrich later converted to Protestantism (not to the majority faith of Catholicism), as he would not have been able to continue his profession as a lawyer at that time in Prussia. Since the Congress of Vienna in 1815, the Rhineland had been ceded to Prussia, where Jews were forbidden to work in the civil service. The father exchanged the original Jewish first name Heschel for Heinrich.

Karl Marx grew up protected and was lovingly supported by his parents, especially by his father. From the dowry of his comparatively wealthy mother Henriette, the Marx family could afford a house near the Porta Nigra, the landmark of Trier. The father recognized Karl's talent and intelligence early on and sent him, as was customary in bourgeois circles at the time, to the humanistic grammar school in Trier. While Karl's grades in mathematics were rather mediocre, the teenager excelled in the classical philological subjects Greek and Latin. Throughout his life, he remained faithful to the ancient treasury of quotations and liked to adorn his texts with it.

At the age of only 17, Marx passed his high school diploma with a grade point average of 2.4. In 1835, he became a regular student of law and cameralistics in Bonn. His father had taken over the career planning of his talented son. The youthful student is said to have joined the fraternity and student association of the "Treveraner" and to have participated in one or another drinking spree. But a romantic side of Marx also came to light during this time: He joined the poetic club "Kränzchen" and wrote one or another sensitive poem. Although he studied diligently and attended numerous colleges and seminars, he was a master of spending money. The father could not transfer the money as quickly as it was spent again. In 1836, Marx became engaged to the sister of his best friend Edgar, Jenny von Westphalen. Jenny was four years older than Marx. Both had known and loved each other since early childhood. The families of Westphalen and Marx knew and understood each other well. Jenny's father Ludwig was a Prussian government councillor and a supporter of Karl Marx. On long hikes with the family, the linguistically gifted Ludwig von Westphalen—he spoke fluent English (he was half Scottish), French, Italian and Spanish—explained to the children the intellectual ideas of his time: from the French Revolution to socialist ideas.

In 1836, Karl Marx transferred to the Friedrich-Wilhelms-University (today: Humboldt-University) in Berlin at the urging of his father. In addition to his obligatory legal lectures, Marx attended philosophical and historical lectures. He devoted himself to an intensive reading of various authors: For example, in his first year of study in Berlin, he worked through Fichte ("Pandekten Bücher"), but also Tacitus ("Germania"), Ovid ("Tristium"), Lessing ("Laokoon"), Winkelmann ("Art History") and Luden ("History of the [T]German People"). He also dealt with criminal law. Even then, the enormous thirst for knowledge of the young, highly gifted man became apparent, who not only dealt with all possible scientific topics, but also tried to think them through and further.

Marx was particularly influenced and impressed by Hegel. Georg Wilhelm Friedrich Hegel was the dominant German philosopher of his time and is considered the most important representative of German Idealism. In this phase of intensive, almost "obsessed" reading, Marx devoured all of Hegel's books. Although Hegel was no longer alive at the time of Marx's reading—he had died of cholera in 1831—his students and his ideas were still influential in Germany. Hegel left behind two opposing schools of thought: the conservative or "Right Hegelians" (also called Old Hegelians) and the "Left Hegelians" (also referred to as Young Hegelians). While the Right Hegelians were state-affirming and praised the freedom of the constitutional monarchy, the Left Hegelians, among them the young Marx, were more radical. Both schools of thought adopted Hegel's "dialectical method". This envisaged a triad of *thesis, antithesis, and synthesis*. Each argument, each thesis, can be assigned, in simplified terms, a counter-thesis, which is then sublated in a synthesis.

Thus, the Right Hegelians saw the Prussian state as being endowed with a successful constitution, emerged in a dialectical process: a state with an efficient bureaucracy, from the thesis: bureaucracy is a gain, antithesis: bureaucracy is an evil due to "self-alienation", synthesis: an efficient bureaucracy, good, high-performing universities with competent and renowned professors, a functioning economy thanks to industrialization and a high level of employment that goes along with it. The Left Hegelians, on the other hand, advocated for a dialectical further development of Prussian society to counter the evils of poverty, state censorship, and the numerous, primarily religious, discriminations. The circle of Left Hegelians regularly met in the "Doctorclub" and debated fiercely in the pubs of Berlin. Marx, at just 20 years old, was one of their spokesmen.

On 10.05.1838, Karl Marx's father Heinrich died at the age of 61 from tuberculosis. The same fate befell four of Karl's siblings, all of whom did not live to see their 25th birthday. Karl Marx was very attached to his father. His sudden death hit him hard, especially since his relatively generous money payments were now limited to a minimum by his mother. Mother Henriette, unlike Heinrich, was not convinced by the activities of her studying son and had to save money for the rest of the family. Overall, the relationship between Karl Marx and his mother was strained—besides the reduced money—he criticized the lack of support for his intellectual pursuits by his mother. Marx then had an advance on his later inheritance paid out.

On 15.04.1841, Marx was promoted to Doctor of Philosophy "in absentia" by the University of Jena at the age of just under 23 with his dissertation "Difference of the Democritean and Epicurean Philosophy of Nature". Here Marx's love for antiquity and philosophy shone through. The work on the difference in thinking of the two Greek philosophers Democritus and Epicurus, both of whom dealt with the world of atoms, was solid, but was not really noticed by either philosophy or classical studies. The path to promotion is interesting: "in absentia" meant in the absence of the candidate. Unlike the usual promotions, a personal defense of the work in a disputation was not expected in this case. Marx only had to send his finished work to the faculty, pay a certain amount, and then received the doctoral certificate by return post. Although Jena was a venerable university, such remote promotions were not unusual due to the chronic lack of money at the time.

Originally, Marx's promotion was only intended as a stopover to habilitation with the goal of becoming a professor. However, since Marx had appeared as a leading Left Hegelian against the Prussian state, he was denied the prospect of becoming a professor. So Marx turned to journalism and became a contributor and editor of the *Rheinische Zeitung* for Politics, Trade and Industry in 1842. This newspaper, founded at the beginning of 1842 by liberal-thinking citizens in Cologne, became the mouthpiece of oppositional currents against Prussia. On 15.10.1842, Marx took over the (chief) editorship of the newspaper, which under him took a further, even more radical, swing towards opposition to the rather conservative Prussia. This could not go well for long. The Prussian censorship authority sent a censor to the *Rheinische Zeitung*, in the end each issue had to be personally approved by the Cologne government president. When Marx and his colleagues did not bow to this censorship and instead circumvented it—the rather simple censorship officials did not understand the explosiveness of the highly intellectual texts and mostly let the provocative parts pass—the issue of the newspaper was banned on 01.04.1843.

In 1843, Karl Marx married his long-time fiancée Jenny von Westphalen. Of the couple's seven children, four died in childhood. Only three daughters survived. Marx and his wife moved to Paris in October 1843, where he published the *German-French Yearbooks* together with Arnold Ruge, a writer and Young Hegelian. Karl Marx's writing style had changed in recent years: Coming from a scientific, Hegelian-influenced style, he increasingly developed into a political journalist who denounced the social and economic grievances of his time. The collaboration of the two editors ended soon, as Ruge felt more committed to Hegel's philosophy and Marx wanted to continue his path as a political economist. In 1844, Marx's first work, "The Economic and Philosophical Manuscripts", was created, which mainly dealt with economic topics and took up the concept of "alienated labor".

In the course of his work as editor of the *German-French Yearbooks*, Marx got to know and appreciate **Friedrich Engels**, the rich son of a successful cotton manufacturer. Together they wrote the work "The Holy Family" (subtitle: "Critique of Critical Critique. Against Bruno Bauer & Consorts"), in which they already laid the foundations of their later work "The Communist Manifesto". In it, both authors—about 90% of the text comes from Karl Marx—criticized the Young Hegelians, who believed that history was merely the further development of human reason, so that political engagement was not necessary. Marx and Engels countered this by stating that history is primarily a social process and one must actively engage in this political process.

As a political journalist, Marx had contributed to the editorial staff of the weekly newspaper *Vorwärts!* published in Paris, which sharply criticized the authoritarian and absolutist course of Prussia. At the same time, Marx increasingly emphasized socialist aspects in his articles. This led to Prussia being able to enforce his expulsion from Paris, and he had to move to Brussels. Engels followed Marx there. At the end of 1845, Marx renounced his Prussian citizenship and became stateless, a status he maintained until his death. In Brussels, Marx published the aforementioned polemic against Proudhon: "Misère de la philosophie. Réponse à la philosophie de la misère de M. Proudhon" in which he criticized the capitalist society in addition to Proudhon's ideas. At the same time, Marx continued to publish articles, this time in the *Deutsche-Brüsseler-Zeitung*.

In early 1846, Marx and Engels founded the "Communist Correspondence Committee". After they had written many articles and papers on socialist and communist ideas, their aim with this association was to unite the revolutionary communists and workers in terms of content and organization into a communist party. In 1847, the "League of the Just", founded by Wilhelm Weitling, an early socialist and first theorist of communism, was renamed by Marx to the "League of Communists". Marx and Engels were then commissioned to write a manifesto, a content and political guideline, for the Communist Party. They published this work, which went down in history as the "Communist Manifesto", on February 21, 1848, in London. The February Revolution of 1848 swept across Europe from Germany and did not stop in Brussels. Marx commuted between Paris and Cologne in the following months, as governments favorable to him were now in office. After his socialist and communist publications in Paris and Cologne, where he wrote for the *Neue Rheinische Zeitung*, Marx went into exile in London with his family from 1849.

In London, Marx's most productive period began. Financially supported by his friend and intellectual companion Friedrich Engels, he used all his literary and journalistic power to pave the way for communism theoretically and practically. In a series of articles in the *Neue Rheinische Zeitung. Politisch-ökonomische Revue*, he described the "class struggles" prevailing in France from his point of view. From 1852, Marx was the London and Europe correspondent for the *New York Daily Tribune*. This also paved the way for Marx's ideas to America and ensured their rapid spread. Wilhelm Pieper, a German philologist and journalistic co-fighter for the revolution, supported him from 1850 as a private secretary and translated Marx's texts into English. In 1859, Marx published numerous articles for the workers' newspaper *Das Volk* and became a correspondent for the *Wiener Presse*.

In London, Karl Marx's main economic works were created, which will be discussed in detail later. In 1859, "Zur Kritik der politischen Ökonomie" was published. This work already contained the systematic foundations of his economic and social ideas, which he then elaborated much more detailed in the first volume of his fundamental work "Das Kapital", published in 1867.

But Marx was not just a theorist. He also wanted to put his ideas of communism into practice. Thus, from 1864 to 1872, he played a leading role in the founding of the "International Workers' Association", also known as the "First International". As with the Communist League, Marx also formulated the theoretical program and statutes here. At the same time, Marx promoted the founding of a revolutionary-oriented, socialist party in the individual German states. Thus, Marx was on everyone's lips not only through his writings and articles but also through his political-practical activities in both Europe and North America.

Private tragedies and illnesses repeatedly set Marx back in his productive work. His wife Jenny died at the end of 1881, and his beloved daughter Jenny died at the beginning of 1883. He himself repeatedly struggled with illnesses and died on March 14, 1883, at just under 65 years of age in London. Marx was buried at the Highgate Cemetery in London. Marx had dedicated his life to improving social conditions. He particularly focused on the miserable situation of the workers and was convinced that social injustices could be improved or eliminated through a different economic and social form. Initially starting as an enthusiastic philosopher and Left Hegelian, he increasingly became a critic of the prevailing conditions over time. In his own analytical, but at the same time sarcastic, sometimes hurtful language, he exposed the inhospitable conditions of his time. Marx engaged in lively discourse with like-minded people in the Western world and also tried to put his theoretical ideas into practice. His ideas fell on fertile ground given the economic and social conditions of his time—he was, however, fiercely fought by the conservative forces, especially in his homeland of Prussia. It is worth considering the basic features of his general political and social theory before we delve into his main economic work, "Das Kapital".

Marx's Theoretical Framework

Marx placed humans at the center of his analysis. They are the bearers of history. They act consciously and systematically according to their ideas. Thus, for Marx, the satisfaction of physical and financial needs such as food, clothing, shelter, and material security is derived from the human will to survive and to live a good life. Economic processes therefore begin in the mind. Without a material and physical basic supply for humans, things like politics, religion, and science are unthinkable. Therefore, the economy plays a crucial role for humans.

At the beginning of every civilization, according to Marx, was the division of labor. Each group of a people or civilization focused on the things they did best: craftsmen on crafts, artists on art, officials on administration, etc. These non-production groups must be fed by the farmers and shepherds. In order to feed all these different groups, which Marx calls *classes*, masses of people working in agriculture and crafts must work hard—in antiquity, slaves were also used for this purpose. The other groups, such as the nobles up to the princes, the priests, the bureaucrats, are beneficiaries of the production of the hard-working. Thus, according to Marx, those employed in agriculture and crafts under sometimes inhumane working conditions are "economically exploited" and at the same time "politically oppressed". Marx and Engels summed up in the "Communist Manifesto": "The history of all hitherto existing society is the history of class struggles" (Marx & Engels, 1983, p. 23).

To escape this, Marx, together with his comrade Engels, demanded the "classless society". Instead of a clear commitment to professions and activities, which are inevitably associated with a class, every human being should be able to choose what he or she is busy with in the future. Instead of always just fishing or philosophizing or raising livestock, a person should be able to do everything at once, as he is no longer tied to an activity according to his class. Marx only hints at the path to the "classless society": through education and self-realization for all, cooperative organization and planning of work, job rotation and above all the abolition of the social and political privileges of the ruling classes and layers in the capitalist social order. The revolutionary transformation of this social order is the goal of the social revolution demanded by Marx.

Private property of the means of production of the rich factory owners and capitalists should be abolished. It is anyway only in the hands of very few, who watch as the masses work themselves to the bone under miserable working conditions, without any prospect of prosperity, let alone wealth. While the bourgeois factory owner is swimming in money and can devote himself to his leisure, the workers, the *proletarians*, are increasingly alienated from their actual physical work. Thus, Marx and Engels write in their "Manifesto of the Communist Party":

> "The work of the proletarians has lost all independent character and thus all charm for the worker through the expansion of machinery and the division of labor. He becomes a mere accessory of the machine, from which only the simplest, most monotonous, most easily learnable manual operation is required. The costs caused by the worker are therefore almost limited to the food he needs for his maintenance and the reproduction of his race. The price of a commodity, and thus of labor, is equal to its production costs. As the repugnance of work increases, so does the wage decrease. Even more, as machinery and division of labor increase, so does the mass of work increase, either by increasing the working hours, or by increasing the work required in time, accelerated running of machines, etc." (Marx & Engels, 1983, p. 31).

Marx's social revolution was not about a violent overthrow of the political order through uprising and civil war. Rather, he saw the upheaval as a long, historical process that could be both revolutionary and evolutionary. Above all, he was concerned with peaceful development. This did not prevent Marx and Engels from formulating very pointedly in their joint "Manifesto of the Communist Party". Especially the last three sentences of the Manifesto became one of the most famous quotes of their work:

"In a word, the Communists support everywhere any revolutionary movement against the existing social and political conditions. In all these movements, they highlight the property question, whatever more or less developed form it may have taken, as the basic question of the movement. Finally, the Communists work everywhere for the connection and understanding of the democratic parties of all countries. The Communists disdain to conceal their views and aims. They openly declare that their aims can only be achieved by the forcible overthrow of all existing social conditions. Let the ruling classes tremble at a Communist revolution. The proletarians have nothing to lose but their chains. They have a world to win. Workers of all countries, unite!" (Marx & Engels, 1983, p. 60).

At the core of his heart, Marx was an interdisciplinary thinker: He came from philosophy, especially Hegel's, whose dialectical method he adopted. His thoughts revolved heavily around the social conditions of his time, which were shaped not only by politics, but primarily by the economic developments ("capitalism") of the time. Marx built on the thought structures of his intellectual comrades or predecessors and further developed his ideas into a self-contained system. For him, the state with its manifestations and structures such as the judiciary was the "superstructure" to the "base", consisting of economic relations. Marx saw the economy as an indispensable part of social relations and accordingly devoted himself intensively to it in his main work "Capital" (cf. Marx, 2009). "Capitalism" was for Marx decisive for the division of society into the working, propertyless *proletariat* (cf. Marx, 2009, p.759) and the wealthy *bourgeoisie (cf. Marx, 2009, p.750)*, who own land, machines and factories. Capitalists and bourgeoisie live off the *"exploitation" of workers (cf. Marx, 2009, p.210 ff.)*, who sell their labor power as a commodity. A third class, the petty bourgeoisie, would increasingly be pushed towards the proletariat. The lower layer of the proletariat, such as beggars and homeless people, Marx also calls *"lumpenproletariat" (cf. Marx & Engels, 1983, p.35)*. Although all people are formally equal before the law, in reality the employee is dependent on the capitalist, socially underprivileged and lives in unequal conditions, which would only be manifested by the state legal order.

The *"surplus value"* of labor produced by the employee (cf. Marx, 2009, p.179ff.)—i.e., the value that the worker earns minus his wage—is absorbed by the capitalist and the worker is *"exploited"*. Since the individual capitalists are in competition with each other with their productions, a declining profit rate—today we would talk about declining profit—can be expected over time. The capitalist entrepreneur would then cut his expenses and try to lower wages, employ fewer workers or increase productivity. Wage cuts were already difficult to enforce back then and would have further deteriorated the economic base of the workers. The same would happen if the workers were laid off. Even productivity gains were only possible through much harder work and fewer breaks, as the use of machines was still limited at that time. The worker becomes increasingly "alienated" and "enslaved" from his work. According to Marx, with the work he takes on primarily to feed his family, the worker physically and psychologically destroys himself. Marx saw the only way out of this miserable situation of the worker in the "proletarian" revolution. Marx's hands-on pragmatism is evident in one of his most famous quotes: "The philosophers have only interpreted the world in various ways; the point is to change it." (cf. Marx, 1845)

Marx's criticism did not stop at religion. He was firmly convinced that religion was only a consolation for people, solely intended to make the misery on earth more bearable with reference to the paradisiacal hereafter, religion was "the opium of the people" (cf. Marx, 1844, p.378ff.). Man is the one who creates religion, not the other way around, religion creates man. Religion is "the sigh of the oppressed creature, the heart of a heartless world" and is only there to mystify unexplainable things. Marx saw religion as part of social relations. In his introduction to the critique of Hegelian philosophy of right, Marx writes "The theory is capable of gripping the masses as soon as it demonstrates ad hominem [to the man; note by the author], and it demonstrates ad hominem as soon as it becomes radical. To be radical is to grasp the matter at its root. But the root for man is man himself." (cf. Marx, 1844, p.378ff.)

When Marxism is mentioned, its philosophy of history is often cited. Marx attempts to trace the developments of history back to a single cause. What are the essential driving forces of historical developments or even changes? For Marx, the answer is clear: It is the material conditions, the previously mentioned division of society into proletarians and capitalists, colloquially, one could also speak of "rich and poor" or "top and bottom". The driving forces of historical development are not philosophical ideas, but the material conditions of society: "It is not the consciousness of man that determines their being, but conversely their social being that determines their consciousness," Marx writes in his preface to the "Critique of Political Economy," the first volume of "Capital". This dependence of historical development on material conditions became known under the term "Historical Materialism". At the end of the development, Marx sees the revolution of the proletariat and the struggle against the bourgeoisie, the "dictatorship of the proletariat" over the bourgeoisie, "The expropriation (dispossession) of the expropriators". All this then culminates in a classless society.

It would be too simple to dismiss Marx's theoretical edifice out of hand as unrealistic and outdated since 1989. Here again, the historical situation of the time should be remembered: Revolutionary developments were the order of the day. The situation of the workers was dramatically worse than today, and the economic system of the time did not have the social structures of today's economic forms in Western Europe. It would go too far at this point to present the extensive reception and criticism of Marx's theoretical edifice. For the purposes of this book, this sketch of Marx's core ideas, especially outside of economics, should suffice. Much more interesting in this context is the analysis of Marx's core theses and ideas on economics, as he expressed them in "Capital". Therefore, we want to deal intensively with Marx's main economic work in the following pages.

Marx worked on *"Capital—Critique of Political Economy"* for almost 20 years. It was finally published in September 1867. Contrary to conventional expectations, the book was not a bestseller. It took four years for the first edition of 1000 copies to be sold. With such a low sales figure, one would not even come close to being included in the circle of economic book bestseller list today. Marx's language style was also too demanding and partly incomprehensible. Even today, the work is not or only very difficult to understand for the layman without introductory commentary. Originally, Marx had intended to publish his main work in four books spread over three volumes. Unfortunately, Marx was too ill and exhausted, so "Capital" remained a fragment. It was the great achievement of Friedrich Engels to compile and edit essential parts of the planned further volumes posthumously from the many manuscripts and excerpts left behind. Engels was able to compile Volume II of "Capital" relatively easily from his friend's estate. For Volume III, he had to supplement some parts in terms of content and combine them into a unified whole. Interestingly, the first volume of Capital, which Marx published in its entirety, was written 2 years after the manuscripts of volumes 2 and 3.

Capital

As Marx writes in his preface to the first edition, he sees "Capital" as a continuation of his work "Critique of Political Economy", which was published 8 years earlier, in 1859. He already points out in this preface the difficulty of understanding, especially the first chapter with the analysis of the commodity. But if one disregards the first chapter on the commodity and especially Chap. 3 with the "value form", one cannot accuse the work of being "difficult to understand" (Marx, 2009, p. 35). Although Marx analyzes mainly the economic conditions in England, the situation is directly transferable to Germany. On the contrary, even worse conditions prevailed in Germany, especially for the workers. Marx writes:

> "What I have to investigate in this work is the capitalist mode of production and the corresponding conditions of production and exchange. Its classical site is England so far. This is why it serves as the main illustration of my theoretical development. However, if the German reader should shrug his shoulders Pharisaically about the conditions of the English industrial and agricultural workers, or reassure himself optimistically that things in Germany are not nearly as bad, I must call out to him: De te fabula narratur!, the story is about you!" (Marx, 2009, p. 35).

Marx was convinced that his work had struck a nerve in his time. His analysis was supported by a broad consensus, especially internationally. At the end of his preface to the first edition, Marx writes with palpable satisfaction:

"The foreign representatives of the English crown express here in dry words that in Germany, France, in short, all civilized states of the European continent, a transformation of the existing relations of capital and labor is as palpable and as inevitable as in England. At the same time, Mr. Wade, Vice President of the United States of North America, declared in public meetings: After the abolition of slavery [it was the time shortly after the American Civil War, in which the northern states were victorious in the fight for the abolition of slavery, note by the author], the transformation of capital and property relations is on the agenda!" (Marx, 2009, p. 37).

Marx divides "Capital" in the first volume, which he calls "The Production Process of Capital," into seven sections with a total of 25 chapters. The first section deals with "Commodity and Money" and the second with the "Transformation of Money into Capital". Sections three, four, and five focus on Marx's "theory of surplus value" in the forms of "absolute" and "relative" surplus value. The sixth section is dedicated to theoretical considerations on "wages," and the seventh is finally reserved for the "accumulation process of capital."

We want to focus on the first volume of Capital, which Marx published before his death and which contains the essential statements of his economic-social theory. Volume 2 and 3 were posthumously published under the title "The Circulation Process of Capital", Volume 3 also posthumously under the title "The Overall Process of Capitalist Production". Volume 2 mainly deals with how the "surplus value" is realized in exchange in the economy. In Volume 3, Marx describes, among other things, how surplus value is transformed into profit, he explains the law of the tendential fall in the rate of profit and outlines the revenues and their sources.

For Marx, the "capitalist mode of production" consists mainly of an accumulation of commodities, today one would probably speak of goods. Consequently, he begins his analysis with the commodity itself. Marx distinguishes between the use value of a commodity, which indicates the usefulness of the thing, and the exchange value. "A use value or good only has a value because abstract human labor is objectified or materialized in it." (Marx, 2009, p. 52). However, commodities are not only objects of use, but also "carriers of value". But how is the exchange value to be calculated? It results from the relative "value ratio of two commodities". The source of the value of a commodity is primarily the labor invested in it. The more labor measured in hours and days is invested in the commodity, the higher is the value of the commodity. It should be noted that Marx had in mind the production conditions of his time with their high proportion of manual labor in the context of mass factory production. Marx knew that strictly speaking, the exchange value cannot be separated from the use value of a commodity. "The commodity is use value or object of use and value." (Marx, 2009, p. 73). Money serves as an "equivalent" to the commodities i.e., it measures the commodity in units of money and thus fulfills a "social function". Money is therefore not only the purpose of production, but for Marx also the embodiment of the wealth of a "capitalist" society.

Marx asks: "Where does the mysterious character of the product of labor come from as soon as it takes on the form of a commodity?" (Marx, 2009, p. 84). For him, the answer is clear: The commodities reflect the social production relations within which they are commodities. Commodities symbolize the labor invested in them within the respective production conditions. Or to put it in the words of Karl Marx: "This fetish character of the commodity world arises […] from the peculiar social character of the labor that produces commodities." (Marx, 2009, p. 85). Marx deliberately uses a religious vocabulary. A "fetish" is usually an object to which supernatural properties are attributed.

The value of commodities is measured in units of money. At the same time, money is the measure of the amount of labor contained in the commodity. A prerequisite for the exchange process of commodities is that they are valued in money, the owners of the commodities want the exchange process, and the legal relations e.g., in terms of legal certainty, support the exchange of goods. However, money increasingly becomes a goal in itself: By being able to buy commodities with money, which in turn represent the social production relations, money itself becomes "magic", the magical formula for access to the world of commodities and a "fetish" in itself, a "money fetish". Marx writes: "The mystery of the money fetish is therefore only the visible, eye-blinding mystery of the commodity fetish." (Marx, 2009, p. 103).

In his third chapter, Marx describes the function of money: "The first function of gold [Marx equates gold with money; note by the author] is to provide the world of goods with the material of their value expression or to represent the values of goods as homonymous quantities, qualitatively identical and quantitatively comparable. Thus, it functions as a general measure of values…" (Marx, 2009, p. 103). In addition, money serves as a "measure of prices", through which the prices or values of goods become comparable to each other. Money first makes the exchange of all kinds of goods possible. Only the exchange "commodity for money for commodity (C-M-C)" (Marx, 2009, p. 113) enables trade. Marx speaks in this context of "metamorphoses", transformations: The first occurs in the exchange of commodity for money, e.g., in the sale of a car or a property. The second, the "final metamorphosis", occurs in the purchase of commodity for money. (From the seller's perspective, it is of course the "first metamorphosis", the sale of money for commodity.) The prerequisites for exchange or purchase and sale are the needs of the buyer and his willingness to pay in the sense of having sufficient money.

In this sense, money becomes a "medium of circulation" because it is "the autonomized value of goods." (Marx, 2009, p. 123). Money eventually becomes the ultimate purpose of economic activity. Those who use money only as a means for their consumer spending are poor. On the other hand, those who can accumulate money as private property and do not have to spend it immediately are considered rich. Money thus becomes a "treasure" and the seller a "treasure builder": "Commodities are sold, not to buy commodities, but to replace the commodity form with the money form. This change of form, from mere mediation of the metabolism, becomes an end in itself. The alienated form of the commodity is prevented from functioning as its absolutely alienable form or only disappearing money form. The money thus petrifies into a treasure, and the commodity seller becomes a treasure builder." (Marx, 2009, p. 135). The seller is then only concerned with the money and its maximum accumulation. "The drive for treasure building is boundless by nature." (Marx, 2009, p. 138). Greed and avarice are thus preprogrammed. Marx even goes so far as to make drastic statements about human moral behavior: "The treasure builder therefore sacrifices his carnal pleasure to the gold fetish. He takes seriously the gospel of renunciation." (Marx, 2009, p. 138). Money is not only a means of payment and creates creditors and debtors, but also exists in world trade. Since money can be exchanged for gold or silver at any time, it can be used worldwide as a means of payment. At the same time, it represents the "social embodiment of wealth." (Marx, 2009, p. 146).

So how is money transformed into capital? Marx gives the answer to this in his second section, starting with the fourth chapter. Marx gives an interesting answer: In addition to the normal form of commodity circulation according to the scheme Commodity (C) for Money (M) and then Money (M) for Commodity (C)—so I sell my old car, get money for it and buy a new car with it, and probably add something from my savings—there is another form of commodity circulation. I can also buy a commodity with money and then convert it back into money, i.e., it is bought in order to sell again. With this, I pursue solely the purpose of exchanging money for money. If I sell the previously bought commodity at a higher price, I achieve a surplus, which Marx calls "surplus value". Marx calls this surplus value in the process Money for Commodity for Money (M-C-M) "capital". Marx works here with an equation that is supposed to indicate the change in value of the money: M'. In his words, the transformation into capital takes place as follows: "The complete form of this process is therefore M-C-M', where M' = M + d(elta) M, i.e., equal to the originally advanced sum of money plus an increase. I call this increase or the surplus over the original value—*surplus value*. The originally advanced value therefore not only preserves itself in circulation, but in it changes its value size, adds a surplus value or valorizes itself. And this movement transforms it into capital." (Marx, 2009, p. 153).

Marx further writes: "The circulation of money as capital is, on the other hand, an end in itself, for the valorization of value exists only within this constantly renewed movement. The movement of capital is therefore limitless." (Marx, 2009, p. 154). Marx criticizes the unnatural fixation on the accumulation of capital for its own sake, not for the satisfaction of consumption, but for the increase of money possession. This promotes greed and avarice, which has nothing to do with the original barter trade of the economy. Marx refers in his footnote to the differentiation of economy and chrematistics by Aristotle: While the economy focuses on commodity trade for a moderate and successful life, chrematistics aims at boundless enrichment, which Aristotle rejects as immoral. Marx sees in the boundlessness of capital accumulation a misdevelopment, whose bearer is the "capitalist": "As the conscious bearer of this movement (see above), the money owner becomes a capitalist. (…) This absolute greed for enrichment, this passionate hunt for exchange value is common to the capitalist with the treasure builder, but while the treasure builder is only the mad capitalist, the capitalist is the rational treasure builder. The restless increase of exchange value, which the treasure builder strives for by trying to save the money from circulation, is achieved by the wiser capitalist by constantly exposing it to circulation anew." (Marx, 2009, p. 155 f.).

The increase in the value of capital arises from the permanent, "restless" valorization of goods, which each represent the labor power invested in them. Marx understands labor power or labor capacity as the physical and mental abilities of the working person, which he uses to produce the commodity. (Marx, 2009, p. 169). However, the labor power of the individual human being should only be sold for a certain period of time, "otherwise he sells it wholesale, once and for all, thus he sells himself, transforms himself from a free man into a slave, from a commodity owner into a commodity." (Marx, 2009, p. 169). The worker thus provides his labor power as a commodity, he sells it. His physically and mentally expended, consumed labor power must be restored by the worker, and therefore he must provide for himself and his family for the necessary things of daily needs such as food, clothing, shelter etc. Because only by providing for his family will the availability of labor power be ensured over the generations in the future.

Because the worker provides his labor power to the employer at the beginning of the month, but is only paid at the end of the month, the worker "credits" the employer. Already at the end of the second section, Marx makes it clear that the distribution of power between worker and employer is extremely unequal: "The former money owner steps forward as a capitalist, the labor power owner follows him as his worker; the one smirking meaningfully and businesslike, the other shy, reluctant, like someone who has brought his own skin to market and has nothing else to expect than the—tannery." (Marx, 2009, p. 178). Marx will return to this in the following sections.

In the third section of his work "Capital", Marx describes the production of "absolute surplus value" compared to "relative surplus value", which he discusses in detail in the fourth section. Marx saw labor as a commodity and thus a use value. The seller of his labor power is the worker, the buyer of this labor power is the capitalist, i.e., the entrepreneur. The worker produces a value that corresponds to his wage and beyond. If you subtract the wage from the work performed by the worker and the value thus created, e.g., in a product creation, the (absolute) surplus value of the work remains for the capitalist. Let's assume, for example, that the worker produces a shoe in 8 hours, which is sold on the market for €50 at the end and the worker himself receives €30 wages for it, then the worker has created an absolute surplus value of €20, i.e., €50–€30; for simplicity's sake, the material costs as input factors of the shoe have not been included. If the worker manages to produce the shoe in 7 hours, he can already start with a second shoe and thus create more value in a working day. The worker achieves this relative surplus value through his experience or his higher productivity.

Marx saw the work process as a "metabolism between man and nature": "Work is first of all a process between man and nature, a process in which he mediates his metabolism with nature through his own action, regulates and controls it." (Marx, 2009, p. 179).

At the same time, from the capitalist and entrepreneur's perspective, the worker's work process is the "consumption process of labor power": By employing the worker's labor power for the production of his goods, the capitalist becomes the consumer of the worker's labor power. However, according to Marx, clear rules apply to the "consumption process": "The worker works under the control of the capitalist, to whom his work belongs. The capitalist ensures that the work is carried out properly and that the means of production are used appropriately, i.e., no raw material is wasted and the work instrument is spared, i.e., only destroyed as far as its use in work requires. Secondly, however: The product is the property of the capitalist, not of the immediate producer, the worker. The capitalist, for example, pays the daily value of labor power." (Marx, 2009, p. 187).

The entrepreneur has the option to extend the working day at his discretion, and thus there is "no limit to surplus labor" (third section, 8th chapter). In the fourth section (10th chapter), Marx defines the concept of "relative surplus value". For him, surplus value is relative when it does not change absolutely—the worker's working day remains the same—but "… a part of the working time, which the worker has so far actually consumed for himself, is transformed into working time for the capitalist." (Marx, 2009, p. 301). Surplus value is therefore only created because the worker does not work into his pocket, but "relatively more" into the company's pocket. In the 12th chapter of the fourth section, Marx analyzes the division of labor and its increase in productivity. However, this is bought at the cost of a monotonous and dulling activity. In the fifth section, Marx once again clarifies his view on absolute and relative surplus value: The worker is and remains the productive producer of surplus value, he "toils", but gets nothing from it.

In the sixth section, Marx outlines the wage in the form of piece and time wages: In both cases, the entrepreneur also appropriates the unpaid surplus labor of the worker, thus practically drawing off working time and surplus value. The fool is always just the worker. In the seventh and last section of Volume 1, Marx delves into the accumulation process of capital. Originally, farmers and simple craft businesses produced the necessary goods for life. In the capitalist system, the many producers are displaced by a few "usurpers", i.e., capitalist entrepreneurs. Means of production and producer are separated from each other. The worker "produces" the surplus value, the entrepreneur only provides the "capital". Two different classes emerge, the working class and the "capitalist class". The rural population is dispossessed of their land, they are "expropriated". Capital is increasingly concentrated and centralized in the hands of individual entrepreneurs. According to Marx, however, this leads to recurring crises, profits fall, workers have to be laid off. An "industrial reserve army" is created. Marx looked especially to England and saw the "poorly paid" British working class, wandering miners looking for the next job, and an emerging agricultural proletariat.

According to Marx, the crises of the capitalist economic system then lead—and here he is mistaken as a prophet—to the collapse of capitalism. Workers and the people as a whole join together and collectively own the means of production and the land. Thus, capitalism is replaced by a communist synthesis. In the 25th chapter of the seventh section, the final chapter of Volume 1, Marx once again points out the economic situation in the British colonies: There he finds the same pattern of economy as in the motherland. The capitalists, the entrepreneurs accumulate their capital, lure cheap labor and wage earners into the country, and the capitalist game continues merrily in the colonies as well. In the last two sentences of the chapter, Marx gets to the point:

"However, we are not concerned here with the state of the colonies. What interests us alone is the secret discovered in the new world by the political economy of the old world and loudly proclaimed: Capitalist production and accumulation, and thus also capitalist private property, require the destruction of private property based on one's own labor, i.e., the expropriation of the worker." (Marx, 2009, p. 717).

The economic theories and thoughts of Karl Marx fill entire libraries. Our focus remains on Volume 1 of Capital, which he completed and published during his lifetime. Volumes 2 and 3 were posthumously compiled by his colleague and friend Friedrich Engels and Marx's wife Jenny and contain thematically compiled articles and manuscripts: Volume 2 primarily deepens the cycle of productive and commodity capital, the turnover of capital, and the circulation of social capital. Marx believed that each individual's capital represents only a fraction of the total social capital. Each entrepreneur symbolically represents only a fraction of the so-called "capitalist class". In Volume 3, Marx deals with the transformation of surplus value into profit and explains the phenomenon of the falling rate of profit. In this context, Marx focuses on a company with a production operation. If production is served by an increasingly higher proportion of machines, then the proportion of human labor in it decreases. Consequently, production becomes more expensive due to the higher costs for the machines. The "surplus value" produced by the workers decreases in relation, the rate of profit decreases. Marx concedes that the "surplus value" cannot be realized in the "circulation process" on the market, as all entrepreneurs want to maximize their profit and compete with each other. This causes prices and returns to fall. Finally, Marx divides the profit into an interest portion and an entrepreneurial profit, as he also deals with the transformation of surplus profit into ground rent.

What remains valid from the ideas and theories of the economist Karl Marx? His impact as a philosopher, sociologist, and economist can hardly be overestimated. On the occasion of his 200th birthday in 2018, a multitude of biographies and articles were published that extensively honor Marx's life and work. In this book, he interests us primarily as an economist. Marx followed the Hegelian dialectic of thesis, antithesis, and synthesis in his theoretical considerations. Less politely expressed, he believed in terms of the economy that every economic or social system is subject to constant change. A set system, thesis (derived from ancient Greek *tithemi* = set), is confronted in a dynamic process by internal contradictions and maldevelopments with another system alternative, i.e., the antithesis or counter-thesis (ancient Greek *anti* = against), and finally replaced by a synthesis (ancient Greek *syn* = with, together) as a "mixed form" that includes elements of the old and new systems.

Marx believed that income between workers and owners is unevenly distributed when looking at individual performance. Thus, the workers and the physical capital produce the value added and in total the social product. But the employee has little of this: While the actual providers of the service, the workers, literally get nothing and only receive what they need to (survive), the entrepreneur and owner get the rest. He, according to Marx, only provides his capital and thus bears the entrepreneurial risk.

The resulting "surplus value" is skimmed off by the "capitalist", the worker is "exploited". He exists on the edge of the subsistence minimum and has to watch how the entrepreneur becomes richer and richer at his expense and accumulates his "capital", i.e., piles it up. The structural change in the economy forces entrepreneurs to rationalize and cut jobs. The resulting army of unemployed, the "industrial reserve army", fights for every job that becomes available and does not or only imperceptibly raise the wage level. Anyone who has a job is glad about it and will not negotiate a higher wage. At the time of Karl Marx, unions and strikes were prohibited.

The increasing competitive pressure leads to a "tendency of the rate of profit to fall", the crises of the capitalist system intensify, and the number of unemployed increases, according to Marx's prediction (antithesis). Marx concluded that the system of capitalism must inevitably collapse, as it cannot survive these inequalities in income distribution and maldevelopments. In the end, a social and economic revolution would give greater importance to equality, communism (synthesis). But Marx was largely wrong with these predictions: After long struggles and political disputes, workers and employees have formed unions, which still form a large and significant counterweight against entrepreneurs today. Wages are now more strongly adjusted to productivity gains, company profits, and the inflation rate. Not all companies are active in the industrial and production sector today. Service companies and small and medium-sized enterprises know much less about "alienation" from work and "exploitation". They are mostly part of the entrepreneurial whole and feel that way—think especially of the start-ups that are sprouting up like mushrooms with many highly motivated young people who see themselves as entrepreneurs in the company. Finally, the modern state with its rules, laws, and measures has contributed to the fact that there is no more child labor, comprehensive health protection regulations have been introduced, and extensive social benefits are provided to the working population in case of illness, old age, and need for care.

Nevertheless, one must admit in the fall of 2019 that the unequal income distribution between the few who already have a lot and the vast majority has continued and further intensified to this day. Never before has the material difference between the one percent of the wealthiest in Germany, but also in other industrialized countries, and the remaining 99 percent of the population been greater than today. It's no wonder that today the "capitalist system" and capitalism are once again under criticism and alternatives are being considered. This would certainly have been in line with Karl Marx's thinking, who demanded a departure from capitalism and a new economic form with more equality. The fact that the practical implementation of the planned economy failed in the countries of the Eastern Bloc and the GDR cannot be blamed on the economic theorist and philosopher Marx. His theories and thoughts on economics are still relevant today and are an integral part of the canon of great economists.

References

Bofinger, P. (2015). Adam Smith. Der Segen des Egoismus. In L. Nienhaus (Hrsg.), *Die Weltverbesserer—66 große Denker, die unser Leben verändern* (S. 31–34). Carl Hanser.

Braunberger, G. (2015). Friedrich List. Der Feuerkopf der Globalisierung. In L. Nienhaus (Hrsg.), *Die Weltverbesserer—66 große Denker, die unser Leben verändern* (S. 23–26). Carl Hanser.

Brost, M. (1999). Immer alles im Lot. Jean-Baptiste Say: Traité d'Économie Politique. *Die Zeit* online vom 27.05.1999. https://www.zeit.de/1999/22/199922.biblio-serie_3_s.xml. Zugegriffen: 14. Okt. 2019.

Daniels, A. (1996). Zölle fürs Vaterland. In N. Piper (Hrsg.), *Die großen Ökonomen. Leben und Werk der wirtschaftswissenschaftlichen Vordenker* (2. Aufl., S. 127–132). Schäffer-Poeschel.

Eltis, W. (1989). David Ricardo. In J. Starbatty (Hrsg.), *Klassiker des ökonomischen Denkens* (2 Bände, S. 188–207). C. H. Beck.

Häuser, K. (1989). Friedrich List. In J. Starbatty (Hrsg.), *Klassiker des ökonomischen Denkens* (2 Bände, S. 225–244). C. H. Beck.

Herrmann, U. (2016). *Kein Kapitalismus ist auch keine Lösung. Die Krise der heutigen Ökonomie oder was wir von Smith, Marx und Keynes lernen können* (3. Aufl.). Westend.

Hoffmann, J. (1992). Alles pendelt sich ein. *Die Zeit* online Nr. 49/1992 vom 27.11.1992. https://www.zeit.de/1992/49/alles-pendelt-sich-ein. Zugegriffen: 14. März 2019.

Hoffmann, T. S. (2009). *Wirtschaftsphilosophie—Ansätze und Perspektiven von der Antike bis heute*. Marix.

Krelle, W. (1989). Jean-Baptiste Say. In J. Starbatty (Hrsg.), *Klassiker des ökonomischen Denkens* (2 Bände, S. 172–187). C. H. Beck.

Kurz, H. D. (1996a). Das System der natürlichen Freiheit. In N. Piper (Hrsg.), *Die großen Ökonomen. Leben und Werk der wirtschaftswissenschaftlichen Vordenker* (2. Aufl., S. 29–36). Schäffer-Poeschel.

Kurz, H. D. (1996b). Geiz der Natur. In N. Piper (Hrsg.), *Die großen Ökonomen. Leben und Werk der wirtschaftswissenschaftlichen Vordenker* (2. Aufl., S. 37–43). Schäffer-Poeschel.

Kurz, H. D. (2015). Karl Marx. Die Entzauberung des Kapitalismus. In L. Nienhaus (Hrsg.), *Die Weltverbesserer—66 große Denker, die unser Leben verändern* (S. 78–81). Carl Hanser.

List, F. (2008). *Friedrich List—das nationale System der politischen Ökonomie, Monographien der List Gesellschaft e.V.*, Bd 25. In (Hrsg) Eugen Wendler. Nomos.

de Marchi, M. (1989). John Stuart Mill. In J. Starbatty (Hrsg.), *Klassiker des ökonomischen Denkens* (2 Bände, S. 266–290). C. H. Beck.

Marx, K. (1844). Zur Kritik der Hegelschen Rechtsphilosophie. Einleitung. MEW Bd.1, S.378ff., zitiert nach Dokument Universität Giessen. www.staff.uni-giessen.de. Zugegriffen: 13. Okt. 2019.

Marx, K. (1845). Thesen über Feuerbach, 11. These, Brüssel, zitiert nach Wikisource. de.m.wikisource.org. Zugegriffen: 13. Okt. 2019.

Marx, K. (2009). *Das Kapital—Kritik der politischen Ökonomie* (Ungekürzte Ausgabe nach der zweiten Auflage von 1872 mit einem Geleitwort von Karl Korsch aus dem Jahre 1932, unveränderter Nachdruck). Anaconda.

Marx, K., & Engels, F. (1983). *Manifest der Kommunistischen Partei*. Nachdruck Reclam.

Mill, J. S. (2004). *Principles of political economy* (Great mind series). Prometheus Books.

von Oertzen, P. (1991). Karl Marx. In W. Euchner (Hrsg.), *Klassiker des Sozialismus* (Bd. 1, S. 139–156). C. H. Beck.

Ott, A. E. (1989). Karl Marx. In J. Starbatty (Hrsg.), *Klassiker des ökonomischen Denkens* (Bd. 2, S. 7–35). C. H. Beck.

von Petersdorff, W. (2015). Thomas Malthus. Der traurige Pastor. In L. Nienhaus (Hrsg.), *Die Weltverbesserer—66 große Denker, die unser Leben verändern* (S. 115–118). Carl Hanser.

Recktenwald, H. C. (1989). Adam Smith. In J. Starbatty (Hrsg.), *Klassiker des ökonomischen Denkens* (2 Bände, S. 134–155). C. H. Beck.

Schipper, L. (2015). John Stuart Mill. Das Glück im Kapitalismus. In L. Nienhaus (Hrsg.), *Die Weltverbesserer—66 große Denker, die unser Leben verändern* (S. 106–109). Carl Hanser.

Smith, A. (2009). *Wohlstand der Nationen* (Nach der Übersetzung von Max Stirner, herausgegeben von Heinrich Schmidt). Anaconda.

Smith, A. (2010). *Theorie der ethischen Gefühle* (Philosophische Bibliothek Felix Meiner Band 605, übersetzt von Eckstein, W. und herausgegeben von Brandt, H.D.). Felix Meiner.

Starbatty, J. (Hrsg.). (1989). *Klassiker des ökonomischen Denkens* (2 Bände). C. H. Beck.

Steinmann, G. (1989). Thomas Robert Malthus. In J. Starbatty (Hrsg.), *Klassiker des ökonomischen Denkens* (2 Bände, S. 156–171). C. H. Beck.

Streminger, G. (2017). *Adam Smith. Wohlstand und Moral—Eine Biographie.* C. H. Beck.

Thornton, P. (2015). *Die großen Ökonomen. 10 Vordenker deren Werk unser Leben verändert hat.* Börsenbuch.

Zank, W. (1996a). Lob der Enthaltsamkeit. In N. Piper (Hrsg.), *Die großen Ökonomen. Leben und Werk der wirtschaftswissenschaftlichen Vordenker* (2. Aufl., S. 44–49). Schäffer-Poeschel.

Zank, W. (1996b). Freiheit und Sozialismus. In N. Piper (Hrsg.), *Die großen Ökonomen. Leben und Werk der wirtschaftswissenschaftlichen Vordenker* (2. Aufl., S. 55–56). Schäffer-Poeschel.

3

Neoclassical and Recent Past

3.1 The Neoclassicists

Neoclassicism is not simply a further development of classicism as "Neo-Classicism", but arose from the efforts and struggles of individual economists to redesign their field. At the center of this further development of the economic discipline were several representatives from different countries and with diverse intellectual backgrounds: the logician and economist William Stanley Jevons from Liverpool, the Austrian doctor of law and journalist Carl Menger, who only later qualified in economics, the Frenchman Léon Walras, a trained natural scientist and novelist, the mathematician Alfred Marshall from London, and the Italian engineer Vilfredo Pareto. They were all united in their attempt to put economics on a new basis in terms of its principles and methods. Thus, Jevons criticized the methodological equality of the different scientific disciplines. In his opinion, the individual sciences should try to develop their own principles and methods. The same applies to economics. Thus, Jevons formulated the core problem of economics as an optimization problem: What type of labor input maximizes the utility of a product given values for population, productive forces, and land conditions? Alfred Marshall, as a mathematician, was more oriented towards the exact sciences, mathematics, physics, and the natural sciences. In his opinion, economic issues should be approached according to a rational-analytical research method. However, he warned the guild of economists against too intensive use of mathematics. It distracts too much from the actual economic problems, its gain in knowledge is very limited and rather tempts to elegant mathematical playfulness than to serious economic analysis.

The economic reality was described by the neoclassicists (cf. Part I, Sect. 3.1) in a very ideal-typical way: A market with many demanders and suppliers is assumed, a so-called atomistic market. The providers of products and services react to the price and adjust their offered product quantities: The higher the price, the more is offered. Furthermore, it is—unrealistically—assumed that the products are all comparable, i.e., homogeneous, and there is complete transparency regarding the goods offered. It is also assumed that there are no barriers to market entry and every new provider has free market access. Prices reflect the scarcity of a good: the scarcer a good, the higher its price. All economic participants as consumers or providers have complete information. The scarcity of individual products is known and conscious to everyone. The image of man as Homo oeconomicus enters the everyday life of economic models. Emotional-psychological elements of being human are ignored, individual differences in the reception and evaluation of market information do not exist. All people are equal, completely rational and informed about the market situation at all times. We will return to a detailed critique of this assumption of the neoclassicists at the end of this book.

According to the rational principle of economics, shaped by mathematics and the exact natural sciences, companies do not exist as value communities with corporate culture and their own history as well as people at their head who offer various products and services, but as pure production functions. The relationships between the individual employees and groups of a company, the human, social science side of the company, are not of interest to the neoclassicists for reasons of simplification. I have explained this problem of neglecting human perspectives and what an alternative could look like in detail in my "Book Limits of Economic Thinking" (Pietsch, 2017, p. 101 ff.).

The production function indicates how many products can be manufactured with a given production technology and labor input. For example, one can consider how many cars can be produced in a factory with correspondingly modern production technology and which workforce. The quality, i.e., the competence of the workforce, plays as little a role as the relationships between the employees. The methodological and leadership skills of the employees and management are just as little considered as the psychosocial conditions of production, e.g., the motivation of the workers, their ambition, teamwork, social interaction in the sense of the general working climate.

Supply and demand are brought into equilibrium in the neoclassical model in the shortest possible time. Spatial differences and individual preferences for products and brands play as little a role as the cultural context. The company focuses exclusively on the production function and neglects state activities or framework conditions set by the government. At best, one can say that the neoclassical economic model describes a theoretical ideal image of the economy, which is best approached mathematically in the model. The benefit for the demander is brought to the fore. Above all, the question is asked what benefit an additional unit of a good brings compared to the additional costs. If you treat yourself to a second liter of beer at the Munich Oktoberfest, you can certainly assume a higher additional benefit than when buying the sixth beer. This marginal consideration of the benefits and costs of an additional unit of a good also entered neoclassicism as the mathematical marginal principle. If one takes this model as a starting point, one can gradually lift the ideal and largely unrealistic individual assumptions of the model and describe the resulting effect.

How did this scientific development come about? From the foundation of classics like Adam Smith, the moral philosopher and his colleagues, to a model shaped by mathematical and natural sciences full of unrealistic assumptions that still have a significant influence on economic theory today? To understand this, we will now look at the biographies, intellectual development, and core ideas of the main representatives of neoclassicism:

If there is such a person as the founder of a new economic school, it is **Alfred Marshall** (cf. Rieter, 1989, p. 135 ff.; Oltmanns, 1996a, p. 75 ff.). His economic approaches and methods, which in some ways build on Jevons' thought structure, are still influential today and laid the foundation for neoclassical thinking in economics. Alfred Marshall was born in 1842 as the son of a cashier at the Bank of England in London. His strict father did not provide little Alfred with a happy childhood. Dominated by the idea that his son must become a priest, Marshall had to cram Latin, Greek, and Hebrew, subjects important for theology, even outside of school. Marshall, on the other hand, preferred to occupy himself with chess and his favorite subject, mathematics. In 1861, against his father's will, he began studying mathematics at St. John's College in Cambridge at the age of 19. His uncle financially supported him in this. Four years later, in 1865, Marshall graduated with top grades in mathematics and received a scholarship, supplementing his income with private math tutoring. This left him with enough money to devote himself to his studies.

Like many economists and scientists of his time, Marshall also dealt with different disciplines. In 1867, Marshall joined the discussion circle "Cambridge's Grote Club" and discussed the social situation in England with philosophers, economists, and politically interested individuals, among other things. He was particularly interested in the causes of poverty. He studied the works of classics like Adam Smith and David Ricardo and dealt intensively with economic phenomena. In 1868, Marshall took up a teaching position in the subject of *Moral Science* and lectured on logic, ethics, and political economy. He never saw himself as a pure theorist, although he liked to dress the classical economic doctrine in mathematical formulas. The mathematician in him seemed to shine through. Marshall visited the industrial centers of his time and tried to understand the economic issues and trading activities of his time through practical observation and analysis. During this time, the basic framework of his main work "Principles of Economics" was created, which he only published 20 years later.

The new element in his analysis was primarily the methodology: Marshall was one of the first to use the supply and demand curves still used today to determine the price of goods and the equilibrium quantity, namely where the supply and demand curves intersect. In Cambridge, Marshall gave special economic courses for women. There he also met his future wife, who was one of his first students. According to the celibate regulations for scholars in Oxford and Cambridge at that time, Marshall had to end his scholarship after he married 3 years later. Therefore, Marshall took up a professorship at the newly founded college in Bristol and became its rector ("Principal") at the same time. In 1883, he temporarily took over a lectureship in political economy at the University of Oxford, until he finally received a chair in political economy at his home university Cambridge in 1885. (At that time, the celibate regulations for scholars were relaxed.) He held this chair until his retirement in 1908. There, he first tried to establish economics as an independent science and separate it from the hitherto affiliated Moral Science Faculty. Adam Smith, as the founder of economics and moral philosophy, clearly has an influence here.

Marshall saw the main reason for dealing with economic issues in the analysis of poverty and the economic possibilities for its elimination. He was particularly interested in how it would be possible to lead a dignified life without poverty, without having to endure the harsh working conditions of the time. Marshall was of the opinion that there was no original economic research method. In a practical science like economics, any method is allowed that makes it possible to theoretically capture and analyze the real conditions of economic life. In his bestseller "Principles of Economics", which is still read today, the new term for economics in English shines through: instead of "Political Economy", Marshall named his main work "Principles of Economics", in reference to the natural sciences like "physics" and "mathematics". In 1890, he founded the Royal Economic Society with colleagues, an association of economists with a corresponding professional organ, the *Economic Journal.* Finally, Marshall reformed economic teaching and established it as an equal science at the University of Cambridge: The Cambridge School of Economics was born. Marshall was a very well-known scientist in his time, whose advice was highly sought after in the highest political and social circles. He died in Cambridge at the age of almost 82.

Marshall influenced economic theory with his advanced supply and demand diagrams. To focus on a few elements of the economy, he introduced partial analysis (lat. *pars* = the part) and kept the other, non-considered elements constant in his observations. He called this Latin *ceteris paribus*, roughly: all other things being equal. As a mathematician, Marshall introduced various mathematical methods into economics to ensure the statements were comprehensible. He developed and refined the so-called elasticity analysis, a method for calculating the effects of individual parameters on the overall result. With elasticity analysis, he could determine, for example, how demand changes if the price changes marginally, i.e., slightly, for example by 1 %. Furthermore, Marshall investigated under what conditions a market equilibrium arises, where supply and demand balance each other. The supply side was determined by a representative firm and its production function, which realizes a certain output with given input factors. For Marshall, the demander was the well-informed consumer known from Homo economicus, who wants to satisfy his needs with the goods that provide him with the maximum benefit. Where the benefit of each additional unit of a good decreases with increasing quantity according to the marginal principle. Think again of the sixth beer at Oktoberfest compared to the second.

Marshall had to face strong criticism for his theory during his lifetime. The strong mathematization and the lack of consideration of a realistic human image in economics heated the minds of the experts. Had Marshall displaced humans with their ethical and social implications in favor of a theory construct with algebraic formulas and rigid graphics, which was based on a completely unrealistic human image? This assessment does Marshall an injustice. From the beginning of his scientific career, Marshall always insisted on studying economic practice closely and drawing inspiration from it for further research. The reader is reminded of the question of eliminating poverty. Also, Marshall's engagement with philosophy and moral-ethical questions points in a different direction than that of the economist who forgets about people.

On the contrary, Marshall was convinced that entrepreneurship, which only embarks on the ruthless journey for profit without considering the common good, is definitely going in the wrong direction. He supported the idea of free entrepreneurship, even flirted with the redistribution of wealth to the poor, at least in parts, and was thus not far from the ideas of the socialists of his time. Marshall was by no means an advocate of the pure construct of Homo economicus. At the same time, he was aware that the mathematical marginal principle is not universally applicable. He was well aware that economic behavior is fed by a multitude of different motives, which are moral, social, psychological, and technological in nature. Marshall saw the economist also as a teacher and educator of people towards a more efficient producer and a wiser consumer—for him, economics was also a pedagogical element.

Nevertheless, Marshall was clear that the establishment of economics as an independent science demanded its own methods and principles, which he modeled after the exact natural sciences. However, he left the door open for new approaches. Marshall was convinced that each time and each country, against the background of the current economic situation, requires its own principles, methods, and doctrines. He even warned his research colleagues against seeing mathematics as a master key, as a suitable means to seemingly solve and handle all economic problems exactly mathematically. Too strong mathematization of real social and economic problems would distract too much from the actual conditions. He said this, even though he was a passionate mathematician! The science of biology with its analogy as a social organism could also provide a number of insights for economics. Focusing solely on mathematics as an auxiliary science of economics falls short. Thus, evolutionary research with its laws of mutation (change) and selection of individual species also helps economic models as an analogy for the rise and fall of individual national economies. This example alone proves that not only mathematics, but also other sciences, in this case biology, could contribute to economics.

As a quintessence of Marshall's work, it can be stated that his contribution to the establishment of economics as an independent science is undisputed. His "Principles of Economics" has influenced many generations of students to this day. Marshall shaped the graphical representation of supply and demand diagrams, consumer and producer surplus. The consumer surplus is the part of the price, shown in the form of an area, that the consumer is willing to pay, but does not have to pay due to the real equilibrium price, while the producer surplus is the area that results as the difference between the real equilibrium price and the price that the producer must achieve in order to produce profitably. Although Marshall observed the economy and realized that a multitude of social and human factors influence economic activities, he created a widely formalized economic world with his mathematical concepts and principles. Elasticities, marginal utility consideration, i.e., the marginal principle, Homo oeconomicus, partial analysis with the exclusion of disturbing influences, i.e., ceteris paribus, are the keywords that paved the way to a more formalized economic theory world, which still leaves its traces today. However, this was neither Marshall's pronounced wish nor his only legacy. Nevertheless, he was a significant co-founder of neoclassical economics and paved the way to modernity.

Léon Walras (cf. Oltmanns, 1996b, p. 63 ff.; Felderer, 1989, p. 59 ff.) was born in 1834 in France as the son of a teacher, later professor of philosophy in Évreux in Normandy. He spent his childhood and youth in Paris. He failed the "Concours", the entrance examination of the renowned École polytechnique in Paris, twice due to insufficient mathematical knowledge and began an engineering science study at the École des Mines in Paris in 1854. However, Walras was only moderately interested in his studies and preferred to write novels. His most famous was the novel "Francis" published in 1858, which had autobiographical traits and described his student life in Paris. In addition, he dealt with literature in general, philosophy, art, history, economic policy, and social science in general. Today, one would speak of a general study, i.e., dealing with the intellectual topics of the time.

After completing his studies, he earned his living with various activities that had little to do with his original engineering studies. Thus, Walras was an employee of the railway company Chemins de Fer Du Nord—his father knew the son of Jean-Baptiste Say, who was a railway director there—and a bill of exchange bank. However, his passion was economics. Walras' father had already written some works on economics and social science, which the son wanted and should further develop. With an essay published in 1860, in which he dealt with the guiding principles of Proudhon's work, the social question, Walras participated in a competition as part of an international tax congress in Lausanne. Although he only came in fourth place, he left a lasting impression on the jury of renowned economists. His fervent wish to obtain a chair in economics at a French university was not fulfilled. The existing chairs were occupied by representatives of the current doctrine. His new ideas based on mathematical economics were rejected at the time. The chair allocation was made internally among the conventional subject representatives.

In 1870, there was a surprising turn in Walras' life: He was invited to participate in the tender for the chair of political economy in Lausanne. His impressive contribution to the international tax conference 10 years earlier was still well remembered. Walras won the race for the vacant chair and got the position in Switzerland. It was his most scientifically productive time. He came into contact with the great economists of his time, such as William Stanley Jevons, Alfred Marshall, Carl Menger, Vilfredo Pareto, and Antoine-Augustin Cournot. Since his wife fell seriously ill and he had to support her financially, Walras also gave private lessons and wrote articles under the pseudonym Paul in the *Gazette de Lausanne*. This multiple burden from work led to health problems for Walras. His first wife died, from the dowry of his second wife and his own inheritance he could afford to work as an honorary professor and to be mainly active as a publicist. He no longer gave lectures. His chair was taken over by Vilfredo Pareto. Walras died in Clarens, today's Montreux, in 1910.

Walras' groundbreaking achievement in the field of economics was the development of a *general equilibrium model of the economy*. With the model of complete competition, Walras tried to determine an equilibrium for all economic variables, i.e., prices and quantities of all products and factors of production. So, what quantities of a good are demanded by consumers at what prices that lead the system to an equilibrium? Walras was convinced that a price could only deviate from its equilibrium price in the short term. Rather, the real price fluctuates permanently around the equilibrium price, "it oscillates". Walras distinguished four different markets: goods markets, capital markets, money markets, and markets for factors of production. An equilibrium price is established on each of these markets.

Walras also laid the foundation for essential economic terms that are commonly used today. He described prices as a function of demand and supply, of scarcity, "rareté". He defined market equilibrium based on the supply and demand function—a mathematical construction where the equilibrium price results where the supply and demand function are equal—and explained utility functions, the utility maximum, and the marginal utility consideration. The marginal utility consideration was, alongside the equilibrium theory, the core element of Walras' research. The value of a good was, for him, dependent on the utility it provides. The most valuable are always the first parts of a good, such as a bite of cheese or the first sip of wine. All further sips only have a decreasing utility, until one eventually becomes weary of the wine. In this, he argued with other economists of his time like Jevons and Menger, who were conducting the marginal utility consideration at the same time, about the authorship.

Much more essential, however, was the development of his model of the equilibrium of the four markets he distinguished, which Walras presented in his main work "Elements d'économie politique pure ou Théorie de la richesse sociale", Elements of Pure Political Economy or Theory of Social Wealth. In a complex mathematical procedure, Walras tried to prove that there is at least *one* mathematical solution where all markets are in equilibrium. He could not prove this. This was only achieved in 1936 by the US economist Abraham Wald. Since the mathematical argumentation with vectors etc. could not be well communicated to the broad masses, Walras invented an almost ingenious metaphor for price formation in equilibrium: the auctioneer. This auctioneer first collects purchase and sale orders at an arbitrarily defined price. If demand exceeds supply, there is excess demand, and the auctioneer raises the price in the next round. If the demand at the higher price is then lower than the supply, i.e., there is excess supply, the auctioneer successively lowers the price. Eventually, an equilibrium price is reached where demand is fully satisfied by supply and nothing remains. This happens step by step in all four markets. Walras called this gradual approach to the equilibrium price *tâtonnement,* French for "groping".

Many of Walras' contemporaries saw this general market equilibrium on competitive markets as a clear sign that the state should only provide the framework conditions, i.e., for open markets, competition, and the competition of providers among each other, but should otherwise stay out of the economy. However, this is only half the truth. Walras was quite convinced that the result of the free play of economic forces should be shared with the poor of the population. On the contrary, he had a clear societal and economic vision: taxes should ideally be completely abolished. People lived from their talents and abilities. Land and soil belonged to the state, which financed itself through rent and lease income. The state provides for security and the necessary infrastructure such as schools and universities.

Many contemporaries found Walras' theory too mathematical and did not provide any significant new insights. Not without reason, Walras complained in a letter to a friend that it takes a long time for complex and far-sighted economic theories to prevail. Without a doubt, Walras not only advanced marginal utility analysis, but also contributed much to theory formation in economics through his general equilibrium theory on the four markets he differentiated, and he is not without reason considered one of the co-founders of neoclassicism. Furthermore, Walras was the founder of the "Lausanne School", one of the marginal utility schools. Vilfredo Pareto followed him to his chair of economics at the University of Lausanne.

Vilfredo Pareto (cf. Eisermann, 1989, p. 158 ff.; Graß, 1996, p. 69 ff.; Wagener, 2009, p. 26 ff.) was born in 1848 as Wilfried Fritz Pareto in Paris. The reasons for Pareto's German first names are not fully known. It is suspected that he received them in reference to the German Revolution taking place at the same time, with which his parents sympathized. His father came from a noble Genoese merchant family, his mother was French. In 1858, the family moved back to Northern Italy—the grandfather had to flee Italy for political reasons and had landed in exile in Paris. Pareto studied engineering at the "Politecnico" in Turin, which he completed at only 21 years of age in 1870. Pareto worked as an engineer for almost 20 years, first for a railway company, later for an ironworks. As a senior employee, he was confronted almost daily with the social, economic, and political questions of his time. In addition, he read many scientific works on these subject areas.

After the death of his father in 1874, Pareto moved to Florence and became acquainted with the economic academy in Florence through the mayor. At the age of 26, he was accepted into their ranks as a non-specialist. Between 1877 and 1887, he gave four economic lectures there, which left a lasting impression on the audience. Pareto's interest in economics grew stronger and stronger. In the following years, he repeatedly struggled with whether he should not fully dedicate himself to science. The practical activity as an engineer and manager—as one would say today—appealed to him less and less. After his marriage to a Russian woman in 1890, he published a series of economic articles in the prestigious journal *Giornale degli Economisti,* the journal of economists in Italy. He commented on an article by the then most famous Italian economist, Maffeo Pantaleoni, so expertly that an intensive friendly relationship developed between the two men. It was Panteoni who, with his influence, helped Pareto succeed Walras' chair in Lausanne in 1893. Pareto was almost 45 years old at the time and had spent his entire professional life in practice. His lectures were very well attended right away, his teaching was quickly noticed. Pareto laid out his lectures and further thoughts in his two-volume "Cours d'économie politique", course on political economy. Pareto was successful: His lectures without detailed mathematics met with great resonance. The two-volume introduction to political economy was brilliantly written and a sales success. This led to jealousies with his predecessor Walras, with whom Pareto maintained close contact. Both became estranged from each other. It led to a break.

In 1898, Pareto inherited a large fortune from his parents, which made him independent of further sources of income. He was released from his teaching obligations and devoted himself to intensive research. Pareto had always been a border crosser between economics and sociology from the beginning of his research. Although he still wrote two economic books in Italian: "Manuale di economia politica", French: "Manuel d'économie politique" (Handbook of Political Economy). But even these contained sociological elements, as conversely the main sociological work "Trattato di sociologia generale" (Treatise on General Sociology) published in 1916 also included his economic theories and findings. For Pareto, the connection of both disciplines was essential: Without the intelligent combination of these two key sciences, economics and sociology, a realistic explanation of economic facts would be impossible.

Around the year 1901, Pareto moved to Lake Geneva in Céligny, where he lived in a stately villa. His wife had previously left him. In her place came a French woman, Jeanne Regis, who was about 30 years younger, with whom Pareto had a daughter and whom he married shortly before his death in 1923. The following year, his two-volume work on socialist theories, "Les systèmes socialistes", was published. Although he did not give in to the urging of his friend Panteoni to return to a chair of national economics, Pareto continued to publish articles on economic issues. Pareto was of the opinion that not all economic problems could be solved solely by economic means. In addition, a sociological analysis was urgently needed. From then on, he devoted himself to this topic until his death, which was facilitated by a heart condition.

Pareto's work and scientific research can be divided into economic and sociological subject areas, analogous to the phases of his life. For Pareto, both scientific areas belong together: Although he is best known for his eponymous "Pareto Optimum"—all actions increase welfare under the condition that at least one individual is better off, but no one is worse off—his main work is undoubtedly "Trattato di Sociologia Generale", which deals with the general theory of sociology and on which he had worked for 20 years. Pareto was firmly convinced that scientific progress can only be achieved through observation and experience. Thus, even in the social sciences, the principle applies that laws must be inferred from observed facts in reality. In this process, hypotheses are formulated about certain facts, which are then to be tested and either verified or falsified.

Humans strive to achieve welfare for themselves and their families in material, intellectual, and moral respects. In this context, Pareto distinguishes between objective welfare in the form of utility and subjective welfare, which he calls "ophelimity" (ancient Greek *ophélimos* = useful). As an example, Pareto mentions smoking a cigarette. Subjectively, smoking increases the welfare and well-being of the smoker, but objectively it harms him as it deteriorates his health. In economics, humans act logically and rationally, i.e., they optimize the means-end relationship in decision-making situations and focus on their subjective utility. With this, Pareto introduced the Homo economicus into economic science. However, it is by no means the case that Pareto did not see the abstraction and unreality of this heuristic: Of course, he knew that humans are also capable of non-logical action, such as when they act altruistically, i.e., humanely and cooperatively, instead of selfishly. He was only concerned that science, based on a rational ideal, explains certain processes in reality, then gradually extends the analyses to the non-logical behavior of humans and adjusts the theory accordingly. Because he was also a sociologist, Pareto was able to assess the different facets of human behavior more differentiated.

With the help of the economic factors labor, capital, and land, goods can be produced using certain technologies. However, these are only purchased by the consumer if they satisfy certain needs and provide subjective utility. Instead of the indifference curves that the economist Edgworth had developed before him—indifference curves show which combinations of goods in quality and quantity from the perspective of the individual consumer provide the same utility, i.e., where the consumer is indifferent or indifferent as to which of the two bundles of goods he prefers—Pareto described individually equivalent choices. Every person can usually state whether he prefers the bundle of goods A to the bundle of goods B or which bundles of goods are equivalent from his point of view. However, Pareto was of the opinion that utility is not numerically, i.e., cardinally, exactly measurable and therefore cannot be compared, e.g., in the form of a utility function. Likewise, there would be no diminishing marginal utility of the utility function, according to which the sixth beer is less useful than the second. In general, for Pareto, the mathematical analysis of economics, especially the partial analysis propagated by Alfred Marshall, was a horror, as economics cannot be adequately represented with mathematics.

In contrast to Walras, Pareto defined the economic equilibrium as a state in which all individuals are consistent with a certain price system of a community, i.e., the prevailing price system reflects the different preferences and tastes of the individuals of a community. In such an equilibrium, a maximum subjective utility is given, and it is not possible to increase the utility of individual members without simultaneously harming a part of the members (Pareto efficiency). It is clear here that Pareto, with this definition of economic equilibrium, perceived the individual utility concepts of people as different and accordingly did not add them up.

Pareto was above all a friend of the statistical analysis of empirical, i.e., phenomena occurring in reality. Thus, he was able to prove on the basis of the wealth and income distribution of the people of his time that the statistical correlation of 80:20 usually applies: 80 % of an event is caused by 20 % of the involved factors. Specifically, this means that, for example, 80 % of a nation's wealth is concentrated on only 20 % of the population—currently in Germany it is even only 15 % who own 80 % of the total wealth. The same applies to income distribution. This 80-to-20 rule was incorporated into the literature as the so-called Pareto distribution. To perceive Pareto only as an economist is certainly too short-sighted.

In his "Trattato di Sociologia Generale", Pareto develops a theory of the elite. He generally divides society into the upper class or elite, which consists mainly of the best lawyers, doctors, musicians, writers, richest, etc. There is the ruling, i.e., governing, elite with political offices and the non-ruling, such as the best doctors. Furthermore, Pareto differentiates the nominally affiliated, i.e., inherited, for example through wealth and nobility, and the elites of people who belong to it due to their own merit. In addition to this heterogeneous elite, there is the counterpoint of the lower class, i.e., the rest of society that does not belong to the elite. Pareto believed that the elites are dynamic and not permanent. The ruling class is constantly being replaced by other, emerging elites, who either come from the elite themselves or work their way up from the lower class through their own merit. This "circulation" of the elites—some go down, others go up—is a societal law that exists at all political and economic levels.

This is not the place to fully appreciate the economic and especially the sociological theory of Vilfredo Pareto. The scientific reception of Pareto's work was relatively subdued. This certainly has to do with his somewhat cumbersome, long-winded writing style, which does not always follow a logical structure. In addition, Pareto's major works such as the "Cours" and the "Manuale" have not been translated into German and therefore were not or only little noticed in the German-speaking world. An English translation of the "Trattato" appeared in 1935 under the title "Mind and Society". The "Manuale" was not published in English translation until 1971. In England, the mathematically organized teaching of Alfred Marshall, especially in microeconomics, predominated. Pareto's influence therefore remained largely confined to France and Italy, not only because of the lack of translation.

Unfortunately, this is still largely the case today, apart from the catchy *80-to-20 rule* or the *Pareto optimum.* Only in 2007 did Nobel laureate George Akerlof attempt to integrate some of Pareto's more realistic behavioral assumptions, the so-called non-logical motives for action, into his research. Although Pareto established the ideal type of Homo economicus in economics with his rational-analytical behavioral assumptions, he himself did not believe that humans act so irrationally. He was too much of a sociologist and analyst of human society and the individual for that.

The last neoclassicist to be presented, Carl Menger, also belonged to the Austrian School. Therefore, following the systematics, he will now be described in section 3.2, although he is still counted thematically among the neoclassicists.

3.2 The Austrian School

The Austrian School, also called the *Viennese School* of National Economics, was essentially shaped by its founder Carl Menger and his numerous students. Menger was involved in about 20 habilitations, fundamental scientific works by scientists who were entitled to teach at universities. The reason for the school's name is easy to guess, as they almost all researched in and around Vienna and were imbued with their own view of economics. The researchers of the Austrian School mainly distinguished themselves from the "Historical School" prevailing in Berlin. They vehemently denied that economic phenomena are all dependent on the prevailing culture and historical circumstances, as the representatives of the Historical School in Berlin postulated.

The representatives of the Historical School demanded economic research based on as broad empirical data as possible. Thus, *Gustav von Schmoller,* one of the leading representatives especially of the younger school, meticulously dealt with the medieval city economy, the guilds, mercantilism, and the Prussian administration. Historical detail studies on economic development were supposed to provide insights into economic laws. In contrast to English classicism and the Austrian School, the representatives of the Historical School did not focus on the individual and his needs in economic considerations, but on the community with its values, cultural expressions, and traditions. It is precisely the historical experiences of a people that shape economic actions. Gustav von Schmoller in particular opposed the self-interest of the classicists as the main driving force of the individual with individual ethics: poverty, unemployment and their fight must be at the center of ethically justified economic action. The state must, if in doubt, cushion the unintended negative effects of the market socially and accordingly intervene in the freedom of market events. This idea of social feeding of the market was taken up again in the 20th century in the conception of the social market economy. We will return to this topic when we deal with the Ordo-liberal School (section 3.6).

Vienna was the economic center of trade with the Orient in the second half of the 19th century, and at the same time, it was at the heart of modernization and industrialization in Eastern and Central Europe. Entrepreneurs, scientists, and artists met in the salons of the city, which with nearly 2 million people was the largest German-speaking city, then one of the largest cities in the world. At these meetings, they discussed all pressing questions of the economy: How is value created in the economy, or what value does a good have? What is the significance of interest? How much should the state intervene in the economy? Let's take an example: You go to a supermarket and want to buy a bottle of water. What would you pay at most for it? Probably no more than perhaps 2 € for 1 liter of water. Let's assume you are walking along the beach promenade in southern Spain in early summer and sweating. Only after about 5 kilometers do you see a kiosk offering drinks. The next kiosk or supermarket is not in sight. What would you be willing to pay this time if you are very thirsty? Probably you would also be willing to pay 5 € before you struggle thirsty to the next restaurant or supermarket. Finally, consider what you would be willing to spend on this bottle of water if you were half dehydrated in a desert. Probably all the money you have with you. This example has a lot to do with the Austrian School. Its representatives believed that there is no objective, clearly measurable value for a good or product, but only a subjective one. This is dependent on the individual person, on his general and specific need structure. In our example, the value of the bottle of water certainly depends on how thirsty and capable of suffering you are or want to be etc.

From the perspective of the Austrian School, interest is also a relative, subjective size: Since it is the price for the lender postponing his consumption—he could have bought something with the money—the question is how important the individual lender takes the postponed consumption. If the missed consumption is painful, the interest for the borrowed money will be set higher—and vice versa. Because the values of a good, but also the interest, turn out subjectively different, no state authority, no matter how competent, can succeed in determining the value of a good and the interest. Simply put, the information is lacking. The state is overwhelmed with this task.

Here two core ideas of the representatives of the Austrian School shine through:

1. The human being, with his individual preferences and assessments, is at the center of economics as part of the social sciences and not the natural sciences with their faith in mathematics. The price is an expression of subjective appreciation by the individual at certain occasions—think of the different prices at gas stations for gasoline depending on the time of day and urgency of refueling.
2. The state should stay out of market events as much as possible and only set the framework conditions. Because it is not state institutions or politicians who define the optimal supply of goods, but the price as a signal for the citizen's appreciation and the free market, which should be able to operate as undisturbed as possible.

The Austrian School was founded by **Carl Menger,** whose vita and ideas we will sketch first. Carl Menger (cf. Streissler, 1989, p. 119 ff.; Horn, 2015a, p. 199 ff.; Leube, 1996, p. 91 ff.), actually: Carl Menger, Edler von Wolfensgrün—he later dropped the noble title -, was born in 1840 in Neu-Sandez in Galicia. His father was a lawyer, but died early when Menger was 8 years old, leaving his wife and six children. Through a small inherited fortune, the mother was able to let her sons study. Carl Menger studied law and political science in Vienna and Prague. He initially worked as a journalist and wrote for the official *Lemberger Zeitung,* was co-editor of the *Neues Wiener Tageblatt* and from 1871 editorial secretary of the *Wiener Zeitung.* Previously, he had received his doctorate at the University of Krakow. In 1872 he qualified as a professor with the German constitutional law teacher and economist Lorenz von Stein with a work on the principles of economics. Initially appointed extraordinary professor at the University of Vienna in 1873, Menger was appointed to a new chair for political economy in 1878. For a short time, he also worked as a ministerial secretary in the Ministry Council Presidency.

With his first work after his habilitation on the investigations into the method of social sciences and political economy (cf. Menger, 2005) in particular, Menger triggered the method dispute with the then predominant Berlin *Historical School* around Gustav von Schmoller. From 1876 to 1878, Menger was a private tutor for economics to the 18-year-old Rudolf, Crown Prince of Austria and Hungary, at the instigation of the educator. After that, Menger taught again in Vienna and devoted himself to intensive study of the social sciences. In 1903, due to his deteriorating health, he retired at the age of 63 and was able to continue his research until his death in 1921. He left behind a wife, a son who later became a famous mathematician, and a private library with 25,000 books.

The essential new insight of Carl Menger, which not only made him the founder of the Austrian School, but also a representative of neoclassicism, was the further development of the marginal utility consideration (section 3.1). In general, Menger believed that a good should not be evaluated based on production or labor costs, but solely subjectively from the perspective of the individual. The value of the good for the person arises from the subjectively perceived benefit for the individual. However, this does not mean the average benefit, but the benefit of the last unit, the so-called marginal utility. Let's look at an example: Water is a valuable, but still affordably priced good in our latitudes. The price of water varies not only according to the respective situation (e.g., in the desert or in the supermarket; see above), but also by the quantity. In a basin with 1000 liters of water, an additional liter of water is hardly worth anything. At the Oktoberfest in the heated festival tents, 1 liter of beer, a Maß, is certainly subjectively worth more compared to the previous 2 liters of beer. The price of a good is therefore dependent on what the subjectively perceived value of the last additional unit is. With a water container with a capacity of 1 liter, the second liter makes a more noticeable difference than with a container with 1000 liters.

The subjective aspect of price has fundamental importance for economic theory. Since the price of a good varies individually, no state authority can set the price of this good. Humans err in predicting the future—forecasts are very prone to error. Therefore, the state cannot actively intervene in economic policy, as the consequences for the future are unpredictable. State interventions inhibit private initiative, a state supply of goods must inevitably fail, as there is no universally valid utility function. The state must set the framework, secure it internally and externally, conclude trade agreements or combat natural disasters. It should take care of the poor and weak, create the necessary infrastructure such as road construction, construction of railways, schools, parks etc. Menger and his students, with their ideas, paved the way for American liberalism, which wanted to keep the state as far out of market events as possible.

Joseph Alois Schumpeter (cf. März, 1989, p. 251 ff.; Böhm, 2009a, p. 137 ff.; Piper, 1996, p. 97 ff.; Braunberger, 2015a, p. 249 ff.) must not be missing in any presentation of economic ideas. There are hardly any economists about whom there are as many anecdotes and quotes as about him. Almost every (former) economics student knows the terms "pioneer entrepreneur" or "pioneer profit" (through the short-term establishment of monopolies in the context of innovations). Many also speak in connection with Schumpeter of the term he coined, "creative destruction" of the pioneer entrepreneur, who challenges old established companies. One feels transported to the present day with all the start-ups and new company formations of various kinds, which approach many things differently than traditional companies, yet Schumpeter was already researching at the beginning of the 20th century.

Joseph Alois Schumpeter was born in 1883 in Triesch in Moravia, today's Czech Republic, as the only child of the cloth manufacturer Alois Schumpeter. The father died when the son was 4 years old. The mother moved with Joseph Alois first to Graz, later to Vienna and married Sigismund von Kéler, a field marshal of the imperial and royal army, in 1893. He significantly influenced the education of his stepson. After graduating with honors from the prestigious Theresianum in Vienna in 1901, Joseph Alois Schumpeter wanted to study economics, which at that time was only possible within the framework of a legal study. He studied among others with Böhm-Bawerk, Ludwig von Mises and Emil Lederer, a profound connoisseur of Marxian theory, which greatly impressed Schumpeter. In 1906, Schumpeter was awarded a doctorate in law.

Afterwards, he spent a short time at the seminar of Gustav von Schmoller in Berlin and a year in England, mainly in London, for study purposes. He visited, among others, Alfred Marshall in Cambridge and Francis Edgeworth in Oxford and was a research student at the London School of Economics. Schumpeter thus got to know the essential economic schools of his time. In London, he met his future wife. As the money was running out, Schumpeter worked as a representative for economic affairs in the office of an Italian lawyer in Cairo. There he managed, among other things, the fortune of an Egyptian princess and restructured a sugar refinery. At the same time, Schumpeter worked on his habilitation thesis titled "The Essence and Main Content of Theoretical National Economics". In 1909, he became a private lecturer, a year later an associate professor of political economy at the University of Czernowitz, the capital of the Bukovina region, then the easternmost tip of the Habsburg Empire, now located in Western Ukraine. In 1911, Schumpeter, at only 28 years old, became a full professor of political economy at the University of Graz. In 1913, Schumpeter went to the Columbia University in New York for a research year, where he met and learned from such significant economists as Irving Fisher.

Schumpeter was also politically active. Even during the First World War in 1916, he advocated for ending the war. In 1919, he became a member of the Socialization Commission, which was to determine whether the German coal industry should be socialized, a move that Schumpeter supported. In March 1919, he served as State Secretary in the Ministry of Finance for 7 months. He eventually resigned due to irreconcilable differences with his Social Democratic ministerial colleagues. In 1921, Schumpeter became president of M. L. Biedermann & Co. Bankaktiengesellschaft, a very old Austrian private bank. However, things went badly: the bank went bankrupt in 1924, Schumpeter was liable as a partner with his personal assets and spent years paying off the debts. In 1925, he took up a chair in economic political science at the University of Bonn. In the same year, Schumpeter married for the second time—his marriage to his first wife Gladys had failed relatively early. However, mother and child died during childbirth. In the same year, his own mother also died. These strokes of fate hit Schumpeter hard. He threw himself into scientific work.

After he had already spent two semesters in the academic year 1927/28 and another one in 1930 as a visiting professor at the Department of Economics at Harvard

University, he moved to the USA permanently from 1932. Prior to this, he had given numerous lectures in Japan, which had received a very positive response. Schumpeter eventually accepted a call to Harvard University and was to build a prestigious economic department with his scientific reputation. He succeeded in doing so. His students included none other than Paul A. Samuelson, James Tobin, Richard Musgrave, Wassily Leontief, among others. Schumpeter held numerous honorary positions such as President of the Econometric Society, which dealt with statistical methods in economics and came to new insights there. He was even elected president of the American Economic Association, the most important association of American economists—as the first economist not born in the USA. Finally, he became president of the International Economic Association. In 1937, Schumpeter married for the third time: the economist Elizabeth Firuski. The economic historian ensured that Schumpeter's leftover notes on the topic "History of Economic Analysis" could be published posthumously. Schumpeter died in 1950 of a cerebral hemorrhage in his summer house in Connecticut.

Schumpeter's work can be divided into a European and an American period. In his habilitation thesis "The Essence and Main Content of Theoretical National Economics", with which he quickly made a name for himself in Germany, Schumpeter advocated for an economics oriented towards natural science and mathematics. Only mathematical formulas and equations allowed economic laws to be identified and described. In economic models, assumptions had to be made for simplification, which do not occur in this form in reality—such as the rationally acting Homo oeconomicus—but allow an image of economic development to be traced. Psychological and sociological assumptions had no place in it.

In his theory of economic development, Schumpeter begins the analysis of the economy with a static model. For simplicity's sake, he initially leaves out entrepreneurs and their profits and only considers wages and ground rents. Changes in the sense of a dynamic economic development are mainly generated by the creative entrepreneur. According to Schumpeter, one is an entrepreneur due to one's personality: a person with certain abilities such as initiative, ideas, foresight, perseverance, and assertiveness. The entrepreneur is the bearer of the change mechanism. Not self-interest drives him, but the "joy of shaping". The inventive entrepreneur develops and drives innovations and thus acquires a monopoly position in the short term—one can imagine the position of the company Apple at the beginning of the iPhone boom. This happens until competitors dissolve this monopoly position by imitating the product—here, for example, smartphones in general.

The entrepreneur is driven to permanent innovation by this short-term "pioneer profit". This "creative destruction" of the previous business model of companies—today, in the age of digitization, one would speak of "disruption"—of an industry by the entrepreneur leads to a further development of the entire industry and is the driving force of economic dynamics. Schumpeter attaches great importance to the role of banks: In order to get his projects and new business ideas off the ground, the entrepreneur depends on capital. The banks provide the entrepreneurs with the necessary capital and thus become their biggest supporters. Today, so-called venture capital from external capital providers would also be possible.

Schumpeter's most important work, which has been translated into 20 languages and is one of the classics of political economy, is "Capitalism, Socialism and Democracy", which was already published in the USA.

In it, he dealt with the nature of capitalism, its successes and above all its future. Schumpeter assumes the self-destruction of capitalism—however, not, as Marx predicted, through a violent revolution, but through the structure and nature of capitalism itself. In capitalism, there are entrepreneurs who maximize their profit with their innovations and the incentive to change, stimulate the economy and raise the standard of living of the population. Capitalism initially creates general prosperity and thus makes a social welfare state possible. Also, the concentration on a few large companies that drive innovation and technological progress was beneficial for capitalism as a whole. They achieve product and process innovations, open up new sales and procurement markets, and constantly improve the quality of their products.

However, the classic owner-entrepreneur was increasingly replaced by salaried managers who—according to Schumpeter's view—did not have the same moral obligation to maximize profits and preserve jobs as the owner. The obligation to provide for the employees entrusted to him is no longer as significant to the manager as it is to the owner-entrepreneur. The identification with one's own company is higher among entrepreneurs than among salaried managers, who can switch to another company if in doubt. For the entrepreneur, "his" company is his life's work, which must be protected and preserved under all circumstances. This is one reason for the gradual decline of capitalism.

Another reason would be the emergence of the class of intellectuals. Yes, you read correctly. Schumpeter believed that more and more people are enjoying higher education, but companies do not need a correspondingly increasing number of academically educated executives. Therefore, many highly educated intellectuals would become and remain unemployed. They would be highly dissatisfied and organize protests against the prevailing system of capitalism, which produces many losers. If at the same time the growth rates of the economy stagnate and unemployment continues to rise, then the general dissatisfaction would turn into public discontent. At the latest then, Schumpeter saw the transition from a capitalist to a socialist economic order: The owner-entrepreneur disappears in favor of large companies with salaried managers, and the support of the capitalist economic system in the population shrinks. In a socialist economic order, control over production and means of production is the responsibility of a central authority. This transition to a democratic socialism takes place gradually and is legitimized by democratic elections.

Joseph Alois Schumpeter described tendencies of capitalism that, especially from today's perspective, stimulate thought. Even if the decline of capitalism in the form he described will not occur and the times of a central planning authority are most likely over, some points are still relevant today. It is often rightly criticized that capitalism, globalization produces always winners and losers, even though the overall societal wealth in the countries of the market economic system has significantly increased. Especially today, there is increased discussion about the increasing economic inequality in the population, whether it is related to income or wealth. Pure capitalism seems to produce significantly more losers than winners from the perspective of its critics.

Schumpeter's merit is to have sharpened the view on the importance and the role of the entrepreneur in the economy. At the same time, he left behind a large number of influential students who built on his ideas. Schumpeter left many extensive works, including on the history of economic ideas, the "History of Economic Analysis", which very well reflects the history of the subject. Not least, through his contacts with the most renowned economists of his time, Schumpeter had a very profound overview of the most pressing topics of economic theory and the current state of research and was able to develop his ideas in competition with the best of his peers. In this respect, he also accomplished a "creative destruction" of old theory buildings through his own research.

The quote "Who is only an economist, cannot be a good economist" comes from **Friedrich August von Hayek.** Accordingly, his scientific work is multifaceted. It radiates into various scientific disciplines: psychology, philosophy, evolutionary theory, even theory of science and above all general social science. Hayek is considered one of the most important thinkers of liberalism and developed the ideas of the Austrian School, especially the liberal ideas of Mises, further. Hayek (cf. Böhm, 1996, p. 105 ff.; Böhm, 2009b, p. 228 ff.; Horn, 2015b, p. 57 ff.; Thornton, 2015, p. 137 ff.) was born in 1899 as the son of the physician August von Hayek in Vienna and grew up in a wealthy family. From an early age, he was broadly interested in science. The philosopher Ludwig Wittgenstein was part of his distant circle of relatives. Thus, the young Friedrich dealt with mineralogy, botany, entomology, and evolutionary theory, among other things. After a short military service in 1917, Hayek began studying law at the university in 1918, but also attended courses in economics and psychology. However, he wrote his dissertation in 1923 on theoretical psychology. For better career prospects, Hayek later focused on economics.

Initially, Hayek was very much inspired by socialist ideas. Like many war returnees with him, he was in search of a "better" world. This seemed to him more achievable in socialism than in a capitalist economic system. Only the reading of the work "Socialism" by his academic teacher and mentor Ludwig von Mises brought him away from the idealizing notions of socialism. Hayek was considered Mises' model student in his private seminars. In 1927, he founded and directed the "Austrian Institute for Business Cycle Research" together with von Mises. In early 1931, following a guest lecture at the London School of Economics, Hayek received a professorship. There he met Ludwig Wittgenstein and Karl Popper, two of the most influential philosophers of the 20th century.

Hayek remained in London until 1950 and helped some scientific colleagues to emigrate from Nazi Germany during the NS regime. During this time, in 1944, he also published his most noted work, "The road to serfdom" (Der Weg in die Knechtschaft). From 1950, he taught at the University of Chicago. In 1962, Hayek took up a professorship at the University of Freiburg i. B. and became a board member of the Walter Eucken Institute—the "Freiburg School" will be discussed in detail in section 3.6. He taught there until 1969, became an honorary professor at the University of Salzburg, from which he returned to Freiburg in 1977, where he remained until his death in 1992. In 1974, Hayek received the Alfred Nobel Memorial Prize in Economic Sciences, endowed by the Swedish National Bank, together with Gunnar Myrdal.

In the first phase of his theoretical work, Hayek primarily dealt with business cycle theory. Business cycle fluctuations are due to the differences between the "natural" or equilibrium interest rate, at which planned savings equal planned investment, and the money interest rate formed on the money market, the market interest rate. If the market interest rate falls below the equilibrium interest rate, the state, companies, and households demand more money. The additional money supply leads to business cycle fluctuations when the loans taken out are primarily invested in areas not close to consumption, such as the industrial goods industry. Because in this case, the investments do not become profitable in the short term, but only over a longer period, for example through improved production conditions, more efficient production, and thus through the increased profitability of the companies. Households save because the production of consumer goods is reduced and the supply of consumer goods decreases. However, this increases the price of consumer goods. The demand for money also increases, and the interest rate rises again. However, this chokes off the economy, as companies now have to spend more on their loans. This can only be regulated by a further credit expansion by the banks. The limit of the boom is regulated by the banks' lending. Once this limit is reached and the investment projects stop, a crash occurs.

In doing so, Hayek opposed John Maynard Keynes—we will go into detail about the probably most significant economist of the 20th century in section 3.4—who had claimed that the global economic crisis was a result of too low demand. Keynes had concluded that in times of crisis, the overall economic demand should be stimulated by the state, and therefore state interventions in the free market were necessary. Hayek was of exactly the opposite opinion: In his view, it was precisely the state interventions in the free play of market forces that were the cause of the economic crisis. Above all, Hayek considered the correlation postulated by Keynes between the total demand for goods and services and total employment—the higher the demand, the higher the total employment—to be "a presumption of knowledge". Hayek had no use for a state fine-tuning of the consumption and investment expenditures of companies and the state. Furthermore, the two economists differed in the timing of the analysis: In the short term, more capital would stimulate investment. In the long term, however, the capital would be destroyed because it would be used in industries far from consumption and would not directly increase the companies' profits.

On one point, however, the two great economists of the 20th century agree: An economist can only play a significant role in society if he thinks and works interdisciplinarily. As in his childhood, Hayek is interested in various scientific disciplines throughout his life and has no understanding for an economist who only falls back on his specialist knowledge. Human behavior can only be grasped by integrating social science and psychological findings. If necessary, the economist draws on insights from evolutionary biology or philosophy. The focus is always on gaining knowledge and not on slavishly adhering to scientific boundaries.

Hayek, however, fought his greatest "scientific battle" against socialism. In his 1944 work "The Road to Serfdom" (Hayek, 2007), he criticized the National Socialist economic order in Germany and the fascist one in Italy as developments of socialism: socialism, planned economy, and collectivist economic systems run contrary to human rights and the principles of the rule of law. Hayek was an advocate of a market economy without state intervention. It is therefore not surprising that Hayek advised British Prime Minister Margaret Thatcher in the late 1970s on her path away from the welfare state of Keynesian character during the neoliberal restructuring of state and economy. Hayek advocated free competition and the play of market forces; the state only sets the framework: "The liberal argument is in favor of making the best possible use of the forces of competition as a means of coordinating human efforts, not an argument for leaving things just as they are. It is based on the conviction that, where effective competition can be created, it is a better way of guiding individual efforts than any other." (Hayek, 2007, p. 85 f.). In the following chapters of "The Road to Serfdom," Hayek deals with the apparent "inevitability of planning," which, in his view, does not exist. Planning the economy is incompatible with a free democracy. On the contrary, planned economy and total rule are congruent, as the planned economy includes rule over consumption and the consumer. State interventions, especially in the form of high taxes and social expenditures, are incompatible with growth-oriented economic development. No wonder that Hayek rejected the social market economy in Germany, which he only wanted to accept "without adjectives." In his conclusion at the end of the book, he urgently admonished his contemporaries to maintain a society of free people: "If in the first attempt to create a world of free men we have failed, we must try again. The guiding principle that a policy of freedom for the individual is the only truly progressive policy remains as true today as it was in the nineteenth century." (Hayek, 2007, p. 238). If we have failed in a first attempt to create a world of free people, we must try again. The central guiding principle that the policy of individual freedom is the only progressive policy remains as true today as it was in the nineteenth century (translation by the author).

Although Hayek completely rejected state interventions, he did assign the state the clear task of setting the framework for the economy. Thus, the state is responsible for the legal order and its compliance, for example, for contract freedom, the protection of property, the provision of public goods such as parks, schools, theaters, etc., external and internal security through police, military, etc. It also has the right to levy taxes. Hayek contrasted the opposition of market and planned economy with two types of social order: the grown, spontaneous order "cosmos," which comes about through the behaviors of its members according to clear rules, and the "made" order "taxis," in which orders control the members of society.

3.3 Thorstein Veblen

Thorstein Veblen, the last representative of the Austrian School described here, believed that economists should work more interdisciplinary. Veblen did this to a special degree.

Supply and demand determine the price. This is the universally valid economic rule. The higher the demand and the scarcer the good, the higher the price rises. However, the more the price rises, the lower the demand becomes. But there are exceptions to this economic law: with certain goods or products, demand actually increases with rising prices. These are the so-called luxury goods. Goods that are unaffordable for ordinary people are valued precisely because of this by many rich people—or people who consider themselves to be such. The relationship "increasing demand with increasing price" is called the "Veblen effect" or "snob effect" and is mathematically referred to as positive price elasticity of demand. This was discovered by an economist who is hardly known even among experts: Thorstein Bunde Veblen, rather an outsider in the economic profession and yet a scientist one should remember. Although not a pure economist, he portrayed the society of his time and its behavior very astutely and gained insights that are still valid today:

Thorstein Bunde Veblen (cf. Schipper, 2015, p. 176 ff.; Frenkel, 1996, p. 218 ff.) was born in 1857 as the son of Norwegian immigrants on a farm in Wisconsin. Veblen had eleven siblings and only learned English at school. He attended Carleton College in Northfield, Minnesota. After earning his bachelor's degree in 1880, he briefly worked as a teacher in Madison, Wisconsin, until he began studying philosophy and economics at the prestigious Johns Hopkins University in Baltimore, Maryland, a year later.

There he enjoyed the lectures of such renowned scientists and personalities as the philosopher Charles Sanders Peirce, the founder of philosophical pragmatism, and the economist John Bates Clark, a representative of neoclassicism and the Anglo-American marginal utility school. In 1882, Veblen transferred to the famous Yale University in New Haven, Connecticut, where he earned his Doctor of Philosophy in 1884. The topic of his dissertation, which he wrote under the moral philosopher Noah Porter, was "Ethical Grounds of a Doctrine of Retribution" (Ethical Foundations of a Doctrine of Redistribution).

Veblen had actually had an excellent starting point for an academic career: a top degree from a top university. Nevertheless, he did not find an adequate scientific position. This was often associated, among other things, with prejudices against him, the Norwegian immigrant. This left lifelong traces in his life and led him to adopt a rather critical attitude towards society. Veblen remained unemployed for 7 (!) years and kept himself afloat with activities on his parents' and in-laws' farm—he married in 1888. He translated Icelandic sagas into American English and occasionally worked as a tutor. From 1891, he continued his academic career at Cornell University as a postdoctoral fellow and a year later taught political economy as an assistant, "Fellow", of J. Laurence Laughlin at the newly founded University of Chicago.

For 10 years, from 1895 to 1905, Veblen was the editor of the newly founded *Journal of Political Economy*. During this time, his most famous and influential publications "Why is Economics not an Evolutionary Science?" and "The Theory of the Leisure Class" were published. In 1900, he became an "Assistant Professor", the professorial entry at the University of Chicago, and between the end of 1906 and 1909, he already taught as an "Associate Professor" of economics at Stanford University, California.

From 1911 to 1918, Veblen finally taught as a "Lecturer" on the basis of one-year contracts at the University of Missouri in Columbia. From 1918, he worked as a lecturer at the "New School for Social Research" in New York, which he co-founded. His greatest public impact was experienced by Veblen in the years 1918 and 1919 as the editor of the New York-based literary magazine *The Dial*.

Veblen was rather unstable in his private life: There were always rumors about extramarital relationships. These cost him his position in Chicago. In 1909, he separated from his first wife. In 1914, after the divorce, he married again. But his second wife died as early as 1920. Veblen was granted 9 more scientifically productive years. He spent his last years of life in seclusion in a log cabin, where he died of heart failure in 1929.

Veblen's most famous work "The Theory of the Leisure Class" is less an economic treatise than a sociological social satire. At the center of Veblen's theory of the leisure class is the upper class, which sets the style for the other classes: The "rich and beautiful" buy and consume products only because they know exactly that the poorer classes can never afford them. Ownership of such luxury goods means not only power and social prestige, but demonstrates the clear superiority of these privileged people over their fellow human beings. The actual value of the products is irrelevant to the rich, as long as they can distinguish themselves from other people. Every reader may imagine a number of luxury labels that are reserved for the extremely wealthy class and are gladly bought and displayed offensively. The price does not matter, even if the value of the goods and quality in most cases do not match the purchase value.

Veblen explains the behavior of people by the fact that there was no longer any class differentiation in America around the turn of the century. Social status was no longer recognizable by noble titles or old castles. Only possession and the purchase of certain products differentiate the rich upper class from the rest of the population. Luxury goods become a social distinction feature. Therefore, these are demonstratively acquired and displayed everywhere. At the same time, the members of the upper class show their financial independence through demonstrative idleness. Idleness is not to be understood as doing nothing, as leisure in the classical sense, it is the attempt to deal with topics that are as far removed as possible from productive work, such as refreshing or learning old languages like Latin and Ancient Greek in the sense of a humanistic education. Education is generally used for differentiation as well as cultural activities such as theater and opera visits, painting pictures or learning and training sophisticated manners. As this form of social differentiation is losing more and more weight, Veblen sees in the demonstrative consumption of luxury goods of all kinds an excellent opportunity for people to stand out. This applies to their own consumption and that of their families and friends. Waste as a prerequisite for recognition and social prestige.

At this point, Veblen deviates from his revered academic teacher John Bates Clark, who, like the neoclassicists, still has the rational Homo oeconomicus in mind, who maximizes his utility and has all decision-relevant information at hand. Veblen sharply recognizes that this is not the case at all. The human being, especially the members of the upper class and all those who emulate them, is for him a vain actor determined by his social environment. Social expectations of his environment, his "class", define his consumption behavior and his lifestyle. Every even so nonsensical fashion development is followed, as long as it helps to social differentiation. Not the individual makes his consumption decisions, but the mass of relevant people around him. This applies not only to consumers, but also to entrepreneurs. Although the individual worker and employee is interested in useful, honest work. But the many "industrial captains" and "financial magnates" of his time exploited this way of working with their "predatory, aggressive capitalism" to get a maximum advantage for themselves and to differentiate from other people and classes.

However, Veblen was not a defender of the working class. He had neither pronounced sympathy for them, nor did he see in them a revolutionary potential, as Marx had seen. Veblen had no illusions about the nature of his fellow men: He did not believe that the behavior of the upper class regarding consumption and idleness would change in the foreseeable future. On the contrary, the other classes would continue to try to imitate this behavior and consumption in order to distinguish themselves from the masses, similar to their role models. Veblen placed great hope in engineers and inventors to drive technological progress and to get people to engage more strongly with the rational principles of the world. Technology as a rational part of nature. For him, the behavior of the majority of the "fine people" was deeply irrational. An aspect that behavioral economists like Kahneman, Thaler, and others picked up on. In sum, "The Theory of the Leisure Class" is Veblen's reckoning with the vanities and irrationalities of the society of his time.

Veblen was influenced by various intellectual ideas and schools of thought. Like the Historical School, he believed that economic activities do not originate from the individual alone and in isolation, but that only a holistic approach helps. He believed that human behavior has changed over the course of history and that society as a whole should also be considered in economic contexts. As Veblen showed in his main work, the main driving force for conspicuous consumption is the relevant class, but also society in general and its respective fashion trends. Man is always embedded in a social network that strongly influences him and drives him to irrational behavior.

In addition, Veblen was a follower of Charles Darwin and his theory of evolution. Darwin explained the origin of species through a sequence of changes in environmental conditions and the survival of the best-adapted creatures: Only those creatures that can best adapt their abilities and characteristics to the changing conditions of the environment can survive, i.e., they "are selected". Veblen saw it similarly in economics: New economic systems and options are constantly being developed, and only the best adapted survive. The rest are negatively selected. Contrary to neoclassical economics with its constant equilibrium of markets, Veblen saw permanent changes in the markets in the form of variations and mutations, leading to new systems and transitions to a new economic world. The static model of permanent equilibrium did not lead further from his point of view. Thus, Veblen was a co-founder of "evolutionary economics".

As a student of Charles Sanders Peirce, Veblen, like the American pragmatists, believed that it is not God who guides the universe and controls the world, but man with his free will. People act and change things, also in economics. With Marx, Veblen shared the idea of the small, "parasitic" layer, in whose hands the means of production lie and who tend to exploit their workers. He believed that technology leads to a change in society and its conditions. Similar ideas and thoughts are heard again today on the subject of digitization. We will return to this thought in a later chapter. However, unlike Marx, Veblen did not believe that the "proletariat" would rise up against the authorities or upper class and ignite a revolution (section 2.3). Instead, the lower classes, especially those with social ambition, imitate the behavior of the upper ones in order to also be able to stand out from the masses.

With his extensive work, which we can only deal with in excerpts here, Veblen laid the foundations of the so-called "institutional economics". Simply put, markets are seen as the result of the complex interaction of a number of institutions: individuals, companies, states, society, social norms, attitudes, etc. Here again, Veblen's work at the scientific boundaries between economics and sociology is evident. In his opinion, it is not possible to separate economic phenomena from social and cultural phenomena. As Veblen impressively showed in his main work, economic behaviors are not isolated from social norms and institutions, but also from cultural components. Only through the exploration of the interaction of all "institutions" relevant to humans will it be possible to accurately analyze and predict economic development. Veblen has put man with his real economic behavior back into the focus of research and for this he has overcome the boundaries of economics. Although he is not one of the greatest economists, his main work "The Theory of the Leisure Class" is still worth reading today, and with a slight smile, similarities to the economic activities of people today—especially with regard to their conspicuous consumption behavior—are clearly recognizable.

3.4 John Maynard Keynes

It is not an overstatement to describe John Maynard Keynes as the most significant and influential economist of the 20th century. The "Keynesianism" named after him developed primarily in the decades after the Second World War into the most important economic doctrine and became the economic policy guide for many governments.

His theories were intensively taught at universities—the author himself experienced this in the mid-1980s at the University of Mannheim. Keynes' teachings and his economic philosophy went around the world and shaped entire generations of economists. Researchers who continued and developed his theoretical path filled lecture halls around the world and passed on the ideas of this brilliant researcher.

John Maynard Keynes had a broad interest in the intellectual topics of his time: He was interested in philosophy, history, mathematics, and economics, and collected mainly old books and pictures. This resulted in an extremely impressive collection of works by European, especially English philosophers such as David Hume, John Locke, George Berkeley, but also German classical authors such as Immanuel Kant, Georg Wilhelm Friedrich Hegel, and Gottfried Wilhelm Leibniz. Keynes acquired paintings and drawings by such famous artists as Eugène Delacroix, Paul Cézanne, and others. He was a member of an elite debating club in Cambridge, the "Cambridge Apostles," and the artistic circle of the "Bloomsbury Group," which dealt with avant-garde art. Here he discussed, among others, with such famous writers as Virginia Woolf (then Stephen) and Katherine Mansfield, but also contemporary philosophers like Bertrand Russell and Ludwig Wittgenstein. Keynes was also a frequently consulted advisor to politicians and managers, sat on the board of an insurance company, was an influential publicist, and left behind about a thousand press articles. His estate included about a hundred extensive books, even though he did not live to be 63 years old.

John Maynard Keynes (cf. Scherf, 1989, p. 273 ff.; Hoffmann, 2009, p. 271 ff.; Thornton, 2015, p. 107 ff.; Caspari, 2009, p. 161 ff.; von Weizsäcker, 2015; Herrmann, 2016, p. 153 ff.; Zank, 1996, p. 157 ff.)

was born in 1883 as the oldest of three children of John Neville Keynes, a professor of political economy, and his wife Florence Ada in Cambridge. The ancestors of the old English Keynes family can be traced back to the 11th century, the time of William I ("William the Conqueror"). Keynes' father came from a family of doctors and had worked his way up to a "Fellow" and "Lecturer," i.e., a member of the research community, and lecturer at the University of Cambridge through his studies at Pembroke College in Cambridge. He later became "Registrary" of the university, which in today's German university system corresponds to that of the university chancellor and administrative head. Keynes' mother was the daughter of a Baptist minister and one of the first female students in Cambridge. She later became mayor of Cambridge. Keynes' mother grew up in a Christian environment and passed on her social attitudes and convictions to her children. It was an intellectual and privileged household in which John Maynard Keynes grew up. His younger brother later became a well-known surgeon. Maynard's sister Margret married the later Nobel laureate in medicine A. V. Hill.

In keeping with the elite milieu and ambition of his parental home, young John Maynard attended *the* classic elite school of England, the renowned Eton College. Several representatives of the English royal family and numerous English prime ministers had already attended this school. After his excellent graduation, Keynes studied mathematics, history, and philosophy at King's College, University of Cambridge. He only studied economics insofar as it had a connection to mathematics. After his bachelor's degree, he prepared for the "Civil Service" exam to enter public service. To prepare for this exam, which essentially tests general knowledge and covers many subjects, such as history, politics, but also mathematics and economics, he also studied with Alfred Marshall and read his main work "Principles of Economics" (section 3.1). This book and the partly private lectures with Marshall led Keynes to deal more intensively with economics. After successfully passing the examination for entry into public service, Keynes then joined the "India Office" in London. The result of the examinations angered Keynes, as he had performed poorly in his parade disciplines of mathematics and economics. Moreover, as the second in the ranking by grades, he could not take up his desired position in the "Treasury," the British Ministry of Finance and Economics.

The position at the India Office quickly bored the highly gifted Keynes. Among other things, he had to arrange the purchase of ten breeding bulls and ensure their transport to Bombay. Keynes created an intellectual balance by beginning to write his doctoral thesis on probability theory, "A Treatise on Probability". This work was highly praised by the leading logicians and mathematicians of his time, such as Bertrand Russell and Alfred North Whitehead. In his dissertation, Keynes succeeded in systematically presenting the logical foundations of probability. Nevertheless, he failed to obtain a scholarship at King's College in Cambridge. Nevertheless, he resigned from the India Office after only 2 years in 1908 and began private studies in Cambridge. Alfred Marshall arranged for Keynes to have an unpaid teaching assignment on money, credit, and prices at King's College in Cambridge in early 1909. Two months later, he was appointed "Fellow", i.e., a lecturer. From the very beginning of his teaching career, Keynes was highly skeptical of the heavily mathematized economic theory conveyed by his neoclassical teacher Marshall. Keynes financed his livelihood mainly through his teaching activities, through articles in the prestigious journal *Economist,* and with the help of his father. He was even briefly politically active for the Liberal Party—he had previously been vice president of the Liberal Club at the University of Cambridge—but was quickly disappointed by his first encounters with active politicians and withdrew.

In 1911, Keynes became the editor of the highly prestigious *Economic Journal*. In 1912, he was appointed to the board of the University of Cambridge. A year later, he was asked to participate in the "Royal Commission", which was, among other things, about the founding of a central bank. In 1915, Keynes took a position in the finance department of the Treasury in London, where he worked his way up to become its leader and thinker. Thus, at the end of the First World War, he was a member of the British delegation at the peace negotiations in Versailles. Keynes was appalled by the amount and dimension of the reparations that the Allies wanted to impose on the defeated Germans. In his opinion, these financial demands were designed to weaken and destabilize Germany economically for decades. At the same time, international economic relations would suffer from Germany's prolonged weakness, and the German population would be demoralized. Consequently, Keynes left the negotiations before the final signing of the Treaty of Versailles and resigned from the Treasury. He vented his anger in his book "The Economic Consequences of the Peace". This book, published in England and the USA in 1919, made him instantly famous worldwide.

From 1920 until his early death in 1946, Keynes taught at King's College at the University of Cambridge. Later, like his father, he became Chancellor there and was thus responsible for the finances, among other things, as head of administration. During his term of office, he managed to multiply the college's endowment through clever speculation on the foreign exchange market. Keynes was able to increase his private wealth through currency speculation and targeted investments after initial setbacks to about 60,000 pounds—today's value about 3 million euros.

In the 1920s, a busy publication activity followed. Thus, Keynes revised his doctoral thesis "A Treatise on Probability" and published it in 1921. From 1922, he regularly wrote in the *Manchester Guardian* on economic policy issues. At the same time, he published in the liberal weekly *Nation*. He summarized his monetary considerations collected up to that point in the 1923 publication "Tract on Monetary Reform". This was followed by the two-volume work "A Treatise on Money" from 1927 to 1930.

Throughout his life, Keynes was a political and economic advisor whose opinion was heard in the government and the public. At the end of 1924, Keynes had spread his economic philosophy in his lectures: In his lecture "End of Laissez-Faire", he had extensively discussed market failure, especially in the global economic crisis at the end of the 1920s. Even then, he called for a strong state that must intervene in economic affairs. In 1936, his main work "The General Theory of Employment, Interest and Money" was published, which revolutionized economic science at the time and has had a lasting impact on macroeconomic theory to this day.

In 1937, Keynes suffered his first heart attack and had to reduce his enormous workload. After his recovery, he became an economic advisor to the government in 1940 and participated as the British chief negotiator in the negotiations for a fixed exchange rate system at the conference in Bretton Woods (New Hampshire, USA) in 1944. He was also involved in the preparations for the founding of the International Monetary Fund (IMF) and the World Bank. These negotiations increasingly wore him down, especially as the USA made no secret of their leading position in the new currency fund. In 1941, he became director of the Bank of England and, due to his numerous services to his country, was made a Baron, "Baron Keynes of Tilton in the County of Sussex", and traditionally received a seat in the House of Lords, the upper house of the British Parliament. In 1946, Keynes died in Tilton East Sussex after another heart attack at the age of only 62 from heart failure. His marriage to the ballet dancer Lydia Lopokova, a social event in 1925, remained childless.

John Maynard Keynes left behind an extensive body of work. Even a content presentation of his most famous works would exceed the scope of this work and distract from the essential contents of his main work "General Theory of Employment, Interest and Money". Many economists, especially those who further developed his ideas, were primarily inspired by his magnum opus. Nevertheless, a brief excursion into his other works, which are very revealing for his entire thinking, is permitted here. Already in his dissertation "A Treatise on Probability", the young Keynes pursued the very ambitious goal of outlining the logical foundations of statistics and putting statistics on a new footing. His approach was nothing less than an attempt to revolutionize probability theory. To do this, he dealt with the established theory of probability. For example, Keynes dealt with the Bernoulli theorems and the statistical "law of large numbers". Although his doctoral thesis could not provide any significantly new insights to a statistician at the time, it clearly showed his interest and ability to combine mathematical-statistical knowledge with philosophical considerations.

In Keynes' work on the economic consequences of the Treaty of Versailles, which made him world-famous, he described his reasons for leaving the conference as British chief negotiator. As early as 1919, he presciently recognized that the economic peace conditions in the form of much too high reparations would overwhelm Germany and not allow for economic recovery at all. He characterized the Treaty of Versailles as a peace dictate, which in his view was solely aimed at permanently weakening the former enemy. In a brief economic-historical excursion, Keynes described the rise of the German economy, primarily based on the high investments of entrepreneurs. The Treaty of Versailles, which required Germany to cede its colonies and lose 10 % of its economic area, also ordered reparations of 132 billion gold marks—this was about three times the German gross national product before the war. In his work, Keynes also vividly and psychologically comprehensibly described the individual statesmen of that time, whom he had experienced during the negotiations. He repeatedly pointed out that an economic dismantling and excessive indebtedness of Germany would affect the entire European economy. The economies were already too strongly intertwined at that time.

In his book on the theory of money, "A Treatise on Money", Keynes laid the monetary foundations of his main work. In it, he defined money, "The Nature of Money", and divided it into cash and bank money, analyzed it in detail and described the various forms of money. In the second book, Keynes analyzed the "Value of Money", which for him is mainly determined by the purchasing power of money measured by consumption and the financial return of money as "labor force". Especially in his third book, he laid the conceptual foundations for his main work of the General Theory such as income, profits, savings, investments, but also the relationship between price level and money supply. Keynes dealt with the conditions of economic equilibrium and extensively determined the reasons why the price level is subject to dynamics. He was interested in the causes of fluctuations around equilibrium, insofar as they are caused by monetary or investment factors. Finally, Keynes addressed national and international monetary policy, primarily focusing on the influence of state banks. He looked not only at England, but also across the Atlantic to the USA and considered the workings of the Federal Reserve Bank. The essential results of this book flowed into his main work and will now be examined in detail.

Jean-Baptiste Say had claimed that every supply creates its demand (Section 2.2). According to this thesis, the market economy system with its flexible prices and wages should automatically find a balance in which full employment prevails. For Keynes, this law did not apply: He was firmly convinced that there could also be a balance with unemployment. The state must create the missing overall economic demand through active economic policy. Keynes makes it clear already in his preface to the English edition: "This book is primarily addressed to economists." (Keynes, 2017, p. 9). In this book, Keynes tried to contrast his ideas and his theory with that of classical economics.

For him, the practitioner, it was essentially about describing reality, which in his view is not given in classical economics: "I will argue in the following that the postulates of classical theory are only valid in a special case and not in the normal case, because the situation assumed by this theory is only a limit case of all possible equilibrium situations. Moreover, the properties of the special case from which classical theory starts do not correspond at all to those of the national economy in which we actually live. As a result, its teachings are misleading and, if we try to apply them to real experiences, have devastating effects." (Keynes, 2017, p. 19). That's quite a challenge to classical economic theory right at the beginning of his main work!

In classical economics, "involuntary unemployment" is not envisaged. There can only be short-term, frictional, or voluntary unemployment. In contrast, Keynes sees involuntary, unwanted unemployment as a real occurrence. He defines: "People are involuntarily unemployed when, with a small price increase of wage goods relative to the nominal wage, both the supply of labor at this nominal wage and the total demand for it at this wage are greater than the actual amount of employment." (Keynes, 2017, p. 28). This means that there is by no means a balance in the labor market when nominal wages are too high and employers do not offer as many jobs as are sought by workers. The missing "effective demand" is, for Keynes, the core of the general theory of employment. Demand is primarily made up of the population's consumption—and this, in turn, from the "propensity to consume"—and the investment volume of companies and the state. Specifically, this means that people stimulate the economy and create jobs through their daily purchases, as companies respond to these product sales to consumers with investments.

Keynes clearly recognized the importance of expectations for production and thus for the employment of workers. Companies invest, produce daily based on their presumed sales at a certain price. If I know that I can sell a certain number of goods in a day, then I will produce accordingly. The business reality in the form of sales revenues determines my long-term expectations: "The supply of jobs by companies depends on these various expectations. The *actual results* [emphasis in the original] of production and sales of products only affect employment insofar as they influence future expectations." (Keynes, 2017, p. 53). If business is booming and I can see no end to the boom, I will be more willing as an entrepreneur to create additional jobs to meet the increased demand.

Keynes sees demand as the sum of all consumption expenditures C of a country and the sum of all investments I. Consumption is primarily dependent on a household's available income, i.e., net income. However, Keynes is aware of the fact that net income is only one of many factors influencing consumption decisions, such as individual preference and specific need, e.g., for sports goods.

Keynes considers it essential that, in total, savings are equal to the sum of entrepreneurs' investments: $S = I$. This can be shown relatively simply: The income of a country or household is equal to the value of all goods produced by a country or household. But income is also equal to the sum of all investments and the population's consumption. If savings are derived from net income minus consumption and investments are also equal to income minus consumption, then the total savings of an economy and the total investments must be equal. If I subtract from all goods that an economy produces in a year those that were consumed, i.e., sold, then the investments remain. If I subtract consumption from the total income of all households, then all savings remain. And these correspond to a country's investments. Or to put it another way: "The consumption and investment decisions together determine income." (Keynes, 2017, p. 66).

Key to the investments of entrepreneurs and, derived from that, the necessary volume of employment are future profits. "Today, I believe, on the other hand, that the entrepreneur determines the volume of employment […] with the intention of maximizing his current and his expected future profits. […] The volume of employment most advantageous for maximum profit, on the other hand, depends on the aggregate demand function …" (Keynes, 2017, p. 77). Granting an additional loan to an entrepreneur can encourage him to make additional investments and thus create jobs. In addition to the investments of entrepreneurs, the consumption of the total population is essential for total demand and thus for income and volume of employment. But what does consumption depend on? Keynes takes a clear position on this: "Obviously, the sum that the population spends on its consumption depends in part on 1. the sum of its income, 2. other objective circumstances, and 3. the subjective needs and psychological inclinations and habits of individuals as well as the principles by which income is divided among them." (Keynes, 2017, p. 88).

Interestingly, Keynes, just like with the construct of expectations, primarily focuses on the human psyche. Individual consumption is not just a question of net income, but also a question of "subjective needs": What hobbies do I have? Where do I go on vacation? What fashion do I like? What daily necessities are important to me? Which brands? But also: What part of my income do I want to consume, what part to save, and much more. All of these are individual, deeply subjective consumption desires. And Keynes recognized this very clearly, only: "But in general, we can consider the subjective factors as given." (Keynes, 2017, p. 88). By keeping subjective consumption desires constant—which is not unrealistic when considering individual consumption preferences that do not change significantly quickly, Keynes can focus on the objective factors that determine the "propensity to consume". Keynes defines the "propensity to consume" as the functional relationship between income and consumption levels. It increases when real wages rise, net income increases, and assets change unexpectedly, such as through a lottery win. The interest rate also plays a major role. As is particularly noticeable in the current economic situation with extremely low interest rates, people consume more at low interest rates because an alternative investment at the bank would yield little. Conversely, according to Keynes:

"Any increase in the interest rate would thus noticeably reduce consumption." (Keynes, 2017, p. 90). Savers are more likely to take their money to the bank at rising interest rates to provide for the future, rather than consuming in the present.

Finally, two more aspects influence the population's propensity to consume: tax policy changes such as income or capital gains tax. Today, possible increases in inheritance tax or the introduction of wealth tax in Germany would certainly also be included. Ultimately, citizens' expectations regarding their future income also play a major role. If I am confident of earning significantly higher income in the short or long term, I will likely consume more in the present. If, on the other hand, I have uncertain job prospects because my company is not doing so well, then I will likely save more for the future and the coming uncertain times. However, it is also clear that "as real income increases, a *larger proportion* [emphasis in the original] of income is saved." (Keynes, 2017, p. 93). This can be quickly clarified: An average earner has to spend a higher portion of his income on daily necessities such as food, clothing, rent, etc. than a millionaire or top earner, who can set aside a significantly higher proportion of his income in addition to buying luxury products. A very good depiction of economic reality, even if much of it is taken for granted today.

Although Keynes keeps the subjective factors of the propensity to consume constant in his analysis, he examines the individual determining motives of the lack of propensity to consume, i.e., individual saving (Keynes, 2017, p. 101): On the one hand, there is the building up of reserves to be able to cope with unforeseen risks. On the other hand, people make provisions for their old age, for the education of their children or the financial support of close relatives and relatives. Some hold back on current consumption desires and prefer to benefit from interest and capital gains in order to be able to spend more in the future. Others save to afford a higher standard of living in old age or to enjoy the feeling of financial independence. Finally—people are all different in their behavior—they hold money for short-term speculations or investments, e.g., for a car as a bargain or stocks with short-term potential for appreciation, or want to leave as much money as possible or, on the contrary, hoard money at home out of stinginess. As we can see, Keynes has closely observed people with their sometimes irrational behavior and analyzed the main motives for saving.

The same applies to entrepreneurs or municipal authorities (Keynes, 2017, p. 102). Thus, companies retain a portion of their profits to invest in the future or to increase their equity. At the same time, companies maintain their *liquidity* for partly unplanned short-term expenses. The commercial motives of caution and income improvement prevail. At the same time, Keynes is aware of the fact that the motives of the propensity to consume, i.e., the answer to the question of how much of my income I want to spend or save, depend on various factors: "The strength of all these motives varies greatly depending on the type of institutions and organizations of the economy under consideration, habits shaped by ethnic affiliation, education, religion, and prevailing moral concepts, current hopes and past experiences, the extent and technical level of physical capital, and the existing distribution of wealth and the standard of living achieved." (Keynes, 2017, p. 103). Keynes clearly saw and worked out the psychological and cultural influencing factors of economic activities. He was aware that the Homo oeconomicus with his rational, constant behavior does not exist across all people and cultures. However, in his analysis, he assumed these factors as given and constant: "That is, we assume the essential conditions of subjective motives for saving or consuming as given." (Keynes, 2017, p. 103). In the short term, the reasons for saving, according to Keynes, do not result from changes in the propensity to consume, but from a change in the level of income.

Keynes introduces further terms that are crucial for his economic analysis. Thus, he defines the *marginal propensity to consume*—mathematically speaking a differential calculation—as the amount by which consumption increases when income increases by one unit of money. So if I receive 1 euro more net salary, the marginal propensity to consume indicates what proportion of this additional money I consume. The rest is saved, with the sum of savings equal to the sum of investments. It applies that as income grows, an ever smaller proportion of it is spent on consumption. At some point, I have everything I need and can put the rest in the bank or invest it elsewhere.

Furthermore, Keynes defines the *investment multiplier:* The investment multiplier means that the total income of a state or household increases by a multiple of the increase in investment. This is easily seen: If the state spends 100 million more on investments for transport infrastructure, construction of schools or theaters, etc., additional jobs are created. The demand of construction companies and the companies involved in the construction of schools, but also the demand for teachers increases. More workers or teachers are hired, who in turn consume more. This also increases the profit of other companies, whose products are now in greater demand, so they can employ more staff. These consume more, etc. Such a cycle recovers a multiple of the originally spent 100 million: the increased consumption expenditures, the increased profits, the increased investments of companies with increased profit, etc. The 100 million have thus "multiplied" the income through this cycle.

While Keynes defined the concept of the marginal efficiency of capital entirely mathematically as the marginal product of yield and cost of a capital investment—that is, nothing other than: What is the ratio between an additional unit of my invested capital and the associated costs—he deals intensively with long-term expectations in chapter 12 of his "General Theory". So Keynes takes up again a psychological core theme, which determines the economic behavior of people, in this case especially of entrepreneurs, but also of consumers, in investments. Often he translates his analysis mainly into formulas and mathematical calculations. It is easily forgotten that Keynes is primarily concerned with a deeply human characteristic. "The long-term expectation on which we base our decisions is therefore based not only on the most probable forecast we can make, but also on the *confidence* [emphasis in the original] we have in it—on how high we estimate the probability that our best possible forecast will turn out to be completely wrong. [...] The so-called *state of confidence* ['state of confidence', emphasis in the original] is a factor to which businessmen always pay the highest and most eager attention. Economists, however, have not analyzed it carefully and usually content themselves with dealing with it cursorily." (Keynes, 2017, p. 131).

Keynes clearly criticized his own profession because it largely negates these psychological factors influencing an investment in the future, and he explained the effects of long-term expectations: On the one hand, investors usually know little reliable about the income effect of their investment, especially if it lies years in the future. On the other hand, especially with stock investors, the average expectations of stock investors—expressed in stock prices—are much more significant than the actual expectations of entrepreneurs (Keynes, 2017, p. 133). Keynes even went so far as to claim that future income plays only a subordinate role for the stock price: "In fact, all sorts of considerations go into the stock quotation that have nothing to do with future income." (Keynes, 2017, p. 134). Professional investors and speculators focus their considerations mainly on psychological considerations: Instead of dealing with the trivial realization of a long-term income forecast, they try to anticipate changes in the stock price valuation faster than the broad mass. One seems to hear the psychologist Gasset y Bon ("The Psychology of the Masses") when reading Keynes: "What is important to them [referring to professional investors; note by the author] is not what value an investment really has for a long-term oriented investor, but how the market values it under the influence of mass psychology in three months or a year." (Keynes, 2017, p. 136).

Much more important than the real market situation, according to Keynes, is the prediction, "what the average opinion about the expected average opinion is." (Keynes, 2017, p. 137). Therefore, not the real macroeconomic and business indicators are decisive, but how the average population judges the economic facts. This judgment is usually also influenced by the individual environment, i.e., friends, family, acquaintances, and colleagues, but also by the media. At the end of chapter 12, Keynes settles accounts with the mathematization in economics in favor of human and psychological factors, which in his view largely determine human economic behavior. Thus, a large part of human activities is based more on spontaneous optimism than on the basis of mathematical expectations (Keynes, 2017, p. 141). Keynes finally states dramatically: "In order to be able to assess the prospects of success of an investment, we must therefore also take into account the nervous constitution and hysteria, even the digestion and weather sensitivity of those whose spontaneous activities largely determine these prospects." (Keynes, 2017, p. 142).

Of course, Keynes has deliberately exaggerated in his linguistic image here. But his main concern is to show that economics is not only shaped by mathematical equations and expectations, but that human psychology, "whims, feelings or coincidences" (Keynes, 2017, p. 142) can be responsible for entrepreneurial investments.

In chapters 13 and 14 of his "General Theory," Keynes deals with the general theory of the interest rate. For him, the individual liquidity preference plays a major role, i.e., the question of how much money or parts of my income I want to keep for current consumption—like money in the drawer—and how much I can save for future consumption. The interest rate is the "reward for giving up liquidity in a certain period of time" (Keynes, 2017, p. 145). The liquidity preference arises mainly from the motives of transaction (I want to buy something in the short term), caution (you never know), and speculation (e.g., a stock purchase). An increase in the money supply is accompanied by a falling interest rate: money yields less return at the bank, more money is held. However, the lower the interest rate, the less companies and government institutions have to pay for loans and the more investments are stimulated.

In the following, Keynes goes into more detail on the reasons for liquidity incentives, i.e., the question of why I as an individual want to hold cash or money readily available. Households mainly hold cash to bridge the period between receiving income and spending money. This is the income motive. Entrepreneurs and traders act analogously by holding money to compensate for the time span between receiving sales revenues and purchasing goods (business motive). Here too, the motive of caution applies to both entrepreneurs and private individuals, i.e., holding money for short-term, sometimes unforeseen expenses. Finally, the fourth motive of liquidity preference is the speculation motive, i.e., having money available for short-term speculation. Keynes notes: "… for every kind of circumstances and expectations there is a suitable interest rate" (Keynes, 2017, p. 170). Because the interest rate is a highly psychological phenomenon (Keynes, 2017, p. 173). After all, the long-term interest rate depends not only on the current policy of the central bank, but also on the "expectations of market participants about its future monetary policy" (Keynes, 2017, p. 173).

As can be clearly seen here, Keynes correctly assessed the real conditions in the money market as a combination of economic and psychological factors. Reality is better captured by considering human characteristics, individually and collectively, than by a purely mathematical-logical analysis. In chapter 21 of his work, he once again makes it very clear how he sees the use of mathematics in economics (even though he himself was a trained mathematician!): "Too much of contemporary 'mathematical' [quotation marks in the original] economics is merely inventions that are as imprecise as the premises on which they are based, through which the authors lose sight of the complexity and interdependencies of the real world in a tangle of presumptuous and useless formulas." (Keynes, 2017, p. 248). Finally, as Keynes notes at the end of chapter 15, people hold more or less cash depending on their expectations about future economic development for the reasons mentioned above. In chapters 16 and 17, Keynes further elaborates his views on the nature of capital and the important characteristics of interest and money.

Much more essential for understanding Keynes' main work is chapter 18, in which he attempts nothing less than a reformulation of the general theory of employment. Initially, Keynes assumes some given factors in his explanatory model that will not change at least in the short term. These include the available amount of work, the qualification of the workers, the existing technology, competition, consumer habits and preferences, the social structures of a country, etc. As independent variables, i.e., influencing factors that are deliberately changed to measure the effects on the dependent variables, Keynes chooses the propensity to consume, the marginal efficiency of capital and the interest rate, as well as the liquidity preference, the money supply, and the wage unit as a result of wage settlements. As a dependent variable, Keynes chooses the volume of employment and the national income or social product. Simply put, Keynes wants to determine through this model what influence propensity to consume, interest rate, money supply, etc. have on employment and social product.

Keynes derived the following insights from his model: "… the physical supply conditions in the capital goods industry, the state of confidence with regard to future returns, the psychological attitude to liquidity and the money supply (preferably measured in wage units) together determine the volume of new investments." (Keynes, 2017, p. 207). In plain language, this means that entrepreneurial investments depend on various factors: a combination of real economic indicators such as interest, money supply, wage settlements, and psychological factors such as liquidity preference and long-term expectations of the level of returns. The rule is that an increase in the income of private households increases consumption depending on the propensity to consume, but less strongly than income increases. The higher my income, the lower my consumption share. For investments, there is a negative correlation with interest: the lower the interest, the higher the investments and vice versa. Due to the aforementioned investment multiplier, income increases more than investment performance.

In the following chapters, which are primarily aimed at professional colleagues, Keynes once again addresses nominal wages, prices, and the system of mercantilism. Particularly important for understanding his main work is the concluding chapter 24, in which he primarily addresses social philosophical issues. Thus, Keynes notes with remarkable clarity what has become highly topical again in today's economic situation: "The most glaring faults of our economic system are its inability to provide for full employment, and its arbitrary and unjust distribution of wealth and income." (Keynes, 2017, p. 308). Keynes wrote this in 1936! While unemployment in Germany currently reached a minimum in 2019, countries like Spain and Italy have dramatically high youth unemployment; but the situation for adults there is anything but rosy. Income and wealth are distributed as unequally as never before in Germany and many industrialized countries, especially in the USA. There is no end in sight.

For Keynes, only state intervention is suitable for eliminating grievances such as unemployment and for increasing national income. While there may be occasional cooperation between state agencies and the private sector, he states: "The state must have a guiding influence on the propensity to consume, partly through its tax system, partly by determining the interest rate, and perhaps in other ways as well." (Keynes, 2017, p. 312). In addition, the state must carry out a "reasonably comprehensive investment control" as the "only means of achieving near full employment" (Keynes, 2017, p. 312). These are the only two areas in which the state should interfere more in the economy than before: to increase the propensity to consume and stimulate investments. However, in Keynes' view, the state gains significantly more weight in economic matters. We will see in the following chapter that this philosophy is absolutely contrary to the philosophy of a liberal like Milton Friedman (section 3.5).

In the concluding paragraph of his main work, Keynes once again raises a warning finger: Many contemporaries, especially civil servants and politicians, but also other opinion leaders, according to Keynes, are hardly influenced by new ideas after their studies and as young professionals between the ages of 25 and 30. However, as Keynes perceptively notes, "… the danger of changes sooner or later comes from ideas and not from powerful interest groups, be it for better or for worse" (Keynes, 2017, p. 316). Good ideas therefore prevail, as has been seen worldwide with Keynes. Changes, according to Keynes, are more likely to arise from the implementation of new ideas rather than from the actions of powerful interest groups.

Keynes' impact on his contemporaries and economic theory cannot be overestimated. His sharp analysis of the current situation from an economic, but also psychological perspective, coupled with his explanation of the first global economic crisis, made him the most influential economist and theorist of his time. He highlighted the unacceptability of the economic contract conditions of Versailles and developed a new theory for full employment. Based on realistic assumptions about human economic behavior, both individually and collectively, such as expectations, liquidity preference, or propensity to consume, Keynes initiated a shift in economic policy ideas: Supply does not create demand and thus equilibrium, as Jean-Baptiste Say had claimed. Rather, according to Keynes, there can be equilibrium in unemployment, and thus supply and demand are not automatically balanced, as the global economic crisis has shown.

Keynes sees a way out in state interventions, which boost its own investments through borrowing, influence the propensity to consume, strengthen effective demand through the multiplier effect, and thus increase employment again. Many countries adopted this idea of state strengthening of aggregate demand after the Second World War. In Germany, this was done through global control. Criticism of his approach—state demand was difficult to scale back in times of saving ("austerity")— eventually led to a new, liberal philosophy around Milton Friedman and Friedrich August von Hayek (Section 3.2), who were very skeptical of state interventions and categorically rejected them. Nevertheless, Keynes influenced many generations of economists. His ideas became particularly relevant again during the global financial crisis of 2008, when banks like Lehman Brothers went bankrupt and had to be partially rescued at the taxpayers' expense to save jobs. At that time, then US President Barack Obama, in the Keynesian sense, launched a large-scale, state-funded investment program, which was ultimately successful and stabilized the economy again.

Keynes had a multitude of followers and, without explicitly wanting to, founded his own school of "Keynesianism". As early as 1930, a circle of students had formed around Keynes and his ideas, the "Cambridge Circus". They included such renowned economists as Richard Kahn, Joan Robinson, Piero Sraffa, or James Meade. Also in the USA, an influential network formed that passed on Keynes' ideas and further developed individual aspects. One of the most influential "Keynesians" was Paul A. Samuelson. His textbook "Economics" is the best-selling economics textbook of all time. Generations of economics students around the world were taught by him or read his textbook, including the author of this book. James Tobin, recipient of the Alfred Nobel Memorial Prize in Economic Sciences and inventor and namesake of the "Tobin Tax", or Robert Solow followed Keynes' ideas.

Since the 1980s, such prominent economists and Alfred Nobel Memorial Prize winners as Joseph Stiglitz, George Akerlof, and Michael Spence have continued to develop Keynes' ideas, to this day. (Joseph Stiglitz will be discussed in Section 4.1). The economic theory of the 20th century is unthinkable without the works of John Maynard Keynes. However, the same applies to his most important intellectual opponent and challenger: Milton Friedman.

3.5 Milton Friedman

It is certainly not presumptuous to claim that Milton Friedman, alongside John Maynard Keynes, was the most significant economist of the 20th century. At the same time, he was Keynes' most important academic adversary: While Keynes saw a country's economic salvation in state investment programs, Friedman was a consistent liberal who rejected state interventions in any form. Both founded influential economic traditions of the "Keynesians" versus the "Chicago Boys", as Friedman and his followers or successors were called due to their work at the University of Chicago. Hardly any intellectual, philosophical, and scientific debate has shaped economic theory in recent decades as much as that of these two pioneers. Even today, one can recognize the differences in the scientific views of the two researchers and the associated tools of the individual scientific schools, even though they have since been further developed and adapted to the current time.

Milton Friedman (see Spahn, 2009, p. 282 ff.; Schwarz, 2015, p. 209 ff.; Heuser, 1996, p. 274 ff.; Thornton, 2015, p. 165 ff.; Hoffmann, 2009, p. 279 ff.) was born in 1912 as the fourth child of a Hungarian, Jewish immigrant family in Brooklyn, New York. Young Milton grew up in Rahwah, New Jersey, near New York. When Friedman was 15 years old, his father, who ran a small retail business, died. Only with the help of a scholarship was the highly gifted boy able to study mathematics and economics at the nearby Rutgers University in New Jersey at the age of 16—Friedman had skipped a grade. At just under 20, he completed his studies with a Bachelor of Arts and continued his studies, focusing on economics, at the University of Chicago. In 1933, he earned his Master of Arts there. Friedman then published numerous articles, which were also included in very prestigious journals such as the *Quarterly Journal of Economics* of Harvard University. This made him known early in the world of economists and he received a generous scholarship from the prestigious Columbia University in New York to write his doctoral thesis. In this dissertation, he dealt with the economic situation of members of free professions such as doctors, lawyers, etc.

In 1938, Friedman married Rose Director, also an economist, with whom he later even published jointly, including their autobiography "Two Lucky People", and who became his most important intellectual and human companion. They had a son and a daughter, neither of whom became economists. Their son David became a well-known constitutional lawyer. After completing his doctoral thesis, Friedman worked for the Tax Research Department of the National Bureau of Economic Research, which was affiliated with the US Treasury, from 1941 to 1943. He then worked on the introduction of automatic wage tax deduction to ensure that companies automatically transfer their tax amounts to the Treasury. In retrospect, Friedman recognized this as a "mistake" because he helped provide the state with a machine that inflated the state apparatus even more and destroyed economic and individual freedom. In 1946, Friedman became a professor at the University of Chicago, where he taught for 30 years. He founded the "Chicago School" there.

Friedman was a founding member of the Mont Pelerin Society, founded by Hayek (see section 3.2), a society in which leading liberal intellectuals from around the world, but especially from the USA, joined together in 1947. During his time as a scientist, he mainly dealt with the teachings of John Maynard Keynes, which were very popular worldwide at this time and especially in the 1950s. Friedman believed that the state should not stimulate the economy through increased spending, but through an expansion of the money supply. But more on that later. In his criticism, Friedman primarily targeted Keynes' consumption function as a function of income. In 1957, his work "A Theory of the Consumption Function" was published. In the 1970s, Friedman then developed his supply-side economic theory ("supply side economics"), which he opposed to Keynes' theory with its strong demand focus.

Friedman's main work on the history of monetary policy in the USA, "A Monetary History of the United States, 1867–1960", which he wrote in 1963 with the economist Anna Schwartz, became essential for his theory formation. In this empirical long-term view of almost a hundred years, both economists examined the effects of changes in the money supply on business cycles. They came to the conclusion that the development of the business cycle was primarily due to the development of the money supply. This also applied to the onset of the Great Depression in 1929 and was not due to the lack of state demand, as Keynes had argued. Also in 1963, the popular science work "Capitalism and Freedom" was published, in which Friedman made his philosophy and core economic thoughts known to a wider public and explained them in an understandable way. His fame was also contributed to by television programs titled "Free to Choose", which he designed with his wife Rose and in which both conveyed economic facts in a comparatively simple way. At the same time, Friedman was a long-time columnist for the internationally known magazine *Newsweek*.

Furthermore, he was a member of many high-ranking associations of national and international economists and scientists, such as the American Academy of Arts and Sciences or the National Academy of Sciences. In 1967, Friedman was president of the most important association of economists in the USA, the American Economic Association. Friedman advised the US government and was instrumental in the introduction of flexible exchange rates after the Bretton Woods system of fixed exchange rates collapsed in 1971. He also played a leading role in reducing various taxes, thus preparing the intellectual climate that led to the neoliberal economic program of then US President Reagan in the 1980s. After his retirement in 1977, Friedman worked at the Hoover Institution at Stanford University until his death at the age of 94. Significantly, Friedman, who had fought for individual and economic freedom all his life, received the Presidential Medal of Freedom, the highest civilian award in the USA, from Ronald Reagan in 1988. Friedman was involved in the current economic debate throughout his life. He also had a clear opinion on the Euro, albeit not a good one—Friedman predicted that the first recession would break the Euro apart. He died in 2006 after a long life of research from heart failure.

Already in his dissertation in 1941 titled "Income from Independent Professional Practice", in which he outlined the income generation of independent professions, Friedman attracted the attention of experts. In this work, he argued that government regulation of admission to the independent professions, such as doctors, lawyers, etc., would increase the prices of these services by reducing supply. This would in turn reduce the choice for the "consumer" and thus lead to a significantly worse offer of these services. At the same time, the welfare of the individual citizen would decrease. Furthermore, competition among representatives of the independent professions would be restricted, which in turn would lead to higher income for doctors. However, this could not be in the interest of society and consumers. It can be vividly imagined that these theses did not stir up enthusiasm among the lobbyists of the independent professions. Influential circles in the university could not ultimately prevent the publication of the dissertation, but they could significantly delay it. Thus, Friedman's doctoral thesis was not published until 1946, after the end of the Second World War. Friedman also studied under the liberal economist and social philosopher Frank Knight, who is considered the actual founder of the Chicago School. Knight had, among other things, made Carl Menger's teachings known in the English-speaking world and translated the economic history of the great German sociologist and economist (section 3.2) into English. Menger's liberal moral philosophical teachings and writings were formative for Friedman.

In 1953, Friedman's article "The Methodology of Positive Economics" was published, quoted here from the "Essays in Positive Economics", published by Chicago University Press (Friedman, 1953). In this article, which is still the most frequently cited on the methodology of social sciences, Friedman advocated applying the empirically based research methods of natural sciences to social sciences. The philosopher Karl Raimund Popper, who was from Austria and taught at the London School of Economics, had strongly advocated this approach in his work "The Logic of Scientific Discovery". Positive economics, according to Friedman in his article, is independent of a specific ethical position or normative, i.e., evaluative, judgments of the researcher. It represents "what is", not "what should be". The results of research must be measured against reality. Economics deals with people. Researchers are also people who bring their own opinions and attitudes to certain topics and make objectivity in research difficult.

Friedman explains this in his article using the example of minimum wage. While the goal that everyone should have a "living wage" is relatively uncontroversial, researchers' opinions on the effects of the minimum wage differ significantly: proponents of the minimum wage predict a general increase in lower incomes and a reduction in poverty, assuming constant employment numbers. Opponents, including Friedman, argue with increasing unemployment, as jobs become more expensive for the employer. An effect that overcompensates the positive effects of the minimum wage and thus exacerbates poverty. There will also be similar differences in evaluation between researchers regarding the role of trade unions, price and wage controls, or tariffs, each positive or negative. Positive economics works with a hypothesis-supported theory that explains certain economic phenomena and can be empirically falsified according to Karl Raimund Popper's principle of falsification. A theory is only valid as long as it has not been refuted or demonstrably replaced by a better one. Experiments that capture reality and test these hypotheses are therefore essential for theory formation. Friedman sees a need for action in the conclusion of his article, especially in monetary theory ("The weakest and least satisfactory part of the current economic theory seems to me to be in the field of monetary dynamics...", (Friedman, 1953, p. 26). In the last paragraph of his groundbreaking article, Friedman once again points out that existing hypotheses must be tested and new ones developed (Friedman, 1953, p. 27). Practical examples take precedence over pure theory.

Furthermore, Friedman believed that economists, when describing the best possible course of action in specific economic situations, such as crises, must keep societal welfare in mind. The decision about the best possible economic activity must estimate its predicted consequences. Each forecast, in turn, firmly stands on the shoulders of a positive economic analysis, i.e., a hypothesis tested against reality. Friedman vehemently rejected mathematical theories in economics that did not contribute to the empirical testing of hypotheses as "self-referential". They only revolved around their own system and did not contribute to scientific progress. His research colleagues at the Massachusetts Institute of Technology, who approached economics purely mathematically, were accordingly criticized by Friedman. There, economics degenerated into a mere sub-discipline of mathematics and was nothing more than an "intellectual game". However, he was also aware of the limits of his own method: hypotheses cannot be confirmed one hundred percent. They can—as Popper also taught—at best be rejected or not.

In his 1957 work "Theory of the Consumption Function", Friedman addresses the theory of the greatest economist of his time, John Maynard Keynes. As we have seen in section 3.4, Keynes saw the consumption of private households as a size dependent on total income, but constant. Simply put: The more I earn, the more I can and will spend on my consumption. However, consumption only increases disproportionately: The more I earn, the more I can save as a percentage of my income—apart from the fact that I gradually consume more luxury goods. Keynes argued macroeconomically, i.e., he combined all households in his consideration and assumed that an increase in household income on average across the entire population would bring about an increase in total demand and thus stimulate the economy. Friedman, on the other hand, saw the individual household at the forefront of his considerations: Not the current income determines individual consumption, but the household's expectations regarding its total lifetime income ("permanent income hypothesis"). In this context, Friedman divided income into a permanent part and a transitory one—in terms of salaries, one could think of fixed and variable salary components. So if I am a top earner and have the secure expectation of earning very well in the coming years, and if I already have a high wealth and, for example, high education, then I will not be deterred from my usual consumption level by short-term salary drops or special expenses. The expensive vacations are still possible, even if, for example, high tax back payments are threatened or the bonuses are lower in one year.

Friedman had recognized that the savings rate, i.e., the part of income not spent on consumption, had remained constant in the USA, especially after the Second World War, although the incomes of households had on average increased significantly. He substantiated his considerations with extensive statistical data on income development, just as he had demanded in his methodological treatise on positive economics. However, if one adopts Friedman's idea of income over a lifetime, then the constant savings rates become explainable. If the household assumes a constant income, then it will not or only insignificantly increase its consumption expenditures. According to Friedman, however, this only applies if individuals can actually freely use their wealth to consume or sell goods and services freely on the market. According to Keynes, consumption expenditures would decrease in times of temporary unemployment or low employment.

With the thesis of permanent income, Friedman shook the Keynesian theory. While according to Keynes, with increasing income, only disproportionately more is spent and thus the savings rate increases, the total demand of households would gradually decrease, and the economy would be weakened. According to Friedman, this is not the case because the household always evaluates short-term income increases in the overall context of its lifetime income. The savings rate remains stable in this case. This has political consequences. Keynes had demanded to compensate for the demand gap created by lack of consumption through state investments—think of the construction of parks or schools and apartments, which create additional jobs in the construction industry and lead to higher consumption among the newly hired workers. Friedman, on the other hand, declared such state investments as useless: People would earn less in a recession phase in the short term. But they believe in their lifetime income and will not significantly reduce consumption. State investments to support the economy with their positive effects on consumption, jobs, or income would not work. Additional income would be saved—since consumption remains constant—and the intended increase in demand would fizzle out. Only the state would increase its debts, as the investments would be financed by credit.

In 1963, Friedman, together with the economist Anna Schwartz, authored a major work on the history of money in the USA titled "A Monetary History of the United States, 1867–1960". The National Bureau of Economic Research had commissioned the underlying study. The aim of the analysis was to investigate the impact of money and monetary policy on the economic development of the USA. In the detailed statistical analysis of the development of the money supply, which spanned over 7 years, Friedman and Schwartz came to a surprising realization:

A changed money supply had major effects on the economy and inflation in the USA. While Keynes clearly assumed that the development of the money supply played no major role for the economy, "money doesn't matter", Friedman and Schwartz proved the exact opposite with statistical data. A sharply increasing money supply led in the past to a significant economic upswing, but also to rising inflation. Conversely, a sharply decreased money supply was accompanied by a strong economic downturn and falling inflation.

Friedman and Schwartz primarily attributed the global economic crisis in the 1930s to mistakes in monetary policy by the Federal Reserve, the central bank of the USA. The money supply fell by more than a third, especially in the crisis years from 1929 to 1933. As a result, commercial banks were no longer able to issue new loans, let existing ones expire prematurely, and generally cut back on the amount of credit. Businesses were thus able to invest less, and private customers consume less. In this case, argued Friedman and Schwartz, the Federal Reserve Bank should have provided fresh money to the commercial banks. After the money supply rose sharply again in 1933, the commercial banks and the economy recovered. In the crisis years of 1937/38, the Federal Reserve Bank doubled the minimum reserve rate for commercial banks, i.e., the percentage of money that commercial banks must compulsorily hold at the central bank. This reduced the money supply again and choked off the economy. The two authors saw the main reason for the crisis in the failure of the Federal Reserve Bank, a government institution, which had severely disrupted the free market economy by intervening at the wrong time with the wrong means. As a remedy, Friedman recommended an annual percentage growth of the money supply, aligned with the growth of the production potential. The European Central Bank

(ECB) still monitors the development of the money supply today to prevent such negative impacts on the economy, as described by Friedman and Schwartz.

His analyses of the monetary situation in the USA over the past hundred years led Friedman to the conclusion that Keynes was absolutely wrong with his neglect of monetary policy and especially the money supply. Government investments, as Keynes had suggested, were not only pointless, but even counterproductive: The additional money needed for government investments would have to come either from private households in the form of higher taxes or be borrowed from the capital markets. In the case of higher taxes, this would curb consumption in the long run and choke off the economy. Higher government debt raises interest rates and reduces entrepreneurs' investments. Alternatively, the state or the Federal Reserve Bank should expand the money supply. Because the social product of a country is, in monetary terms, nothing other than the money supply multiplied by the velocity of circulation, i.e., the frequency with which the circulating money is used. Since the velocity of circulation remains relatively constant over the years—the behavior of economic actors is stable in the short term—an increasing money supply results in an increasing social product.

Friedman also opposed the newly discovered and in the Philips curve illustrated presumed correlations between inflation and unemployment: The higher the unemployment, the lower the inflation, and vice versa. Therefore, one could reduce unemployment by accepting higher inflation. The saying of the former Chancellor Helmut Schmidt became famous in this context in the 1970s: "Better 5 % inflation than 5 % unemployment". Friedman countered that unemployment is structurally conditioned—the sought-after qualification does not match the one offered, the mobility of workers is not limitless, workers are temporarily looking for work, etc.—and also cyclical. If you subtract the structurally conditioned unemployment, then there is maximum employment. This leads to rising wages and prices. At the same time, workers, through the unions, enforce higher wages because they want to offset the higher inflation. This increases real wages and thus unemployment. However, unemployment remains in the long term at the level of the "natural rate".

Friedman vehemently rejected the government stimulus programs demanded by Keynes—such as those massively pursued by then US President Barack Obama in the financial market crisis in 2008. It is not the private market economy that causes instabilities in the economy, but the state or central bank with their interventions. Instead, the money supply should grow evenly, tied to certain productivity indicators, to provide both private households and businesses with a stable planning basis and to prevent short-term speculation and associated changes in behavior.

In the following decades, Friedman will repeatedly formulate his theses on individual freedom and the market economy and bring them closer to the widest possible public: Friedman was convinced that the free market economy is the essential means of achieving individual freedom. According to him, the free market economy, free from government interventions, is the most efficient form of economy. It represents the values of choice, challenge, and risk that are important to him. Friedman assigns only a few tasks to the state, such as the protection of private property, the defense of the country, the protection of the poorest from hunger and need.

In his 1963 work *"Capitalism and Freedom"* (Friedman, 2016), Friedman elaborates on his economic philosophy. He firmly believes that economic and political freedom go hand in hand: "Economic institutions play a dual role in achieving a free society. On the one hand, freedom in economic arrangements is understood as a component of freedom, so that economic freedom is already an end in itself. Secondly, economic freedom is an indispensable component in achieving political freedom." (Friedman, 2016, p. 30). Friedman sees the freedom of the individual as the highest good and the ultimate goal of society. The only form of economy to secure this freedom is the "free market economy based on private entrepreneurship" (Friedman, 2016, p. 36).

Friedman compares the role of a state's government to that of a "game master and referee": The government sets the rules for the economy and ensures their compliance as a referee. In addition, the state secures property rights and sets the legal framework in which its citizens operate. The government is also responsible for the monetary system. Friedman summarizes its role as follows: "The organization of economic life through voluntary exchange presupposes that we have created the conditions for maintaining peace and order through the agency of government." Since free and unhindered competition is an essential element of the free market economy, it must be maintained under all circumstances. Collective agreements by companies or monopolies, where one provider dominates the market, must be prevented. The state is called upon not to allow these monopolies in the first place. State intervention for "paternalistic reasons", i.e., out of a misunderstood "paternal" concern for the citizen, is only allowed in exceptional cases, such as to secure property rights. Not allowed are, among other things, price subsidies in agriculture, import taxes or import quotas, state production monitoring, rent controls—one could think of the "rent cap" here -, legally fixed minimum wages, control of radio and television, subsidized housing projects, toll roads and even conscription and pension and retirement programs that must be purchased from a state society (cf. Friedman, 2016, p. 59 f.).

Friedman has a clear opinion on the monetary policy of the Federal Reserve Bank: As he had already noted in his work on the history of money in the USA, the decreasing money supply had been primarily responsible for the recessions of the past decades. However, the responsibility for controlling the money supply lies with a few people, in this case only men, at the Federal Reserve Bank. This is a clear error of the system: "Any system that puts so much power and so many decisions in the hands of a few men, that mistakes—excusable or not—can have such far-reaching consequences, is a bad system." (Friedman, 2016, p. 74). Friedman quotes the French statesman Georges Clemenceau with the words: "Money is too serious a matter to be entrusted to the gentlemen of the central bank." (Friedman, 2016, p. 74). Instead of these authorities in the Federal Reserve Bank, Friedman prefers to rely on legal rules such as the clear determination of the growth rate of the existing money supply.

It is obvious to Friedman that the free market economy can best thrive through free international trade. Therefore, all possible types of trade restrictions should be abolished or reduced. Exceptions may be possible for political and military reasons, such as the ban on the sale of strategically important goods to communist countries. It is interesting in this context how Friedman assesses trade barriers like tariffs, which is of high importance in the current situation: "Our tariffs harm us as well as other countries. We would be better off if we worked without tariffs, even if other countries did not." (Friedman, 2016, p. 96). He relies primarily on flexible exchange rates, as these "are determined by private transactions without government intervention" (Friedman, 2016, p. 90).

Friedman is very critical overall of the state's fiscal policy in terms of state investment programs. It is possible to establish legal rules such as the planning of expenditure programs based on desired state services on the part of the citizen. But in general, for Friedman: "In fiscal and monetary policy—all political considerations aside—we simply do not know enough to be able to use deliberate, intentional, well-considered changes in taxation or spending as effective stabilization mechanisms. If we try anyway, we can almost certainly make things worse." (Friedman, 2016, p. 102). Friedman even comments on the role of the state in education, which is supposed to educate children to be responsible citizens. In this context, the "educational service" can also be provided by private, profit-oriented providers. The state would only have the task of defining a minimum standard in the form of a minimum catalog of teaching material. From the range of state and independent schools, parents could then choose the best possible one for their children. "Parents who decide to send their children to private schools then receive an amount that corresponds approximately to the costs incurred by a training place at a state school, provided that at least this amount is spent on education at a recognized school." (Friedman, 2016, p. 117). These so-called "education vouchers" have become a famous point of Friedman's, which was later often quoted. The same principle also applies to universities, both state and private (here: scholarships) or for vocational education.

In the following chapters of "Capitalism and Freedom", Friedman goes into detail about monopolies and how they arise and how the state should prevent them. He advocates for free choice of profession and speaks out against licenses, as he did in his dissertation on admission to the free professions. Thus, the state interferes with the free choice of profession through the admission of physicians—one could also consider the example of the numerus clausus for medical study places—and reduces the supply of competent doctors, decreases the provision and makes treatments more expensive.

In the tenth chapter, Friedman deals with the question of income distribution. For illustration, he compares life to a lottery in which every person has the same initial capital. Everyone has the same chances, but everyone bets different amounts. Since everyone bets on different numbers and pays a different stake, they also win differently. If one wanted to restore the initial equality after the game, it would be like banning participation in the lottery. The restoration of equality would then be possible, among other things, through progressive taxation. From today's perspective, one would want to add: wealth tax, inheritance tax, etc. To this, Friedman states unequivocally: "I do not doubt that this view contains a piece of truth. However, it can hardly be used as a justification for the current taxation, if only because the taxes are levied *after* [emphasis in the original] it is generally known who has won the prizes in the lottery of life and who has come away empty-handed, and because those who decide on the taxes are usually those who think they have come away empty-handed. Based on these considerations, it might be worth considering letting one generation determine the tax provisions for the yet unborn next generation by vote." (Friedman, 2016, p. 195).

According to Friedman, income should be distributed according to performance criteria. This is the task of the market. Friedman is critical of state measures for income distribution. Thus, the progressive income tax and the inheritance tax are suitable on the one hand to improve equality. On the other hand, especially wealthy taxpayers know enough "emergency exits" of tax avoidance such as depreciation, tax deductibility, tax exemptions, etc., which they consistently use. Depending on the degree of use of tax evasion, citizens of the same income level pay different taxes, which rather increases inequality. Instead, Friedman proposes a "constant proportional tax rate of 23.5 % on the taxable income" (Friedman, 2016, p. 208), which would help prevent tax avoidance and even tax evasion and generate approximately the same state revenues as progressive taxes.

As far as social and welfare measures are concerned, Friedman is rather against public housing. Instead, low-income families should receive financial support, allowing them to freely choose their homes and not all live in the same area, thus counteracting the ghettoization of cities. Friedman rejects the state-set minimum wage as well as agricultural subsidies, as they interfere with the free market and, for example, in the case of minimum wages, make jobs more expensive and thus endanger jobs. From Friedman's point of view, the fight against poverty can be achieved primarily through two measures: on the one hand, through private charity in the form of donations, alms from wealthy private citizens, and on the other hand, through negative taxes, i.e., state grants when offsetting the tax allowance. It is essential that Friedman, in the liberal sense, relies primarily on private civic initiatives and not on the state. On the last pages of his work "Capitalism and Freedom," Friedman once again emphasizes what is most important to him, the liberal philosophy: "The foundation of liberal philosophy is the belief in the dignity of the individual, in his freedom to realize his possibilities in accordance with his personal abilities with the only restriction that he does not limit the freedom of other persons to do the same." (Friedman, 2016, p. 232).

Friedman fought all his life for his libertarian view, especially in economic matters. He used many forums, was not only academic, but also popular scientific on television. He was a contentious liberal who did not make only friends with his radical views. This became particularly clear in 1976 when he was awarded the Alfred Nobel Memorial Prize for Economic Sciences, endowed by the Swedish National Bank. Thousands demonstrated against this award because Friedman had trained influential students ("Chicago Boys") who advised Chile's dictator, Augusto Pinochet, on economic policy in the 1970s and wanted to implement their liberal ideas. Although Friedman did not flirt with Pinochet's dictatorial regime, the liberal economic reforms proposed by his students were very much in his favor. In the early 1980s, Friedman himself became an economic advisor to US President Ronald Reagan and was able to put his liberal ideas into practice. The discussions about lower taxes, reduced government spending, and increased competition, accompanied by privatizations, are unforgettable. These ideas spilled over to Europe at the same time as Margaret Thatcher's government and laid the foundation for the neoliberal economic form. Regardless of what one may think of Friedman's ideas, one thing is certain: Milton Friedman was one of the most influential economists of the 20th century, whose ideas have shaped economic activities more than ever before. A variant of the liberal economic view was represented especially in Germany by the so-called ordoliberals. We will now turn our attention to them.

3.6 The Ordoliberals

As we have seen in the examples of the most significant economists of the 20th century, John Maynard Keynes and Milton Friedman, opinions differ on the extent to which the state should influence economic activity. On the one hand, we have heard extensively from Keynes, who believed that involuntary unemployment at equilibrium could be reduced through targeted state investments. On the other hand, Friedman saw any form of state intervention as a "devil's work" that must be prevented at all costs. In Germany, too, after the Second World War, there was intense debate about a new economic order, which was informed by the experiences of the last decades. On the one hand, people had in mind the classic liberal position of Adam Smith and knew the negative consequences of too lax a "laissez-faire liberalism". On the other hand, the excesses of state interventionism à la Soviet Union and National Socialism in the economy were still too formative to want to adopt this model. Influential economists of the early post-war period such as Walter Eucken, Franz Böhm and Leonhard Miksch, who all taught in Freiburg—hence the term "Freiburg School"—therefore devised a middle way between these two extreme positions of economic design, which combined liberal positions with a state-oriented regulatory framework. This combination of economic elements was named ordoliberalism (lat. ordo, for "order") in reference to the journal *ORDO—Yearbook for the Order of Economy and Society,* founded in 1950.

The core points of this new economic concept were primarily a regulatory framework to be created by the state for a fundamentally market-based economic order. Specifically, the idea of ordoliberalism (cf. Braunberger, 2008) meant that the state has to ensure the citizen's freedom in the market and economic competition. The state is merely responsible for the framework, for the order of the economy, and the maintenance of competition. The state should stay out of the economic process as much as possible. Thus, a functioning system of free prices should prevail in a market characterized by perfect competition, where as many suppliers and demands as possible appear, competing with each other. Anything that restricts the free play of market forces, such as monopolies or oligopolies, should be avoided. In the case of a monopoly, the state has to intervene and restore the competitive situation. There should be free access to the markets, private property of means of production should dominate, and the contracting parties should have freedom of contract among themselves.

Every entrepreneur is responsible for his actions, but also liable in case of damage—think in this context of the "socialization of debts" in the context of bank rescue. In addition, the state should ensure that the value of money remains stable. In general, the state's actions must be predictable and comprehensible. Therefore, a long-term, constant economic policy is part of the ordoliberal concept. Over time, the various representatives of ordoliberalism have thought about the further development of these core ideas and adjusted them accordingly. The emergence of the economic form of the *Social Market Economy*, which has shaped the Federal Republic in the post-war years and to this day, would not have been possible without the theoretical structure of ordoliberalism. Therefore, we want to briefly outline its most important representatives and their essential ideas. We start with a man who is considered the founder of the Freiburg School and of ordoliberalism as a whole: Walter Eucken.

Walter Eucken (cf. Janssen, 2009, p. 187 ff.; Braunberger, 2015b, p. 63 ff.; Oswalt, 1996, p. 195 ff.; Lenel, 1989, p. 292 ff.; Gerken, 2000) was born in 1891 as the son of the philosopher and literature Nobel laureate Rudolf Eucken and his wife Irene, a painter, in Jena. He studied a broad range of subjects in Kiel, Bonn, and Jena, including history, national economics, political and legal science. In 1913, he completed his studies with a doctoral thesis under the national economist Hermann Schumacher, with whom he worked as an assistant at the Friedrich-Wilhelms-University, renamed Humboldt-University in 1949, after his military service in World War I. Eucken habilitated in Berlin in 1921, was a private lecturer until 1925, and was appointed to a chair at the University of Tübingen in the same year, and from 1927 at the University of Freiburg. There, Eucken worked until his death in 1950—he died on a lecture tour in London at not even 60 years old. He was a co-founder of the Freiburg School, which had formed in the early 1930s. In 1933, the philosopher Martin Heidegger became rector of the University of Freiburg for a short time and introduced the National Socialist university constitution there. Eucken, married to an "assimilated Jewess," made no secret of his aversion to National Socialism and openly took a stand against Heidegger and National Socialism. He even held a lecture series in which he advocated for the freedom of thought.

In secret, Eucken met with fellow scientists such as the sociologist Alexander Rüstow or the economist Wilhelm Röpke. They discussed the reconstruction of economy and society after the war and the hoped-for collapse of the hated National Socialism. Eucken was interrogated several times by the Gestapo. However, they could not prove any "suspicious activities," and consequently, he was not imprisoned. After 1945, he advised the French and American military governments as a member of the scientific advisory boards of the newly created Ministry of Economics in Bonn and was thus able to bring his ideas closer to political practice. Eucken was an active mind, a popular intellectual of his time, and had intense dealings with great minds of his time, such as Friedrich August Hayek, the physicist Werner Heisenberg, the painter August Macke, but also with such famous philosophers as Karl Popper and especially with his friend Edmund Husserl, the "father" of phenomenology, a new direction of thought within philosophy.

Eucken's scientific work—his most significant works were "The Foundations of National Economy" and the posthumously published "Principles of Economic Policy"—was primarily concerned with the compatibility of market economic elements with a state regulatory function. In a policy paper from 1946, Eucken already clearly recognized that, in his opinion, both the methods of the National Socialist central administration economy and those of the pure free market economy had failed. Instead, he envisioned an economic system in which the state sets the economic order and the framework conditions, but otherwise stays out of current economic events. The state should ensure that there is complete competition, that economic power accumulations are not possible in the first place, and that the interplay of supply and demand can take its course unhindered at free prices. Eucken also advocated for free world trade, which should help to restore prosperity after the devastating war, but also contribute to peacekeeping.

The formation of cartels should be prevented as well as the establishment of mono- and oligopolies. In economic policy, Eucken called for stronger support for small and medium-sized enterprises. In his endeavor to create the ideal of perfect competition, he naturally rejected nationalizations and all types of abolition of private property. Nor did he want to allow central control of the economy, which in his opinion had already failed during the time of National Socialism. In his conception, which was primarily ethically shaped, man has a free will and can freely shape his framework of order, the state, but also the economy according to his ideas. With his ideas, which he exchanged with other friendly scientists, he set the intellectual milestones for the path into the post-war period and the new economic order in Germany.

Alfred Müller-Armack and Ludwig Erhard

Alfred Müller-Armack is far from being as well-known in the economists' guild today as the previously portrayed pioneers of the economy. Hardly anyone knows that this seemingly inconspicuous university professor became the namesake of the "Social Market Economy", which was the basis of Germany's unprecedented economic recovery in the years after the war. It is rumored that Alfred Müller-Armack coined the term during a monastery stay: a middle ground between the central administrative economy of the National Socialists and the free market economy. He placed great emphasis on always capitalizing the attribute "social" when used with the market economy: the *Social Market Economy*.

Alfred August Arnold Müller, as his full name was, was born in 1901 in Essen as the son of a plant manager of the Krupp company (see, among others, Lingen, 2019). Later he took his mother's maiden name and published from 1929 under the double name *Müller-Armack*. After graduating from high school, Müller-Armack studied national economics in Giessen, Freiburg, Munich and Cologne with a focus on political science, economic history and social sciences. In self-study, he also dealt extensively with philosophical and legal issues. In 1923, Müller-Armack received his doctorate in Cologne with a thesis on the crisis problem in theoretical social economics. He mainly dealt with the emergence and overcoming of economic crises and chose an interdisciplinary approach from sociology and economics. This was followed in 1926 by his habilitation on the economic theory of economic policy. Müller-Armack was deeply engaged with the intellectual currents of his time, especially with the topics of sociology, theology, philosophy and of course economics. Philosophers who dealt with the nature of man, such as Max Scheler, Helmuth Plessner and Nicolai Hartmann, influenced his thinking as much as Max Weber, Werner Sombart, Ferdinand Tönnies and other great sociologists.

Müller-Armack became a lecturer and from 1934, at only 33 years old, an extraordinary professor, the youngest in Germany at the time. In 1938 he moved to the University of Münster and in 1940 received a chair for National Economics and Cultural Sociology with a focus on Sociology of Religion. (Max Weber sends his regards.) From 1950 he taught and researched again at the University of Cologne, where he was also head of the Institute for Applied Research and the Institute for Economic Policy. His time during National Socialism is critically discussed: On the one hand, Müller-Armack joined the NSDAP as early as 1933 and wrote a book on "State Idea and Economic Order in the New Reich", which was evaluated as regime-supporting. On the other hand, serious sources prove that his National Socialist commitment was doubted. After the end of the war and National Socialism, Müller-Armack set about conceiving a new economic order that should combine the elements of a free market economy with Christian social ethics. Similar to the Freiburg School, the state should create the framework and ensure competition so that the free play of market forces is guaranteed. State interventions to correct economic policy misdevelopments were only allowed in exceptional cases.

After the Second World War, Müller-Armack joined the CDU. In 1947, his most significant work, which was to lay the theoretical foundations of the social market economy, was published: "Economic Steering and Market Economy". Ludwig Erhard, the Minister of Economics, later Chancellor and "Father of the Economic Miracle", read it with enthusiasm. In 1948, Müller-Armack was elected to the Scientific Advisory Board of the United Economic Area of the "Western Zones", i.e., the British,

US, and French occupation zones. In 1952, Minister of Economics Ludwig Erhard brought Müller-Armack into his ministry and entrusted him with the management of the Department of Economic Policy. He became Ludwig Erhard's most important employee and close confidant, thus having the opportunity to implement his theoretical elaborations in "Economic Steering and Market Economy" in economic practice. In 1958, Müller-Armack became State Secretary for European Affairs in the Ministry of Economics and at the same time a member of the Board of Directors of the European Investment Bank. After the change of government in 1963, he left the office of State Secretary and resumed his teaching activities at the University of Cologne as an honorary professor. He took on numerous honorary positions, including the leadership of the Konrad Adenauer Foundation and—2 months after Erhard's death—also the chairmanship of the newly founded Ludwig Erhard Foundation. After his emeritus in 1970, he was granted 8 more productive years. Müller-Armack died after a short, severe illness in 1978 in Cologne.

Müller-Armack's most significant work, *"Economic Steering and Market Economy"* (Müller-Armack, 1990), will be the focus of consideration here. With it, Müller-Armack laid the intellectual foundations of the successful formula of the social market economy. The starting point for the newly conceived economic order was the economic form of state economic control prevailing under the National Socialists. Therefore, Müller-Armack described this structure of the economy in its manifestations, advantages, and disadvantages. He first characterized the economic control of the National Socialists in Germany: "Instead of the steering of the economic process by the market process, a central steering takes place, whereby, as in the case of German economic control, the individual businesses are primarily private profit-making businesses. In this respect, economic control maintains a clear boundary against the complete nationalization of the means of production." (Müller-Armack, 1990, p. 16).

He specified the economic control: "Prices, wages, courses, and interest rates were subject to strict regulation, while on the other hand, the state financed investments in favor of general expenditure through an expansive credit and monetary policy." (Müller-Armack, 1990, p. 17). Economic control is characterized by a "material allocation through quotas, rationing, urgency levels, investment bans, emission bans, and in the social area the allocation of labor or the prevention of job changes" (Müller-Armack, 1990, p. 18). The central control of prices and quantities eliminates the autonomy of the consumer, he cannot freely decide on his consumption decisions, savings, and capital formation. Demand and production are decoupled, as the controlled economy also governs with price stops and the steering function is lost. The entrepreneur is restricted in his entrepreneurial freedom by the determination of the price, the wage stop, and the purchase and sales quota, and cannot plan, invest, and make profits as he wants, "… because those freedoms of action have been taken from the entrepreneurial pursuit of profit …" (Müller-Armack, 1990 p. 28). At the same time, there is a lack of incentive for innovation and profitable further development of the business. The needs of the consumer no longer shine through, the scarcity of economic goods is no longer indicated. The "creative" entrepreneur (surely meant in the sense of Schumpeter; section 3.2) is no longer required.

Foreign trade was also state-controlled or regulated through import and export restrictions, foreign trade monopolies, fixed exchange rates, and compulsory foreign exchange management (Müller-Armack, 1990, p. 42).

Even technical progress was not achievable due to the lack of profit motivation or was limited to "war-important" areas. Even unprofitable productions were subsidized by the state and thus made possible. Müller-Armack concludes: "The claim of economic control to be the absolutely superior economic system cannot be accepted after all this." (Müller-Armack, 1990, p. 62). But what was to replace the state-controlled economy? He advocated a "controlled market economy" between the poles of the liberal market economy on the one hand and economic control on the other. In the second part of his fundamental work, Müller-Armack describes in detail how he imagines the controlled market economy, the "Social Market Economy".

First, Müller-Armack presents the market economy in its pure form. The market economy is the "strict subordination of all economic processes to consumption, which gives the determining signals to the production movement through its valuations expressed in prices" (Müller-Armack, 1990, p. 78). This means not only free price formation, but also free decision on production quantities and money supply. Free competition ensures the competition of the best providers and prevents monopolies. Consumer wishes and their needs are thus better taken into account. Müller-Armack characterizes the liberal market economy: "Thus, one was essentially content to advocate for internal trade and traffic freedom and to eliminate state influence from international exchange and currency policy. Free trade and automatic gold currency, freedom of trade and internal freedom of economic areas, plus the creation of a formally rational, substantively neutral market law …" (Müller-Armack, 1990, p. 92). But he clearly recognizes: "It was a consequential error of economic liberalism to see the market economic distribution as socially and politically satisfying." (Müller-Armack, 1990, p. 93).

A statement that has regained enormous importance today in times of increasing economic inequality in the population.

Müller-Armack urgently warned that it was time to design a new economic order: "The two alternatives between which economic policy has so far moved, the purely liberal market economy and economic control, are internally exhausted, and for us it can only be a matter of developing a new third form, which does not present itself as a vague mixture, as a party compromise, but as a synthesis gained from the full possibilities of our present." (Müller-Armack, 1990, p. 96). This economic policy synthesis should be the Social Market Economy. In the following, Müller-Armack describes the essential principles of the Social Market Economy as he envisioned it.

First, a "flexible price and value calculation" (Müller-Armack, 1990, p. 99) should be created, i.e., a free price system that reflects the scarcity of products and aligns supply with demand. Economic policy must primarily concern itself with active competition policy that stimulates competition, eliminates monopolies or prevents their formation. The value of money should be kept stable. Above all, however, economic policy should follow a clear, strategic plan and not consist of erratic individual measures as before. Interventions in price policy, "state price interventions", are justifiable in exceptional cases "in view of price fluctuations that do not have a production-controlling function ..." (Müller-Armack, 1990, p. 109). It should also be possible to limit credit expansion by influencing interest rate formation (Müller-Armack, 1990, p. 112). At the same time, Müller-Armack believed that "interest rate formation cannot simply be seen as an automatic mechanism regulated by competition, but requires state regulation, precisely in order to maintain the competitive structure in the goods markets" (Müller-Armack, 1990, p. 112).

The economic structure cannot have a moral task in the sense that values and moral convictions are created. Nevertheless, it applies: "This is about the possibility of an economic policy that sees in double optics, which on the one hand takes into account the necessities of the market economy, but on the other hand does not lack the determined will to achieve the social and cultural goals we envisage." (Müller-Armack, 1990, p. 116). In social policy, Müller-Armack is firmly convinced that "it is … economically quite unproblematic to standardize a state minimum wage as a so-called order tax, which essentially keeps at the level of the equilibrium wage, in order to avoid arbitrary individual wage reductions" (Müller-Armack, 1990, p. 119). How prescient the namesake of the Social Market Economy anticipated the state-defined minimum wages from today's perspective! Instead of determining market prices, Müller-Armack rather advocated for a state redistribution of income through taxation of higher incomes and the state granting of child allowances, rent and housing construction subsidies. He also advocated for the promotion of crafts and small and medium-sized entrepreneurs.

In the construction industry, Müller-Armack called for a limitation on rent increases (Müller-Armack, 1990, p. 125), and that as early as 1947! The state should either build new apartments itself or grant discounted loans to private or "non-profit" builders. This should stimulate housing construction and create more supply for affordable apartments. In general, a "framework control" of the housing and construction industry is compatible with a market economy (Müller-Armack, 1990, p. 127). Since the pure market economy endangers the existence of smaller and medium-sized companies, especially the existence of agricultural businesses, the state can certainly intervene. It is compatible with the market economy to carry out a "conscious influence on the forms of operation" (Müller-Armack, 1990, p. 135). Foreign trade should essentially be left to market forces, but must be measured against the goal of industrialization and employment levels. The theory of comparative cost advantages in international trade developed by Ricardo is still valid and creates prosperity. At most, a currency adjustment fund could be set up to regulate the capital fluctuations associated with trade in goods.

In monetary policy, Müller-Armack recommends state control in the sense of a restrictive control of money issuance, accompanied by a currency correction, i.e., revaluations and devaluations. The goal must be to keep the value of money stable. The purchasing power of private and public households should be observed and, if in doubt, "skimmed off", either by "depositing the notional purchasing power in accounts and blocking them up to a certain quota" or by "creating an approximate balance of the country and provincial budgets" (both quotes from Müller-Armack, 1990, p. 148). In economic policy, the primary objective is to create approximate full employment. However, it is no longer necessary to think of measures of economic control from earlier times, which resulted in employment in unfree and unproductive employment relationships. The goal is a balanced state budget with no permanent new debt. However, a state economic policy is necessary, because it applies: "Without such temporary state leadership of the economy, it may be difficult to get by in the future." (Müller-Armack, 1990, p. 153). A remarkably noteworthy and prescient statement, considering the current economic situation. Nevertheless, Müller-Armack clearly sees the limits of state engagement in credit expansion and investment programs.

Müller-Armack saw no alternative to the "determined transition to the market economy as an unavoidable prerequisite for reconstruction" (Müller-Armack, 1990,

p. 156). The clear decision for an "economically appropriate organization" (Müller-Armack, 1990, p. 157) had become the central question for people in post-war Europe. Müller-Armack, with his ideas on the social market economy and its practical implementation together with Ludwig Erhard, laid the foundation for the unprecedented success, the "economic miracle" of the post-war period in the Federal Republic of Germany. The social market economy will always be associated with his name, even if Müller-Armack as a person and his achievements as an economist recede into the background. He was always concerned with an ethical and social design of the economic form. Accordingly, he clearly formulates the core of his concern in his concluding sentence: "We are not committing ourselves to an insensitive form of organization, but can be sure that we can follow our social and ethical convictions on the way there." (Müller-Armack, 1990, p. 157). However, Müller-Armack would never have been able to put his ideas on the social market economy into practice without another economist and politician: Ludwig Erhard.

Numerous biographies have been written about **Ludwig Erhard,** the "father of the economic miracle" after the Second World War (see, among others, Mierzejewski, 2005), numerous prizes have been named after him, as well as a foundation. In 1949, during the decisive phase at the beginning of the Federal Republic of Germany, he was Minister of Economics, and even Chancellor in 1963. Here we are primarily interested in his economic policy ideas. A brief biographical sketch should suffice for our purposes (see Mierzejewski, 2005, especially p. 13 ff.). Ludwig Erhard was born in Fürth in 1897. He was supposed to follow in his father's footsteps and take over the business as a textile merchant. However, a severe injury from the First World War prevented him from standing for long periods behind the shop counter. Initially, he studied at the Nuremberg School of Commerce from 1919 to 1922, graduating with a degree in business administration. He then moved to the University of Frankfurt to study business administration and sociology. He received his doctorate in 1925. Finally, Erhard worked as an assistant at the Institute for Economic Observation at the Nuremberg School of Commerce, where he later became deputy director. However, his habilitation with the topic "Overcoming the Economic Crisis through Economic Policy Influence" failed. There were different opinions about the reasons later. He himself attributed his failure in habilitation to the influence of the National Socialists.

From 1942 to 1945, Erhard headed the Institute for Industrial Research. After the war, his meteoric rise began: Initially working as an economic advisor in his hometown of Fürth, he was appointed by the US military government as the Minister of Commerce for the Bavarian State Government. As early as 1947, he became the head of the expert commission "Special Office for Money and Credit" in the administration of the finances of the British-US "Bizone" and prepared the currency reform. In 1948, he became the director of the Administration for Economy for all western occupation zones. Since 1947, he had been accompanying his practical work as an honorary professor at the University of Munich. In 1950, he received a call to the University of Bonn. In 1949, Erhard was elected to the first German Bundestag via the CDU and was immediately entrusted with the office of the first Federal Minister of Economics in Konrad Adenauer's cabinet. He was close to the ordoliberal position and was so enthusiastic about Alfred Müller-Armack's description of the social market economy that he brought him into his ministry and drove the practical realization of the concept. Free competition was, for him as for most ordoliberals, the core objective in the economy, which the state should ensure.

Already Vice Chancellor since 1957, Erhard was elected Chancellor of the Federal Republic of Germany in 1963 following Adenauer's resignation. In 1966, he was voted out by the first grand coalition under Chancellor Kiesinger. His three years in government are considered rather unsuccessful. After his time as Chancellor, he remained a member of the Bundestag until his death in 1977 and took care of the foundation named after him in 1967, which was to carry on his scientific and political legacy. He was buried in Gmund am Tegernsee, where he had lived with his family since 1953.

Although Erhard had published several works on economics during his lifetime, such as "Germany's Return to the World Market" in 1953 or "German Economic Policy" in 1962, his book "Prosperity for All" published in 1957 became a bestseller. It was not only published at the right time during the peak of the economic miracle, but was also very popular and easy to understand, so that even economic laymen could understand and follow his work well. For Erhard, competition in the economy was the decisive goal that needed to be maintained. Competition stimulates rivalry, forces companies to constantly improve performance and innovate while simultaneously increasing productivity and quality. However, the state must ensure that this free competition can actually thrive. Any approaches to reducing competition, such as oligopoly or monopoly formations, which bring with them the concentration of power of the providers, were absolutely to be prevented. Along with free competition and increasing productivity, the wages of the working population should grow.

It is worth taking a closer look at Erhard's most popular work, "Prosperity for All", on the following pages

(Erhard, 1964). For Erhard, it was essential that an antitrust law existed quasi as an "economic basic law" that let free competition run unhindered in order to increase the prosperity of the people. The goal must be to increase the national economic yield before distribution in the population, so that the cake to be distributed would become larger for everyone (Erhard, 1964, p. 10). The state must indeed stand up for the weak and pay social benefits. However, these are primarily linked to the increase in the gross social product. In order to be able to pay the state's services to the citizens, expenditure discipline is necessary. Otherwise, taxes would have to be increased, which would choke off the economy. Free entrepreneurs must be able to supply free consumers with goods in order to guarantee material prosperity and the supply of the population. Stable, free prices and a fixed currency are the cornerstones for the economy, which the state has to ensure. If prices are subject to high fluctuations, for example in the case of high inflation and thus devaluation of money, citizens can no longer trust the value of money and ensure their consumption. Furthermore, currency fluctuations can lead to an increase in the prices of imported goods, which leads to additional uncertainty.

Erhard abolished the price regulations set by the allied victors as quickly as possible. Liberalization of foreign trade was also essential for him: "Between October 1949 and December 1950, exports tripled." (Erhard, 1964, p. 42). This was mainly due to tough international competition. German products were in high demand not only domestically, but also quickly abroad due to the high backlog demand. The newly formed social market economy was challenged by numerous crises, including the Korea crisis at the beginning of the 1950s. However, Erhard and his team managed to keep the market economy on track, as he writes: "Here the triad was achieved, which should be the ideal image for every market economist of modern character: With increasing production and productivity and in these relations nevertheless rising nominal wages, the increase in prosperity thanks to stable or even falling prices benefits everyone." (Erhard, 1964, p. 65).

The enormous backlog of the population after the deprivation-filled war and post-war years was satisfied by an increase in production, which in turn brought salary and wage increases for employees, workers, and civil servants. This then allowed for a further increase in the level of consumption. The standard of living in Germany continued to rise incessantly. By 1954, the phase of absolute economic boom had been reached, with full employment within reach. During this phase, Erhard insisted on not ruining the "overheating" economy with high demand and good prospects through dramatically rising prices and inflationary tendencies: "Such considerations [prevention of inflationary tendencies, note by the author] prompted me, despite much resistance and despite much head-shaking in those turbulent months, to *oppose any avoidable price increase* […] to *fight.*" (Erhard, 1964, p. 92, emphasis in the original). And further (Erhard, 1964, p. 97, emphasis in the original): "The maintenance of *monetary stability* is the indispensable prerequisite for balanced economic growth and for genuine and secured social progress." Erhard categorically rejected a planned economy and central control of the economy.

Erhard saw himself primarily as Minister of Economics and not obligated to the interests of individual groups. His highest maxim was the welfare of the people. In his own words: "The measure and *judge* of the good and evil of *economic policy* are not dogmas or group positions, but exclusively the human being, the *consumer,* the people. An economic policy is only to be considered good as long as it benefits and blesses mankind in general." (Erhard, 1964, p. 133, emphasis in the original). In this context, the freedom of competition must be preserved, freedom as the "highest value of the community" (Erhard, 1964, p. 136). Erhard strictly rejected cartels of any kind. Economic progress, economic growth should benefit the consumer alone and not the entrepreneur who exploits his economic power. The quality and price of a product should encourage the consumer to buy and thus influence the direction and quantity of the entrepreneur's production. Erhard was an advocate of steadily increasing economic power. Only a strong national economy can distribute to all citizens. For his dictum was: "Those who devote their attention to distribution problems are repeatedly tempted to distribute more than the national economy is able to give according to productivity." (Erhard, 1964, p. 216).

Erhard also turned to philosophical and societal issues. Thus, in the 10th chapter of his book "Prosperity for All," he dealt with the question of whether prosperity leads to materialism, i.e., a life solely in pursuit of material values? Erhard countered: "… the better we succeed in *increasing prosperity,* the less often people will sink into a purely material lifestyle and mentality" (Erhard, 1964, p. 222, emphasis in the original). At the same time, he looks presciently into the future and already raises the question of "work-life balance" in 1957 (!): "We will certainly reach the point where the question is rightly asked whether it is still right and useful to produce more goods, more material prosperity, or whether it is not more sensible to gain more leisure, more reflection, more leisure and more recreation by renouncing this "progress"." (Erhard, 1964, p. 233). A wise statement, very relevant for today's time. His comments on economic theory are also current: "Economic events do not follow mechanical laws. The economy does not have a life of its own in the sense of a soulless automatism, but it is carried by people and shaped by people. [...] One should therefore not underestimate the method of psychological influence." (Erhard, 1964, p. 236). Economics is not a natural science, it has to do with people and is carried by people!

On the one hand, Erhard did not want to follow the "night watchman state" of pure liberalism at all. State interventions in the economic sense within the framework of credit granting, monetary and fiscal policy, price stabilization, and the maintenance of free competition are absolutely necessary. On the other hand, he decidedly opposed a "welfare state": "The social market economy cannot thrive if the underlying intellectual attitude, i.e., the willingness to take responsibility for one's own fate and to participate in an honest free competition through striving for performance improvement, is condemned to die out by supposed social measures in neighboring areas." (Erhard, 1964, p. 245). People should retain responsibility for themselves and their well-being. The state only supports in cases of hardship and need. An integrative Europe was an economic must for Erhard, at that time still with freely convertible currencies. He even goes further and extends the arc to world trade: "For me, it is a matter of course that anyone who advocates a free economic society at home also belongs to the pioneers of a global division of labor and close intergovernmental cooperation." (Erhard, 1964, p. 302). Tariff barriers should be eliminated just like trade barriers of all kinds. This wisdom is currently highly relevant due to trade protectionist measures.

It is undisputed that Ludwig Erhard, with his economic policy, made a significant contribution to the economic well-being of the still young Federal Republic. He was thus a prominent, if not the most prominent representative of the ordoliberal school, who put the theoretical ideas into practice together with his employee Alfred

Müller-Armack. This idea of the social market economy as a synthesis of two economic forms from central control and free market economy still exists today, but must be readjusted to the present time. How this could happen will be outlined in section 6.2 about the future. But first, we want to deal with the present: the time after the economic crisis.

References

Böhm, S. (1996). Die Verfassung der Freiheit. In N. Piper (Hrsg.), *Die großen Ökonomen. Leben und Werk der wirtschaftswissenschaftlichen Vordenker* (2., überarb. Aufl., S. 105–111). Schäffer-Poeschel.
Böhm, S. (2009a). Joseph A. Schumpeter. In H. D. Kurz (Hrsg.), *Klassiker des ökonomischen Denkens* (Bd. 2, S. 137–160). C. H. Beck.
Böhm, S. (2009b). Friedrich August von Hayek. In H. D. Kurz (Hrsg.), *Klassiker des ökonomischen Denkens* (Bd. 2, S. 228–249). C. H. Beck.
Braunberger, G. (2008). Ordoliberalismus. Das verwaiste Erbe der Freiburger Schule. *FAZ* 19.06.2008. https://www.faz.net/aktuell/ordoliberalismus-das-verwaiste-erbe-der-freiburger-schule-1912163-p2.html. Zugegriffen: 20. März 2019.
Braunberger, G. (2015a). Joseph Schumpeter, Vergesst mir die Banken nicht. In L. Nienhaus (Hrsg.), *Die Weltverbesserer – 66 große Denker, die unser Leben verändern* (S. 249–253). Carl Hanser.
Braunberger, G. (2015b). Walter Eucken. Der wahre Neoliberale. In L. Nienhaus (Hrsg.), *Die Weltverbesserer – 66 große Denker, die unser Leben verändern* (S. 63–67). Carl Hanser.
Caspari, V. (2009). John Maynard Keynes. In H. D. Kurz (Hrsg.), *Klassiker des ökonomischen Denkens* (Bd. 2, S. 161–186). C. H. Beck.

Eisermann, G. (1989). Vilfredo Pareto. In J. Starbatty (Hrsg.), *Klassiker des ökonomischen Denkens* (Bd. 2, S. 158–174). C. H. Beck.

Erhard, L. (1964). *8. Auflage, bearbeitet von Wolfram Langer.* https://www.ludwig-erhard.de/wp-content/uploads/wohlstand_fuer_alle1.pdf. Zugegriffen: 17. Juni 2018.

Felderer, B. (1989). Léon Walras. In J. Starbatty (Hrsg.), *Klassiker des ökonomischen Denkens* (Bd. 2, S. 59–75). C. H. Beck.

Frenkel, R. (1996). Gelächter im Gottesdienst. In N. Piper (Hrsg.), *Die großen Ökonomen. Leben und Werk der wirtschaftswissenschaftlichen Vordenker* (2., überarb. Aufl., S. 218–222). Schäffer-Poeschel.

Friedman, M. (1953). *Essays in positive economics.* Chicago: University of Chicago Press. https://pdfs.semanticscholar.org/4af4/acabcbae145c9d21bca3cfb34fdbb55282a0.pdf. Zugegriffen: 23. Juni 2018.

Friedman, M. (2016). *Kapitalismus und Freiheit* (11. Aufl. mit einem Geleitwort von Horst Siebert). Piper.

Gerken, L. (Hrsg.). (2000). *Walter Eucken und sein Werk. Rückblick auf den Vordenker der Sozialen Marktwirtschaft* (Untersuchungen zur Ordnungstheorie und Ordnungspolitik (Walter Eucken Institut), Bd. 41). Mohr Siebeck.

Graß, R.-D. (1996). Marx der Bourgeoisie. In N. Piper (Hrsg.), *Die großen Ökonomen. Leben und Werk der wirtschaftswissenschaftlichen Vordenker* (2., überarb. Aufl., S. 69–74). Schäffer-Poeschel.

Hayek, F. A. (2007). *The road to serfdom text and documents. Nachdruck der Originalversion von 1944.* The University of Chicago Press.

Herrmann, U. (2016). *Kein Kapitalismus ist auch keine Lösung. Die Krise der heutigen Ökonomie oder was wir von Smith, Marx und Keynes lernen können* (3. Aufl.). Westend.

Heuser, U. J. (1996). Geld, Freiheit, Ideologie. In N. Piper (Hrsg.), *Die großen Ökonomen. Leben und Werk der wirtschaftswissenschaftlichen Vordenker* (2., überarb. Aufl., S. 274–280). Schäffer-Poeschel.

Hoffmann, T. S. (2009). *Wirtschaftsphilosophie – Ansätze und Perspektiven von der Antike bis heute*. Marix.
Horn, K. (2015a). Carl Menger. Die Preise richten sich nicht nach den Kosten. In L. Nienhaus (Hrsg.), *Die Weltverbesserer – 66 große Denker, die unser Leben verändern* (S. 199–202). Carl Hanser.
Horn, K. (2015b). Friedrich August von Hayek. Wider die Anmaßung von Wissen. In L. Nienhaus (Hrsg.), *Die Weltverbesserer – 66 große Denker, die unser Leben verändern* (S. 57–59). Carl Hanser.
Janssen, H. (2009). Walter Eucken. In H. D. Kurz (Hrsg.), *Klassiker des ökonomischen Denkens* (Bd. 2, S. 187–204). C. H. Beck.
Keynes, J. M. (2017). *Allgemeine Theorie der Beschäftigung, des Zinses und des Geldes* (Neuübersetzung von Nicola Liebert). Duncker & Humblot.
Lenel, H. O. (1989). Walter Eucken. In J. Starbatty (Hrsg.), *Klassiker des ökonomischen Denkens* (Bd. 2, S. 292–311). C. H. Beck.
Leube, K. R. (1996). Das Ich und der Wert. In N. Piper (Hrsg.), *Die großen Ökonomen. Leben und Werk der wirtschaftswissenschaftlichen Vordenker* (2., überarb. Aufl., S. 91–96). Schäffer-Poeschel.
Lingen, M. (2019). *Alfred Müller-Armack*. Internetseite der Konrad-Adenauer-Stiftung. https://www.kas.de/web/geschichte-der-cdu/personen/biogramm-detail/-/content/alfred-mueller-armack-v1. Zugegriffen: 20. März 2019.
März, E. (1989). Joseph Alois Schumpeter. In J. Starbatty (Hrsg.), *Klassiker des ökonomischen Denkens* (Bd. 1, S. 251–272). C. H. Beck.
Menger, C. (2005): *Untersuchungen über die Methode der Socialwissenschaften, und der Politischen Oekonomie insbesondere*. Elibron Classics Replica Edition (facsimile Nachdruck der Originalausgabe von 1883 von Duncker & Humblot Leipzig). Adamant Media Corporation.
Mierzejewski, A. C. (2005). *Ludwig Erhard. Der Wegbereiter der Sozialen Marktwirtschaft. Biografie*. Siedler.

Müller-Armack, A. (1990). *Wirtschaftslenkung und Marktwirtschaft* (Sonderausgabe). Kastell.

Oltmanns, T. (1996a). Ökonomie gegen die Armut. In N. Piper (Hrsg.), *Die großen Ökonomen. Leben und Werk der wirtschaftswissenschaftlichen Vordenker* (2., überarb. Aufl., S. 75–81). Schäffer-Poeschel.

Oltmanns, T. (1996b). Die Weisheit des Auktionators. In N. Piper (Hrsg.), *Die großen Ökonomen. Leben und Werk der wirtschaftswissenschaftlichen Vordenker* (2., überarb. Aufl., S. 63–68). Schäffer-Poeschel.

Oswalt, W. (1996). Die Ordnung der Freiheit. In N. Piper (Hrsg.), *Die großen Ökonomen. Leben und Werk der wirtschaftswissenschaftlichen Vordenker* (2., überarb. Aufl., S. 195–207). Schäffer-Poeschel.

Pietsch, D. (2017). *Grenzen des ökonomischen Denkens – Wo bleibt der Mensch in der Wirtschaft?* Eul/Lohmar.

Piper, N. (1996). Der Unternehmer als Pionier. In *Die großen Ökonomen. Leben und Werk der wirtschaftswissenschaftlichen Vordenker* (2., überarb. Aufl., S. 97–104). Schäffer-Poeschel.

Rieter, H. (1989). Alfred Marshall. In J. Starbatty (Hrsg.), *Klassiker des ökonomischen Denkens* (Bd. 2, S. 135–157). C. H. Beck.

Scherf, H. (1989). John Maynard Keynes. In J. Starbatty (Hrsg.), Thomas Morus. *Klassiker des ökonomischen Denkens* (2. Bd., S. 273–291). C. H. Beck.

Schipper, L. (2015). Thorstein Veblen. Spott auf die feinen Leute. In L. Nienhaus (Hrsg.), *Die Weltverbesserer – 66 große Denker, die unser Leben verändern* (S. 176–180). Carl Hanser.

Schwarz, G. (2015). Milton Friedman. Konsequent liberal. In L. Nienhaus (Hrsg.), *Die Weltverbesserer – 66 große Denker, die unser Leben verändern* (S. 209–212). Carl Hanser.

Spahn, H.-P. (2009). Milton Friedman. In H. D. Kurz (Hrsg.), *Klassiker des ökonomischen Denkens* (Bd. 2, S. 282–300). C. H. Beck.

Streissler, E. (1989). Carl Menger. In J. Starbatty (Hrsg.), *Klassiker des ökonomischen Denkens* (Bd. 2, S. 119–134). C. H. Beck.

Thornton, P. (2015). *Die großen Ökonomen. 10 Vordenker deren Werk unser Leben verändert hat.* Börsenbuch.

von Weizsäcker, C. C. (2015). John Maynard Keynes. In L. Nienhaus (Hrsg.), *Die Weltverbesserer – 66 große Denker, die unser Leben verändern* (S. 16–19). Carl Hanser.

Wagener, H.-J. (2009). Vilfredo Pareto. In H. D. Kurz (Hrsg.), *Klassiker des ökonomischen Denkens* (Bd. 2, S. 26–47). C. H. Beck.

Zank, W. (1996). Der Staat als Hebel. In N. Piper (Hrsg.), *Die großen Ökonomen. Leben und Werk der wirtschaftswissenschaftlichen Vordenker* (2., überarb. Aufl., S. 157–162). Schäffer-Poeschel.

4

Present

Any selection of economists and their ideas is primarily subjective. It depends on whether I am operating within a national framework and looking at it from a German perspective or perhaps from an Asian or American perspective. In almost every country, there are outstanding economists who have a significant influence on the shaping of the economy and economic ideas in general. In Germany, this is recorded annually in the excellent economist ranking of the *Frankfurter Allgemeine Zeitung* (FAZ). It meticulously notes which economists are mentioned in which media with how many quotes and how often they are consulted in politics. This reflects the practical relevance of economists. In addition, the quotes in relevant research media, the "Top Journals", are counted and condensed into an overall index. Those economists who are at the top of the national table have proven in the past year that they occupy an outstanding position both in research and in practice. Based solely on this list, 100 German or

German-speaking economists and their core ideas would be mentioned here.

Looking across the Atlantic and trying to portray the most influential US economists of recent years and decades, one certainly cannot ignore *Gary Becker,* who tried to capture social phenomena such as the choice of spouse economically in a cost-benefit calculation. Or *Paul Krugman,* the great macroeconomist and advocate of world trade, who regularly attracts millions of readers with his blog. Also, *Richard Musgrave,* the world-renowned financial scientist, or *Robert Shiller,* who has brilliantly outlined the capital markets and their developments with his psychological ideas ("irrational exuberance"). Finally, *Paul Samuelson, John Nash* or *John Kenneth Galbraight* with their commitment to the weak and the building of counterpower ("countervailing power") against overpowering corporations. We would find in almost every country, if it comes to finding great and outstanding economists of the recent past or the present.

However, I am not concerned with completeness. I want to give you, dear readers, an impression of what the currently pressing questions of economists are and what core messages they convey. This applies not only, but especially after the time of the economic crisis in 2008. In Part II of this book, I then want to take a look at the future of economic topics based on these topics and messages and overlay my critical view. The following selected and briefly outlined economists have mainly dealt with two sets of problems:

1. *Ethical questions of economics* especially the *growing global inequality* and the task of economics, especially to serve people. These questions have been mainly addressed by the American economist and globalization critic *Joseph Stiglitz* and the Indian economic

philosopher *Amartya Sen*. I would like to let these two economists speak exemplarily on these issues.
2. The *critics of the rational human image and behavioral economists,* both of whom have tried in recent decades to examine the irrationality of human behavior more closely and thus to represent reality much better in economic theory. As core representatives of behavioral economics, I want to mainly pick up the ideas of *Daniel Kahneman* and *Richard Thaler.* Both American economists have also received the Alfred Nobel Memorial Prize for Economic Sciences, Daniel Kahneman in 2002 and Richard Thaler in 2017.

As described above, I am aware that with this selection of topics and researchers, I have neither nearly described the current trends in global economic theory nor provided an objective overview of the countless research fields such as micro and macroeconomics, fiscal science, foreign trade, economic policy, business ethics, etc. If you look at the list of Nobel laureates in economics alone (see, among others, Karier, 2010), you will find *"Keynesians"* (Paul A. Samuleson, Robert M. Solow, James Tobin, Franco Modigliani, K. Gunnar Myrdal and others), *game theorists* (among others, John F. Nash, Reinhard Selten), the microeconomists of the *Chicago School* (Gary S. Becker, George J. Stigler, Ronald H. Coase and others). Furthermore, there are *theorists of the equilibrium model* (among others, Kenneth J. Arrow, Gerard Debreu), *foreign trade economists* (Bertil G. Ohlin, Paul R. Krugman, Robert A. Mundell and others) or also researchers who mainly dealt with the formulaic representation of the economy such as Jan Tinbergen, Trygve Haavelmo and James Heckman. They had not reached their peak of research only after the economic crisis, but set their own, globally recognized accents in economics. However, as mentioned, I had to make a selection of researchers, which is of course deeply subjective. Nevertheless, I think that the description of the following economists and their ideas provides a good insight into the economic issues that concern them and all of us today. I would like to describe these economists and their core topics in the following according to the grouping outlined above. I will start with the "ethicists" who mainly address inequality and the negative effects of globalization.

4.1 The Ethicists

The US economist **Joseph E. Stiglitz** (see, among others, Plickert, 2008), who teaches at Columbia University in Manhattan, comes from a Jewish family. He first studied mathematics, then economics at Amherst College and received his doctorate from the world-famous Massachusetts Institute of Technology (MIT) in Boston. Stiglitz held professorships at many outstanding universities. He was initially a professor of economics at Yale University, then at Stanford University, Oxford University, and Princeton University. In addition, he taught at the French elite schools École polytechnique and L'institut d'études politiques de Paris ("Sciences Po") in Paris. From 1993, he advised US President Bill Clinton and became Chief Economist of the World Bank in 1997. Stiglitz was and is represented in various committees with his expertise, among other things, he was president of the International Economic Association, the global association of economists. In addition, he is a co-founder of the "Institute for New Economic Thinking", founded in 2009, which deals with new approaches within economics. In 2001, he received the Alfred Nobel Memorial Prize in Economic Sciences for his work on the relationship between information and markets, together with George Akerlof and Michael Spence.

Stiglitz conducted research in a number of economic areas such as risk aversion in human behavior, which he mathematically proved. He researched the optimal supply of public goods in fiscal science and explained in a model of efficiency wage named after him and his colleague Shapiro that unemployment can also exist in equilibrium. Among other things, they found out that wages do not fall deeply enough in recessions to give companies the incentive to hire more people. Stiglitz received the Nobel Memorial Prize for his microeconomic theory of asymmetric information in markets (see Schmidt, 2001): This is best illustrated by the simple example of the insurance industry: Insurance entrepreneurs and policyholders take out insurance, e.g. car insurance. Both parties have different information about the probability of damage. Of course, an insurance company can refer to average damage data per age, per vehicle category, according to the period of driving license possession, etc., and calculate the insurance sum actuarially from this. However, this excludes a forecast of individual driving behavior. Only the policyholder can assess the forecast, as only he knows his driving behavior and can influence it in the specific driving situation. Both, the insurance company and the policyholder, therefore, do not have the same information, but "asymmetric".

Stiglitz then mathematically demonstrated that the insurance company is better off if it knows the policyholder's probability of damage. The policyholder must disclose this and can thus expect a lower insurance sum, as no safety surcharge has to be calculated. The disclosure of the probability of damage is possible today, for example, by the policyholder revealing his own driving behavior data. This can be done actively or in the future by allowing the vehicle data to be evaluated, such as how often the sports mode was used, at what speed, etc. The same can be imagined for health insurance, where there is a bonus for regular health checks and sharing the information with the insurance company. Stiglitz called this model, in which the uninformed market side attempts to eliminate the information asymmetry by such probing, the "screening" model.

Stiglitz is known to a wider public primarily as a critic of globalization (cf. Stiglitz, 2002) and as a warner of unequal societies (cf. Stiglitz, 2015). He also frequently commented on various other current economic issues. For example, he warned against Spain's rigid austerity policy ("anti-austerity policy"), criticized rating agencies as partly responsible for the financial crisis with their opportunistic rating behavior, initially in favor of the banks and later, in the crisis, against them. In his opinion, the euro mainly benefits Germany with its export surpluses, while other countries can no longer counteract through devaluations. In the financial crisis, Stiglitz primarily criticized the Obama administration for its bank bailout at the expense of taxpayers. Thus, profits would be privatized in good times by the banks and in bad times, such as the financial crisis, losses would be absorbed by the state and thus "socialized". In this context, Stiglitz spoke of a "socialism for the rich". The positions of Joseph Stiglitz on economics always consistently followed the perspective of the poor and poorer in the population: What does the poorer part of the population get from globalization? What results from this in the form of unequal societies etc.?

In his book "The Shadows of Globalization" (original: "Globalization and Its Discontents", Stiglitz, 2002), he sees globalization, measured by the goal of combating poverty, among other things, in developing countries as rather negative. Globalization essentially benefits the already rich industrialized countries and not the developing countries with a high proportion of poor population. Thus, developing countries are rather underrepresented in committees on essential economic issues, such as in the World Bank or the International Monetary Fund (IMF). Only the USA has a veto right in these committees. The work of the committees is largely opaque, there is a lack of an independent global (arbitration) court. The IMF only follows the ideology of free markets and the interests of the financial industry and multinational companies. In addition, Stiglitz calls for a new global social contract in which a fair trade order prevails, which gives all participants a fair share of the trade profits. In principle, he considers free trade with the use of comparative advantages, as Ricardo had taught, to be sensible, warns against tariffs and protectionism in general. He criticizes the neoliberal doctrine, in his view, many privatizations have gone wrong, such as with the Mexican banks.

Stiglitz also sets a clear emphasis against the growing inequality in society in his book "Rich and Poor. The growing inequality in our society" (original: "The Great Divide. Unequal societies and what we can do about them", Stiglitz, 2015). The book consists of a consolidation of some recent Stiglitz articles on the subject of inequality. The economist denounces the growing inequality between the 1 % of the richest part of the world population and the remaining 99 %. Fewer and fewer super-rich own as much wealth as the poorer half of the population, currently about 3.8 billion people. The top one percent of Americans own 40 % of all private US wealth and 25 % of the total annual income. 25 years ago, the top one percent only accounted for 12 % of this income and 33 % of the wealth (cf. Stiglitz, 2015, p. 88).

For Stiglitz, the causes of growing inequality lie primarily in neoliberal economic policy, beginning with

President George W. Bush. Tax relief mainly benefited the rich. Deregulation and privatization mainly helped those who are not dependent on state aid. Mass unemployment and wage dumping weakened the middle class. The rich are favored by low taxation and socialization of losses in the financial crisis. Above all, Stiglitz criticizes the theory that what benefits the rich, such as lower taxes, also benefits the poor. Wealth is not the prerequisite for mass ascent from poverty - on the contrary. Equal opportunities between rich and poor are not given: poor children do not receive a good education, for example at expensive private schools. Accordingly, they do not get one of the coveted, well-paid jobs, if they get a job at all. Unemployment and low income weaken domestic demand. Since this affects the large number of the population, it leads to a cyclical dampening.

With his criticism of the prevailing conditions, the growing inequality, especially in the USA, but also in the rest of the world, Stiglitz puts the entire authority of his expertise and his Nobel Prize for the poorer of society in the balance and thus aims in the same direction as the poverty researcher Atkinson. The second "ethical" economist to be mentioned in this context, the Indian economist and philosopher Amartya Sen, argues in a similar direction.

Amartya Kumar Sen (see, among others, Köhler, 2006; Gaertner, 2009, p. 354 ff.; Schipper, 2015, p. 150 ff.) was born in 1933 in West Bengal, an Indian state on the border with Bangladesh, and grew up in an educated and well-off family. His father was a professor of chemistry at the University of Dhaka, a state school in the capital of Bangladesh. The famine and experiences of extreme poverty in Bangladesh shaped Sen, although he himself was spared. He studied economics at the prestigious Presidency College in Kolkata and moved to the University of

Cambridge after his bachelor's degree. The Adam Smith Prize awarded to him enabled him to study a subject of his choice for four years. He chose philosophy because, in his opinion, it cannot be separated from economics. (We remember that the founder of modern economics, Adam Smith, was a moral philosopher, section 2.1). Like Stiglitz, Sen taught and researched at the world's most prestigious universities and institutions: at the Massachusetts Institute of Technology, in Stanford, Berkeley, Harvard, at the Delhi School of Economics, the London School of Economics and Oxford University. In Oxford, he taught political economy in addition to economics. Sen is a co-founder of the World Institute for Development Economics Research of the United Nations University (UNU-WIDER) in Helsinki, Finland, and was president of the American Economic Association, the association of American economists, in 1994. From 1988 to 1998, Sen taught philosophy and economics at Harvard University. Between 1998 and 2004, he was the rector of the prestigious Trinity College in Dublin and then returned to Harvard University, where he still teaches as an emeritus. In 1998, Sen received the Alfred Nobel Memorial Prize in Economic Sciences for his work on welfare economics, the standard of living in general, and the theory of economic development.

Amartya Sen has dedicated his life to the issues of social inequality, distributive justice, and the fight against poverty and oppression (see Köhler, 2006). In doing so, he has always moved between economics, philosophy, and also the social sciences. In his opinion, it is not enough to deal with the basics of welfare economics to combat poverty and inequality in the world. A just economy also includes a just social order with a corresponding political institution. To this end, all members of society must discuss in responsibility for their fate how they want to live together.

For this, every citizen needs a say. Moreover, pure income is not the only thing that makes people happy: even with a high income and great wealth, one can be unhappy if one lives in a country where there is no freedom and oppression. Egoistic self-interest, the economic paradigm par excellence, is not the only driving force of people. In addition, there are other values that significantly influence human behavior.

Thus, Sen developed a *Human Development Index* together with the Pakistani economist Mahbub ul Haq and the British economist Meghnad Desai (see Klier, 2009), i.e., an index of human development, which is used by the United Nations as an indicator of a country's prosperity. With this index, a report on human development has been published annually since 1990. This takes into account other factors that define the standard of living in addition to gross national product per capita. For example, the average life expectancy is integrated for each country, as well as an education index, which indicates how many years a 5-year-old child will attend school on average. A geometric mean is formed from the dimensions of life expectancy index, education index, and income index.

In order to represent and measure individual and societal welfare, Sen developed his own concept: the *capability approach* (see Klier, 2009). As already explained, Sen had recognized that the wealth of a nation cannot be measured solely by income. Consequently, the question must be asked what a person needs for a happy and fulfilled life. The essential prerequisite is the basic material security, which enables a life free from hunger, thirst, and cold. However, these are only elementary things. But what capabilities does a person need beyond that to realize himself in his life? This question concerns not only income or wealth, but also health in terms of life expectancy, living in peace, the observance of human rights, and sufficient educational opportunities for all people in society. In connection with the questions of the capability approach, Sen has worked closely with the moral philosopher Martha Nussbaum, among others. This again shows Sen's closeness to philosophy, which he never decoupled from economic developments.

In his 1999 book "Development as Freedom" (German: "Ökonomie für den Menschen", cf. Sen, 2000), Sen summarizes his core theses. It is based on six lectures between 1996 and 1997, which Sen gave as a "Presidential Fellow" at the World Bank in New York. Although the average life expectancy of people worldwide is higher than ever before, and the democratic form of government is now the dominant one in the world, there is still scarcity, poverty, and oppression in certain parts of the world. In addition to ongoing poverty and famines, fundamental political freedoms and basic rights, especially for women, are being trampled upon. The environment is threatened as never before, depriving the economy of all its foundations and ruining the health of humanity. According to Sen, the freedom of the individual is the highest commandment and social obligation. A country, the world, can only develop if the prevailing lack of freedom is eliminated. Only this gives people the freedom to participate in life, to take advantage of educational opportunities, to promote health, and to lead a good life. Freedom does not only refer to political freedom in the sense of freedom of political participation in elections or peaceful protests, but also to the important freedom of exchange and trade.

Sen distinguishes five types of freedom (cf. Sen, 2000, p. 71 ff.): political, economic, social freedom in the sense of social opportunities, guarantees for transparency, and finally social security. Only under these conditions is prosperity possible. However, individual prosperity does not only depend on the absolute level of income or wealth. For example, people with disabilities or diseases have different needs and require a higher income to maintain a certain standard of living than comparable people without disabilities or healthy people. Environmental conditions vary between countries and result in higher costs, e.g., for warmer clothing and heating or air conditioning. Not to mention the varying degree of environmental pollution. Countries also differ in the extent of their social security systems or the rate of crime and violence, which, despite comparable income, affect the quality of life. In some wealthier countries, the poorer parts of the population are more likely to be excluded from education and active participation in the community than is the case in poorer countries (e.g., in the case of private schools compared to generally lower-quality public schools in the USA). Finally, income is also relative when compared to the number of family members it has to be distributed among.

Poor people are not only materially poor and struggle with living conditions, they are also literally "poor in opportunities for realization". This is especially true in relation to education. In Germany, we can tell a tale about the rate of high school graduates or high school students in poorer families compared to the wealthier ones. Unemployment also leads to a lack of opportunities for realization. While the market in its free form can lead to an increase in prosperity through economic growth, Sen warns against an uncritical view of the market: "No matter how you look at it, a critical public discussion is an indispensable prerequisite for good welfare policy, because the way and extent to which markets are to be used cannot be decided on the basis of a grand general formula or any general attitude that either wants to leave everything to the market or take everything away from it." (Sen, 2000, p. 153).

Sen sees the form of government of democracy as best suited for human freedom and economic growth. For him, however, the commitment to women's self-determination is a key element in strengthening prosperity and especially freedom. Universal access to education and qualified vocational training for women is a good step towards reducing gender inequalities in some developing countries. Sen advocates for the unconditional observance and strengthening of human rights and advocates for social justice. Values are particularly important to Sen in the capitalist economic system: mutual trust between business partners, adherence to codes of conduct and signed contracts, etc. This also applies to dealing with nature, which must be conserved and taken into account in business actions.

Sen finds the definition of the rational decision-maker in economics, who only seeks his personal advantage, too narrowly defined. It would be better to integrate human values such as compassion and duty. Thus, he writes in his work "Ökonomie für den Menschen" (Sen, 2000, p. 321): "If you help a needy person because his misery weighs heavily on your heart, then you are acting out of compassion. However, if visible misery does not make you particularly unhappy, but instead leads you to the decision to change a system that seems unjust to you - or more generally, if your decision is not solely based on the fact that the sight of misery distresses you - then you are acting out of a sense of duty."

Sen is a boundary crosser, especially between economics and philosophy. With his ethically weighing positions on morality, the fight against poverty and famines, he puts his finger on the wound of modern times. He defines types of justice, puts the economic welfare definition on a broader basis, and thus brings a higher degree of humanity into the economic discussion. Not everyone likes this, but it enriches the discussion and leads to a true "economy for the people".

4.2 The Behavioral Economists

Daniel Kahneman (see, among others, Heuser, 2012; Thornton, 2015, p. 241 ff.) was born in 1934 as the son of a Jewish family from Lithuania in Tel Aviv. Kahneman's family emigrated from Lithuania to Paris and had to go into hiding after the occupation of France by the Wehrmacht. After the war, Kahneman emigrated to Palestine and studied mathematics and psychology at the Hebrew University of Jerusalem. After military service, he was briefly employed as a psychologist for the Israeli army and developed assessment tests for the selection of officer candidates there. Afterwards, Kahneman studied and received his doctorate in psychology at the University of California. After teaching positions as a professor of psychology at the Hebrew University of Jerusalem, the University of British Columbia in Canada, and the University of California in Berkeley, he has held a professorship in public and international affairs psychology at Princeton University in New Jersey near New York since 1993 and is now emeritus. He received the Alfred Nobel Memorial Prize in Economic Sciences in 2002, together with Vernon L. Smith, a representative of experimental economics.

Richard H. Thaler (see, among others, Straubhaar, 2017) was born in 1945 in East Orange, New Jersey, as the son of a teacher and later real estate agent and an actuary. Thaler studied at Case Western University (Bachelor) and the University of Rochester (Master) and also received his doctorate there. After 4 years as an assistant professor in Rochester, he moved to the prestigious Cornell University in New York, which is one of the eight most prestigious universities in the world. Since 1995, Thaler has been teaching at the University of Chicago. He was a visiting professor at the Massachusetts Institute of Technology. In 2015, he was president of the American Economic Association, the American association of economists. In 2017, Thaler received the Alfred Nobel Memorial Prize in Economic Sciences.

Kahneman and Thaler, who conducted research together with the prematurely deceased psychologist Amos Tversky, primarily criticized the neoclassical assumption of Homo economicus, the rational decision-maker and consumer, who has complete information transparency and can make the most efficient choice for him at any time between different alternatives. Through a multitude of empirical studies, Kahneman, Thaler, and Tversky found out what we all already intuitively knew: Humans are by no means infallible beings who decide and act purely according to rational criteria. On the contrary: We feel compassion for our fellow human beings, donate and help without expecting anything in return, react emotionally, have different characters, and are often unpredictable in our behavior.

Through their experiments, the three behavioral economists found out that, for example, humans in a decision-making situation with insufficient information rely on rules of thumb and established the "General Theory of Employment, Interest, and Money". Thus, consumers increasingly reach for well-known brands such as cornflakes when they are overwhelmed by the multitude of cornflakes variants on the supermarket shelf. The brand creates trust, they have had good experiences with it, and its price-performance ratio is known to be good. This is how uncertainties in decision-making are overcome. The findings of Kahneman et al. can be roughly divided into three categories (see Pietsch, 2017, p. 160 ff.):

1. *Motivational effects,* which deal with the motivation of individual people and their economic behavior.
2. *Cognitive effects,* which deal with "thinking errors" - Kahneman has written an international bestseller with his book "Thinking, Fast and Slow" (see Kahneman, 2012), in which he prepares the different versions of thinking errors for a broad audience.
3. *Behavioral effects,* which deal with irrational behaviors of people.

In the following, let's look at the "irrational" economic behaviors based on specific findings.

Motivational Effects

People tend to fear a loss more than they are pleased by the prospect of a gain *(loss aversion)*. In an experiment by Kahneman and Tversky, the subjects could choose between a gain of $100 and one of $200, with the latter only given a 50 % probability. Although the probability of occurrence is the same in both cases (a 100 % chance of winning €100 is statistically exactly the same as a 50 % chance of winning €200!), almost all subjects chose the "safe" option of a €100 gain. With a certain willingness to take risks, one could have won twice as much, namely €200. People are mostly afraid of making losses and giving back what they thought was already secure.

Tversky and Kahneman identified another effect in relation to the price of goods. In an experiment, they were able to demonstrate that the price for an item, in this case a cup, varied greatly depending on whether I am the buyer or the seller of this cup. Thus, buyers were only willing to pay an average price of $2.87, while sellers set an average price of $7.12. The two behavioral economists explained the different price with the different value that buyers and sellers attach to the item. While the value of a good that one owns has an intuitively higher value, the buyer is more dispassionate. He is familiar with the situation of not owning the item, while the seller experiences this as a "loss".

Cognitive Effects

Prices usually follow the logic of supply and demand. The higher the demand and the smaller the supply, the higher the price can be set, and vice versa. However, in an experiment, Tversky and Kahneman were able to overturn this logic. Students were asked to note down the maximum price they were willing to pay for a list of products. But before the students noted down the prices, they were asked about their social security number, which is quite common in the USA. At the end of the experiment, the two researchers came to a very surprising and rationally incomprehensible finding: Those students who had higher social security numbers were also generally willing to pay a higher price than the other students with the lower number. The one has nothing to do with the other, you might rightly say. But that's how it was. Tversky and Kahneman's explanation is: People are influenced by their current environmental information, in this case the social security number. This is called the "anchoring effect" in behavioral economics.

You can try the experiment yourself among your acquaintances and talk about real estate prices in Munich. With another group, you talk about real estate prices in a small town in a sparsely populated area of Germany, such as Mecklenburg-Vorpommern. Afterwards, both groups look at some properties, and you ask for the maximum price your acquaintances are willing to pay. It will be interesting to see whether the "Munich" group is willing to pay a higher price than the "Mecklenburg-Vorpommern" group.

Richard Thaler was able to prove in an experiment that every person has a reference value for the price of a certain product in their head. In this specific experiment, it was about a radio with a purchase price of $25. This was roughly the reference value that the potential buyer had in mind. Now this potential buyer gets advice from a good friend to visit a nearby electronics store where the same radio only costs $20. Since he can save $5 and follow his friend's advice, the man decides to buy the radio for $20 in the neighboring radio store. Thaler then applies the same situation to the purchase of a television, which also costs $5 less in the neighboring store than in the local specialty store. However, the absolute price is $500 and the reduced price is $495. In the last example, the prices are $5000 and $4995. At least in the last case, the customer will consider whether, despite his friend's advice, he is willing to take the detour to the neighboring specialty store to save another $5. With this, Thaler was able to show that it is not the absolute, but the relative price difference to the customer's perceived reference value that is decisive.

Formulations are also crucial. In one experiment, a looming Asian disease was described that threatened the lives of 600 people. Two subsequent programs were described with their effects and were to be chosen by the test participants as the most suitable measure against this deadly disease: In the first program, 200 of the 600 people will definitely be saved through the appropriate defense measures and medication. In the second program, there is a one-third chance that 600 people will be saved, and a two-thirds chance that no one will be saved. For your information: The probability of dying is the same in both programs. If 200 people in the first program are sure to survive, that's a rate of one third. If in the second program the probability of survival of the 600 people is one third, this means nothing other than that statistically speaking 200 people will survive and 400 will die.

Although the probability of dying or surviving is the same in both cases, 72 % of respondents chose the first program (200 people will definitely be saved), while only 28 % voted for the second program. Behavioral economists like Thaler took advantage of this approach of positive formulation and gentle nudging for the population to change human economic behavior. Consider organ donation: While in Germany (still) every organ donor must actively give their consent to organ donation and then receive an organ donor card, in neighboring Netherlands every citizen is automatically declared an organ donor, unless they actively object ("opt-out solution", is also under discussion in Germany).

Behavioral Effects
Imagine the following scenario: You buy a theater ticket for $10, which in today's prices and converted to Germany might be €50. On the way to the theater, you lose the ticket. Would you replace the lost ticket and, assuming there are still comparable tickets available, buy a new theater ticket? While you ponder, let it be revealed that in Thaler's experiment, 46 % of the subjects answered yes to this question and 54 % said no. Now let's take the second case: On the way to the theater, you don't lose the theater ticket, but $10, which in today's prices and converted to Germany is also €50. You have not yet purchased a ticket. Would you still buy a theater ticket at the box office despite the lost money? Again, while you ponder, it is revealed that in the experiment by Thaler et al., 88 % of the subjects stated they would still want to pay the admission price, while only 12 % spoke against it.

How does this difference in economic action come about? In both cases, $10 (or €50) was lost, once in the form of the theater ticket, the other time in the form of money. The difference, according to the researchers, arises from the *"mental booking"* of the process to different accounts, the so-called "mental accounting". Even without profound accounting knowledge, one can explain: In the first case, the costs of the theater visit double, as a replacement ticket must be purchased. The additional costs are therefore allocated to the "account" theater visit. In the second case, you have merely lost $10 of your assets; you mentally book the loss as a loss of assets and not to the "account" theater visit. Therefore, you subsequently buy the ticket. The difference between the two processes is therefore merely the way you mentally book or evaluate the process. Such behavioral patterns are also observed in the financial world, in "Behavioral Finance" i.e., the behavior-oriented financing doctrine. If I expect a rising value of a stock, e.g., from €50 to €55, then I will invest more in these stocks to be able to sell them later minus taxes and transaction costs with profit. But if I am not the only one who has these expectations regarding this stock, because they have already been announced in various newspaper articles, then the effect will quickly evaporate, and the prices of the stock will develop towards the general expected value. The stock market is psychology and partly irrational behavior.

From these selected examples, it may have become clear what behavioral economists Kahneman, Tversky, and Thaler are getting at: Human behavior is partly irrational (see, for example, the social security number as a price reference) and only partially predictable. In my opinion, this integration of psychological effects into economic behaviors is already moving in the right direction. The real person shines through here and does not wither as a being to be optimized mathematically. Behavioral economics has often been criticized for the fact that the experiments mainly take place in the laboratory and do not adequately reflect reality. At the same time, a comprehensive theory draft is missed. The truth probably lies somewhere in between. It is clear that humans are more than a rational being who always makes the optimal decision based on complete information. To be fair, it must be said that this was also an assumption in neoclassical theory to simplify the model, a decision heuristic.

However, the results of the experiments in behavioral economics gradually reveal the psychological and social foundations of humans. This interdisciplinary approach thus results in a great gain in knowledge for economics. Not for nothing have Kahneman (see Kahneman, 2012) and Thaler (independently of each other) received the Alfred Nobel Memorial Prize for Economic Sciences in 2002 and 2017. But the path drawn here does not end here, but must be continued towards greater interdisciplinarity. As we have already seen, the Alfred Nobel Memorial Prize winner of 2014, Jean Tirole, in his latest work "The Economics of the Common Good" (see Tirole, 2017) points the way in the right direction: The human being as an individual personality with psychological laws, equipped with a fallible brain, surrounded and embedded in the culture and tradition of his social environment, also acts economically anything but rationally (see Tirole, 2017, p.122 ff.). Behavioral economists have made a crucial contribution to highlighting this.

What remains after reading the various authors and theories from antiquity to modern times as the essence of economic thinking, and how should one imagine the future? I try to give answers to this in the two chapters of Part II of this book.

References

Gaertner, W. (2009). Amartya Sen. In H. D. Kurz (Hrsg.), *Klassiker des ökonomischen Denkens* (Bd. 2, S. 354–372). Beck.

Heuser, U. J. (2012). Schreck der Ökonomen. *Die Zeit* 16.05.2012. https://www.zeit.de/2012/21/L-P-Kahneman/komplettansicht. Zugegriffen: 20. März 2019

Kahneman, D. (2012). *Schnelles Denken, langsames Denken*. Penguin.

Karier, T. (2010). *Intellectual capital – Forty years of the Nobel Prize in economics*. Cambridge University Press.

Klier, A. (2009). Amartya Kumar Sen & Martha Craven Nussbaum. Jedem nach seinen Befähigungen. https://www.alexander-klier.net/wp-content/uploads/2012/06/Artikel-Bef%C3%A4higungen.pdf. Zugegriffen: 20. März 2019.

Köhler, B. (2006). Serie Ökonomen: Amartya Sen: Das Gewissen der Ökonomie. *Bilanz* 14.03.2006. https://www.bilanz.ch/unternehmen/serie-oekonomen-amartya-sen-das-gewissen-der-oekonomie#. Zugegriffen: 20. März 2019.

Pietsch, D. (2017). *Grenzen des ökonomischen Denkens – Wo bleibt der Mensch in der Wirtschaft?* Eul/Lohmar.

Plickert, P. (2008). Joseph Stiglitz. Kassandra der Finanzkrise. *FAZ* 06.10.2008. https://www.faz.net/aktuell/beruf-chance/mein-weg/joseph-stiglitz-kassandra-der-finanzkrise-1714311.html?printPagedArticle=true#pageIndex_0. Zugegriffen: 20. März 2019.

Schipper, L. (2015). Amartya Sen. Anwalt der Armen. In L. Nienhaus (Hrsg.), *Die Weltverbesserer – 66 große Denker, die unser Leben verändern* (S. 150–153). Hanser.

Schmidt, R. H. (2001). Nobelpreis. Rütteln an den Grundfesten. *Die Zeit* 18.10.2001. https://www.zeit.de/2001/43/200143_nobelpreis.xml/komplettansicht. Zugegriffen: 20. März 2019.

Sen, A. (2000). *Ökonomie für den Menschen – Wege zu Gerechtigkeit und Solidarität in der Marktwirtschaft*. Hanser (Titel der Originalausgabe (1999) Development as freedom. Oxford University Press).

Stiglitz, J. E. (2002). *Globalization and Its Discontents.* Norton.
Stiglitz, J. E. (2015). *The great divide – Unequal societies and what we can do about them.* Norton.
Straubhaar. (2017) Dieser Nobelpreisträger brach mit allen Heiligtümern. *Die Welt* 10.10.2017. https://www.welt.de/wirtschaft/article169490204/Dieser-Nobelpreistraeger-brach-mit-allen-Heiligtuemern.html. Zugegriffen: 20. März 2019.
Thornton, P. (2015). *Die großen Ökonomen. 10 Vordenker, deren Werk unser Leben verändert hat.* Börsenbuch.
Tirole, J. (2017). *Economics for the common good.* Princeton University Press.

Part II

Current and Future Challenges of the Economy

After we have dealt with the history of economic ideas and their essential representatives in Part I of this book, we want to approach the current and future topics of the economy, armed with this knowledge. However, before we do that, I would like to use the following chapter to summarize the findings of our journey through economics so far and to organize the conceptual tools (Chap. II. 5.1). In addition, we will get to know the nature and logic of economic research with its models (Chap. II. 5.2) and learn why they are so important, but also see their limits. We also want to look at the contribution other sciences can make to economic theory (Chap. II. 5.3), such as the social sciences, psychology, and mathematics. The latter has been viewed critically lately, and I will try to explain why this is the case (Chap. II. 5.4). As in every science, one also encounters the limits of theory formation in economics (Chap. II. 5.5). This happens especially where the human being and his activities in economic theory are forgotten.

In Chap. 6 of Part II of this book, we will address the most pressing questions of today's economy and ask ourselves how these issues will develop in the future. We begin our analysis with the question of justice in the economy (Chap. II. 6.1). In recent years, the economic form of capitalism in general, and specifically the social market economy in Germany, has come under criticism (Chap. II. 6.2). The topic of ethical action in the economy has also become increasingly important (Chap. II. 6.3). In the daily economy and its pursuit of "always higher, always further, always faster," one eventually reaches a natural limit (Chap. II. 6.4). Added to this are the influences of globalization and digitalization (Chap. II. 6.5). Drought summers in Germany and parts of Europe, overfishing and pollution of the world's oceans with plastic waste, as well as the discussion about CO_2 and NO_x values have led to ecology gaining an increasingly important role in its interaction with the economy (Chap. II. 6.6). And what does the future work society actually look like (Chap.II. 6.7)? How do we achieve an economy that creates more value for everyone and not just a few (Chap.II. 6.8)? Finally: What challenges do we face in an economy in uncertain times?

5

The Quintessence of Economic Thinking

5.1 Essential Ideas of Economics

The first thinkers of economic ideas were not economists, they were primarily philosophers. As the ancient Greek name already suggests, they were friends of wisdom or science. They dealt with the core questions of humanity such as coexistence, ethics, with humans themselves, anthropology, and with living together in a state. In addition, the nature surrounding them was of outstanding interest to them. Thus, the "Presocratics" dealt with the question of the primal substance of the world and the primal ground of being (cf. Kirk et al., 2001). Sometimes water was considered for this (Thales of Miletus), sometimes air (Anaximenes), others invoked an infinite, the so-called *apeiron* as a term for the primal substance. Empedocles considered four elements and their mixture as the primal substance: earth, water, air, and fire. Parmenides finally saw in "being" the primal ground of the world.

Anaxagoras looked at the entire universe and recognized a beautiful, purposeful order (cosmos) in it. Pythagoras and his students were fascinated by the numbers and their ratios existing in the world. This is also where the "Pythagorean theorem" from geometry, which all students have to learn, originates.

From the time before, from the beginnings of humanity, the Stone Age (cf. Bick, 2012), no economic considerations are known. The daily struggle for survival was about food and self-sufficiency. During the time of the Babylonian and Egyptian high cultures, the core economic considerations mainly revolved around the question of how agricultural production can be increased, e.g., through more efficient water regulation and the type of cultivation. This ensured the nutrition of a growing population. Considerations for the distribution of food were also in the foreground. The more division of labor the production became and the further apart the goods to be exchanged were, the more long-distance trade was conducted along the river courses and seas. The exchange of goods for goods was gradually replaced by the introduction of a money economy (cf. Vaupel & Kaul, 2016) and the emergence of banking with the granting of credit. However, there are still no or no significant records of economic ideas or laws on these topics. Only the classical Greek philosophers like the outstanding Plato and his student Aristotle, the teacher of Alexander the Great, began to deal with questions of economics within their philosophical system.

In Plato's main philosophical work, "Politeia" (cf. Hülser, 1991, Volume V), the state, we find the first approaches to an economic theory. There, Plato describes man in the polis as an economic subject with vital needs for food, clothing, and shelter. To obtain these necessary goods, man must work, but brings different talents with

5 The Quintessence of Economic Thinking

him. The division of labor in general and the specialization in certain activities and professions lead to an increase in productivity. The exchange of individual goods should take place fairly and within a cooperatively designed working society. In Plato's ideal world, cooperation in the economic world is harmonious and without competition and conflict. However, Plato was not naive and clearly recognized even then that this is at best a deceptive idyll. He was greatly troubled by the greed of his contemporaries for ever more wealth, the "pleonexia". Against this, Plato proposes a rule of philosophers, wise men, who take care of the state and the fight against greed. Plato was more concerned with the ethical dimension of economic action: the greed of man for wealth as an egoistic behavior that withdraws from the common good and the state. The individual and the family become more important than the state, which we all represent. As a concrete measure against egoism, Plato proposes the abolition of private property, especially for the ruling class of the state. The elite of the state should not worry about their own wealth, but about the fate of the state. The moral integrity of the ruler is in the foreground here. Instead of a high fortune, the statesman should rather strive for the virtue of prudence in life. Material things become secondary.

Aristotle, a student of Plato and one of the most significant philosophers of the Western world, gave economics its name. Derived from "oikos" (house) and "nomos" (law), one could translate economics as "household management theory". Thus, Aristotle develops in his three books on the "Oikonomia" (cf. Brodersen, 2006) his ideas on household rule, the relationship between man and woman, father and children, and master and slaves. In the second book, he deals with the financial history of Greek and Persian states, including the question of how to increase state revenues, and in the third book with the laws of man and marriage. Aristotle primarily sees economics as the art of household management: it provides the material basis for the family and its members and thus ensures a good life. He views private property and the pursuit of wealth positively, as they ensure efficient household and state management. He therefore views economics pragmatically as a technique for securing a good life. As with his teacher Plato, the ethical dimension of economic activities is at the forefront: Aristotle rejects profit maximization as mere accumulation of wealth beyond the necessary measure as immoral. Similarly, in his work "Nicomachean Ethics" (cf. Aristotle, 2007), he describes that the exchange of goods brought about by division of labor must be "fair". The type of justice meant here is that of reciprocity: an exchange must always involve an equivalent exchange of goods for goods or goods for money.

In the Middle Ages, the philosopher Thomas Aquinas took up essential thoughts of Aristotle and developed them further. It is no surprise that in a time of intense religiosity, especially within the framework of Christianity, the ethical dimension of economic action was even more in the foreground than it was with Plato and Aristotle. In his main work "Summa Theologiae" (The Sum of Theology; cf. Aquinas, 1985), Thomas demands that in the trade of goods both parties should have the same benefit. This includes, among other things, that all information for price formation should be disclosed. Thus, the seller of wheat should give the buyer information about how productive the harvest was in total, in order to estimate the offer and thus a scarcity of the goods. The price should be fair, "iustum pretium", a demand that can already be read in Aristotle. Thomas, strictly faithful to the Bible, advocated a general prohibition of interest and branded any interest taken when lending money as usury. Many scholars of this time focused their philosophical

5 The Quintessence of Economic Thinking 263

treatises on ethical topics, especially on how to reconcile the findings of Western philosophy with Christian faith. Therefore, the topics of the justice of exchange, but also of economic activity in general, were more in the foreground of considerations.

This only changed at the beginning of the modern era. In the 18th century, especially from the second half onwards, the population, especially in Europe, began to increase again, after it had declined sharply in the 17th century, mainly as a result of large and long-lasting wars, especially the Thirty Years' War. The population was still largely fed by agriculture. Consequently, the considerations of the economic thinkers of that time mainly revolved around the laws of agriculture. To this end, the Frenchman François Quesnay developed the first overall model of an economy. Quesnay was one of the main representatives of the "Physiocrats"—Physiocracy means the rule of nature—whose core idea was that the economy functions according to the model of natural processes (cf. in the following Zank, 1993). If the economy is left to this natural order, "laisser faire", all forces lead to a balance that marks the best possible state of the economy. State interventions are categorically rejected. This vehement rejection of state correction of the economy is a response to the system of mercantilism, which began mainly in France. The goal of mercantilism was to strengthen the power of a state by accumulating as much wealth as possible. This was to be achieved with state promotion of trade, which was to bring as much money as possible into the state coffers and ensure a small outflow. The more money or gold in the state coffers, the better. Protective tariffs were also used when it came to supporting the domestic economy. Against this, the Physiocrats demanded that not the balance of trade, but agricultural production should provide for the prosperity of a people. Therefore, the state should not promote trade, but, if at all, agricultural production.

François Quesnay, who was a physician by profession and also the king's personal physician, created an initial economic cycle model ("tableau économique"). He divided the citizens into three "classes": the first class, the farmers, fishermen, and miners, whom he referred to as the "productive class," were responsible for the production of new goods and thus for the wealth of the country. The second class, the class of landowners or also called the "distributive class," lived off the proceeds of production minus the payment of the farmers. The third class, the "sterile class," such as craftsmen, employees, merchants, lived from their work for the landowners or the administration of agricultural yields. The individual classes are interconnected in this economic cycle. The farmers pay rent to the landowners and live from the sale of agricultural products. The landowners sell the agricultural products on to the "sterile class," who convert these goods into commercial goods and resell them. If the state wants to promote the economy, it must above all strengthen agriculture by, among other things, abolishing serfdom and making agricultural methods more efficient, according to the opinion of the Physiocrats (Zank, 1993).

As we have seen from the previous explanations, the economic insights of the thinkers described were merely marginal phenomena in a philosophical overall work and dealt with selected economic issues. And when the thinkers dealt with these topics, they were all not specialists in economics, but rather generalists like the philosophers Plato and Aristotle or physicians like François Quesnay. The founder of modern economics, the Scot Adam Smith, was also a moral philosopher by profession. Smith, like Plato and Aristotle, was more of a generalist, mentally engaged in various sciences. In his efforts to

5 The Quintessence of Economic Thinking

secure a position as a university lecturer, Smith gave public lectures in Edinburgh on a comprehensive range of topics. He lectured on legal topics as well as on English literature and rhetoric, but also on philosophy in general. Only at the age of 27 was he appointed Professor of Logic at the University of Glasgow. Two years later, he became Professor of Moral Philosophy. During this time, his first major work, "The Theory of Moral Sentiments" (see Smith, 2010), in which he dealt with human nature and its relationship to society, was created. Only at the age of 53, after his career as a philosophy professor, did he complete his main economic work "The Wealth of Nations" (2009).

Smith's main theme was, as he succinctly formulated in the title of his book, how the wealth of nations is created (see Smith, 2009). In this context, Smith examines a variety of topics such as the principles of division of labor, the formation of wages and prices based on supply and demand, and the functions of money and the financial system. Smith saw free trade across national borders as a crucial source of a nation's wealth. Production could become more efficient through specialization in certain work processes and division of labor. The goods produced more cost-effectively as a result can then be sold and exported internationally in free trade. A significant aspect of Adam Smith's theory relates to human characteristics: From Smith's perspective, the entrepreneur's egoism does not prevent wealth, on the contrary, the entrepreneur advances the economy as a whole by pursuing his own interests.

The explanation is relatively simple: In his pursuit of profit, the entrepreneur tries to satisfy customer needs and produce high-quality goods in an increasingly efficient production system. Since all successful entrepreneurs act in this way—and are guided by the "invisible hand"—the products are always made more customer-friendly and efficiently. The economy as a whole thus becomes increasingly competitive, and the wealth of the nation grows. However, this only applies, according to Smith, if entrepreneurs think and act in the long term. Smith also advocated for fair income distribution, as the worker only receives an incentive to work hard and productively through high and fair wages. After all, he can thereby adequately feed himself and his family.

With the increasing industrialization, especially in England and Germany, the conditions of economic activity also change. The economists of that time naturally pick up on these changes. Thus, the transition from manual to machine production in factories using masses of workers is anything but smooth. Production in the factories becomes increasingly divided, the individual only sees a tiny section of the total product. At the same time, the workers experience a production environment that is anything but optimal for their health: Long, often dull and repetitive tasks require a robust physical and mental constitution. Meanwhile, the safety and hygienic working conditions are extremely deficient. The workers, who mostly live with their families near the factories in miserable wooden huts and barracks, surrounded by dirt and mud, are often overworked and can hardly recover. Even children have to help out, as the parents often do not earn enough to feed the family. The average wage of a worker is far from sufficient for a decent standard of living.

In this depressing situation for the worker and his family, the economic theory of Karl Marx comes into play, who, together with Friedrich Engels, the wealthy son of a spinning mill owner, analyzed the situation of the time (see Marx & Engels, 1983) and recommended a revolution. In his pursuit of profit, the entrepreneur tries to use the "surplus value" (see Marx, 2009) produced by the worker on the resulting good for himself and to pay the worker only the wage he needs to maintain his labor power. Because the entrepreneur owns the means of production, he can enjoy the fruits of the worker's labor without adequately sharing the profit. This leads to the "impoverishment" of the worker and an increasing proletarianization. The worker becomes increasingly "alienated" from his work and no longer identifies with the product of his efforts. The entrepreneur optimizes his capital investment on the backs of the workers, he "exploits" them. This leads to a "class struggle" of the entrepreneurs or the "bourgeoisie" against the workers: While the worker "impoverishes", the entrepreneur and owner of the means of production "accumulates" capital. Consequently, Marx calls on the workers and "proletarians" across national borders to revolt against these conditions and establish a new, socialist system. The core idea should be communism (lat. *communis* = general, common), the common ownership of all means of production.

While Karl Marx presented a comparatively closed economic and social system, other economists focused on essential individual aspects of the economy. For example, David Ricardo explained how trade between individual nations came about and why it makes sense even if a country can produce all goods in a more efficient production ratio itself (see Fischer, 2011). According to Ricardo, the reason for this lies in the gains from specialization: A country focuses on the production of the good in which it has fewer production disadvantages compared to another country and leaves it to the other country to focus on those goods in which it has even greater production advantages. Other economists, such as the Frenchman Jean-Baptiste Say, made a name for himself with the "Say's Theorem" named after him (see Hoffmann, 1992): Every production, every offer, according to him, creates its own demand. The overproduction of a good in one country will be balanced out at the latest by the underproduction of the same good in another country. The Englishman John Stewart Mill, who saw himself as a political economist, saw an ideal economic order in a market system with the greatest possible personal freedom and yet fair market results (see Schipper, 2015).

Often, economists, who were originally philosophers, sociological and political thinkers, had to respond to current economic crises and develop a concept that could be used in practice. This was also the case with the most influential economist of the 20th century, the Englishman John Maynard Keynes. After studying philosophy, mathematics, and economics at the University of Cambridge, Keynes worked in the India Office of the British government, then in the British Treasury, and then returned to the university as a professor. As a member of the British delegation at the Versailles peace negotiations at the end of the First World War, he already recognized that the reparations imposed on Germany and the German economy represented an economic and political catastrophe. In his work "The Economic Consequences of the Peace" (1919, German: "Die ökonomischen Konsequenzen des Friedens"), which made him internationally known, Keynes denounced the economically and politically unfulfillable reparations burdens. It already demonstrated the visionary, but also pragmatic views in Keynes' economic theory.

This was particularly evident in the face of the global economic crisis that broke out in 1929, which spread from the New York Stock Exchange across the entire United States. Contrary to Jean-Baptiste Say's assumption, the supply does not create its own market. The situation is roughly comparable to today's, even though there is currently no economic crisis (see Keynes, 2017): The interest rate controls the supply and demand for money. The

5 The Quintessence of Economic Thinking

higher the interest rate, the more money is saved and deposited at the bank and the less is spent. The bank invests the money and puts it to work. If the interest rate is very low or zero, it is not worth investing, and cash is rather held. This "liquidity trap"—i.e., households prefer to save cash rather than spend it—leads to low consumption, thus no demand is generated and goods and services are less in demand. Consequently, fewer workers and employees are needed for their production and provision, leading to mass unemployment. As a remedy, Keynes recommends replacing the missing demand from the private sector with state demand. Through increased construction of highways and real estate, investment in private companies, etc., entrepreneurial activities are strengthened, labor is increasingly in demand, and unemployment is reduced. The state thus stimulates entrepreneurial activity. If the state's investments are financed by loans on the capital market, the interest rate also rises, people hold less cash and deposit it again at the bank. Due to the increased demand on the capital market, the interest rate rises. For private investors and savers, it then becomes attractive again to hold money at the bank at higher interest rates.

Economists have dealt with a plethora of different topics over the past decades, the description of which would go beyond the scope here. For example, they theorized about the economic backgrounds of marriage. Nobel laureate Gary Becker claimed that spouses did not marry for love, but out of rational calculation (cf. Siedenbiedel, 2013). The family was comparable to a small factory, which brought more prosperity to each individual family member through the division of labor between man and woman. Others, like Joan Robinson, argued that economics should explain life and primarily address issues of unemployment and exploitation. There was often disagreement about the proportion of equality and freedom in the economy. Thus, the dispute among economists ignited over the question of how much influence the state should have in the economy. Starting from the ideal economic form to the question of whether the state should only set the framework conditions such as the legal and tax framework, the determination of property relations, the maintenance of free competition or the defense of the state against attacks from within and from outside. Representatives of a socialist, rather balancing approach advocated for increased state intervention in favor of the poor, weak and socially marginalized. Keywords such as wealth and inheritance tax, minimum wage and pension, but also state control of large corporations, unconditional basic income require a strong influence of the state in the form of a partial redistribution of market economic results. The aim is primarily to combat the ever-increasing inequality in society: because the poor are getting poorer or stagnating at a low level, and the rich are getting richer. Economists who research and argue in this direction include the economic philosopher and Nobel laureate Amartya Sen, the Englishman Anthony Atkinson, the American Joseph Stiglitz, also a Nobel laureate, and John Kenneth Galbraight. Some, like the social philosopher John Rawls, focus their intellectual efforts on the essence of justice.

The opposing position of an economist relying on the free forces of the market was or is represented mainly by economists like Friedrich von Hayek, Ludwig Mises and Milton Friedman (Friedman, 2016): The state should only set the framework conditions such as the legal system, the legislative, executive and judiciary and interfere as little as possible in the economy. A good example is the mandatory health insurance in the USA, "Obamacare": From the perspective of economists demanding equality and protection of the poor and weak, this state health insurance is a blessing, as it provides about 20 million of the poorest Americans with sometimes severe health restrictions with insurance coverage (cf. Holderied, 2010). This gives the insured a reasonably adequate medical care, which they could not otherwise afford for financial reasons. Advocates of freedom, on the other hand, see this mandatory health insurance as an unreasonable restriction of the individual freedom of choice of citizens. In addition, the insurance is unprofitable and makes the rich insured pay for the care of poorer fellow citizens, which would be equivalent to a communist approach (Schmitt, 2013; Eschbacher, 2017).

But not only philosophical considerations drive economists. In recent decades, against the background of a forced mathematization of economics, numerous mathematical models have been described that are based on a rational homo oeconomicus. Using extensive mathematical formulas and statistics, the influences of various aspects of monetary policy, but also fiscal policy and foreign trade on the overall economy were calculated. Section 5.1 will go into more detail on the importance of mathematics in economics.

Recently, however, a more realistic image of humans has been approached again and the sometimes highly irrational behavior of humans in the economy has been taken up. Under the keyword "behavioral economics", irrational behavior patterns of consumers and people in economic activities have been empirically examined. It could be shown that people behave very intuitively in economic terms and their behavior depends on the type of question or simply on misperceptions. About 50 years ago, an attempt was made to approach the real nature of the economically thinking and acting human being by dealing with the strategic-tactical behavior of humans within the framework of game theory. What is the most tactically clever behavior if I am accused as a criminal and could betray my companion? If I betray him, I show myself cooperative and can hope for leniency in punishment. If neither I nor my companion say anything, we can in doubt not be convicted of the act, as there are no circumstantial evidence. If my companion betrays me, and I hope for his loyalty, then I will in doubt be punished the hardest of us both. This situation, known as the "prisoner's dilemma", illuminates the real life world of people in economic everyday questions more than the mathematical models.

As this brief summary of the core topics of well-known economists (see Hoffmann, 2009; Karier, 2010; Piper, 1996; Kurz, 2009; Nienhaus, 2015; Starbatty, 1989; Thornton, 2015) shows, the range of economic topics is very broad. Many theories and core ideas have now become common knowledge among economists, but also among laypeople. From my point of view, two things are interesting:

1. The economists *worked/work interdisciplinarily*, were or are versatile intellectuals of their time with different academic backgrounds. They used/use the entire range of sciences, be it social, natural or engineering sciences. The only thing that was and is essential is the gain in knowledge that they drew and draw from the application of knowledge from other areas.
2. Many great economists were partly employed in practice for a long time and were thus able to confront their theoretical ideas with practice and vice versa, draw inspiration for their theoretical considerations from their practice. If they also worked empirically with data from the real economy, they came to concrete and comprehensible results. Economists can of course also be "just" researchers—nowadays, due to the complexity of scientific knowledge formation, specialization is

indispensable—but practical experience has obviously not harmed.

5.2 The Logic of Economic Research

In section 5.1 we have compiled the essential findings of the economic profession over the centuries in a brief overview. To better evaluate these findings, it is worth dealing with some basic assumptions of economic research. Economists work primarily with models to explain complex economic facts. Models represent a simplified image of reality and serve to illustrate explanations. To get as accurate a picture as possible of the effects, for example, of an interest rate increase on a particular market—think here of the increase in the interest rate of the European Central Bank—a model is chosen to simulate the effects. It is assumed that only the variable(s) under consideration, in our example the interest rate, changes and all other influencing factors remain the same. In the language of economists, this is called (lat.) "ceteris paribus", or roughly "all other things being equal". This is intended to exclude other factors from influencing economic development other than the interest rate under consideration. At the same time, it is assumed that all information necessary for decision-making is available and transparent, i.e. there is complete market transparency. At the same time, the often criticized Homo oeconomicus is assumed as the acting person, i.e. the always rationally acting, self-seeking person without regard for his fellow human beings.

Since the financial crisis 10 years ago, a rethink has begun among economists. None of them saw the crisis coming, no one had the reality "on the radar" in their complex models. The economic profession and its representatives became largely "duds" (see Nienhaus, 2009), who did not see the crisis coming even with their most sophisticated mathematical models. Reality was simply ignored. The models stood in their apparent elegance and expressiveness for themselves, but not for the reality surrounding them. The mutual dependence of the individual elements of an economy, including consumption, investments, interest rate, foreign trade, monetary policy, etc., is so great that it is not sufficient to pick out individual elements, change them and leave all other factors untouched. If you look at the consumption decisions to buy a house, for example—one of the factors that led to the financial crisis, triggered by the "real estate bubble" in the USA—you will quickly realize that they are not just a question of the interest rate.

Let's take a specific family with two small children and one earner. Of course, the interest rate plays a role in whether and how much real estate I can or want to afford. The lower the interest rate, the greater my willingness to take out a loan from the bank. The lower the interest rate, the higher the loan amount I am willing to take on, and the more I reduce my equity capital. I would consider this factor in an economic model and keep the other factors constant ("ceteris paribus"). But this is where the problem already begins. The currently 7.5 billion people in the world are all different. They differ in their risk tolerance—depending on whether they have a lot of equity or little to none. Knowledge about house financing and impending ancillary costs varies: Some are good calculators, plan the ancillary costs down to the decimal point and are accordingly not surprised. Others are overwhelmed by the high ancillary costs or overestimate their financial possibilities. During the financial crisis, banks granted families with no equity at all and an annual income of less than $50,000 loans of $300,000! It is easy to understand that this could not end well.

5 The Quintessence of Economic Thinking

In addition to purely financial economic factors, other things play a role when buying a house. My family, my friends, and acquaintances influence the purchase of the house. The location, size, and price of the selected house depend on my needs, the space required, the location of the nearest school, and how representative the neighborhood is. Do I want to impress my neighbors, friends, and relatives with my house, is the house my status symbol, and do I want to present myself as particularly financially potent? Do I have experience in building a house, do I choose the right company, the right bank? In the context of the financial crisis, commission-hungry representatives of banks and construction companies often met inexperienced builders who not only underestimated their monthly burden but also overestimated the quality of construction. Media and traditional advertising in the US did their part and advertised for home ownership at low interest rates and low monthly burden. Anyone who thought highly of themselves and wanted to do something for themselves and their family bought a home now. The incentive to buy houses was further increased by betting on rising property prices. After a few years, the home should not only be paid for but also have risen exorbitantly in value. The timely sale of the house promised hefty profits and at the same time hedged the risk of not being able to service the loans. However, after the market had collapsed, the monthly installments could no longer be serviced, the house that had to be sold by force was no longer worth anything, as many homeowners in the US followed this example. The US financial crisis eventually spilled over to Europe.

As can be easily seen from this example, models are only as good as they are able to represent the complex reality in a somewhat true-to-nature way. The problem is not only the forced averaging, the average citizen becomes the object of analysis and not the individual real person. Much more serious is the poor predictive quality, as the individual variables do not remain constant, but influence each other. So-called experts who announce a real estate bubble can unsettle the markets just as much as corresponding media reports and inadvertently promote overheating of the market. In contrast to positive science, which operates with clear, natural scientific rules and laws such as that of free fall, economics is a social science that deals with people. Human behavior cannot be dressed in mathematical formulas and "derived". This applies to individual household decisions in microeconomics as well as to the summary at the country level in macroeconomics. Rather, it is necessary to work more interdisciplinary, i.e., to draw on the findings of neighboring sciences such as sociology, psychology, but also neuroscience, in order to set up more realistic economic models and forecasts.

5.3 Contributions From Other Disciplines

Even the ancient Greeks dealt with economics. Aristotle treated economics as part of human activities. Adam Smith, the founder of modern economics, was a trained moral philosopher and analyzed the economic behavior of people from a philosophical perspective (cf. Smith, 2009, 2010). Today, economics is often dominated by mathematics, elegant equations, and vivid graphics, in which the fictional character of Homo oeconomicus rules: the rational, self-interested person who, based on his unlimited knowledge, optimizes his life in economic terms according to all the rules of the art. But is it really the purpose of an economy to focus primarily on numbers, data, and facts and forget about the people behind it? I have

5 The Quintessence of Economic Thinking

already discussed this in detail in my 2017 work "Limits of Economic Thinking—Where is the Human in the Economy" (cf. Pietsch, 2017) and would like to explain here only the core thoughts of an economy that researches beyond the narrow disciplinary boundaries.

The importance of an interdisciplinary view of economic theory becomes clear with a simple example from the everyday life of most people. Let's assume an employee changes his job because the new job seems more interesting to him and it advances him professionally and personally. In addition, he also receives more money per month. However, the job change is associated with a longer commute and is difficult and cumbersome to reach by public transport. What alternatives are there? After public transport is ruled out as an option, there are the possibilities of driving your own car, forming a carpool with colleagues, joining a ride-sharing center like "BlaBlaCar", or renting a car via car sharing. Since the latter is rather ruled out as an alternative due to the high costs, the lack of daily availability, and the limitation to city centers, the other alternatives are analyzed in more detail.

In this example, economic theory primarily considers the needs, or in the language of economics, the "preferences" or "preference structure" of the customer, in this case the employee, and their available budget. When in doubt, the customer will opt for the cheapest variant and try to form a carpool with colleagues. However, if he wants to drive to work more flexibly, alone and undisturbed, he will likely want to drive his own car. As a result, from the multitude of alternatives, the one that is the most cost-effective according to the individual needs of the customer is selected. This can be represented mathematically and graphically by a budget line (budget constraint of the household) that intersects an isoquant (set of all factor combinations that produce the same output quantity).

The budget line embodies the financial resources available per month and the isoquant curve the selectable combination of costs of owning a car compared to the costs of carpooling. This would be a purely economic consideration. But have we described all the influencing factors in the decision about the various alternatives? I don't think so.

It starts with the fact that the decision between carpooling with colleagues or using a carpooling service is a matter of personality. Some people love being around others, are very communicative, flexible, and prefer to choose the carpooling service as an alternative, which definitely represents the most cost-effective variant. Others, on the other hand, are infatuated with their own car and love being independent, are rather morning grouches and do not want to share their car under any circumstances. They generally reject a carpooling service as too inflexible because they don't want to drive to work every day with strangers. This would not change even if future generations of cars were to drive autonomously, i.e., self-controlled. This is still a relatively trivial explanation of the differences in human behavior that can contradict the economic decision: Thus, the more expensive option of driving with one's own car can be preferred to the carpooling service or carpooling for personal reasons. This could still be explained with a different "preference structure" of the customer.

But what happens when the employee decides to buy a new car or a car for the first time because the many trips to the more distant workplace are better and more comfortable to manage with a new car? What criteria are used to acquire a new car? Is it bought or leased, paid for in cash or financed by credit? This is certainly a question of budget and is therefore covered by traditional economic theory. But who decides about the brand of the car, the engine power, etc.? Decisions when choosing a new car

5 The Quintessence of Economic Thinking 279

do not only depend on the budget. It is a question of attitude towards certain car brands. Do I know the local dealer? What about their service performance? What were my experiences with certain brands in the past? Do I want to drive a different brand for a change? The family usually has a say: children strongly influence the choice of brand, as well as engine power or color. The same applies to friends, acquaintances, relatives or work colleagues who recommend certain brands or models. Test reports are read, relevant websites are consulted, manufacturers' advertising is compared. Is my car a status symbol for me, as is often the case in Germany? Do I want to stand out from my neighbor or impress friends and relatives? Especially for vehicles in the upper middle class and luxury class, the theory still applies that the Norwegian economist and sociologist Thorstein Veblen (Sec. I.3.3) described in his work "The Theory of the Leisure Class" (see Veblen, 2007): the higher the price, the greater the demand for goods that primarily bring prestige to their owners.

Admittedly, this is a greatly simplified representation of economic decisions. However, it clearly shows that economic actions are primarily what they have always been: actions of not always rationally deciding people who not only have their budget in mind, but also other factors. Sociologists have extensively studied the social mechanisms of the purchasing process, starting with the influence of group pressure through the "peer group", the peers or the people in one's own circle who influence my decisions and whom I want to impress. Think especially of teenagers who want to stand out or show belonging to a group through certain clothing accessories. Psychologists have extensively studied the construct of consumer attitudes towards individual brands or consumption in general. They have come across psychological phenomena such as *cognitive dissonance* (see Festinger, 2001). Simply put, humans always try to maintain their emotional balance. This also applies to consumption decisions. On the one hand, I have bought an excellent car from my point of view and on the other hand, I have spent a lot of money that is then missing elsewhere. So I will try to strengthen my decision by reading more test reports about the car after the purchase, asking friends about their positive experience with the new car, etc., in order to justify the high price to myself.

However, this is only part of the whole picture. Brain researchers and neurobiologists are studying the brain waves and the feeling of happiness that buying a car triggers in humans. For example, the happiness hormone endorphin is released, and certain reward areas in the brainstem are activated. The list of potential disciplines that can contribute to the analysis of a car purchase is large and growing. It is not clear why economic theory focuses only on mathematical optimization models and follows a quasi-scientific approach. It is simply not true that a science only makes statements when it is measurable and can make elegant deterministic statements like mathematics or physics. Economics is a social science with humans as protagonists. I am therefore convinced that the interdisciplinary possibilities are far from exhausted. Essential questions of economics, especially ethical questions known from philosophy, are for example:

Is capitalism with the social market economy as a manifestation in Germany still the right economic model? Am I allowed to sell or consume everything that is available for purchase? Are there ethical boundaries, such as with weapons or organs? What about justice? Should economic theory increasingly address the question of how the ever-increasing inequality in society can be analyzed and prevented? Can there be an economy in the service of people that ensures that all people not only have enough to eat, but can also live well? Many questions can only be solved in an interdisciplinary dialogue. Almost every discipline can make a substantial contribution here (for a presentation of selected theoretical approaches of individual [social] sciences, see Pietsch, 2014, especially p. 35 ff.). Mathematics alone cannot solve these questions. Adam Smith and Aristotle would have looked with astonishment at economic theory and its fixation on mathematics. For them, an analysis of the economy including all available knowledge, regardless of the discipline, was a matter of course. But this is far from the case in modern economic theory. I will therefore go into a little more detail about the role of mathematics in economics.

5.4 Mathematics in Economic Theory

The use of mathematics in economic theory undoubtedly brings a number of advantages. First, it forces the researcher to a clear model of reality that can be described in mathematical structures. The assumptions about certain, verifiable economic facts can be clearly described. All researchers in a certain field "speak the same language" and can only disagree about the basic assumptions. The mathematical results are clear and can be derived and understood based on the rules of total or partial differentiation. Mathematics forces the scientist to express himself unambiguously and to write down and specify the logic of the arguments. Similar to the natural sciences, certain statements about economic developments can also be confirmed or refuted in economics as a social science. This is done with elegant formulas, equations, and understandable graphs and functions. The result of the mathematical derivation is understandable and comprehensible for all interested—and in the language of mathematics trained—readers. Intuitive relationships can then be empirically and mathematically verified and proven.

As compelling as the arguments for the use of mathematics may seem, they neglect the fact that in economic theory we are dealing with real flesh-and-blood people. These people, as we have already shown, do not act according to the model of Homo economicus: people have compassion for other people, act irrationally, orient themselves to their reference group of family, friends and acquaintances, and are influenced by the masses. I am aware that the construct of Homo economicus is a heuristic, a simplified model assumption, to develop, for example, economic policy measures without regard to a possibly irrationally acting individual. The Homo economicus, similar to mathematics, follows an ideal model that all economic interventions should be oriented towards.

The mathematization of economics is relatively new. Although economists such as Walras, Pareto, Cournot, and Heinrich von Thünen had already formalized their work using mathematics in the 19th century, it was not until the 20th century that this was pushed forward, up to Kenneth Arrow, Gérard Debreu, and Paul Samuelson in the 1940s and 1950s. Even today, it is difficult to get purely qualitative work into the most renowned economic journals. There is still a veritable belief in mathematics among professionals. But this comes at a price. Today, economics students first learn about mathematical models and their elegant derivations of total differentiation in the Lagrange method. Thomas Piketty, a French economist, became instantly world-famous in 2014 with his book "Capital in the 21st Century" (cf. Piketty, 2014). In it, he writes about the importance of mathematics in economics (Piketty, 2014, p. 53):

5 The Quintessence of Economic Thinking

> Let's put it bluntly: The discipline of economics has not shed its childish fondness for mathematics and for purely theoretical and often very ideological speculations, which comes at the expense of historical research and cooperation with other social sciences. All too often, economists primarily deal with small mathematical problems that only they themselves are interested in, which allows them to easily attach the label of scientificity to themselves and to evade the much more complicated questions that the world around them raises.

Even if one does not want to fully agree with this very pointed statement by Piketty, it does hit a sore spot. Despite all the undeniable advantages of a mathematical approach, it falls short in a social science. But what would be the alternative to this?

The main criticism of economic theory arose in 2008 when the economic and financial crisis could not be predicted by economists and their guild (cf. also Chap. II.5.2). In addition to pure mathematical laws, psychological and sociological factors also play a role: homeowners who took on loans they could never repay with their income; lenders who, driven by high commissions, did not hesitate to grant risky loans to borrowers without any equity. With the prospect of future increases in property values and the sale after a few years with profit, homeowners were lured. When the housing bubble burst and homeowners could no longer service their loans, the banks were left with their "bad loans", the US economy was the first to plunge into the crisis and dragged the economic world with it. Homeowners tried to sell their houses in a panic to at least pay off some of the debt. The oversupply on the housing market caused prices to collapse, and homeowners could no longer service their loans. The banks went bankrupt or—even worse—had to be rescued by the state because they were classified as "systemically important".

Why couldn't this crisis be predicted (cf. among others Nienhaus, 2009)? In addition to the economic laws of supply and demand, human factors play a role. The greed of lenders for high commissions without any security. The greed of homeowners betting on permanently rising prices and promising themselves high profits. Banks betting on increasing returns on their lent capital. The media accompanied this development closely and amplified it, without having originally caused it. Panic in the housing market increased and then spread to other markets. Since many households could no longer service their loans, they also did not have enough money left for everyday life, let alone for vacations or larger purchases like cars etc. Consumption collapsed and with it the demand for many goods. The manufacturers of these goods laid off their employees because they were not selling as much and their profits were falling. The laid-off employees in turn had to further cut back on consumption. Many of these issues are dependent on psychological and sociological factors.

Of course, mathematics can be used to elegantly model the assumptions of the housing bubble. But the effects themselves could not be predicted, as they primarily revolved around the actions of people in relation to other people. These are not always *Homines oeconomici*, who act rationally and can be described mathematically. But they are human. And that's a good thing. The alternative to the purely mathematical derivation of economic problems is the inclusion of other social sciences in predicting economic developments. Even at the risk that the results of the prediction are not as exact and clear as the mathematical results.

5.5 Limits of Economic Theory

In the preceding chapters, I have already described some inadequacies or limits of economic theory. Economics as a social science cannot do without the most important findings of other social sciences such as sociology, anthropology, and psychology. Even insights from philosophy in the form of ethical discussions or brain research must be taken into account when describing and predicting economic behavior. Of course, mathematics also has its place, which forces logical thinking and can lead to interesting results on the basis of clear basic assumptions in a model or research design. However, mathematics should not be overemphasized, and the human being should still be at the center of considerations. After all, it's all about him. We have seen that humans do not resemble the ideal of the *Homo oeconomicus,* who is equipped with perfect information and always acts rationally and selfishly in every situation and can estimate the consequences of his actions. But there are other points that show the limits of economic thinking.

At this point, I do not want to list all the findings and explanations of my previous work "Limits of Economic Thinking. Where is the human being in economics?" (cf. Pietsch, 2017). Nevertheless, I want to give some food for thought in all due brevity, which I have detailed in a ten-point program in the above-mentioned work (cf. Pietsch, 2017, p. 228 ff.). There, in addition to the lack of rationality of human action, the critical view of mathematics in economics, and the obligation to include other social sciences in the analysis of economic action, I have pointed out further limits.

While it is commendable that econometric models make statistical predictions based on past data, such as about economic development or growth forecasts, the future is thus written against the background of the past, taking into account numerous influencing factors such as interest rate and money supply development. Correlations of the past, so-called statistical correlations, are extrapolated into the future. However, it applies to economic forecasts that they become increasingly uncertain the further into the future they are supposed to occur. This is mainly due to the fact that the statistical data used is not always reliable, that structural breaks or changes are not always predictable. People also react to forecasts: if economic downturns are predicted, many people start to prepare for the supposedly worse times and save their money rather than consume, which burdens the economy (additionally). The same applies in the reverse case for predicted upswings. Economic forecasts can often only be certain trend statements for a manageable time.

Economists are not free from political judgments and currents. Interesting in this context is, for example, the question of increasing inequality in Germany. Economists who are more politically "left" see, based on empirical data and their own experiences, that the gap between rich and poor in Germany has clearly increased in recent years. In contrast, conservative economists see the opposite: both groups would have benefited from growing prosperity in Germany. Left and right economists access similar statistical databases but come to different conclusions. Ultimately, this is only human: every social scientist is trapped in his own view of things. This includes my own socialization, i.e., how I grew up, as well as my political attitude, which I have acquired over the course of my life. If I stand up for the poor and weak of society, then I will welcome a wealth tax, a higher inheritance tax, or a tax on very high incomes, a "rich tax," more than an economist who does not want to "punish" the "high performers" of

5 The Quintessence of Economic Thinking

society for their ability and diligence "to the detriment of all". The intense discussions between proponents of a strong state in the economy and the liberal representatives of a lean state testify to the predominantly political discussion that overlays the economic one. The discussion between a representative of the "Keynesian school" and a proponent of Friedman's liberal ideas when it comes to diagnosing the economy is also interesting.

The insights of the past of economic theory and its core representatives are given too little consideration. As an economics student in the first semester, I vainly looked forward to an introductory event that would have familiarized me with the core ideas of economic theory. Analogous to philosophy or sociology, the ideas of the outstanding and formative economists of the past and present should be dealt with at the very beginning of the study of economics—similar to the presentation in this book. Of course, any such selection is subjective, and some authors and great representatives of the subject are missing, who another author would certainly have chosen. Certain economists were presented too briefly or, on the contrary, more intensively than personal taste dictates according to some readers. But you can never please everyone!

However, it misses the core statement that a further development of economic theory is only possible when one has internalized the previous approaches and ideas and can build on this solid intellectual foundation. Especially since, as we have seen, a canon of undeniable classics has emerged. No student of economics can avoid Adam Smith, Karl Marx or John Maynard Keynes and Milton Friedman. Often, it is even worth reading the original works, so that one can immerse oneself in the respective thought world of the authors and the circumstances of the time. In this way, one also expands the current theory, which helps to derive certain laws of economics using mathematical formulas. Only after my studies in business administration did I enjoy studying the classics of economics intensively in my free time, and was able to gain a great deal from it personally. It helps not only to understand the different approaches and ideas about the economy. In addition, one quickly realizes that economic ideas have a "boom" at certain times.

After the war, the question was about an adequate economic form for the young Federal Republic of Germany. The idea of a "social market economy" was quickly born, which combined the freedom of individual economic action with the social component. At that time, this was not only a small revolution, but also the start of the well-known economic miracle of the post-war period. Everyone quickly became better off than before, the scarcity management was relatively quickly replaced by a competitive, growing economy that benefited all citizens. Today, this can no longer be said so unreservedly. The question of inequality and the different participation in economic prosperity in Germany raises doubts about the current economic form. It is certainly sensible to rethink the success model of the social market economy and make it future-proof for the era of digitalization, so to speak, to design a social market economy 2.0. However, this can only be done with a solid knowledge of the economic ideas of the past.

While knowledge of the history of economic ideas is more a matter for experts or interested laypeople, basic economic knowledge is increasingly becoming part of general education. As I write these lines, a scientific analysis of economic knowledge in Germany by the weekly newspaper *Die Zeit* has just attracted attention (cf. Heuser, 2018). Without the basic knowledge of supply and demand, interest calculation or forms of money investment, no responsible citizen can manage today. Hardly anyone

5 The Quintessence of Economic Thinking

knows the current amount of a Hartz IV rate or the distribution of wealth in Germany. How are major life projects to be mastered, such as buying a property, if I have not previously learned the basic rules of interest calculation, the principle of repayment and the numerous incidental costs? The authors of *Die Zeit* rightly point out that especially the well-paid, better-educated classes have a higher household income, and are also better trained economically and can therefore increase their wealth more competently.

How can this deficiency be remedied? It would be helpful to make economics a compulsory subject in all schools. Depending on the level of prior knowledge, the basic rules of economics can then be taught and tailored specifically to the respective target group. It has never harmed anyone to know the calculation of interest and compound interest, to know that the price is determined by supply and demand, or how high the Hartz IV rate is. Here too, it does no harm to pass on the essential ideas of the great economists in simplified form to the eager students. In this way, children and young people not only come into contact with practical economic topics, but also get a first impression of the basic considerations in the subject of economics. Perhaps it even helps some students to develop an early enthusiasm for economics.

What is missing, in my view, is an economic vision for the future of German society, an "economic narrative". As hinted at earlier, we are all—especially the experts—called upon to critically question the existing economic order and to adapt or redesign it on the basis of the developments that are already foreseeable today. Specifically, it is about the question of whether the social market economy, which is already 70 years old in its essential contents, can and should continue to exist in the same way for the next 70 years. Does this also apply to the system of capitalism as such? In the coming years, digitalization will completely revolutionize the economy, millions of jobs will disappear as a result and will have to be recreated elsewhere. This new or modified form of economy will have to provide answers to the growing inequality of incomes and wealth. In what kind of economy do we want to live? How do we shape our daily coexistence on this basis? Is the social market economy really still social, or do we need to make profound changes? Do we have a vision of the economy of tomorrow? Do we have a new economic narrative?

Politics is currently called upon to think not only about the future of the parties—the governing parties have already announced this as I write these lines. The economic form of the social market economy and its concrete further development to cope with future challenges must necessarily be at the forefront of considerations. What is needed is an economy that serves people—and not the other way around! In this context, I would like to say a few words about the construct of man in economic theory.

When economics is criticized, the artificial *Homo oeconomicus* is often brought into the field. The *economic man*, it is said, is always and at all times acting rationally, knowing the exact benefits of products and services and getting the most out of his money (Pietsch, 2017, p. 15 ff.). This type of person has complete information about the market and offers and can select the best offer for his taste and wallet based on this. The higher the price for a product rises, the less it is demanded, according to economic theory. Against the background of my limited budget, I choose the combination of products that provides the most benefit for me. Let's take a concrete example to illustrate this idea: I have 30 euros available and have to consider how many pizzas I can buy for myself and my family. Alternatively, I can treat myself to hamburgers at the neighboring fast-food "restaurant". I also want to drink enough. Assuming my family consists of three people, I first have to ask my wife and son about their food and drink preferences. Now I have to decide according to my preferences whether I buy the two pizzas for my wife and me including a soft drink each and a large hamburger with fries for my 30 euros or forego a pizza in favor of another hamburger, which is cheaper. Or I forego my own drink, as this is the only way to finance all food preferences with the given budget.

This is how economic decisions are made in everyday life. The hamburgers or pizzas available for the given budget are, economically speaking, the bundle of goods measured by individual preferences, i.e., in our example, what my family likes to eat. In the graphical representation, the budget line limits what has been said. And where the bundle of goods intersects the budget line, the lunch that is possible with my financial means results. But this only applies if all family members behave rationally, i.e., sensibly, and we distribute the money as well as possible. This is how the decision about lunch would be made according to microeconomic household theory (cf. Mankiw & Taylor, 2012, p. 539 ff., especially p. 550). But does this correspond to reality? Do we actually always act so comprehensibly and rationally in practice that we only have the maximization of benefits against the background of a limited budget in mind for all decisions?

What would this example look like if a family member gave up food or at least a drink to be able to give another, e.g., my son, a dessert in addition to his beloved pizza? In other words: Are we always selfishly acting people who always consider how we can get the most out of it for ourselves? What role do our feelings and emotions for the next person play in this? Such behavior, which puts the other person more in the foreground, i.e., altruistic behavior, is completely ignored. Why, for example, do two of the richest men in the world, Bill Gates and Warren Buffet, donate most of their wealth and spend it on charitable projects, such as education for poorer children, and only bequeath a fraction of their wealth to their descendants? Why are Hermès bags and Rolex watches increasingly in demand, even though prices rise every year? The sociologist Thorstein Veblen called this phenomenon the "snob effect". I buy myself a social status and show who and especially how financially potent I am. I compare myself with my fellow human beings and show them very clearly that I "perform more, and earn more" and can therefore afford much more expensive products than the people next door.

After all, in society and in economic matters, the person with his mistakes and weaknesses plays a major role. We compare ourselves with neighbors, acquaintances, relatives, and friends. Who has the biggest house, the most expensive car, or the prettier dress? Who has the more exciting job with the more lucrative income? We feel more comfortable when we are perceived as the richest in a row house settlement than when we are the poorest in a villa area. Holidays are often chosen by sounding names: Sylt sounds more sophisticated than Osterode, Marbella more chic than Torremolinos. In Mallorca, only the trendy places like Port d'Andratx with its marina are worth mentioning. Depending on the social class, the "Ballermann" in Mallorca is frowned upon. Even the smallest ones are integrated into the status competition: The selection of the right kindergarten with foreign language training in the right district sets standards. It continues with the right clothes and the right hobby. Everything that is expensive is just good enough for the offspring.

5 The Quintessence of Economic Thinking 293

The American psychologists and Nobel laureates in economics, Daniel Kahneman and Amos Tversky, have found in their decades-long research that human behavior is often irrational (cf. Pietsch, 2017, p. 159 ff.): For example, we are more likely to agree to surgery if the survival probability is given as 90 % compared to the statement of the death probability as 10 %, which is the same result. Decisions are therefore dependent on how the problem is formulated. This is called "framing" in technical terms, depending on the context or frame, English "frame", the question is asked. Prices are demonstrably estimated higher when test subjects in the experiment are first asked for their social security number, this is called "anchoring", anchor value. *Intuition* plays a big role in decisions (cf. Pietsch, 2017, p. 161). Kahneman mentions an intuitive decision situation using the purchase of a baseball and a bat (cf. Pietsch, 2017, p. 17 f.): Baseball and bat cost together $1.10; the bat is supposed to cost one dollar more than the ball. So how much do the bat and ball each cost? The intuitively correct solution is: The bat costs $1 and the ball 10 cents, together $1.10. But is this solution correct? No. As can be easily determined, in this intuitive solution the bat is only 90 cents more expensive than the ball. So the solution cannot be correct. The correct solution is: The bat costs $1.05 and the ball only 5 cents. Both together cost $1.10, with the bat being one dollar more expensive than the ball in this correct solution. Would you have also intuitively fallen for it? So much for the rationality of decisions.

Two more examples are intended to demonstrate the very limited usability of the *Homo-oeconomicus* model: the maximization of income and profit (cf. Pietsch, 2017, p. 9 ff.).

1. Income Maximization

If every human being acted rationally according to the schema of Homo oeconomicus, we would all try to get the maximum income for our work and the time invested. But is this really the case? It starts with the fact that every human being brings different inclinations and abilities. One person is skilled in crafts and practical matters, the next is more adept in intellectual matters. Not everyone wants to become a craftsman entrepreneur or work in companies just because they then get the most money for their working time. Following this logic, as many people as possible should work for a large company in metropolises like Düsseldorf, Munich or Frankfurt, as that's where the most money is paid. They would have to focus on in-demand trades such as electrical engineering or mechatronics during their training, for example, to be accepted by the large car manufacturers. Then everyone should try to make a career as quickly as possible in order to earn as much money as possible against the background of their education. But this also means doing a lot of overtime, showing above-average commitment, accepting stays abroad and much more.

On the other side of the spectrum, after graduation, professions such as investment banker, management consultant, fund manager etc. should be pursued with the prospect of making as much money as possible in a short time. Corresponding courses of study such as business administration or business mathematics etc. should be chosen accordingly often. Even if "traditional" courses of study such as law, engineering or humanities such as history, German studies, psychology and philosophy were chosen, a job should be sought that allows a maximum income. Thankfully, this is not the case! People choose, if they have a choice at all, the training that best suits their inclinations and abilities, even if the income does not match. Fortunately, many young people still want to train in road construction or in nursing and healing professions. Men and women study humanities, foreign languages or other disciplines regardless of later income.

The personal commitment at the workplace and the career development is fortunately increasingly made dependent on the compatibility of work and family. More and more parents collectively or individually take time off, "sabbaticals", to see their children grow up. People work because they mostly enjoy their work, they are appreciated by their colleagues and bosses and they see their work as meaningful at best. Psychologists call this motivation independent of income "intrinsic", coming from within and from the task, as opposed to "extrinsic" motivation, which comes from outside the work, such as from income and status. The weekly and lifetime working hours are increasingly adapted to personal needs for participation in family activities or the desire for sufficient private life. Paid or unpaid breaks from the job are becoming more and more the rule. Because people are different, there are also those who take the classic career path with a strong focus on income and status.

2. Profit Maximization

The entrepreneur as Homo oeconomicus always tries to maximize his profit. For this purpose, mathematical differential equations, a calculation method for determining so-called maxima, are used in economic theory. The profit is economically derived from the total revenue minus the costs incurred for it. The revenue is obtained by multiplying the selling price by the quantity of products or services sold. The total costs consist of the costs for the production of the product, such as development and production, but also the costs for the purchase of raw materials, machines, as well as labor costs in development, production, sales, and administration. Without going into the business details, I can say, simplifying, that I achieve the maximum profit by keeping the costs as low as possible and the revenue as high as possible. Does the entrepreneur always strive for maximum profit? He should at least theoretically.

However, this already varies according to the form of the company. Let's take a corporation in the form of a stock corporation. The board and top managers are obliged to their employees, shareholders, and the supervisory board controlling them to generate maximum growth. For this, they analyze market conditions, competition, and customers, define goals and visions, design strategies, derive measures, and control their compliance. But no one

> can say whether the strategies for the future are correct, as they often reach far into the future and market developments, trends, and customer orientations must be estimated many years in advance. Take, for example, a car design that determines the design 5 to 7 years before the vehicle's market launch, which should therefore inspire customers in the medium-term future. Furthermore, the models are usually designed for a life cycle of 7 years and sold worldwide. The design must still be current worldwide at the end of this cycle. No one can see into the future, so perfect rational planning for profit maximization is impossible. Because no one can take into account all eventualities in the long term.
>
> If the entrepreneur is also the owner, many other influencing factors will play a role in addition to profit maximization. Ethical considerations play a major role. Today's entrepreneurs, like those in the past, are often aware of their special responsibility: for their employees and their jobs, for the environment and its preservation. They reject child labor, often do not produce in countries that are very cheap but produce under inhumane conditions for the sake of maximizing profit. There are black sheep, of course. But they are, thank God, rare. Employed managers of large corporations must, of course, adhere to the same legally anchored ethical principles and must not tolerate child labor or exploitation of workers. Independent entrepreneurs, on the other hand, usually have more freedom to accept restrictions on profits in favor of their own ethical basic convictions. In the long term, however, they too must generate profits in order to successfully operate in the market and maintain their jobs.

Of course, the Homo oeconomicus is a construct, a heuristic or auxiliary size, to make basic thoughts about the economic behavior of people. However, it should not be limited to interpreting this model too narrowly and forgetting the specifically human aspect. Humans have a value system that is shaped by origin, upbringing, education, and the environment. Economic decisions are not made in isolation, but depend on reference groups, media influence, cultural influences, and, as we have seen, are subject to psychologically conditioned misconceptions.

In sum, it must be stated that the trend of economic science is slowly moving back towards the "gradual reunification of the social sciences" (see Tirole, 2017, p.152). Findings from sciences such as sociology, psychology, but also humanities such as philosophy and history or other adjacent areas should be used together to explain or predict human economic behavior. This is primarily a realization from the depressing economic crisis of 2008, which hardly any renowned economist had foreseen. Since then, people have been talking about the "crisis of economics". The still existing mathematics-heavy mainstream economics will inevitably have to be ended in the future. I am convinced of that. Humans cannot be described with formulas and abstract models.

We have seen it in this chapter: Humans do not always naturally strive to be faster, higher, and further, but there are also limits to growth and economic striving for more income and profit. What are the topics of the economy of tomorrow that urgently need to be discussed? Let's take a look at them in chapter 6.

References

Aquin, T. (1985). *Summe der Theologie* (3 Bände). Bernhart, J. (Hrsg.). Kröner.

Aristoteles. (2007). *Nikomachische Ethik* (2. Aufl.). Tusculum.

Bick, A. (2012). *Die Steinzeit* (2., Korr. u. ak. Aufl.). Theiss in Wissenschaftliche Buchgesellschaft (WBG).

Brodersen, K. (Hrsg.). (2006). *Aristoteles – 77 Tricks zur Steigerung der Staatseinnahmen, Oikonomika II*. Reclam.

Eschbacher, V. (2017). Warum Republikaner Obamacare verabscheuen. *Tiroler Tageszeitung* 24.02.2017. https://www.tt.com/politik/weltpolitik/12664194/warum-republikaner-obamacare-verabscheuen. Zugegriffen: 29. Mai 2019.

Festinger, L. (2001). *A theory of cognitive dissonance* (Combined Academic Publ. Zuerst veröffentlicht 1957). Stanford University Press.

Fischer, M. (2011). Der Freihändler. *Wirtschaftswoche* 04.12.2011. https://www.wiwo.de/politik/konjunktur/david-ricardo-der-freihaendler/5886714.html. Zugegriffen: 14. März 2019.

Friedman, M. (2016). *Kapitalismus und Freiheit* (11. Aufl. mit einem Geleitwort von Horst Siebert). Piper.

Heuser, U. J. (2018). Ökonomie: Was wissen Sie über Wirtschaft? *Die Zeit* 31.01.2018. https://www.zeit.de/2018/06/oekonomie-wirtschaft-grundwissen. Zugegriffen: 14. März 2019.

Hoffmann, J. (1992). Alles pendelt sich ein. *Die Zeit* Nr. 49/1992 vom 27.11.1992. https://www.zeit.de/1992/49/alles-pendelt-sich-ein. Zugegriffen: 14. März 2019.

Hoffmann, T. S. (2009). *Wirtschaftsphilosophie – Ansätze und Perspektiven von der Antike bis heute*. Marix.

Holderied, T. (2010). Ich weiß nicht, was ich ohne Obamacare tun soll. *jetzt* 06.05.2017. https://www.jetzt.de/usa/junge-amerikaner-sagen-ihre-meinung-zu-obamacare. Zugegriffen: 14. März 2019.

Hülser, K. H. (Hrsg.). (1991). *Platon. Sämtliche Werke griechisch und deutsch* (Bd. 10). Insel.

Karier, T. (2010). *Intellectual capital – forty years of the nobel prize in economics*. Cambridge University Press.

Keynes, J. M. (2017). *Allgemeine Theorie der Beschäftigung, des Zinses und des Geldes* (Neuübersetzung von Nicola Liebert). Duncker & Humblot.

Kirk, G. S., Raven, J. E., & Schofield, J. (2001). *Die vorsokratischen Philosophen. Einführung, Texte und Kommentare*. Metzler.

Kurz, H. D. (Hrsg.). (2009). *Klassiker des ökonomischen Denkens* (2 Bände). Beck.

Mankiw, G. N., & Taylor, M. P. (2012). *Grundzüge der Volkswirtschaftslehre* (5., überarb. u. erweit. Aufl.). Schäffer-Poeschel.

Marx, K. (2009). *Das Kapital – Kritik der politischen Ökonomie* (Ungekürzte Ausgabe nach der zweiten Auflage von 1872 mit einem Geleitwort von Karl Korsch aus dem Jahre 1932, unveränderter Nachdruck). Anaconda.

Marx, K., & Engels, F. (1983). *Manifest der Kommunistischen Partei*. Reclam (Nachdruck).

Nienhaus, L. (2009). *Die Blindgänger: Warum die Ökonomen auch künftige Krisen nicht erkennen werden*. Campus.

Nienhaus, L. (Hrsg.). (2015). *Die Weltverbesserer – 66 große Denker, die unser Leben verändern*. Hanser.

Pietsch, D. (2014). *Mensch und Welt – Versuch einer Gesamtbetrachtung*. Eul/Lohmar.

Pietsch, D. (2017). *Grenzen des ökonomischen Denkens – Wo bleibt der Mensch in der Wirtschaft?* Eul/Lohmar.

Piketty, T. (2014). *Capital in the twenty-first century*. Harvard University Press. Deutsche Ausgabe: *Das Kapital im 21. Jahrhundert*. Beck.

Piper, N. (Hrsg.). (1996). *Die großen Ökonomen. Leben und Werk der wirtschaftswissenschaftlichen Vordenker* (2., überarb. Aufl.). Schäffer-Poeschel.

Schipper, L. (2015). John Stuart Mill. Das Glück im Kapitalismus. In L. Nienhaus (Hrsg.), *Die Weltverbesserer – 66 große Denker, die unser Leben verändern* (S. 106–109). Hanser.

Schmitt, U. (2013). „Obamacare" ist Teufelswerk – und absoluter Renner. *Die Welt* 06.10.2013. https://www.welt.de/politik/ausland/article120662017/Obamacare-ist-Teufelswerk-und-absoluter-Renner.html. Zugegriffen: 29. Mai 2019.

Siedenbiedel, C. (2013). Ökonom Gary Becker: Gegensätze ziehen sich an. *FAZ* 01.08.2013. https://www.faz.net/aktuell/wirtschaft/menschen-wirtschaft/oekonom-gary-becker-gegensaetze-ziehen-sich-an-12308018.html. Zugegriffen: 14. März 2019.

Smith, A. (2009). *Wohlstand der Nationen* (Nach der Übersetzung von Max Stirner, herausgegeben von Heinrich Schmidt). Anaconda.

Smith, A. (2010). *Theorie der ethischen Gefühle* (Philosophische Bibliothek Felix Meiner Band 605, übersetzt von Eckstein, W. und herausgegeben von Brandt, H.D.). Felix Meiner.

Starbatty, J. (Hrsg.). (1989). *Klassiker des ökonomischen Denkens* (Bd. 2). Beck.

Thornton, P. (2015). *Die großen Ökonomen. 10 Vordenker deren Werk unser Leben verändert hat.* Börsenbuch.

Tirole, J. (2017). *Economics for the common good.* Princeton University Press.

Vaupel, M., & Kaul, V. (2016). *Die Geschichte(n) des Geldes. Von der Kaurischnecke zum Goldstandard – So entwickelte sich das Finanzsystem.* Börsenmedien AG.

Veblen, T. (2007). *Theorie der feinen Leute: Eine ökonomische Untersuchung der Institutionen.* Fischer Taschenbuch.

Zank, W. (1993). Reiche Bauern, reiches Land. *Die Zeit* Nr. 8/1993. https://www.zeit.de/1993/08. Zugegriffen: 19. Febr. 1993.

6

The Most Pressing Issues of Tomorrow's Economy

We are almost at the end of our journey through economics. What remains is a look at the most pressing questions of tomorrow's economy. There are a number of unresolved problems and challenges that we should all deal with. I would like to briefly outline these, well aware that any selection is subjective. Let's start with what I consider to be the most pressing issue: the question of justice and how economics can contribute to solving this problem.

6.1 Justice

Let's now compare two completely contrasting scenes from everyday life:

In the *first scene*, we see, among other things, the countless homeless people in this world who, under unspeakable hygienic and climatic conditions, sometimes without a roof over their heads, barely survive and have to worry every day about how they will survive the day. Having almost nothing, they are sometimes robbed while sleeping and thus lose the very least they may have been able to save from their old life or have begged for. We have all encountered people in our lives who have reached the bottom of society, who see no way out of their situation. But also those in the expensive metropolises, who have a roof over their heads and can less and less afford the sometimes horrendous rents, are struggling to survive. The worst off are those who are unemployed and have no assets to fall back on, as well as single mothers or fathers who can barely manage to feed their children, let alone prepare them for a successful life.

Not much better off are the many poorly paid wage earners and those in the care professions, who are not adequately paid despite their socially valuable professions. They work until they drop, and at the end of the month it is at best enough to feed the family, if they have not inherited or have a well-earning life partner. Not to forget the numerous retirees who, despite a lifetime of self-sacrificing professional activity, could not put aside enough to enjoy their last phase of life with their meager pension. There are more and more professional groups and people who are in this situation, not only in a comparatively rich country like Germany or in the USA. And incomes are even declining in the lower and middle part of society, due to unemployment, increasing part-time work and tough competition in the labor market.

According to a statistic (see Feldenkirchen, 2015), the annual income of a typical middle-class American family fell by an average of $5,000 between 1999 and 2015. 58 % of income increases since 2008 (the year of the economic crisis!) have gone to the top one percent of the population. 0.1 % of the U.S. population, or one in a thousand residents, amassed as much wealth as the entire wealth of the bottom 90 % of the population, or the bottom 900 of these 1,000 Americans! The top 25 hedge fund managers in the U.S. earned as much in 2013 as 533,000 public school teachers, namely $24 billion (see Feldenkirchen, 2015). Studies by the international development organization Oxfam, published in time for the annual World Economic Forum in Davos, have shown that the eight richest people on this planet own exactly the same wealth, namely $426 billion, as the entire poorer half of the population combined, a total of 3.7 billion people (see Oxfam, 2017). The world's 2043 billionaires are opposed by 3.7 billion people in relative poverty. 82 % of the total global wealth growth in 2017 went to the one percent of the wealthiest people in the world. In contrast, the poor half of the world's population, 3.7 billion people, got nothing (see Oxfam, 2018).

Even in Germany, the divide between rich and poor is intensifying. The German Institute for Economic Research (DIW) has supplemented the data from the European Central Bank's (ECB) wealth survey with information from rich lists, such as those published annually by the *Manager Magazin*. As a result, the 45 richest households in Germany own as much as the poorer half of the population, more than 40 million people (see Diekmann, 2018). Both groups had assets of 214 billion EUR each in 2014.

Even if we do not subscribe to the old class struggle proclamations of Marx and Engels, this distribution of wealth should give us pause for thought. We have not yet spoken of the large number of children who must live in poverty and who must either succumb to or escape from starvation, instead of being able to prepare for a long and hopefully successful life. In some parts of this world, there is war, and the children affected by it, as well as their parents and grandparents, try to survive or flee, risking their lives to escape to supposed prosperity. If that is not bad enough—the difference between a poor child born in a war zone, fighting for its life, and a child of wealthy parents in a rich, peaceful country is due to pure chance. Added to this is the fact that wealth on the one hand and poverty or lack of prospects on the other hand are "inherited". We all know the discussion well enough that a child from a simple background with parents from a non-academic milieu can hardly climb the ladder of success like a top manager perfectly prepared by his family, even in wealthy Germany: It starts already in school, where the non-academic parents neither have the time and money nor the capacity and confidence to send their child to a higher school, let alone to university. Where there is nothing, nothing can be inherited, not even the absolute confidence to make something of oneself in life. Apart from the fact that the necessary network of one's own family also plays a role in life.

The *second scene of everyday life,* on the other hand, looks different, much more pleasing from the perspective of those involved. The people of the top one percent of society in terms of wealth would not have to worry too much about their daily existence. They live in large houses, mostly with additional holiday homes or even yachts, do not have to worry about their daily meal and go on vacation several times a year. The dream destinations of the world are explored, no matter the cost. Their children attend expensive private schools or boarding schools, stay among their own kind and enjoy the best possible education. The richest of the rich can live very well from their earned or inherited wealth and save for retirement in good time. A good example of the diverging social gap are the property owners in the metropolitan regions, who are becoming increasingly wealthy due to the rise in property prices, while at the same time many of their tenants can no longer afford the rising rents. For 2019, average rent increases of 5 % are forecast in Germany (as of 26.12.2018; Spiegel Online, 2018).

Since the parents are very well, mostly academically educated, they will also have their children educated through the best schools and universities at home and abroad. None of these children would have to study seriously to finance their lives. Student apartments are not rented elaborately, but bought outright, preferably in the trendiest neighborhoods. Thus, the offspring is not only excellently educated, but can also meet their peers at private elite universities and establish an extremely valuable network of relationships for life. In addition, most of them receive from their family the indispensable self-confidence, optimism and—not to forget—the manners needed to be successful in life. It is no coincidence that company leaders and board members of large companies often have successful parents and ancestors.

Now it is not the case that this chapter is being written at the end to stir up social envy or even provide arguments for why a redistribution from top to bottom according to the communist principle would be appropriate. On the contrary. This admittedly pointed depiction of the division of society into rich and poor or into 1 % versus 99 % is intended to sharpen the mind to the challenges that the economy of the future is confronted with. It is, in my opinion, the task of economics—and economic theory and research—to mitigate these differences, this social gradient. It cannot be that in the poorer parts of this world hunger, misery and war prevail, while people in other parts live in "luxury and abundance". Let it be said again: It is not about taking something away from the well-off and "better earners" and giving it one-to-one to the poor. It's not that simple, and it won't be implemented that way. In all the focus on the successful or "rich and beautiful" of this world, we must not forget that their wealth is mostly hard-earned, often at the expense of health. No top manager or politician or entrepreneur lies on the lazy skin and waits in his hammock for his next paycheck.

The task of economics and economists in the future will be to consider how society can become more economically fair. What tools must be used to at least enable the poor in society to participate more? Of course, there are numerous more or less sensible proposals for redistribution, such as the wealth tax, the higher inheritance tax, or the progressive income tax, which disproportionately taxes higher incomes and taxes top incomes of about 1 million EUR at almost 100 %. Furthermore, there are considerations for expanding a free state infrastructure such as educational institutions or tables for free nutrition. Existing outstanding commitment of helpful citizens must continue to be supported. For example, how can I motivate volunteers and entrepreneurs for the common good or offer them incentives to do more? Are approaches to the "economy for the common good", which measure and reward the societal well-being of companies, going in the right direction? Why are there no sponsorships between "young" and "old", such as young people and old, experienced managers or craftsmen, to start new companies, to not let the experience of the "old" go to waste? Why are there no sponsorships between "rich" and "poor"? A "rich" person who gives his "poor" counterpart useful tips from his professional life or life in general? In the USA, there are a number of these success stories of how people have successfully made it from dishwasher to millionaire. Why don't these rich people let the other 99 % share in their experiences? It is often not only experience or financial means that are lacking, but also the shining role model, will, and confidence to dare to experiment.

Who doesn't fondly remember the touching film "The Pursuit of Happyness" (2006), in which Will Smith plays

6 The Most Pressing Issues of Tomorrow's Economy

an unsuccessful sales representative who, in his quest to rise, receives an unpaid internship at an investment bank. Only the best candidate gets the chance for a permanent position. But before the decision is made, the protagonist, separated from his wife due to rent arrears, has to continue to struggle as a sales representative with his young son. In between, in every free minute, he has to cram for his exam to prepare as an investment banker—he has to become the best, otherwise the job won't work out. Nevertheless, father and son literally end up on the street, once they even miss the night in a homeless shelter. They have to—this is the low point—sleep in a public toilet. *They have nothing left but themselves.* In the end, Will Smith, who brilliantly plays this desperate father, manages with indomitable will and diligence, but also with the goodwill of his successful bosses, to secure the permanent position at the investment bank. He made it and becomes one of the most successful investment bankers in the USA. This handover between "rich" and "poor" must be encouraged more, for the benefit of all.

The aim here cannot be to provide a complete list of all possibilities for reducing injustice. However, the economy of tomorrow must provide an answer to this if it wants to serve the most important thing in the world: the human being.

So how can the economy be more aligned with the interests of all people, making it fairer for everyone? Here, it can only be about some exemplary suggestions. Of course, not everyone, like Will Smith in the aforementioned film, can become an investment banker. Not all people are lucky and can seize the offered opportunity and assert themselves against many applicants. Of course, there will always be people who are not so favored by luck and who, despite hard work, receive a low wage and already struggle with finding a flat. What is needed is a successful mix of equal opportunities and state welfare to make the economy fairer. Nobody can help being born into their family. Some are simply lucky and are born in a rich country like Germany or the USA and then perhaps even into a wealthy family. Others are less fortunate and experience how their parents have to get by daily with their meager financial means. However, all people must fundamentally receive the same opportunities.

It starts very concretely with education. Of course, children from wealthy households will have it easier, for example through targeted promotion of talents, whether they are musical, artistic, or athletic. However, if all children have a right to a daycare place, as is already the case in Germany, they can be promoted regardless of their parents' wallet. Why doesn't educational support start at kindergarten age, and children from poorer families can receive a kind of "daycare BAföG" and thus be specifically supported according to their talents? Learning musical instruments, promoting mental and physical abilities should be worth financial support to the state. Money that, as a rule, only financially well-off families can afford. The targeted promotion of children from poorer families could ensure that their intellectual talents are recognized in time and all children are specifically prepared for higher education. Financial support for children from poorer families already in pre-school and school age in the form of "scholarships" would enable particularly talented children, in exceptional cases depending on their abilities, to also be taught in private schools or even boarding schools. In individual cases, such financial support already exists. This could be further expanded.

It must be possible for particularly talented children and young people to study at the best universities in the country. The growing number of fee-based private universities should not be an obstacle to this. These too should be open to talented young people of all classes and be financially supported by the state. There is still a lot of room for improvement. Especially in Germany, too many educational paths are still dependent on the wallet and the education of one's own parents.

The stronger ones must support the weaker ones. This principle underlies the solidarity community. This would mean that those who have a higher income and wealth pay disproportionately for the poorer parts of society. This is already taken into account, for example, in Germany and many countries through a progressive income tax: the income tax rate gradually increases with the level of income until it reaches its maximum of currently 42 %. The wealthiest part of the population, from an income of around 250,000 EUR for singles or 500,000 EUR for jointly taxed married couples, already pays a "wealth tax" of 45 % from this amount (see, among others, Kaufmann, 2017). There is not much room for increase when considering that the motivation of those with a high income to perform more decreases with increasing tax rate. Attempts, as common in France or Scandinavia, to withhold well over half of the income from the state, should therefore be viewed with caution.

In Germany, there are always considerations about the wealth tax and increasing the inheritance tax. The thoughts behind this are not without a certain logic. Large fortunes are often inherited and not earned. It therefore makes sense to consider how this "unearned" wealth can serve the general public to some extent. However, such cases need to be examined more closely and differentiated: First, it depends on the size of the estates to be inherited. Second, it depends on how this wealth was acquired and whether it is tied up in a company or not. The aim cannot be to tax the grandmother's house, which the grandchild inherits and which has only a small value, to a considerable extent. This is regulated in Germany, for example, by the fact that inheritance tax only applies from a certain amount to be inherited, for example 400,000 EUR when parents pass on to their children, and increases progressively with the inheritance amount. For larger estates to be inherited, considerable inheritance taxes are already due today. For companies to be inherited, it must be ensured that the companies are not endangered in their existence by the inheritance tax. Therefore, the inheritance tax should not be too high when continuing the company.

A wealth tax, as already exists in other countries, can serve the general public on the one hand, as it promotes the redistribution from richer to poorer layers. On the other hand, similar to the inheritance tax, wealth that has already been built up from taxed income is taxed a second time. In particular, those who have worked hard in their lives, perhaps founded a company and taken risks, are asked to pay for their work again. When we think about how to make a society more just, we need to consider whether redistributive measures are really fair from all perspectives. Rather, we should rely more on the stronger voluntarily supporting the weaker. Even if this sounds naive at first glance, it is a way to let the solidarity community have its say.

Why shouldn't the wealthy of this society provide the talented, poor children and young people of this world with the scholarships mentioned above through a "solidarity fund"? There are already many who advocate for free daily school meals. Why shouldn't state-subsidized scholarships be set up for talented and willing children and young people? If people's educational biography no longer depends solely on the education and (financial) support of the parental home, it may be possible to break the education cycle i.e., high education of parents, high education of children and vice versa, and pave the way for more people to a sufficient and successful life. In my opinion, more can be achieved through this increase in equal opportunities in different starting situations than through a pure (wealth tax) levy, which is very controversial in society. I will further deepen similar ideas in section 6.8 about a social utopia, for example, the unconditional basic income and the (state-guaranteed) right to a roof over the head for all citizens of a state. These would all be good first steps to make a society and an economy more just. Is capitalism the right economic form for this?

6.2 Capitalism as a Model on the Way Out?

After the fall of the Berlin Wall and the collapse of the communist states and the Soviet Union, many observers were clear that, in addition to the political system, the socialist economic system had run its course. Capitalism, the market economy, had successfully displaced socialism and the planned economy. Capitalism was considered without alternative for a long time. However, in recent years, not only intellectuals have increasingly doubted whether capitalism itself is the answer to the pressing questions of the time and the economy. Since Marx, capitalism has been understood as an economic and social order characterized primarily by a market order of supply and demand and by private property of goods and means of production. In addition, the goal of capitalism is to "accumulate capital" (see Marx, 2009) i.e., the continuous striving for profit and profit of companies and individuals acting therein.

Criticism of capitalism has now become multivocal: In addition to the topics known from Marx's analysis such as "exploitation of workers", "alienation of labor" and "impoverishment of the masses" (Marx, 2009), new, more current ones have been added. Everywhere, the increase in income and wealth inequality among the population is denounced. Many criticize the pursuit of ever higher profits at any cost by some entrepreneurs and companies. Finally, the primacy of selfishness and profit-seeking over the common good and the welfare of the majority of citizens in a state is criticized. Personal enrichment, according to the harshest critics of capitalism, comes at the expense of the poorer population, who have nothing of the increasing wealth in the hands of a few, nationally and internationally. The state is increasingly pushed back, especially in the model country of capitalism, the USA. Public debt is rising as taxes—mostly for the wealthy part of the population—are dramatically decreasing. This, in turn, comes at the expense of the welfare state and the associated infrastructure, ranging from social benefits to pensions and educational and health facilities. Not only their number, but also the quality is continuously decreasing.

The gap between rich and poor, in the view of many citizens in the world, is continually widening, between the wealthy and the indebted, those with good jobs and the unemployed, those with the best education and opportunities in the labor market and the low-skilled. High crime rates and the increase in violence in some cities are the result. The poverty problem is intensifying. Citizens' awareness of the community, the sense of justice in society is increasingly lost, the individual dominates the scene at the expense of the community. The elbow mentality of "every-man-for-himself" is intensifying, the common good thinking is increasingly disappearing. Everything seems to be subordinated to the dictate of productivity increase and profit maximization. Pope Francis once put it very pointedly: "This economy kills." (Evangelii Gaudium). So far the critical voices on capitalism, which

6 The Most Pressing Issues of Tomorrow's Economy

could be extended at will and are not only heard in designated "left" circles of countries around the globe. Even if one does not want to join this very critical tenor, the thought of increasing concern among the population remains.

On the other hand, it is rightly said, "No capitalism is also no solution" (Herrmann, 2016). Ultimately, capitalism has brought prosperity, not just for a few, but for all. As we have already seen, the introduction of the social market economy in Germany with the founding of the Federal Republic of Germany in 1949 brought at least in the 1950s "economic miracle years" the "prosperity for all" promised by Ludwig Erhard (cf. Erhard, 1964). This economic form is based on the market economy, i.e., the free play of supply and demand based on privately owned means of production and the pursuit of profit. However, in this model, as we have read in section 3.6 about the idea givers Müller-Armack and Ludwig Erhard, the state does not only ensure the framework conditions. So not only are the legal regulations enacted that the entrepreneur and the merchant have to observe, and public infrastructure is provided for, for schools and educational institutions, the health system, public parks or swimming pools as well as internal and external security. All this would also be provided by a purely market economic system of Anglo-Saxon character. The state ensures private property, freedom of contract and open markets, free price formation, a stable monetary system and above all free, unhindered competition.

In addition, however, the social market economy ensures that the state intervenes in the result of the economic process and socially corrects too large inequalities in the result. Progressive tax rates ensure that higher incomes are taxed disproportionately. Those in need are supported by unemployment and social assistance, retirees receive a transfer payment from the state. High assets are taxed after deducting a certain allowance when inherited. Families with children also receive tax allowances, and spouses benefit from spousal splitting. The state support program is supplemented by numerous private and voluntary initiatives that try to alleviate the greatest need in Germany. This is what the model of the social market economy, which has been successful in Germany for many decades, looks like in brief, which supports the individual in his pursuit of profit and at the same time provides relief in social emergencies. Above all, however, this concept ensures that not only the self-healing and control forces of the market are relied on, but the state performs an active balancing and ordering function.

But what role does economics and especially economic theory now play? In the concrete design of a country's economic form, various functions and structures of the economy can be tailored to the prevailing guiding principle: more equality or more freedom (cf. also my detailed explanations in my work "Limits of Economic Thinking", Pietsch, 2017, p. 165 ff.).

If I want to increase the *equality of a society* within the framework of a market economy principle, I must use certain instruments more intensively. For example, as can be seen in the Scandinavian countries, income tax would have to be significantly increased. There, even relatively low incomes are taxed more heavily than in Germany, and high incomes are taxed disproportionately high at about 60 %. After taxes, top incomes should only leave 20 % of the yield for the employee. One should not orient oneself on the concrete numbers, they can be lower in one case or another, depending on how much one wants to promote equality within the population. A wealth tax on capital and real estate, stocks etc., as well as an inheritance tax that would primarily affect higher wealth, would have to

6 The Most Pressing Issues of Tomorrow's Economy 315

be introduced. An increased minimum wage—ideally at a 35-hour week—would be supplemented by a *basic income without work*. All income sources of a state would have to be analyzed and increased in their percentage factor, with the exception of value-added tax, which rather affects the "small" incomes. All luxury goods would be subject to a "luxury tax". The money collected in this way would be spent on social support services, such as social assistance, unemployment support, higher pensions, state funding of educational and health facilities, and generally state transfers for the less privileged of this society, whether they are low earners, single parents or in need of care. In sum, this model stands for "more state" and less free market economy. With these measures, a higher equality in society could be achieved if that is the economic objective.

If, on the other hand, I want to emphasize the *freedom of society*, the freedom of opportunities and individual performance in a society, I must take different paths. While the "model of equality" assumes a human image of a needy, not always autonomously acting individual, the "libertarian model" emphasizes the self-sufficient, confident, mature citizen who can provide for himself and his family in every situation of his life and only needs state support in exceptional cases. Here, the state should interfere as little as possible in the market results. Such a model was realized in the 1980s under then US President Ronald Reagan and British Prime Minister Margaret Thatcher ("Reaganomics and Thatcherism"). The core element of this economic order is the almost unhindered, free play of market forces. Taxes are generally drastically reduced: income and corporate taxes are lowered, as currently again by the Trump administration in the USA. Wealth taxes. Inheritance taxes are also drastically reduced. Taxes on real estate do not exist, nor do taxes on luxury goods. The money thus lost to the state and therefore missing is not fully compensated by a higher motivation of companies and employees, who are now allowed to keep more of their wages or profits, consume and invest more, and thus stimulate the domestic economy. This missing money must be partly sacrificed at the expense of state infrastructure services and social assistance. Thus, less money is available for state schools and universities, for the health system and public facilities such as parks, theaters, museums, playgrounds etc. The politically responsible and above all the citizens must form their own opinion about these two extreme variants of the market economy—more equality or more freedom—in democratic elections.

The task of economics will be to give policy recommendations to the state on the basis of empirical studies, i.e. numbers, data and facts, for example about the benefits of the minimum wage or a wealth tax, and coherent theoretical structures, and thus to guide the design of the optimal economic form in appropriate channels. Only in this way can capitalism become a "civilized" (Dönhoff, 1997) or a "compassionate" capitalism for all, on which the mentioned points of criticism largely bounce off. Defining this and successfully implementing it in practice or accompanying the implementation will be a major challenge for the economic profession of the future. Capitalism is not a model that is running out. However, an important task is to make capitalism more moral.

6.3 Economy and Ethics

Not everything that is economically efficient and effective is also ethically justifiable. The necessity of a moral framework for economic activities has become increasingly indisputable in recent years. It is not for nothing that more and more future leaders around the globe are being

6 The Most Pressing Issues of Tomorrow's Economy

familiarized with the ethical and moral prerequisites in the context of the subject "Business Ethics" or its Anglo-Saxon variant "Business Ethics". Ethical problems in economics can essentially be identified on three levels (cf. among others Küng, 2010):

- On the individual level, e.g. among the executives and participants of economic activity
- At the level of companies and institutions that significantly intervene in the economic process
- At the level of the conception and further development of the economic system as such

What ethical challenges are we talking about? Every reasonable person knows that slave labor is forbidden today, as is child labor. No one in Germany would think of subjecting workers to any form of mental or physical torture. It goes without saying that companies should neither produce in such countries where these practices are even remotely tolerated, nor cooperate with partners who support these conditions. The individual consumer should also be interested in the manufacturing conditions of the products he prefers, as he can also ensure with his purchasing behavior that these practices are not supported or "have no market". Nevertheless, there are many examples of ethically questionable methods of doing business that urgently need correction and above all the establishment of clear rules to avoid such behavior.

The list of possible transgressions is long. It's about corruption, where a certain misconduct by managers or simple employees is rewarded with money payments or benefits in kind. Thus, a tender by state and non-state bodies can result in contract awards to the company of the payer of these bribes through a secret payment to foreign accounts with the respective decision-makers.

Major sporting competitions and events can be directed to certain countries or cities through payments to decision-makers. Administrative processes can be simplified or influenced in some countries by the payment of large sums of money in favor of the paying company or institution. For example, customs clearance can be facilitated, the transport of urgent goods accelerated, or even the entry of certain people into a country made possible. Buyers and purchasing managers of larger companies are often the target of corrupt behavior. Since they often have the authority to decide from which suppliers certain parts or components needed for production are purchased, and it often involves very large quantities, there is a risk that this decision will be influenced by the respective supplier through illegal methods.

Corruption is just one form of ethical misconduct. Collusions or cartel formations are other examples. Companies, especially in a market with only a few powerful players, could collude in their behavior, e.g., to determine prices or production quantities that allow all participants to make the greatest possible profit at the expense of the consumer. Not all collusions are ethically condemnable, some are even necessary. There are cases where an industry agrees on certain standards for the benefit of the consumer, e.g., on what charging devices for electric cars should be provided or what size suitcases should comply with in order to optimally use the available space when traveling in the trunk or on an airplane. Sometimes it's just about the legislator issuing new standards for an industry, with the help of which these requirements are to be implemented in practice. There are certain ISO standards (International Standards Organisation, ISO) that set technological standards to facilitate international trade in goods and services, in which the manufacturers also participate, such as in the size of child seats.

6 The Most Pressing Issues of Tomorrow's Economy

However, the general rule is that all agreements between companies and institutions to reduce competition between them or to increase the profits of the participating companies at the expense of the end customer are prohibited. The same applies to the use of a monopoly position, for example to increase prices.

Another example of the need to comply with ethical rules are ecological aspects of economic activity. It should not have escaped anyone's notice that nature has been and is being sustainably damaged by human activities, especially by economic behavior. Keywords are global warming, toxic waste exports, fracking. The latter is a method of extracting natural gas, in which the rock layers in the earth are destroyed with water and chemicals to extract the gas accumulated in them. The danger of fracking is that toxic chemicals can contaminate groundwater (see, among others, Merkel, 2013), enter rivers and bodies of water and kill fish and other creatures there. Furthermore, the air can be contaminated by escaping toxic gases. The tensions already existing in the earth's interior are further intensified by fracking and increase the risk of earthquakes. Other environmental sins caused by economic activities are the deforestation of rainforests (see Reuter, 2014) to get valuable wood or to gain agriculturally usable land, the worldwide overfishing of the seas (see Honey, 2016) and chemicals with a dubious reputation such as glyphosate, which are used for pest control in agriculture, can endanger the harvest and users and are therefore rightly controversial (see Oberhuber, 2015).

The Internet offers further opportunities for unethical behavior, as this medium, through buying and selling, relies much more heavily on mutual trust than personal consumption. The beginnings of the company eBay are a vivid example of this. Every buyer and seller goes through various security procedures to ensure the seriousness of the transaction. Especially the payment process on the Internet carries numerous risks and is subject to an extensive security system. Nevertheless, money payments over the Internet are no more protected from hacker attacks than personal data. All mentioned forms of unethical behavior also exist in the world of the Internet: from corruption to agreements to fraud and "rip-offs". Due to the often anonymous handling of the buying and selling process, the possibilities of fraud have become more complex, such as payment without sending or receiving goods, and can only be combated by strict security standards and measures, such as reliability ratings, deleting dubious accounts, or setting up "Internet police departments", etc.

I would like to touch on just two more examples of unethical behavior in business, the treatment of animals and any form of discrimination, before I briefly outline approaches to correcting such practices.

The dignified *treatment of animals* (cf. Precht, 2016) has rightly become a very sensitive point in the public perception of products and companies. Images of battery cages for chickens, kept in the tightest of spaces to produce a "product" that can be sold to the customer, have become a symbol of inhumane behavior towards animals. Not without reason must it be stated on the packaging of eggs how these eggs were "produced" and how the chickens were treated in the process. Another example is the use of animal testing in cosmetics development. Thus, animals have to suffer and are sometimes killed so that the intolerance of shower gel or make-up for humans can be demonstrated. Although all animal testing in the cosmetics industry was banned by the EU Commission in 2003, this only applies to EU member states, and there are still companies that relocate to countries where these practices continue to exist. Animal welfare organizations like PETA

e. V. rightly mobilize against this and regularly publish "positive lists" of cosmetics companies (cf. Animal Welfare Association, 2019) that clearly take a stand against animal testing, including such prominent names as "Lush" or "Body Shop". Only through the publication of positive examples and the branding of negative behavior can a correction of unethical business practices be achieved.

Another case of unethical behavior in business is *discrimination*. No person should be discriminated against because of their race, religion, sexual orientation, nationality, cultural affiliation, or even their gender. This starts with the selection of new employees, who should not be rejected based on their picture or foreign-sounding names in application documents. It continues with pay, the type of job, where the appropriate education should be the only determining factor. Pay should be based solely on the qualifications and expertise of the candidates and should not be affected by whether he or she is a man or a woman, belongs to a certain ethnicity, religion, or nationality, or has a certain sexual orientation. Only the presumed and actual performance should be the deciding factor, even if the latter is usually not objectively measurable.

The outlined examples of unethical behavior can be carried out both individually, i.e., by individuals, as well as by companies and institutions and the people acting within them. Rules for correction must be defined at both levels to avoid abuse. Recently, the economic system of "capitalism" has come under strong public criticism. I have already given an insight into the problem of business ethics at the system level in section 6.2. The following mechanisms and measures are being discussed or already applied to correct unethical behavior or to prevent it from arising in the first place (cf. among others Lütge & Uhl, 2017, p. 173 ff.):

- Quality seals such as *Fair Trade* to certify fair trade are intended to ensure that the entire manufacturing and trading process is fair, i.e., based on mutual give and take. The coffee trade can serve as a concrete example. Fair Trade aims to qualitatively improve the living and working conditions of small farmers and their families by passing on a slightly higher consumer price than usual to the farmers. They simply receive significantly more for the harvested coffee beans. If a minimum price is guaranteed to the farmers, their incomes are put on a secure basis, and the supply of the families is secured, even if the harvest is once worse. At the same time, the compatibility of ecology and economy can be promoted by trading and consuming more environmentally friendly organic products.
- A quality seal can also be awarded based on criteria that prohibit certain forms of work, such as child labor, or unreasonable working conditions or hours. In the same direction are considerations about the minimum wage, which ensures a sufficient salary for workers.
- At the corporate level, binding *codes of ethics* have been established that, in addition to a mission, such as: "We want to act ethically because we too bear responsibility for our society and our environment," define clear core values of the company, such as appreciation, responsibility, prohibition of any discrimination, etc. From this, clear norms and rules for daily cooperation in the company and dealing with customers and society are to be defined, such as "We are committed to our employees and our customers. We bear responsibility for society and the environment." etc.
- In recent years, *compliance* departments and areas have proven their worth in companies, which are supposed to ensure that corporate and individual misconduct is identified in time and appropriately punished. This

6 The Most Pressing Issues of Tomorrow's Economy

ranges from combating corruption to uncovering bribes and unethical behavior such as discrimination based on ethnicity, religion, or unequal treatment of customers. Essential here is the training and sensitization of managers and employees. These measures can be supported by databases in which the acceptance of small gifts in the sense of transparency is documented as well as anonymous hints about possible misconduct of individual employees ("whistleblowing").

- Sometimes, a reminder of the model of the "honorable merchant," to whom virtues such as honesty, responsibility, decency, care, sustainability, and role model function belong, is also sufficient. It is essential that misconduct is consistently and publicly punished, leaving no room for interpretation.
- Finally, the consumer, we can all ensure with our buying behavior that we no longer do business with companies that do not commit to Fair Trade or undermine ethical standards.

However, ethical considerations do not end with fair dealings in the economy and with nature. The goal of the economy, optimization, must also be viewed against the background of ethical considerations.

The essence of the economy is optimization. This is how you read it or something similar in critical reports in newspapers and magazines. You hear it in lectures at economic faculties in Germany and the world. The goal is "higher, faster, further," mathematically speaking: the optimum. The economic principle of maximum results with given input or achieving results with minimum input. When the principle of the optimum, the best possible, is transferred to social processes, the approach seems strange: Do I get the most out of my friendships? Do I minimize my costs by asking my relatives and acquaintances to support me?

Do I maintain relationships only to get the maximum possible for me? Such an attitude would not only be strange in friendships but would quickly lead to the end of even long relationships without mutual give and take, the principle of every friendship. But in economics, this principle of optimization is still the core. But how did the long journey from barter economy and division of labor specialization of the Stone Age, antiquity, through the Middle Ages to the modern age and modern times proceed?

While at the beginning of economic activity, as we have seen, the concern for adequate nutrition for the family and the clan was paramount, barter trade became increasingly important. People now produced more than they needed themselves and exchanged the rest. The trading partners were increasingly distant from each other, and the ever more efficient logistics eventually even enabled trade between far-flung countries. Money as a medium of exchange helped in preserving the value of the traded goods and could be spent in various ways. Initially only for personal needs or those of the family and clan, later for a rather pointless accumulation of wealth that could not be spent even over several generations. With the advent of machines in the context of industrialization and the ever-growing companies, entrepreneurial profit became increasingly important. While in the medieval guilds the supply of individual members was still very much in the foreground, the emerging large companies had to use the money invested by the financier, the "capitalist", sensibly to generate a corresponding return.

A classic entrepreneur would never think of investing his money in a process for the production of certain products if he did not simultaneously hope to increase his invested capital. This incentive to earn money has been the basic condition for successful entrepreneurship since the introduction of money. This is still a legitimate incentive

6 The Most Pressing Issues of Tomorrow's Economy

for entrepreneurs of all kinds today, to receive compensation for the emerging risk and the success of the company and the preservation of jobs. This has always been the aim of financiers and entrepreneurs, to maximize the return on the invested capital or to achieve the highest possible return. From this, the demand for profit maximization was derived in economic theory. In Karl Marx's terms, this was still "the surplus value" of capital (cf. Marx, 2009). But why is the principle of profit maximization so important for the entrepreneur?

First, we need to understand how a company's profit is generated. Simplified, a company must try to sell as many products and services as possible at a high price that can be enforced on the market. This turnover in the form of received funds must be so high that it can finance all the costs incurred for employees, machines, factory halls and buildings, land, etc., and ideally, there is still something left over that the entrepreneur and his family need to live and that the invested capital is appropriately interest-bearing. Would you as an entrepreneur invest your hard-earned money, let's say a few hundred thousand euros, as a financier in a company that does not make a profit and you would receive at least 1–2 % interest on your invested capital from the bank as an alternative? Probably not. The company's profit allows all associated costs to be covered, such as paying the wages of employees and thus creating secure jobs. At the same time, however, you must always continue to invest in the future, e.g., in new products, machines, and halls. Perhaps you also need to establish branches in other countries or even invest in growth sectors. For all this, you need a high company profit, most of which you have to reinvest in the company.

In today's times, many large companies and corporations exist that have many financiers in the form of shareholders who want to benefit from the success of the company. This is legitimate, as the shareholders also bear part of the entrepreneurial risk depending on the amount of money they have invested in the company. Nowadays, entrepreneurs and financiers are different people. The tasks of the entrepreneur are taken over by employed managers in large corporations, whose mandate is to use the shareholders' invested capital as best as possible, to advance the company and to maintain thousands of jobs. The logic is: The higher the entrepreneurial profit—usually measured at the end of the fiscal year—the more secure are the jobs of the employees, the more can be invested in the future, and the greater is the confidence of the financiers that their invested capital is very well invested in this company. In the language of the stock exchange: The share price rises. At the same time, the company, measured by market capitalization, becomes more valuable and can be bought up by other companies with increasing difficulty.

So the managers at the top of the company, depending on the legal form the board or the managing directors, do everything they can to maximize the company's profit. Are there limits to increasing corporate profits, or is any means justified in the pursuit of profit? Let's remember the beginnings of economic activity: Here, the provision for the individual and the family—equivalent to today's employee of a company—was the goal of entrepreneurial action and striving. If the profit is achieved by offering ever better, high-quality products at reasonable prices, and if the customers thereby gain added value, there is nothing to object to. Both, customer and company, are satisfied, the former with the product and the latter with the profit. If the profit is fairly distributed among employees and management or financiers in the form of dividends, then there is nothing to object to. Wise company leaders invest in the future of the company in a timely manner based on market and competitive observation in the form of new products, other markets, or growth sectors. This ensures that the company is crisis-proof in the future and jobs are preserved. Profits must always be higher, as wages, material costs, and much more increase in the context of inflation and must be compensated accordingly.

A good example of such a solid business model with a decent profit that meets the above criteria are the commercial banks of the past. Customers benefited from the banks by seeing their money safely stored in their accounts and receiving interest for it. At the same time, they could borrow money in the form of loans at good market conditions, which they could repay according to a clear plan. Many entrepreneurs, especially in the medium-sized sector in Germany, were thus able to provide themselves with money on the capital market for their investments in the future of their company, expand and thus secure jobs. The banks benefited from the interest-bearing funds or the investment of their customers' deposited capital on the capital market and made a decent profit. It had to be the consideration of every management, of the employed entrepreneurs, how to further increase the profit in order to have even more money available for the company's future provision.

However, optimizing for the sake of optimizing is not the solution. Profit maximization as the guiding principle of economics is necessary (cf. Mankiw & Taylor, 2012, p. 353 ff.). However, it does not justify all means and does not answer the question of the "sufficient profit" or how much profit is enough. Profit maximization of course applies not only to companies, but also to states. Every state and its representatives will strive to increase state revenues so high that all tasks of the state can be financed and the state does not go into debt. Unfortunately, this is hardly granted to any state in the world. The state deficit, which arises when state expenditure is higher than state revenue, is the rule everywhere and is even increasing in most states on earth. The aim of the state government must therefore be to take in more through taxes, fees, levies and money flows from abroad than it spends on all state activities such as the construction of roads, public buildings, defense, culture, education, social affairs and much more. It thus behaves analogously to the actions of an entrepreneur. We will see later that the fiscal policy of states cannot be so easily compared with entrepreneurial action. However, the principle of profit maximization remains the same in both cases.

Let me say a word about *utility maximization.* Economic theory assumes that the customer or consumer tries to maximize his utility when buying goods or products (cf. among others Mankiw & Taylor, 2012, p. 522). The optimization idea from the consumer's point of view is what profit maximization is for the entrepreneur. Although the benefit for the customer is difficult to determine, let alone measure, in individual cases, this principle is based on the idea that the customer wants to get the maximum benefit for himself with his existing financial budget. So I try to book a relaxing family vacation in the sun of Spain as cheaply as possible through various vacation portals and offers on the net. This ensures that I get the highest benefit for myself and my family with the vacation. As simple as this principle sounds, its implementation in practice is difficult. Are vacations actually comparable? Do I have complete transparency over all offers for my planned vacation in Spain? This idea of utility maximization comes from the model of the *Homo oeconomicus,* an idealized human being who always acts rationally, knows all decision alternatives and always strives for personal optimization. In economics, money plays a crucial role in optimization. Let's lose a few thoughts about money itself.

6 The Most Pressing Issues of Tomorrow's Economy

These remarks clearly show a thematic change from the Stone Age necessity of exchange and division of labor towards the optimization of distribution and economic justice. To put it bluntly: It was a long way from the Stone Age, ancient and medieval economy of supply and the "fair" exchange of an Aristotle or Thomas Aquinas to the "accumulation of capital" in the hands of a few during the industrialization at Marx and finally the question of justice today. The eight richest people today amass a fortune equal to the lower half of humanity, or a good 3.7 billion people (cf. Oxfam, 2017). Let's take a closer look at this topic of wealth concentration.

Our ancestors in the Neolithic Age exchanged tools, jewelry and raw materials for food and everyday necessities, i.e., goods for goods. As early as many millennia later, around 3100 BC, the ancient Egyptians first used gold as a means of payment, unit of account and store of value (cf. Haidacher, 2015, p. 34). In the city-state of Athens, the Greek drachma was already used as a coin with a pictorial symbol as a means of payment in 600 BC. Money is increasingly developing from a means of payment for the purpose of exchange to an object of wealth and property among the ancient Greeks (cf. Vaupel & Kaul, 2016). In Caesar's time, money was also used to finance one's own rise with the help of one's army, and coins were minted with one's own likeness (cf. Bank Association, 2018). Money was then seen as an expression of power and served to secure it and for propaganda purposes. In the 9th century AD, the mark was first mentioned in writing as a unit of weight and means of payment in the area of North Germania (cf. Bavarian Coin Office, 2019). Money was thus a key component of the economy.

With the introduction of money as a means of exchange and store of value, a detrimental development of *more and more, faster and faster,* partly against the rules, began.

Until then, the focus was primarily on the self-sufficiency of the members of a community with the essentials for life and survival. Economic activities were a necessary maxim due to the respective circumstances to ensure pure survival. With the advent of money in the form of gold, silver, and other precious metals, this function of life assurance was supplemented by the new function of wealth accumulation for the purpose of prosperity and its increase: It became possible to accumulate money for the sake of money and not primarily to exchange it for goods that were acquired from other communities or countries as part of the division of labor. The British economist David Ricardo illustrated his theory of comparative cost advantages at the beginning of the 19th century using the exchange of wine and cloth: One country focuses on the production of wine, which it can produce better than another country due to the more favorable climate and greater experience, which focuses on the production of cloth (cf. Eltis, 1989). Both countries benefit from the exchange of goods and thus increase the prosperity of their population.

Soon, however, it was no longer about increasing the prosperity of the members of a community or a country, but about money itself. Money was suddenly associated with wealth, riches, power, fulfillment of all dreams, a better life. The function of money as a medium of exchange was repurposed as a measure of the financial potency of individual members of society. People who did not have the prosperity of their country in mind, but their own innate greed for profit. The pursuit of power over material things, people, status, and image became increasingly important. Luxury consumption was made possible by the availability of an almost infinite amount of money, thus enabling the acquisition of a multitude of houses that no person can ever inhabit simultaneously. In this way, lands

6 The Most Pressing Issues of Tomorrow's Economy 331

could be bought up that one can hardly traverse oneself, or simply clothing and jewelry could be purchased in a quantity whose partial sale would be sufficient to support a multitude of poor, starving people.

Of course, this is a very simplified representation of today's reality, and of course, it has rarely been so extreme in the past. There was already the division into rich and poor. The probably richest family in the late Middle Ages, the trading dynasty of the Fuggers from Augsburg, was deeply rooted in their Christian faith and donated generously to the poor people. They created numerous almost free accommodations for the poor workers and day laborers of the area and supported poor families with free food. Economic activities for the benefit of the community like those of the Fuggers, however, increasingly degenerated into a rapid accumulation of money for individuals for their own pleasure. But one must not confuse this with the fact that the entrepreneur in the market economy system must achieve an appropriate remuneration for his investments. This is the legitimate pursuit of an entrepreneur. He too is responsible for the well-being of his family and his entrusted employees and secures their jobs through his entrepreneurial risk-taking actions. The entrepreneurial profit ensures his own prosperity and that of his employees.

However, efforts seem to have gone awry to make as much money as possible in the shortest possible time, without regard for the well-being of the other members of society who are also affected. The greed of the individual, who does not use his economic activities as in the centuries before to achieve "prosperity for all" (Erhard, 1964), but merely satisfies his greed for money by legally pursuing economic activities that only aim at his material prosperity and create no additional value beyond that. In contrast, numerous large, but also medium-sized companies, among others in the automotive and mechanical engineering industry in Germany, produce globally very sought-after products such as cars, machines, and other engineering products with the seal "Made in Germany". They create and secure many thousands of jobs, make a decent profit, and ensure the prosperity of the cities and municipalities that host them through the abundant business taxes. They all *create value* and legitimately retain a part of their profits to remunerate all those involved in the value creation.

But what about those who engage in speculative trading on the stock markets, such as betting on rising food prices and realizing profits at the expense of the poorest? A gamble with a long lever to individual wealth, coupled with the senseless, extremely detrimental increase in the cost of essential foodstuffs—stock speculation in general, which no longer follows business economic laws, but only hopes to realize stock purchases and sales with the prospect of the quickest possible profit. The pinnacle of speculation are the so-called short sales (cf. among others Schömann-Finck, 2011), in which a seller sells securities, goods etc. that he does not even own at this point in time, but which are only borrowed ("short sale"). This serves only the purpose of acquiring these only borrowed securities at a later date (at the starting point) cheaper and then to make a profit through the positive difference between selling and buying price, the so-called *Short Position*. Of course, every entrepreneur and trader of goods tries to buy the items e.g. for his supermarket cheaper than he sells them to his end customers. With a small but significant difference: He sells goods of daily need to his customers and thus increases their welfare. Short sales only increase the seller's account, nothing else. Therefore, they have been rightly banned in Germany since 2010 (cf. Schömann-Finck, 2011).

The economic crisis of 2008 was, to a large extent, triggered by the real estate market and the "sub-prime loans" (cf. among others Kohlenberg & Uchatius, 2008): At that time, average American earners were granted cheap loans by unscrupulous bank employees, sometimes without any equity, which they could never repay in their lives. The loan was associated with the hope of providing a roof over the head for their own family and selling the house with a decent increase in value after a certain speculation period. The excess demand for these houses certainly justified this increase in value. The winners were mainly the credit brokers, who pocketed lavish commissions. When this automatic mechanism subsided with the collapse of demand in the housing market and the borrowers had to sell their over-indebted houses below value, the US banking system and soon the entire world economy wobbled with it. The greed of these credit brokers plunged families into ruin, they themselves pocketed the commissions until the end.

As we have seen, the introduction of money into the economy has not only brought positive aspects, because now one no longer had to offer extensive stocks of goods for exchange, but could rely on money as a store of value and medium of exchange. Nevertheless, people have always used money not only to create wealth, but also to enrich themselves. This happened, as we know, not always in a legal way. But, the question is, does a lot of money also make you happy? More precisely: How much money does a person need for happiness? And can happiness be increased further, the more money an individual has? Is there a limit to this? If money alone does not make you happy, does the economy contribute to the well-being of people? We want to take a closer look at these topics in section 6.4.

6.4 Limits of Growth

In 1972, the sensational book "The Limits of Growth" by the American economist Dennis Meadows was published (Meadows, 1972). It was based on a study commissioned by the Club of Rome, an association of scientists and experts from various disciplines from more than 30 countries, founded in 1968. The core message of the book, which alarmed the world public, was that the economic and population growth of the time, i.e. in 1972, projected into the future, would lead to a shortage of food, enormous environmental pollution and a massive shortage of raw materials. All this would lead, according to Meadows and his co-authors, to the collapse of the world economy before the year 2100, a drastic decline in prosperity and the inability to secure the nutrition of the world population. This ominous trend must be urgently counteracted, for example through birth control and enforced environmental protection in the sense of a more economical use of vital, non-renewable resources.

Even if one does not want to fully agree with these negative scenarios from the past, it is still useful to consider where the limits of economic growth lie. The most current reference to these limits can be seen today in China. Anyone who has had the opportunity to travel to China in recent years, especially to China's capital Beijing, has been negatively affected by the extent of air pollution there. Hardly a day goes by without the fine dust pollution exceeding many times the amount still tolerable for health (see Lee, 2017) and people being able to leave their house without filter masks. The culprits are not only the coal-fired power plants, but also the massive nitrogen pollution from industrial chimneys, as well as the rampant road traffic. It is no coincidence that China has now become a pioneer in promoting alternative vehicle drives. There is even

6 The Most Pressing Issues of Tomorrow's Economy   335

talk of a mandatory quota for electric vehicles of 10 % from 2019 to reduce smog (see Giesen & Hägler, 2017). In China, the limits of growth are most clearly seen in industrial emissions. A similar discussion took place many years ago regarding the use of sprays of all kinds containing chlorofluorocarbons, which gradually destroy the ozone layer (for the discussion 25 years after the CFC ban see Knauer, 2015).

Non-renewable resources such as crude oil and minerals like nickel and copper set similar natural limits to growth. The consequence of the increasing scarcity of these resources (see, for example, Bräutigam, 2013) are rising raw material prices, which are becoming increasingly unaffordable, especially for poorer countries. Rainforests are being deforested, oil fields will eventually be completely depleted, as will ivory, which costs numerous elephants their lives each year. Not only the lives of these large mammals are endangered by the growing demand for ivory, but also those of other animal species (see Habekuß, 2019). OECD economists have been concluding for years that further economic growth as before will lead to water scarcity, increased environmental pollution, climate change, and declining biodiversity. It is no coincidence that resource-saving production methods have been used for years, resources are recovered ("recycled") or replaced by other, renewable resources—for example, plastic is to be made from corn in the future.

These examples of the limits of economic growth have long been known and have deeply ingrained themselves in the consciousness of people in industrialized countries. Numerous climate forums and summits of recent years have been at least partially successful in combating climate change. However, when we talk about the limits of growth, we also need to think about the societal conditions of growth. How much consumption is enough? Do I really need a new smartphone or laptop every other year? How many shoes, bags, coats, or suits do I need during the year? Isn't my old suit still good enough, my old shirts and shoes, or my second-generation tablet computer? Do I really need to have the latest generation to be able to join the conversation? Today's generation of consumers is more open-minded, better educated, and more critical. They are not so easily seduced by the marketing measures of the providers. The best example is the "sharing economy", the economy of sharing: Instead of owning a car, cars are simply rented on occasion and used for transport from A to B. Hotel rooms are replaced by temporarily rented private apartments at the holiday destination via providers like Airbnb. Ownership itself is no longer a status symbol, but merely a means to an end. Consumption today is more conscious: "organic" instead of normal, vegetarian or vegan instead of meat, without packaging and only recyclable goods.

Even the richest people in the world do not always want to go higher, faster, further. Bill Gates and Warren Buffet, for example, put most of their wealth into foundations to use it for charitable purposes. Young mothers and fathers often do not want to make a career as quickly as possible, earn as much money as possible in a short time, and then indulge in status consumption. Today, it is becoming more and more the rule that young couples share child-rearing, to see the children grow up in shared parental leave, part-time work, foregoing the big career. The "work-life balance" is becoming more and more important: more time instead of more consumption, more children than professional titles, less money in doubt and therefore more of the children and one's life partner. These new tendencies in society—admittedly mainly in the rich industrialized countries—lead to a restriction of consumption. A new modesty is emerging that does not always strive for higher, further, and faster—professionally and privately.

6 The Most Pressing Issues of Tomorrow's Economy

Thankfully, lifespans are getting longer and longer. Many people today do not want to live just to work, but also to enjoy their lives. Some high earners around the age of 60 decide they have worked enough, retire early from their careers, and start a new, more leisure-oriented life. They are then no longer available to companies. Many are no longer willing to take the step for the last bit of additional money or extra pension. They want to secure a certain standard of living, but forgo more income and provision in favor of quality of life. They no longer need a large house and prefer to move to smaller apartments closer to the city center. Or they move to the sunny south of Spain for the winter and live more relaxed and at lower costs in an idyll. Some are enthralled by a short stay in a monastery, a place of seclusion and silence, a time of inner reflection and leisure. The topics of time, time for oneself, and modesty are becoming increasingly important, not only in old age but in general. Instead of "always higher, faster, and richer," a certain minimum of quality of life, time for oneself and one's loved ones comes into play. All of this does not necessarily have to lead to less consumption. Often, however, this is the case. The lower income over a lifetime often leads to more happiness and not to additional consumption. The limits of economic growth are not only a result of the limitation of natural resources, but are also rooted in us humans ourselves.

The economic principle is essentially based on achieving the maximum result with a given use of resources or ensuring a predetermined goal with minimal resource use. At the same time, it is assumed that the economy is always growing and that this best serves the prosperity of all, as consumption desires can be better satisfied and more and more citizens can find well-paid work. Is this permanent growth maxim still realistic in today's time, but especially in the future? Is it really the case that a permanently growing economy automatically enables higher prosperity for all and therefore should be pursued with all might? I want to subject this question to a critical analysis.

The Oldenburg economist Niko Paech questions the positive effects of a permanently growing economy. In his "post-growth economy" (Paech, 2012), he advocates the approach that it must be possible to get by without growth in gross social product and to allow a reduced level of consumption. Money alone does not make you happy: beyond a certain income level, a further increase in salary does not increase individual well-being or happiness in life. At some point, I have earned enough money, bought the essential things in life, such as a property, a car, and enough money for my hobbies and the security of the family. It is also questionable whether an increase in economic performance can effectively combat hunger and poverty, let alone in terms of ecological impacts. Natural resources are scarce and are reaching their natural limit with further use by the economy. The media reports are full of the smog-infested cities in China, but also in India, where industrial emissions drastically reduce the quality of life of the population.

Much speaks for steady economic growth. Jobs are created, the salaries paid help to secure the families of the employees and to consume. A trade surplus, where domestic goods are more popular abroad than foreign goods at home, brings money into the country. This can be used for public infrastructure such as parks, schools, theaters, etc. More work means more taxes, money that can be made available to the weak in society such as children, retirees, the sick and those in need of care, but also the unemployed and people with disabilities through social transfers. As long as natural resources are available in sufficient quantities, this is not a problem. The problem only arises when the blessings of the social market economy in

6 The Most Pressing Issues of Tomorrow's Economy

Germany no longer reach everyone. Doubts about this wealth-promoting function for all citizens are appropriate.

There is much criticism that the growth of an economy is increasingly benefiting fewer people. The rise in property prices with the fight for scarce living space, especially in the metropolises, is leading to an increasing two-class society (cf. Fricke, 2018): on the one hand, the property owners, whose wealth from property is constantly increasing due to increased demand, on the other hand, the tenants, who can afford less and less living space due to the constant rent increases. Wages are only rising moderately, barely above the inflation rate, and the investment bankers in the upper floors can look forward to dramatic salary increases. The profits of the companies mainly benefit the employees working in them, while the unemployed and welfare recipients get nothing. Of course, these employees have to work hard for their money. The property owners also had to work hard for their property once, unless they inherited everything. Nevertheless, the gap between the haves and the have-nots shows that economic growth does not automatically create "prosperity for all" (Erhard, 1964), even if Germany is still comparatively well off. The wealth gap is widening.

At the same time, an increase in economic performance is often bought with an increase in raw material consumption. The CO_2 emissions per capita are far too high to be able to maintain the two-degree climate protection target. Each of us knows enough examples from our own environment of natural resources that are finite and can reach their end faster through permanent economic growth. This is also a question of the compatibility of ecology and economy.

How can these negative consequences of the economy be avoided in a "post-growth economy"? Niko Paech sees a possibility in the downsizing of the industrial system:

A regional and self-sufficient economy of the communal members of a society should take the place of the previous one, which advocates more strongly for each other (cf. Paech, 2019). Instead of toiling 40 hours in the factory, they should rather work only 20 hours and devote the rest of the time to the community. This can be in the form of craft services for the community, through self-sufficiency with food to a certain degree in their own gardens by growing plants and keeping animals. The consumption needs of individual members of a society can also be covered by exchanging or giving away no longer needed goods, e.g., children's clothing or toys, to increase the usage duration of everyday items. Wear parts of washing machines can be repaired more often, clothes can be sewn and exchanged, computers can be dismantled and recycled. This reduces the acute consumption need, one can get by with less money and does not necessarily have to rely on a growing economy. According to Paech, monetary is replaced by social capital. The person in the community with his network of exchange and self-sufficiency replaces growth to a certain extent. However, a company and the economy as a whole cannot generally do without growth in order to help employees and the population to a certain income or prosperity.

Regardless of whether one grants such a "post-growth economy" chances of realization or not, every person today must ask themselves whether it always has to be more, better, richer, or whether they can be satisfied with a certain level of consumption. Do I always have to have more than my neighbor? Do I need different variants of every piece of clothing? Can I live in more than one house or apartment at the same time? The question that those who professionally deal with economics and politics must ask is: Do we necessarily need an ever-increasing growth of the national economy, or do we not first have to start looking at the gap between rich and poor, between winners and losers of this economy, and consider how we can reduce this discrepancy instead of increasing it? The best would of course be both: growth of the national economy *and* a reduction of the discrepancies. Perhaps then with an appropriate growth of the economy, it will be easier to achieve prosperity for all. What applies nationally is of outstanding importance with regard to the global economy.

6.5 Globalization and Digitization

Globalization, worldwide trade, is not a new phenomenon. Already in antiquity, goods of all kinds were sold and traded to the most remote corners of the far-flung Roman Empire. In the Middle Ages, the Augsburg Fuggers created a nearly worldwide trade empire. However, worldwide trade has entered a new stage of development in recent years through the Internet. Transport and communication costs have dropped dramatically, just think of sea and air transport or telephone calls between continents. The tariff level has not only dropped to a historical low with the creation of the EU internal market, which would not fundamentally change even with the UK's exit from the EU ("Brexit"). Between 1960 and 2008 alone, foreign trade increased by a factor of 15.5 at constant prices (cf. Federal Agency for Civic Education, 2018). The number of internationally active companies has more than octupled from the end of the 1960s to 2008 (cf. Pietsch, 2017, p. 65).

Over the years, global brands have emerged that promise the same standard everywhere in the world: Fast food chains like McDonald's or Pizza Hut exist everywhere. Television formats like "Voice of Germany" or "Who Wants to Be a Millionaire?" are marketed globally. Stars of acting and music are known worldwide. News about events of global importance are shared on social networks and online games like "Clash of Clans" are played worldwide. The fashion of global brands is already available everywhere in the world. Luxury brands like Gucci, Hermès, Prada or Louis Vuitton can be found in luxury boutiques all over the world, as well as sports goods from Puma, Adidas or Nike.

Globalization creates a worldwide market with 7.5 billion potential consumers. According to Ricardo's theory of comparative cost advantages (cf. Eltis, 1989, especially p. 200), countries can specialize in certain products, Germany for example in automobiles and machines, and thus reap specialization gains. But not everyone in the world benefits from the increased prosperity through global trade. The profits mainly benefit the industrialized countries (EU, USA, Australia, parts of Asia such as China). However, especially in the poor countries of the world, particularly in the countries south of the Sahara, but also in countries like India, the number of people who have to get by with the equivalent of $1.25 per day and head is still increasing. All of Africa contributes only 3.1 % of the global economic output, measured by gross domestic product (GDP). The countries with the highest GDP, USA, China, Japan, Germany, UK, together account for about 51 % of the global GDP (cf. Federal Agency for Civic Education bpb, 2016).

Globalization brings with it far-reaching ecological consequences in addition to economic effects. In the search for marketable timber, forests are being substantially cleared worldwide, and water is being excessively used for thermal power plants. Alternative energy sources such as wind or solar energy are not yet sufficient to meet global energy needs. Therefore, coal and nuclear power plants remain in operation in individual countries for an unforeseeable period. Global trade flows are accompanied by global financial transactions. Money flows around the world to generate profits on stock exchanges, in hedge funds or private equity companies. Often, these transactions serve to hedge currencies or commodity trade. In some cases, such as in the form of highly speculative financial derivatives, they are used solely to gamble, without any productive function for the global economy, they are supposed to generate astronomical profits for individual banks, as happened in the financial crisis in 2008. The profits were then "individualized", especially among the investment bankers, the losses were then "socialized" through the state and ultimately the citizens (cf. among others Hank & Petersdorff, 2013). Therefore, the effects of globalization on the economy and society must be viewed in a differentiated manner.

Another element of current and future economic development is digitization. The effects of digitization on the world of work become most apparent when looking at individual sectors as examples. Due to their importance, we focus on the automotive industry in Germany, where the incisions caused by the digital world will be very significant. The automotive industry is facing its biggest upheaval in decades. In addition to the increasing electrification of cars—from hybrid models that combine an electric motor and a conventional combustion engine, to the electric motor with range extender, to the purely electrically powered car—the market will be dominated by autonomous and interconnected cars. Furthermore, the proportion of vehicles shared through car sharing will increase worldwide. When asking what effects digitization will have on the automotive industry, the mentioned trends will play a major role.

In a large-scale study, the international management consultancy McKinsey 2015 (cf. McKinsey, 2015) intensively questioned over 3000 customers, about 1000 each in Germany, the USA and China, about the effects of networking and autonomous driving. All customers had recently bought a car. These results were compared with those of a survey of 20 top executives from selected car manufacturers. The results shed an interesting light on the future development of the automotive industry against the backdrop of digitization.

The authors of the study found that the cars of tomorrow will increasingly integrate the communication and information services of social media: In the foreseeable future, drivers in every car will have access to their emails, SMS, WhatsApp or social media such as Facebook or Instagram. Today, all kinds of smartphones are already used to play music via Bluetooth connections or to install apps that allow the car to be used remotely. For example, the current location and fuel level can be queried from a distance and the auxiliary heater can be switched on. In the future, the direct exchange of data between the vehicle and the outside world will be possible without a smartphone. Traffic, weather and road conditions will be retrieved from the cloud in the future. This will simplify route planning and the search for a parking space with a corresponding electric charging station. Vehicles will communicate with each other to report the next traffic jam in time, up to the automatic adjustment of speed. Internet access in the car allows in principle the same activities as at home at the desk: For example, online orders could be placed using voice control, news could be retrieved or YouTube videos could be watched. But also car-specific services are possible such as hotlines, online bookable workshop appointments including online remote diagnosis as well as test drives or feedback to the manufacturer.

Autonomous driving will be implemented by car manufacturers in several stages. Today, a driver of a current

7-series BMW model can already park his car remotely in his garage or a parking space. Driver assistance systems such as lane change warning, brake force booster with collision warning etc. support the driver. Parking assistants enable parking while the driver takes his hand off the steering wheel. In the next stage, it will be possible, for example, to drive with "autopilot" for a certain time in slow city traffic or on the motorway. Then the car steers autonomously via distance measurement and navigation and only requests the driver to take over the steering wheel and control again in unclear or dangerous situations via an acoustic signal. In the last stage, the car will take over the control completely autonomously, the driver can sit back and relax and enjoy the journey or go about his work.

What do these trends mean for companies, jobs and society?

Business
For businesses, digitization and the direct communication it enables with their customers offer an undeniable advantage: they can tailor their offerings directly to their users or customers. For example, if a customer listens to classical music in the car, often travels to Italy, and then uses a concierge service to suggest suitable restaurants including navigation to them. He uses car sharing in big cities, e.g., during a weekend visit to Berlin, and his app shows him where the next free parking space is and how to get there. In addition, the customer enjoys his car and prefers sporty driving. If he allows the manufacturer to participate in the use of individual services in the car through his consent, specific offers can be actively compiled for the customer. Thus, in the case mentioned above, the manufacturer can actively arrange concert tickets in his hometown or surroundings for the lover of classical music, offer events for sporty driving with a comparable or next higher model,

or show the car sharing offer in certain cities that are also booked as holiday destinations. Furthermore, workshop appointments can be announced online and arranged immediately if the customer wishes. He defines how much information he wants to reveal about himself and his activities. The highest commandment is the sovereignty over one's own data and the sensible handling of these in mutual agreement and for mutual benefit.

Digitization also means building up new knowledge and skills among employees, training them accordingly or simply hiring employees with the appropriate knowledge. This not only means recruiting employees who can analyze data, but also software and app developers who can develop the processes and the necessary data infrastructure in the latest, "agile" technology. Individual companies like Google, Apple, Amazon etc. are moving closer together with car manufacturers and insurance companies to create a common benefit for their customers, as we have seen in the example mentioned above. Jobs are being converted, for example from combustion engines more towards electromobility and services. Traditional self-driving cars are supplemented or partially replaced by autonomous ones.

The culture of companies will also change in the coming years towards flatter hierarchies, self-determined, agile teams, in which the old-style bosses develop into moderators or coaches. The fight for the best talents will also be reflected in the corresponding start-up culture. Gone are the days of hierarchically thinking bosses with ties and large anterooms. It will increasingly be the technically participating, founder-oriented executives without airs who will set the tone in the future. The single office as a status symbol has served its purpose. What counts are the cool working atmosphere and an exciting topic or project, be it app or software development or a new online model. No more 1000-page concepts will be written, but prototypes will be developed directly with which future products can be anticipated.

Jobs

Certainly, some jobs will disappear or become significantly fewer in the coming years, such as jobs related to the combustion engine or those of insurance agents. Books, for example, are increasingly being bought online thanks to Amazon, thus reducing the number of jobs in stationary bookstores. The estimates regarding the extent of a change in the working world vary. The philosopher Richard David Precht (cf. Precht, 2018, p. 23 ff.) predicts that in the coming years there will be fewer and fewer people who will have an eight-hour working day. Millions of jobs could disappear along with the typical employee jobs. Computers and robots are supposed to take over the job in the future by handling standardized processes such as an insurance application online or robots increasingly taking over production. Transports from A to B will in the future be taken over by autonomously driving cars or transporters or—in the case of letters or parcels—by drones. Autonomous cars will be booked via a flat rate for a certain time via smartphone app. Likewise, according to Precht, computers could replace legal expertise in the context of artificial intelligence. Today, Google is already used to search for medical symptoms and a suitable diagnosis is prepared before going to the doctor. This eliminates thousands of jobs. The missing income would then have to be covered by a basic income (cf. Precht, 2018, p. 125 ff.). Education in the sense of knowledge of digital content and further education will become even more important in the future.

Society

The age of the internet will bring enormous advantages. Most people in the world have a computer, tablet and/or smartphone and an internet connection. This keeps them constantly connected: with family, friends, acquaintances, colleagues, but also like-minded people in corresponding forums. They use social media like Facebook or Instagram, communicate via WhatsApp, chat via Skype or Zoom. They share videos, photos, voice messages, blog their thoughts, follow friends and stars and rate them through corresponding likes. Modern television is the relevant YouTube channels, online games partly replace the game on the street.

The digital world is increasingly replacing personal contact. This can be seen as very regrettable, but it does not change the fact itself. Especially young people communicate almost exclusively online via their smartphones. Personal conversations and phone calls are becoming less important. Trends are almost exclusively coming from the digital world, but globally and around the clock. Social networks are increasingly replacing the real ones made of flesh and blood. However, bullying also takes place in the online world. Crimes do not stop at the online world either. Sociologists view the increasing digitalization of communication in society critically (cf. exemplarily Hurtz, 2017), as it can lead to a creeping loneliness and social alienation. You can also play football realistically on the Playstation or Xbox without leaving your room.

Like everything in life, the increasing digitalization of society has two sides: On the one hand, you are confronted daily with other opinions from other countries, making you more open-minded and better informed. Universities are increasingly recording their events on video and uploading them to YouTube; some world-renowned universities like Harvard even offer online courses

6 The Most Pressing Issues of Tomorrow's Economy

for the masses as part of the "Massive Open Online Courses" (MOOC; cf. Harvard, 2019). Knowledge and information differences between countries are decreasing more and more, as everyone can access the same information and news pool. It is becoming increasingly easier to acquire knowledge. The use of new technologies is becoming an increasingly self-evident tool for the new generation of "digital natives". Thanks to Wikipedia, numerous online libraries of universities and information pages on the Internet, knowledge is becoming increasingly freely available. Knowledge is increasing.

The negative sides are also obvious. In addition to the increasing loneliness and isolation of people "off-line" while living "online", the handling of personal data is very critical. Data that has once been uploaded to social networks is usually stored for life. Search queries on Google and Co. allow an exact data analysis of the user. Amazon offers similar items when searching for an item with a reference to people who have gone through the same search path and bought ("People who bought this item also bought …"). People are almost constantly on the Internet. They exchange ideas, read news, shop, upload photos and videos or watch them. Emails are sometimes written faster today than saying hello. Employers or superiors expect an immediate response to inquiries, sometimes even on weekends. Permanent availability is defined as the standard of the modern age. Not only the correct answer counts, but also the reaction time. Employees and other citizens increasingly feel stressed, overwhelmed and sometimes suffer from chronic exhaustion. High internet consumption sometimes leads to addiction, for example to computer games.

At the end of this short section on digitalization, the questions must be asked, which aspects—negative or positive—will predominate and how we can manage to bring society and economy into line with digitalization. Or as Precht puts it with regard to the upheavals caused by digitalization: In what kind of society do we want to live? I would add the economic component to this question: *In what kind of economy do we want to live?* In an economy that is there for people and not the other way around? What could such an economy look like? The path that the Federal Republic of Germany took after the devastating World War with the social market economy was basically correct. Today it is important to strengthen the "social" component of this market economy (further). Specifically, it could look like this:

We want to live in an economy where no one has to go hungry and everyone has a roof over their head. Everyone should be able to satisfy their basic needs—sufficient food, clothing, shelter—and have enough money left over to do something for their health and to relax on vacation. Health care should be affordable for everyone. Even today, there are still enough people in wealthy Germany who (for various reasons) fall out of statutory health insurance. The economy cannot be obliged to ensure that every job seeker gets a suitable job. This is good and not possible in a market economy without centralist, planning interventions by the state. However, these people without a job could be secured by an unconditional basic income. Especially in times of digitalization, when many jobs are being lost, this could be a way to compensate for a permanent or temporary job loss.

The economy should be supported more than before by the solidarity community. This should not only apply the proven methods of progressive income taxation or inheritance tax, which bring about a certain redistribution of wealth from the "stronger" to the "weaker". In addition, the "civil society" is called upon: The willingness to donate and help, especially of the part of the population that is materially better off, is great. This was not only shown by the willingness to help at the beginning of the refugee crisis, for example at Munich's main train station. Internationally, many, especially very wealthy people, are willing to donate a not insignificant part of their wealth, for example to restore burnt-out parts of historically significant buildings like Notre Dame in Paris.

It should be an economy where the young help the old with their ideas, their knowledge of new media and technology in general. In return, the old share their life experience with the young and support them with advice and action. Thus, the older ones with their extensive professional experience could help the younger ones to choose the right job or the right training. "Coaching" is the keyword here, not only for the new generation of executives, but also for the collaboration between young and old. With a little more solidarity and community thinking, many would already be helped. This active collaboration between the individual parts of society, but also the economy, would be desirable. This would lead to a "New Social Market Economy" against the background of the challenges of digitization, ecology and globalization. The right impulses from society are just missing. Someone has to make the start.

6.6 Economy and Ecology

Economy and ecology inherently pursue different objectives. The economy strives for efficiency, for the least possible use of factors to achieve a certain target quantity, or tries to achieve the maximum result with given means. Ecology is primarily concerned with a harmonious coexistence of living beings, whether human or animal, and a careful handling of the respective habitat. The potential negative consequences for the environment are accepted in the economy as unavoidable collateral damage. The economic pursuit of wealth accumulation with simultaneous cost optimization and clear competitive orientation is opposed by the ecological law of life in harmony with nature. Much has already been done: For example, fluorocarbon-containing (CFC) sprays have been banned, and the Kyoto targets for reducing CO_2 emissions underline humanity's will to leave nature as unharmed as possible for future generations. However, there is still much to do. The economy of the future must be measured by its contribution to improving the ecological situation in the world. Further growth, without considering the negative consequences of economic action on the human ecosystem, i.e., a continuation as before, cannot exist. We only have one world. Even if the thought is not new, it remains crucial for economic thoughts about the future.

The ecological core challenges of the economy are all well known: raw material and fossil energy reserves are limited and cannot be further exploited without sustainably disturbing the natural balance. Thus, oil will only be available in limited quantities, as will certain metals such as lithium for battery production or plastics. Starting points here are all forms of recycling, whether of metal, plastics, paper, or the replacement by biodegradable substances. A good example of an urgently needed corrective intervention in the strong resource use is plastic waste. According to the Federal Environment Agency, up to 500,000 tons of plastics are transported into the seas in the EU each year (see Federal Environment Agency, 2018a). All types of plastic packaging pose a major problem for the environment. According to the Federal Environment Agency, about 18.2 million tons of packaging waste were produced in Germany in 2016 (see Federal Environment Agency, 2019). This was the highest value in years. This development is also easily observable in the habits of daily life: books are still often sold shrink-wrapped in plastic for protection. The reader may want to browse a copy in the bookstore. In the end, however, he wants to take home or give away a new packaged book. At the same time, publishers usually only take back books in packaged form from the bookseller as returns. The trend towards fast food or "coffee to go" is increasing, and with it the packaging. Online ordering is increasing. Amazon delivers more and more directly to the front door, including packaging. The number of one- and two-person households is increasing, especially among older people, and with it the smaller portions of food or household utensils that must be packaged per individual (single portions instead of family packs).

Now, not all packaging is the same. Recyclable fabric bags, for example, are better suited for transporting books than plastic bags. Reusable packaging helps to reduce waste. Deposit bottles have the advantage that they are more likely to be returned due to the economic incentive. Here too, the consumer can actively contribute to increasing sustainability by choosing the right packaging or by taking a previously purchased packaging, such as a shopping bag, back to the store to transport the new goods. The different recycling rate of the packaging is largely predetermined: for example, 75 % of glass packaging, 70 % of paper, cardboard or carton packaging and 60 % of aluminum packaging are recycled according to regulations (see Federal Environment Agency, 2019).

The result of such an ecologically unsustainable strategy is that the proportion of plastic particles in the sea is now six times higher than that of plankton (see Krieger, 2016), which fish urgently need as food. With the consumption of fish, which inevitably also ingest plastic waste with their food today, humans are ultimately indirectly exposed to plastic waste again. Currently, only just under 30 % of the (continuously growing) plastic waste in the EU is recycled (see European Parliament, 2018). The objective already exists to curb the consumption of plastics throughout the EU. Whether the practical implementation will succeed will be shown over time. Certainly, economic approaches such as the introduction of a tax on plastics should also be considered. However, humans must also participate by preferring certain products, e.g., those with an environmentally friendly label, and avoiding others, generally consuming less, or using certain products such as electrical and electronic devices for longer.

A second ecological challenge lies in production and energy generation. Pollutants such as dangerous chemicals or radioactive material burden the environment. Unwanted by-products of the production of industrial products can contaminate soil, water, and air sustainably. In recent months, there has been much discussion about the consequences of using the pesticide glyphosate in agriculture. Its long-term effects on nature are unclear. Therefore, glyphosate should initially not be used or only used under strict conditions (see Oberhuber, 2015). Similar caution is advised when using so-called biocides in the environment (see Federal Environment Agency, 2018b Biocides). Cleaning and disinfecting agents, wood preservatives, but also mosquito spray and ant poison are potentially dangerous for the environment, humans, and animals according to the Federal Environment Agency and must be subjected to strict control. The same applies to the residues of certain drugs in drinking water.

The long transport routes to bring mass products to consumers should not be underestimated. Everyone knows the distances that certain products cover to end up in the refrigerated section of the local supermarket. The advantage of a large selection of fresh products such

6 The Most Pressing Issues of Tomorrow's Economy

as strawberries or fish at competitive prices is offset by the environmental impact resulting from long logistics routes: All modes of transport consume energy, whether train, truck, ship, or airplane. The latter two modes of transport consume large amounts of diesel or kerosene, respectively, and therefore have a corresponding pollutant load in the form of CO_2 and NO_X (see Flämig, 2018). Even if it is assumed that more and more renewable energy, e.g., in the form of electric drives in trucks and ships, will be used, it will take several years before the emission load can be significantly reduced.

These core challenges may suffice at this point to demonstrate the necessity of a compelling interaction between economy and ecology (see, among others, Müller, 2015, especially p. 187 ff.). There are hardly any limits to the economic approaches to sustainability. Non-environmentally conscious actions of individuals, but also of companies, can be economically sanctioned, for example through fines, special levies, or taxes on certain substances or chemicals. Recycling quotas can be prescribed as well as the mandatory introduction of reusable packaging, deposit bottles, etc. Increased consumer education can lead to more conscious consumption, such as avoiding plastic bags or extended use of certain electronic products. Essential for the economy and its research is the trend towards sustainability. This starts in the minds of economic actors: The environment as a limited resource that needs to be preserved for future generations. A clean environment is not available for free: It costs money, requires attentive action, and the willingness of all participants to be sustainable. Responsibility for the community instead of self-interest, timely and long-term provision instead of short-term action without regard for the consequences for the environment and people. This also applies on a global scale, as environmental pollution does not stop at national or continental borders. The economy and its researchers and idea providers are challenged to provide politics and society with the best possible strategies and tools to adequately meet the ecological challenges. A big task is coming up for the economy!

Approaches to an ecology-oriented economy already concern the objective. Thus, the goal of environmental protection could be incorporated into a kind of economic constitution. The same applies to the objectives of individual companies. For example, companies could commit to using environmental resources as gently as possible, to use sustainable materials, or to no longer use certain materials at all. For example, certain publishers no longer use plastic films to protect their new books, but only connect both book covers with a symbolic adhesive strip. The automotive industry is fully committed to electromobility or hydrogen drives in the future, with the electricity being generated from sustainable energy. Resources such as water can be reused in production. Recycling of plastic bottles or steel in all forms helps to keep the cycle of production and consumption in manageable quantities ("Circular Economy").

The "Sharing Economy", i.e., the economy that aims to share products among various customers, also helps to protect the environment. Apartments are shared via providers like Airbnb, so that existing living space is used by several people, at least temporarily. Cars are shared in car sharing, thus being used and utilized more efficiently. If this is done with electric vehicles, the environment is doubly protected: on the one hand by reducing the number of people who buy a car and on the other hand by environmentally friendly electric drives. This paves the way for a "post-carbon society" (cf. futureInstitute: Megatrend Neo-Ecology, 2019), i.e., a society that does without coal as an energy carrier. Companies can "educate" their customers to behave more environmentally conscious by advertising for more sustainable products. They can evaluate and select suppliers according to certified environmental standards. Production processes can be continuously optimized to improve the ecological balance in the production of products.

Further approaches for a sustainable economy could be the promotion of organic products and the approach to keep the logistics between customers and producers as short and lean as possible ("direct trade"). This is supported by the attitude of consumers, but also employees of the companies: A conscious handling of resources is maintained, which tends more towards minimalism than towards maximalism. A longer use of durable consumer goods, but also textiles is aimed for, thus going against the trend of buying a new, fashionable piece of clothing every season. The goal is a conscious renunciation of environmentally harmful products and generally a reduction of consumption and thus the minimization of one's own waste (cf. futureInstitute: Megatrend Neo-Ecology, 2019). These are just a few exemplary approaches that should suffice as a sketch here.

6.7 The Working Society of Tomorrow

Nowadays, the term "Industry 4.0" is often mentioned in many specialist symposia and meetings of representatives of the economy with politics (cf. Merz, 2015). The term is not only supposed to herald the future, so to speak as version 4.0, but refers to the nomenclature common in software updates in releases, i.e., new versions. The future of work will therefore increasingly be determined by the latest IT technology. If version 4.0 is at the doorstep, there must have been previous editions of the industrial world.

The "versioning", one could also say, the individual industrial revolutions, begins with the introduction of mechanical production technology in the late 18th century (1.0), which was followed by division of labor mass production "of Fordian character" thanks to electrification at the beginning of the 20th century (2.0). The increasing use of electronics and information technology ignited the next stage in the middle of the 20th century and enabled further automation of production (3.0).

The provisional conclusion was now the fourth stage of the industrial revolution with the Internet as infrastructure. Physical objects such as machines, logistics and storage systems, operating resources etc. are connected via the Internet in such a way that they can independently trigger actions and control each other on the basis of exchanged information. This is generally called the "Internet of Things" (cf. Schipper, 2015). Examples of such automated cooperation of individual elements of production are e.g., driverless transport vehicles, inventory of stock levels with the help of autonomous flying robots, the drones, automatic single-piece production of shoes or textiles, networking of machines and plants.

What does this industrial revolution 4.0 mean for the activities of tomorrow's workers? It is clear that simple activities, such as the transport from A to B, in production, machine operation and manual data entry will be replaced to a large extent by the new technology (cf. Eckert, 2018). Control and monitoring functions of skilled workers will be automated to a greater extent than before and will no longer require the same high qualification as before. Required goods and commodities could be machine-disposed and called up in time without the employee's intervention. What remains are activities such as demanding maintenance and repair tasks, certain manual production skills, e.g., on the production line, but above all more complex coordination, control and decision-making functions. Profound knowledge of IT systems is becoming increasingly important, as is the complex interplay of the entire production process. Programming skills and the ability to control and coordinate complex systems in interaction are becoming increasingly important for the skilled worker of old. For management, Industry 4.0 means that certain planning, control and coordination activities are passed on to the skilled workers. They are given an even stronger control and coordination function than before, which is not made easier by a growing number of figures, data and facts.

These outlined challenges primarily concern the manufacturing industry. In general, not only will new media and communication tools change the world of work, but above all a new emerging generation of workers who will approach work with different attitudes (cf. Rövekamp, 2016). The primacy of profession and career will increasingly give way to the desire to lead a happy life and enjoy a comfortable living. The big luxury car or a single office with an anteroom is no longer desirable, but rather a demanding, interesting job that allows a lot of freedom and self-realization, but also more leisure time for hobbies, family, and social engagement. Luxury products like cars or apartments are increasingly being shared and seen purely functionally, i.e., it will be about driving the car from A to B, staying in the rented holiday accommodation. The upcoming generation, at least in Western countries, does not want to live to work, but to work to live.

Work is increasingly taking place independent of location and time (cf. among others Lange, 2018): whether in a café with a cappuccino with a smartphone or laptop within reach, or from home, or on a park bench. Many activities such as programming jobs for apps or other internet applications are assigned on the basis of specific target specifications such as allowed time, required quality, etc., the fulfillment of which is the task of self-determined teams. The currently popular method of agile programming according to the so-called Scrum method in companies points the way to this autonomous working method of the development teams. Hierarchies are becoming increasingly unimportant: The times of impressively looking leaders of all kinds, often men in the past, with their well-fitting suits and fashionable ties and the formal address of the employees will soon finally belong to the past. The trend is towards jeans and sneakers or at most to "Smart Casual", a more elegant but casual outfit. The tie as a symbol of sovereignty has definitely served its purpose. The atmosphere is rather casual. People work in small teams that devote themselves to their project work. The formula of the confidential "you" is becoming more and more the rule rather than the exception. The new world of work and its work culture will correspond to that of the countless start-ups, as they started their triumphant march around the world years ago, especially in Silicon Valley, California. A laptop and smartphone are often completely sufficient as basic equipment.

However, some activities will not be possible without the physical effort of people. Members of the nursing professions will continue to be physically and psychologically challenged in an aging country like Germany—despite the progress of technology. Employees in the catering industry will still—thank God—serve food and drinks. The path to the robot or drone is still far. Saleswomen and salesmen will continue to advise customers in stationary stores, although the internet is also penetrating these areas with time-independent online purchases. Even classic housework does not do itself. Many topics remain focused on people, although technology will significantly improve working life in such areas as well.

This upheaval of the world of work in the course of Economy 4.0, as I would like to call it in reference to Industry 4.0, will only succeed through investment in education. From an early age, children must not only be properly instructed in the use of computers and smartphones, but also specifically prepared for the changes in the world of work. Adult workers must resort to the diverse offers of further education agencies more often than today. You are never too old to learn something new. It is motivating to see that these further education efforts are anchored in most party programs in Germany and that the preparation of citizens for the digital age is being promoted. Only in this way is a life with a future-proof job possible. The alternative would be the long-term unemployment of a part of the left-behind population, which inevitably goes hand in hand with the loss of human dignity. This must be avoided at all costs. But what would an economy look like that makes people happy and promises a good life? Wouldn't it be a good idea to think intensively about this at the end of our journey? We also want to shed light on what happiness actually means. In section 6.8 we will also design an "economy of the good life".

6.8 The Economy of the Good Life

As we have seen, economic action is an activity given to man in his world. Even our ancestors traded and exchanged, initially goods for goods, later goods for money. Already here, as we have found, misdevelopments emerged, such as in the form of unrestrained greed, to possess money for the sake of money and not as an equivalent for the exchange of goods of daily life. But does money actually make people happy?

First, let's briefly deal with the term happiness. Interestingly, in English there are essentially two terms for happiness: There is the term *luck,* which can be translated as lottery luck, random luck. A player who makes a big win in the casino or in the lottery is happy in this sense, not as a result of his lifestyle, he just had "luck in the game". The second term *Happiness* is the one we are considering: life happiness, satisfaction with oneself and one's life circumstances. This life happiness is to be found. The ancient Greeks used a fitting word for this, *eudaimonia,* the blissfulness, which everyone should strive for. The founding fathers of the United States of America wrote the pursuit of happiness, "the Pursuit of Happiness", into their Declaration of Independence. But does money, or more generally, the economy make us happier?

There seems to be agreement that happiness first and foremost depends on whether one is physically and mentally healthy and does not suffer any lack. Some philosophers went so far as to say that happiness is the absence of pain or a state of "peace of mind", the *ataraxia* (Epicurus). Of course, each of you can imagine moments of happiness: health, a cheerful family with children, many friends, meaningful work, a beautiful home, grandchildren and much more. Not all of these moments of happiness have to do with the economy.

If you keep in mind the most important elements of happiness, physical and mental health and absence of deprivation—the US psychologist Abraham Maslow called this the lowest category of needs in his hierarchy of needs—then we quickly agree that this can only be achieved with a certain income. But does a high income and thus more money per month make people happier? The happiness research of economics, the "Happiness Economics" (cf. Weimann et al., 2011), has been dealing with this topic for several decades. The discussion was

6 The Most Pressing Issues of Tomorrow's Economy

triggered by the US researcher Richard Easterlin, who showed the limits of happiness with the Easterlin Paradox named after him: In his study, he showed that while an individual becomes happier with a higher income, this has no effect on the happiness of an entire nation. The British economist Angus Deaton, who received the Alfred Nobel Memorial Prize for Economic Sciences in 2015, was able to prove from 450,000 interviews with Americans that people's sense of happiness increased up to an annual gross income of 75,000 dollars (cf. Ettel & Zschäpitz, 2015). After that, an increase in income had no further detectable effects on the feelings of happiness of the citizens surveyed.

However, this is only half the truth, because Deaton and his colleague Daniel Kahneman, also a recipient of the Alfred Nobel Memorial Prize for Economics in 2002, found in another study (cf. Faigle, 2010) that life satisfaction grows with increasing income, continuously, although the feeling of happiness does not intensify further. Apparently, it is enough for people to secure a certain basic supply of food, clothing and housing, plus health care, perhaps to go on vacation once or twice a year and, if things go very well, to pay off a property at some point. However, the reverse is true that in Germany below a monthly net income of 1200 EUR, every increase of 100 EUR has three times as much impact on the feeling of happiness as above 1200 EUR. This is intuitively understandable: People who do not have enough money for the bare necessities such as food, clothing, a roof over their heads and health care, cannot objectively be called happy. An increase in income of just 100 EUR per month already significantly increases the scope for living, especially if you have to calculate down to the last cent.

Happiness research has also shown that in countries that are objectively poor, such as Bhutan or Bangladesh, and that have been measuring not only material wealth but also the state of happiness of the entire population for decades (cf. Wallacher, 2007), this state of happiness is higher than in some much wealthier countries. It is a truism that happiness is an individual phenomenon and depends on many factors, such as partnership, family, a happy childhood, fulfilling work, friends, etc. Nevertheless, material wealth, money, is a decisive factor. Money enables the purchase of things that increase personal well-being, such as a beautiful house, a great car, a nice vacation, etc. However, the influence of money on a healthy lifestyle should not be underestimated: I can live healthier, eat healthier, go for regular medical check-ups, dress warmer, etc. Higher incomes are associated with higher pension payments, a house that provides security in old age. However, this positive correlation between high income and life satisfaction or happiness only works up to a certain limit. After that, the increases in happiness decrease more and more. Those who have enough, a little more money hardly elicits a smile, and other things like personal crises or experiences become more important. On the other hand, many more men in the younger generation want to participate in the upbringing of their children, forgo a big career in favor of their offspring, and also take parental leave. Some workers in their mid-50s want to give up a high income in favor of a higher quality of life and retire early from their careers. More money does not always bring more individual happiness.

Two aspects of the topic of economy and happiness should be mentioned here. First: Not absolute, but relative wealth is decisive for most people's sense of happiness from a certain minimum income. Neighbors compare who has the more imposing house, the larger garden, or the nicer car. Especially men compare their supposed incomes or their professional position. To put it bluntly: A man who has the larger row house in a less affluent neighborhood is more satisfied than a man who lives in a posh suburb of Munich, but has by far the smallest property there.

Secondly: What matters is what you do with the additional money. There are many personalities in society, but also ordinary citizens, who put themselves materially or personally at the service of a charitable institution, support the homeless, donate food for the food bank, found and finance a non-profit institution to support citizens in social difficulties. Or they award educational scholarships to poor students and sponsor school meals for primary school children all over Germany (cf. exemplarily Hasse, 2012). There is not enough space here to present and appreciate all these examples.

Now that we have thought about what happiness in the economy can be, I would like to sketch an "economy of the good life" in the following. I do not want to describe an economy as it is, but as I think it could be, even though the concrete design could be very difficult. Nevertheless, the sketching of such a "social utopia" in the sense of a target image is important.

One of the most famous sentences of the famous US President John F. Kennedy (1961) is: "Ask not what your country can do for you—ask what you can do for your country." I would like to reformulate this quote for my purposes and formulate the goal of an economy as I imagine it: *One should not ask what man can do for the economy, but what the economy can do for man.* The world does not revolve around the economy—although one could get that impression again and again—but around man. And he should also be at the center of economic considerations. In the following, I would like to describe, admittedly somewhat idealized, a social utopia in which the economy puts man back at the center.

I do not want to label it with any "label" that can then be marketed, but rather define a desirable target state from my point of view, how the economy could serve man. Without an idea, a *narrative,* a mission, to which we all want to move our economic activities, I believe nothing new can emerge. Not without reason, great companies started with a clear mission. The social market economy also started after the Second World War with an idea. In the following, I want to sketch individual elements of this mission, which I call social utopia. Although the term utopia, as a non-place, from ancient Greek *ou topos* for "no place, nowhere", signals that this idea is not easily realizable, I still want to dare to stimulate a way of acting. If we all agree on the target state, it might be easier for us to find and go the way there together. The fact that I focus on Germany for the sake of simplicity does not mean that individual elements do not also apply worldwide.

No one has to starve in Germany, thank God. This is already a great achievement of the social market economy and its actors. The welfare state guarantees social benefits for the needy, the mandatory health and nursing care insurances finance the costs of doctor visits as well as hospital and nursing home stays. Numerous soup kitchens, such as the food banks or other charitable institutions and homeless shelters, provide food and shelter for the poorest part of the population. It is a hard life full of deprivation, poverty, and illness, but the state at least ensures survival. But that cannot be all. Is it really sufficient that in Germany no one has to starve or even freeze to death anymore? Can we as a society be satisfied with that? Shouldn't a country as rich as Germany also guarantee its poorest citizens a decent, a dignified life? And what role can economics play in this?

From my point of view, the first thing that needs to be changed is the objective of economics. The goal of economics, "No one should starve in Germany" (There are still too many people, but also children, who are hungry in Germany today!), must become the more ambitious goal "In Germany, all people must be able to live decently". What sounds like an unrealistic demand, I would like to try to fill with life in the following. It is completely clear that many elements of what I will now present as a proposal already exist in one form or another. However, I would like to rely much more on voluntariness and the compassion of fellow citizens, especially the wealthier ones, and less on state coercion. I will explain what this means in concrete terms in the following.

The first question we need to answer is: What do we understand by a decent life? Without becoming too philosophical, we can pin this down to a few basic needs of life. Thus, the basic needs of every human being's daily life must be satisfied: enough to eat and drink, suitable clothing for all seasons, a roof over one's head. In case of illness, a quick visit to the doctor must be possible. This is part of the basic security of human life. However, this is not yet enough for a decent life. This includes an interesting job, for many a family, but also enough leisure time to pursue hobbies, take care of loved ones, or simply rest or go on vacation. A corresponding leisure offer or even vacation must be affordable. Many people in Germany cannot afford this today. Often, this is only possible with a well-paid job, in metropolitan areas sometimes even with two for dual earners. Such a job, in turn, can only be obtained with a corresponding education. This is probably what most people in this country imagine a decent or even good life to be. I am not talking about a life of luxury after winning a million in the lottery, but about a life free of material worries at least.

However, the reality today is that many people live on Hartz IV and have to get by on about 400 EUR per month per person. Many are homeless or can barely afford their apartment. Despite decades of hard work, the pension is not enough in old age to finance housing and life. Not to mention vacation and possible hobbies. What can be saved is passed on to the children. Christmas presents often fall by the wayside or have to be saved elsewhere. If we now transfer our thought of a decent life for all citizens as the goal of a successful economy to the material prerequisites, this means:

- All citizens need a material basic security that enables them to feed themselves adequately and ideally balanced, to dress and to afford a sufficiently large accommodation with affordable rent.
- They all need affordable comprehensive health and nursing care.
- There must be time left for all citizens to pursue their hobbies, whether they are sports or cultural, and to go on vacation at least once a year.
- A good education should prepare all citizens for the respective suitable profession, which at the end of a working life leads to a pension with which they can afford the above-mentioned points of a decent life, always provided they have managed their money normally.

What contribution can economics make to this, or what basic prerequisites must be given?

It is undisputed that the wealthy part of the population, at least the upper half, can afford this decent life without the state and already lives decently and well today, at least materially. So it is about the lower half of the population, strictly speaking about the lower third, which has little or no wealth or is in debt. Since the lower third of the population includes many people who have no work and/or no housing and thus no chance of self-financing, this population group would have to receive money from another source. This could be, for example, an unconditional basic income (cf. Bohmeyer & Cornelsen, 2019). The higher this is per capita, the more likely it is to cover basic needs. The exact amount is difficult to determine, but depends on the respective place of residence and the costs incurred there. Thus, an income in Munich will have to be higher than in a small town in Mecklenburg-Vorpommern. If we base this on a family with two children, then we will have to set at least 1000 EUR per month per person in order to finance rent, clothing and nutrition in a city with average living costs and still have time for hobbies or vacation.

The question is whether all citizens should receive an unconditional basic income in the interest of fairness, or only those up to a certain wealth or annual income. Let's assume that every citizen received this unconditional basic income, then alternatively, every wealthy citizen could completely or at least partially forego their basic income in favor of needy citizens. The basic income would be paid until the end of life and would not be offset against the pension. This would ensure that there is enough money available for a decent life even in old age. The state would have to promote and rent out missing apartments at subsidized prices, like the classic social housing. The rent could be offset against the unconditional basic income. Just as every child today has a right to a daycare place—even in the expensive metropolises—every citizen would have a right to an apartment. This right would greatly increase the pressure to build apartments.

The ideas for financing such an unconditional basic income are numerous and have already been discussed in various party programs in Germany, but also in other countries. The proposals range from a higher inheritance or income tax (especially for top earners) to a progressive wealth tax (the higher the wealth, the higher the tax rate) to a financial transaction tax (Precht, 2018, p. 135 ff.) e.g. on stock purchases and sales. These are not new ideas. What is new from my point of view is the stronger consideration of voluntariness, the appeal to the solidarity of all citizens: In order to enable the poorest of the population and thus all of us to live a good life, one could also imagine a solidarity fund of the rich and better-off in society. Every wealthy or well-earning middle-class citizen, or anyone who wants or can afford to, could voluntarily pay into the solidarity fund for the benefit of the lower third of the population.

What at first glance seems like an unrealistic undertaking, a social fantasy, turns out to be not so absurd on second glance. If you look at the general willingness of the population to donate, for example in famines or for war victims etc., you will quickly see that there are many, especially wealthy people in Germany, who like to donate considerable sums to charitable organizations. If a part of this money were paid into such a solidarity fund for Germany, many unconditional basic incomes and/or social housing could be financed. As a concrete and pragmatic implementation of this proposal, imagine, for example, an additional field in the tax return where a citizen voluntarily enters a certain donation amount at his discretion, perhaps in the amount of a per mille up to one percent of his annual income. For an average income of 42,000 EUR, this would be a sum of 42 to 420 EUR, but for an income millionaire it would already be 1,000 to 10,000 EUR. Not yet included are the generous donors who annually—or in high-income years—pour far more than one percent of their income into the state's coffers.

As naive as it sounds at first, this idea is not. The money collected annually via the tax office for the solidarity fund would then be invested by a regional and

6 The Most Pressing Issues of Tomorrow's Economy

locally subdivided committee of reputable and experienced experts into various social projects such as housing construction, free daycare, elderly care places or educational institutions. The prioritization is taken over by a committee of local politicians, social experts etc., who, in addition to prioritizing the funds according to the need of the institutions or groups of people eligible for funding, control the use of funds. This would create an additional social budget at all levels, which could ensure that not only does no one in Germany have to go hungry anymore, but also that they can live relatively well. This would be a possible way towards a *New Social Market Economy*, a market economy that serves people and ensures a good life.

Such a social utopia, if it became reality, would have a positive impact on the prosperity of the population. The implementation of the legal claim to a roof over one's head would not only help the homeless or those who already cannot find a cheap apartment, especially in the big metropolises, to improve their living conditions enormously. At the same time, it would benefit the construction industry and all the economic sectors dependent on it, and create or secure jobs. The unconditional basic income would give many people, e.g. low earners, more flexibility to choose a job that best suits their inclinations, even if it is low paid. Nevertheless, they could lead a decent life. If, for example, the financial transaction tax were used to finance it, those affected by this tax would not have to fear significant losses in terms of their prosperity. A financial transaction tax is a tax on transactions in the financial market, which is mainly levied on stock trading.

Poor families, especially their children, often lack the appropriate role models, people who have managed to make something of their lives, to take up an interesting profession or even to accumulate wealth. Often, the marginalized part of the population lacks courage, self-confidence and trust in their own abilities to embark on the path from a good education to a successful or interesting profession. Every person has unique talents that need to be found and promoted. Role models can help with this. For example, successful women and men could go to social hotspot schools and tell how they worked their way up and why they got so far.

Our society lacks the partnership of young and old, rich and poor, successful and marginalized. To help directionless youth, successful entrepreneurs could act as mentors, demonstrating how they started their journey. This could provide young people with a perspective—an incentive that shows them how to learn, what the right attitude is, and what matters in life. If the top and bottom of the social pyramid voluntarily work together, how much more can be achieved in Germany? It doesn't always have to be about state-mandated compulsory measures. Why can't civil society in Germany shoulder more? If this were to happen, such a social utopia of the economy of good life in Germany or elsewhere in the world would no longer be a pipe dream.

6.9 Outlook: Economy in Uncertain Times

In March 2020, the Corona pandemic briefly brought the world economy to the brink of collapse: In Germany, economic performance, measured by gross domestic product, fell by 4.9 % in 2020 compared to the previous year (see Statistisches Bundesamt, 2021; Pietsch, 2022, Chap. 8). In the second quarter of 2020, the German economy experienced a historic slump of 9.7 % compared to 2019. The state was temporarily forced to save the economy through various support services for companies such as short-time work compensation and aid, leading to a state financing deficit of 139.6 billion EUR. Individual sectors were particularly affected by the pandemic: Air traffic in 2020 fell by almost 75 % to just under 58 million passengers at the 24 largest airports in Germany, compared to 2019. The tourism industry recorded only 32 million overnight guests from abroad in 2020 compared to 2019, a drop of two thirds. The restaurant industry's turnover in Germany also shrank by almost half. In contrast, online trade flourished. It rose by 27.8 % from March 2020 to January 2021 compared to the comparable previous year period. Despite short-time work with state compensation at 67 % of the wage level, real wages fell by 1.1 %.

Large events of all kinds had to be cancelled, schools were closed and switched to remote learning. *The pandemic hit a country that was not adequately prepared for it.* Teachers and frustrated families with small or school-age children were responsible for the complete organization and not only required a high tolerance for frustration, but also brought them to the brink of physical and mental exhaustion. *Home office* and *homeschooling* had to be managed in parallel in some cases. Those who were able to work from home were still lucky. Well-situated parents with academic education could not only provide their children with the necessary infrastructure in the form of computers and laptops for homeschooling, but also with advice and assistance. An unbeatable advantage compared to families from socially disadvantaged or educationally distant households.

The question of *how much restriction of freedom* was possible and really necessary or allowed was particularly controversial in society. The rift temporarily went through the entire society in Germany, but also internationally with their different models of lockdown or later opening.

Demonstrations from the perspective of opponents of the Corona measures on the streets alternated with the urgent appeals of epidemiologists to get vaccinated and to comply with all distance and hygiene rules. The most pressing question was: On what criteria do I decide a lockdown, which sectors and businesses should be affected? Later, after the introduction of vaccinations, the crucial question was *which G-regulation should apply* i.e., vaccinated, recovered, tested, or *"boosted"* and whether vaccination can be made mandatory.

Especially for our purposes, the question is significant whether the balance between the health or survival of particularly vulnerable groups and the economy was decided correctly. Was the decision made too quickly and sustainably *against freedom and prosperity?* Of course, one can always discuss whether the lockdown measures could have been avoided in individual cases—for example, restaurant operators and sports event organizers had developed a detailed hygiene concept—but overall it was certainly correct to temporarily shut down the economy to protect health.

Lockdowns, of course, always involve the restriction of civil rights, which must inevitably be accepted. Everyone has the right to free movement, freedom of assembly, consumption, etc. The liberal way of life *per se* is therefore a great good that needs to be protected. However, the measures to contain the spread of the Corona virus have saved many lives, especially those of the elderly and weak, but also people with pre-existing conditions. The argument of some liberal economic ethicists (see, for example, Lütge & Esfeld, 2021) that the costs and benefits of the Corona measures are out of proportion and that the lockdowns imposed by the government are unjustifiable, is not very convincing. The principle still applies: *Every human life that could be saved by a Corona measure, every vaccination carried out, was worth this effort and the sacrifices!* The horrific images from the overcrowded intensive care units in Bergamo and elsewhere in 2020 remain unforgettable. At that time, doctors had to make the almost inhuman ethical decision of who would be connected to the ventilator or remain connected and who would not in case of doubt ("triage"). No one should have to make such a decision about life and death again, and we should never have to see these images again!

The balance of the Corona pandemic is shocking (see Radtke, 2022): As of March 2022, at the time of writing these lines, more than *6 million people worldwide have died from the Sars-CoV-2 pandemic.* With the worldwide confirmed cumulative number of confirmed SARS-CoV-2 infections of more than 448 million, the mortality rate (lethality rate) is therefore just over 1.3 %. The unofficial, statistically unrecorded number, is likely to be much higher. Although most of the affected people have thankfully recovered, many of them suffer from long-term damage ("Long Covid"). The long-lasting symptoms include, among others, reduced resilience, breathing problems or permanent taste and smell impairments (see Ärzteblatt, 2021). These people are marked for life.

The infection rate, the course of Covid-19 and recovery are of course also a question of vaccinations. *Boosted,* i.e., people vaccinated three times, have a lower risk of becoming seriously ill or even dying. There were considerable differences worldwide in the impact of the pandemic, not only in terms of vaccination rates, but also the amounts of vaccine available. While in the rich industrialized countries of the West such as Europe, North America but also in large parts of Asia, the vaccinations were sometimes sluggish but mostly successful, the *poorer countries were not able to do so to the same extent.* They lacked both the financial and technological capabilities i.e., patents and production lines, to procure enough vaccine in the shortest possible time for their population and thus prevent worse. It was therefore an encouraging sign of international solidarity that it was decided at the G7 summit in June 2021 in Cornwall to provide one billion vaccine doses to poorer countries (see Spiegel online from 11.06.2021).

The most impressive images were those of the hospital and nursing staff. They struggled at the forefront, risking their own health to the edge of their capacity limits (and sometimes beyond) for the well-being of their patients. They all deserve our *great and lasting appreciation*. They should finally receive the *payment* that is appropriate for them and their activity. Therefore, the salary structures must be fundamentally reconsidered. Hospitals should focus less on purely business factors such as rigid cost management, but place greater emphasis on the human factor of care and treatment: The appropriate equipment and payment of medical staff *must, if necessary, be at the expense of the business return.*

But not only Corona has clearly shown us how important the economy has become for us humans. The *flood disaster* also rightly focused on human solidarity and help: Many volunteers from all over Germany personally helped to eliminate the flood damage. Extensive financial aid was immediately promised by the federal government, states and municipalities to alleviate the hardship and enable the reconstruction of the affected regions. A 30 billion EUR reconstruction fund was set up, which was divided into immediate and reconstruction aid and should at least compensate for the material damage (see Biegger, 2022).

Likewise, the war in Ukraine, which was only a few weeks old at the time of writing these lines, was fought not only, but primarily *with economic instruments*: Extensive

6 The Most Pressing Issues of Tomorrow's Economy

and severe economic sanctions were imposed immediately after the start of Russian military actions in Ukraine. They range from financial restrictions to the cessation of business activities in Russia, freezing of assets, among others, of the oligarchs, to the exclusion of Russian banks from the international SWIFT payment system (see, among others, European Council, 2022). Even a possible import stop of Russian gas and oil is being discussed. Of course, the great human tragedy of the suffering population in Ukraine must rightly be at the forefront of attention. Destroyed cities, houses, and buildings, a traumatized population, especially countless *affected children.* They all lead a life under hygienically and safety-wise unworthy conditions in air-raid shelters. Children who have to spend their birthdays, silent with fear, in emergency shelters with their mothers—the fathers have to defend their country—and hope for a near peace. Extensive aid deliveries with food, medicines, and everyday items are just as much an *encouraging sign of worldwide solidarity* as monetary donations and the acceptance of several million Ukrainian refugees in various European countries.

As vitally important as these questions of humanity are, we must also ask ourselves the question of economic impacts in the course of this book. Specifically: What economic consequences will these greatest challenges of humanity in a long time, the Corona pandemic, the flood disaster, and the war in Ukraine have? I would like to focus on 5 points in the following (see also Pietsch, 2021, p. 417 ff.):

1. How will *digitization* change life in Germany? How will we work in the future?
2. What do the Corona pandemic and the war mean for the much-vaunted *globalization?*

3. To what extent will the pandemic and war increase *public debt* and the already existing *economic inequality* within the population but also between countries?
4. What do ecological disasters like the flood disaster mean for the interplay between economy and ecology? Don't we now have to act *globally even faster and more consistently?*
5. Based on the experiences in the Ukraine war, don't *economic sanctions as "negative free trade"* have to be included in the economic toolbox? *Economic sanctions as a legitimate "weapon"* in the fight against aggressors?

Working in the Age of Pandemic-Induced Digitization
I don't know how it is for you: Can you still remember your own work routine or that of your children, grandchildren, or friends and acquaintances *before* the pandemic? We often got up early in the morning, quickly took care of the children after our own breakfast, and then plunged into the hectic rush hour. We were either on the way to work with public transport, our own car, or by bicycle. The bus and subway schedules determined life, sometimes tightly packed on the individual seats, where important documents were quickly read, be it tasks for school, university, or simply for the upcoming office appointments. The morning traffic jam with its streams of cars engulfed us and we were often annoyed by the amount of time we spent getting to school, university, the office, or generally to work. Some of us also had to quickly catch the next plane or train to travel from A to B.

Most of us, therefore, had a long odyssey of waiting, traffic jams, changing trains, queuing, etc. behind us. In the office, we often rushed from appointment to appointment in different meeting rooms, sometimes at physically different locations with the corresponding journeys and the search for a parking space. At the end of the working

6 The Most Pressing Issues of Tomorrow's Economy

day, everything went backwards only in reverse: We were stuck in traffic again, maybe picked up the children from school or daycare in a hurry, before the evening finally welcomed us to our free time. Most of the time, we were too tired or exhausted from the day's strains to enjoy the short free time with family or friends. For many of us, this was or is similar to the typical work and professional routine. *But that is long gone.*

Since the beginning of the Corona pandemic in March 2020, office life has been taking place almost exclusively virtually, i.e., in online meetings à la Skype, Teams, Zoom, etc. These existed before, but they were supplemented by personal meetings and in-person meetings, including shared lunches or coffee breaks and conversations with colleagues. The changes in the working world were already underway before Corona. The *pandemic only acted as an accelerant for digitalization.* Even before Corona, the world of status-oriented individual offices was slowly dying out. Open-plan offices were more the rule, as was working in (agile) teams, the "first-name basis and sneaker" culture, and jeans instead of suits or costumes. While most people still had their own workspace before Corona, which they could set up individually, the increasing proportion of work from home is leading to denser workspaces and shared desks. Companies have recognized a cost efficiency here that they are using accordingly: More home office means less office space, equals less cost. This is legitimate from the companies' perspective, but it reinforces the trend towards home office. Apart from the fact that many employees have set up in their own four walls and created new routines in a pleasant environment. The trend is now towards making the *offices more attractive* again in order to have more colleagues on site.

However, virtual work at home hardly gave most employees any time. Instead of the early commute to the office, people started earlier and used the time to read and respond to the first emails before the first appointment or to prepare for the upcoming appointment. In some cases, the time saved on commuting to the office was also used to bring forward the first appointment of the day. The same applied in the evening, as all you had to do at your desk at home was to close your laptop. After all, you were already at home and could seamlessly transition into your free time. Needless to say, business trips also largely fell by the wayside, as contacts nationally and internationally were *just a click away*. And lo and behold: It worked that way too, even though virtual meetings cannot replace personal meetings in the medium to long term. Team events or coffee rounds can also be organized virtually. But it's not the same. Anyone who has worked in a company for a longer period of time knows that nothing beats an occasional *personal exchange* over dinner with national and international colleagues.

Which changes from the Corona era will survive the transition to the post-pandemic era? How will we work in the future (see also Precht, 2022, especially p. 98 ff.)? The *end of mandatory attendance* is likely to come for all those in companies who can do their work from home. Companies like SAP have already announced that they will allow work from home for the entire week if necessary or desired (see White, 2022). This is of course easier to imagine in the field of software development, as people are already working virtually on different software modules in agile teams today. The location of work will play almost no role in the future, what matters is only the leadership culture, which is based on trust, team orientation, cohesion, and result orientation. In the future, the path will lead towards a *"hybrid working"* (see also Rau, 2021), in which the forms of traditional office work merge with virtual work from home (wherever this home will be!) into a unity.

In the future, corporate management will have to ensure the right balance between presence and home work: The performance evaluation of employees must be even more consistently based on clear goals than before, as the personal experience of individual employees on site can no longer be assumed. There must be *no disadvantages or differing treatment of employees,* no matter where they work. Perhaps certain appointments will have to be defined as face-to-face events, such as personnel talks or sustainable strategy workshops. Employees with constant customer contact will probably also have to meet their most important customers at least once a year on site in order not to jeopardize personal contact and to be able to build trust. It will become unavoidable to define certain standards in the individual companies as to what hybrid working should look like. Specifically: How many days a week can home office be used? Which meetings and topics need to be clarified on site, what technical equipment should be made available to employees, etc. There will certainly be *differences in hierarchy* in terms of presence. Board members will certainly have to be present on site more often than, for example, software developers.

But do employees even want such hybrid work? Do the ideas of companies and employees align? A survey by the Institute for Employment and Occupational Research (IAB) as part of the study "Home Office in Times of Corona—Use, Obstacles and Future Desires" (cf. IAB, 2021) concludes that the Corona pandemic has further accelerated the trend towards home office. *81 % of those who had the opportunity to work from home did so fully or partially, and almost two-thirds of respondents were satisfied with working from home. Only 7 % of respondents*

(!) can imagine a complete return to office life on site. The greatest challenges arose in the technical infrastructure i.e., equipment, infrastructure such as WLAN, capacity of the lines, access to company networks, etc.

However, the disadvantages of home office work were also clearly named: The culture of presence was replaced by purely virtual meetings. The valued personal exchange with colleagues, for example over coffee, was missing. It also became clear that the physical proximity to the workplace quickly blurs the *boundaries between work and leisure.* In the future, mature employees will be required who can cope on their own without permanent presence and the advice of their superiors. This requires bosses who trust their employees, communicate with them more frequently to inquire about their well-being and can give professional tips. Specifically, this means that the working culture on the company side must focus more on *trust, appreciation and goal orientation.* Employees who need to bring even more self-organization, personal responsibility and flexibility in the future, coupled with even more digital competence, are in demand. Only in this way will companies and all of us as employees be prepared for the *world of work after Corona.*

Globalization in Times of Pandemic and War
The Corona pandemic and also the war in Ukraine have shown one thing above all: The interdependence of companies within the framework of the global economy. At the beginning of the Corona pandemic, production lines were shut down at short notice. National borders had to be closed to prevent a national spread of the virus. Goods flows could no longer cross borders, production necessary materials, raw materials or even entire modules were stuck at the borders. Global supply chains could no longer be served. Many everyday items could only be stocked locally.

6 The Most Pressing Issues of Tomorrow's Economy

We all still remember with horror the panic buying of toilet paper. Discussions soon arose that spoke of a *new de-globalization* (cf. Dullien, 2021).

The war in Ukraine also forced a rethink: Many companies ended their business activities, stopped selling products and gradually withdrew from Russia. At the same time, many spare parts, such as wiring harnesses, could no longer be delivered from Ukraine. Days and weeks of production interruptions were the result. The initiated harsh but legitimate economic sanctions did their part. Thus, the gradual import stop of Russian goods led to a shortage of supply in Germany and to a rise in prices and inflation. The vulnerability of globalization was most evident in the uncertain times of the pandemic and war.

According to an analysis by the Institute for Macroeconomics and Economic Research (IMK), a *de-globalization* is indeed to be expected (cf. Dullien, 2021). The reason for this is that many countries will move towards sourcing central products of daily life nationally or even locally. Based on a risk analysis of supply chains, companies will be increasingly forced to source certain raw materials and preliminary products at least in the medium term from the national market. However, this *re-nationalization of supply chains* is only possible to a limited extent if additional complexity, inefficiencies and rising costs are accepted (cf. ter Haseborg, 2021). Companies should therefore establish a so-called early warning system for their supply chains that allows flexible redirection. In addition, it must always be expected that there will be further pandemics or trade and customs conflicts in the future. Therefore, a *correct mix of regional and international production structures and supply chains* is recommended in order to be able to react in time to crises.

Despite all setbacks and some de-globalization tendencies, globalization will not be stopped. We will have to continue living with it, but: *It will have to change.* The head of the Global Politics and Development department of the Friedrich-Ebert-Foundation, Jochen Steinhilber (cf. Steinhilber, 2021), predicts a slowed down globalization *("Slowbalization")* and explains his assessment based on five different trends:

1. Companies will *diversify their supply chains more,* i.e., include additional suppliers domestically and abroad, to reduce the risk of dependence on a single supplier. In particular, supplementing supply chains in the domestic market prevents a crisis or pandemic-related failure.
2. *The role of the state will change.* The Corona pandemic has swung the pendulum a little *more towards the state.* According to Steinhilber, this will remain the case in the post-Corona era. The state has proven itself in times of crisis as a manager, stabilizer, and preserver, especially where markets fail. Concrete examples include the billion-dollar aid packages for the economy to save key industries and companies, the Corona emergency aid, the proven short-time work allowance, and much more. For instance, US President Joe Biden has put together a trillion-dollar investment package to rescue the faltering US economy and stimulate the global economy at the same time. However, the protection and strengthening of the common good must be weighed against economic freedom, which is rather counteracted by state intervention. We remember the controversy between John Maynard Keynes and Milton Friedman (see Sect. 3.4 and 3.5, pp. 175 ff., especially p. 200): While Keynes wanted to strengthen the overall economic demand through a state investment program, Friedman essentially rejected all kinds of state interventions.

Especially in times of crisis, such as during the financial crisis of 2008, it becomes apparent that the market

6 The Most Pressing Issues of Tomorrow's Economy

alone cannot mitigate the consequences of a pandemic, a flood disaster, or a war. Particularly the poorer part of the population, but also many small and medium-sized enterprises that cannot fall back on a large financial cushion, *must be supported by the state.* This can, of course, only happen temporarily and once, so as not to permanently paralyze competition and the free play of market forces. Therefore, the role of the state will have to be discussed more in the context of the global economy in the future.

3. Despite the *global* impact of the pandemic, the *challenges will have to be solved purely nationally.* Each country had to define the right rules and economic strategies for itself and its population to emerge from the crisis as best as possible. This affected the lockdown regulations, the type and intensity of economic aid, the vaccination strategy, and finally the approach and timing of relaxations. Purely financially, there were significant differences worldwide: Wealthy industrialized countries like Germany, the USA, or Great Britain with a well-filled state purse could protect the domestic economy, provide state aid to companies, or ensure sufficient vaccine more than, for example, the poorer economies of South America or Africa. The support of poorer countries from economic strength is primarily an *ethical imperative* for the rich countries. It was all the more gratifying that billions of vaccine doses were allocated to African countries, among others, after the supply of the own population with sufficient vaccine had been ensured.

4. States are gradually exerting more influence in the global economy to their advantage. Steinhilber rightly refers to this as *"thinking in spheres of influence".* Economic policy measures such as tariffs, sanctions, control of raw materials, are used reciprocally as a means to achieve political goals. An example of this is

the highly controversial discussion about the coverage of the 5G mobile network in Germany by the Chinese mobile phone provider Huawei.
5. Not only the war in Ukraine or the pandemic of the last two years have damaged the global economy. In general, the era of ongoing economic growth seems to be over globally. According to the American economist Larry Summers, a secular stagnation, *"the secular stagnation",* (see Steinhilber, 2021) is emerging worldwide. Even China, which in recent years has been a guarantee of annual double-digit economic growth measured by gross domestic product, is now "only" calculating with single-digit growth rates. In addition to the pandemic experiences of the last two years and the bleak prospects of the war in Ukraine, the reasons lie primarily in demographic development, growing inequality, and state over-indebtedness. I would like to briefly discuss the last two reasons in the following.

Combating Inequality and Rising National Debt
The Corona pandemic will further exacerbate inequality between and within countries. While wealthier countries were able to boost their pandemic-stricken economies through state aid and billion-dollar investment programs, poorer countries are still staggering (see Unmüßig, 2022 for the following). As of January 2022, only 5 % of the population in low-income countries were fully vaccinated. Over 160 million people worldwide fell into poverty due to the pandemic. By 2030, another 207 million could follow. Western industrialized countries, on the other hand, had easier access to vaccine doses, which they could not only finance but also partially produce in their own country. The fight for the scarce vaccine doses was won mainly by these countries, especially in the early stages. There is nothing wrong with each country wanting to provide for

itself and its own citizens first in order to escape the pandemic. However, it must be noted that vaccination rates remained relatively low in poorer countries for a long time (see Unmüßig, 2022).

There were also further differences within individual countries in the fight against the pandemic: Blessed are those who could work from home during the pandemic. In addition to office activities, it was mainly high-paying specialist jobs such as software developers, project managers, etc., that found working from home much easier. Nursing and social and educational professions such as social workers could not benefit from the advantages of a home office and were particularly challenged. The hardest hit, however, were the *households with lower incomes,* who had only limited access to health services. In addition, their jobs were often threatened with cuts: Especially those working in low-paid but particularly affected sectors such as tourism or gastronomy were disproportionately reduced during the pandemic (see also Steinhilber, 2021). This was especially true for the less qualified. It will be particularly important in the time after the pandemic—whenever that will be—to distribute the financial burdens on several shoulders and not to be borne by those countries and population groups that are already struggling to cope with life (see Pietsch, 2020, p. 237 ff. for selected measures to combat inequality). In addition, we must not leave the next generation with a huge mountain of debt that they will somehow have to pay off. According to the motto: After us, the deluge.

In addition, *global poverty will continue to rise as a result of the pandemic* (see Unmüßig, 2022). We cannot be indifferent to this. Poorer countries had to go further into debt to protect and provide for their populations, while at the same time the economic cycle was throttled or completely choked off. It is not only the ethical duty of wealthier countries to support economic reconstruction, but it is also in their own interest: A low vaccination status benefits no one and can threaten wealthier countries with a new pandemic wave due to increased incidences (see Steinhilber, 2021). In addition to worldwide financial support for poorer countries in the course of accelerating vaccinations, consideration must also be given to at least a *temporary lifting of global patent protection.* We all live together on this one earth. Although each country has to deal with the pandemic on its own (and still has to), we *must practice international solidarity with poorer countries.* This is especially true in today's dramatic times for the population of war-torn Ukraine. The acceptance of refugees for their protection from war and terror is a matter of course. We were also helped when our grandmothers and grandfathers had to flee from the affected war zones. This is not only about protection and security, but also about peace and democracy. Prosperity and health must *arrive globally in the future and must not stop with a few.*

Accelerated Integration of Ecology and Economy

The flood disaster of 2021 at the latest should have caused the last doubters in Germany to rethink: Climate change is hardly stoppable and has hit us all with full force. An end to climate disasters is not in sight. As these lines were being written, the east coast of Australia, especially the region around Sydney, was hit by a century flood (cf. Senzel, 2022). First, there were several years of extreme drought and resulting devastating bush and forest fires. Then this flood. The causes are clear: Climate change increases the risk of a flood, as the heated atmosphere absorbs more water and the intensity and frequency of rainfall dramatically increases. In the population of Australia, traditionally considered the country with the most climate deniers worldwide, a rethinking process

6 The Most Pressing Issues of Tomorrow's Economy

has already begun (cf. Senzel, 2022). Now, in the face of these increasingly frequent climate disasters, the timetable for implementing ecological measures must be massively accelerated: Every measure for CO_2 reduction, for the transition to renewable energies etc. is to be prioritized and if possible *implemented more quickly than previously planned.* This will not only apply to Germany, but worldwide. What initially sounds like a trivial realization will be *a Herculean task for the next years and decades!* when it comes to concrete implementation on the ground.

Economic Sanctions as a Legitimate Weapon in Wartime
No one knows how long the pandemic will continue to hold us in its grip. The same applies to the war in Ukraine. What we do know is that the *economy has become vital for all of us.* How quickly the supply of essentials can break off and war can cause supply chains to implode, we have all painfully experienced. Even the simple trip to the gas station shows us how dependent we are on the principle of supply and demand: When raw materials like gas and oil become scarce, we feel it directly in our wallets. Wars are now fought, among other things, *with the means of economic sanctions.* The state and its actors must increasingly intervene in the economy, not only to set the framework as ordoliberal economists thought, but also to secure the supply of the population and to stabilize companies. We will have to re-question the role of the state in the economy.

The broad-based economic sanctions against Russia, from the import ban on aircraft spare parts to financial markets, banks, IT sector, and personal sanctions against President Putin and his closest circle (cf. Schröder, 2022), are having an effect. Although the current conduct of war will not be influenced in the short term by these sanctions, it will lead to a significant weakening of the Russian economy in the medium to long term. The ruble has already lost significantly in value. A potential import embargo for Russian oil and gas will also cause the lucrative revenues in the billions to collapse. Economic sanctions, however, tend to have a medium to long-term effect and can increase the cohesion of the affected population with the government. A *reactance effect,* known from psychology, which further unites those affected by a commonly experienced external pressure. It will also be important to find a way out of the sanctions spiral, provided Russia is willing to end the war.

What Will Change in the Future?
Let us take a brief look into the future at the end of this chapter and outline the economic challenges *that we will have to master, especially in the time after the Corona pandemic.* In my view, these will primarily be the following (cf. among others Pietsch, 2021, p. 418 ff.):

- *The pandemic has acted like a fire accelerator on digitization.* In the future, life and work in the offline and online world will have to merge into a harmonious whole. Digital capability will become the central competence of the future not only for our children, but for all of us. The *world society will increasingly become a hybrid society:* A society that must find the optimal balance between the virtual and the "real" world for itself. This will certainly dramatically change the way we work and probably also cost jobs. However, it does not help to resist the development. On the contrary, we must actively confront and embrace it.
- The *globalization will have to change.* It will be crucial to shape globalization in such a way that especially the poorer and weaker in the world benefit the most from it. Or as the Bonn philosopher Markus Gabriel puts

6 The Most Pressing Issues of Tomorrow's Economy

it: *"…we must bring about a kind of globalization that produces an ethical cohesion of all people (…)."* (Gabriel in Gabriel & Scobel, 2021, p. 293). We must advocate for a global prosperity that reaches everyone and not just a few. A globalization that is therefore more oriented towards people and takes into account those who should benefit most from it.

- The pandemic has clearly shown us that *the environment benefits from life in the virtual world.* The reduction in the number of trips and international meetings and their replacement with virtual meetings have indeed caused the internet capacity to glow, but they have also cleared the streets and thus significantly reduced pollution. No one seriously disputes anymore that we urgently need to change course to ward off the impending climate catastrophe. We have *not a problem of knowledge, but a problem of implementation.* The horrific images of the flood disaster of 2021 should remind us and urge us to accelerate the initiated ecological measures by at least one power. This will not only benefit the environment, but also the biodiversity of animals. The issue of ecology must continue to be at the top of the ethical agenda of the economy.
- The pandemic and the horrific images of war have also made it clear: *The world has become a bit closer and more solidary.* The vast majority of citizens in countries worldwide have adhered to the rules of the pandemic, whether it was the mask mandate, the distance and hygiene rules, the curfew and contact restrictions, or the vaccinations. The younger ones were considerate of the older and more frail, the healthy of the sick. They bought groceries for those who could no longer do so. Many took in war refugees from Ukraine or donated money and everyday necessities for the population threatened by death. We *are all in the same boat.*

Hardly anyone does not know at least one case in their family, circle of friends and acquaintances, or colleagues who was affected by Corona or has relatives in Ukraine. Managers trusted their employees regarding their work from home, who confirmed the trust placed in them and reliably delivered their results in a work method unfamiliar to them.

- The *role of the state will have to be rethought*. As important as short-time work benefits, Corona emergency aid, or individual state participations or support of entire sectors such as the tourism industry were, they were active interventions in the market's control mechanism. The pendulum of discussions will swing between a state that only sets the framework and ensures competition and an "interventionist state" that should keep the population away from the undue hardships of war, pandemics, or weather disasters but also the increasing inequality. This is not only a question of political sentiment, but practically the question of what kind of state we want to live in in the future. Should the state be a guarantor of prosperity and supply for the weakest among us or only accompany and secure the free market economy? The discussion promises to be exciting.
- The *inequality of society has further intensified in most countries and also between countries*. We must counteract this massively. Not only the pandemic, but also ecological disasters and wars could happen in the future, which none of us hope for. The pandemic, as we have seen, has increased social differences—just think of the different conditions of homeschooling. This tendency is expected to continue in the coming years (cf. Fratzscher, 2022, p. 227). Ecological disasters hit especially countries that already today hardly have the

6 The Most Pressing Issues of Tomorrow's Economy

money to feed their population sufficiently, like the countries of Sub-Saharan Africa. Even the flood disaster in a rich country like Germany has shown what financial losses threaten the affected people, some of whom have lost everything. War will also force many people into poverty, who give up everything they have painstakingly built up by fleeing. The gap will widen.

- *We are leaving the next generation with a high national debt due to the pandemic.* For example, the federal budget's expenditures increased from around 343 billion EUR in 2019 to 508 billion EUR in 2020 (cf. Pietsch, 2021, p. 423). Just in the period from January to October 2020, the federal budget had a deficit of a good 89 billion EUR. The state quota in Germany increased by almost 20 % in 2020 compared to 2019 and is currently 54 %. This high debt must be repaid as quickly as possible. The strong shoulders must carry more than the weak ones. *Intergenerational justice is also an ethical imperative:* The next generation should not also have to financially clean up the pandemic for us. They have already suffered enough under the Corona rules.

Despite all challenges, we must look forward and address the pressing issues. If it is true that *the greatest challenges of the coming years* and decades will not only be ecological, but *primarily economic,* then it is time to deal more intensively with these pressing issues. I hope that this book has made a contribution to understanding the economic issues of the past, present, and also the future better. Only in this way are we better prepared for all eventualities that threaten us economically in the coming years.

References

Ärzteblatt. (2021). Long COVID: Patienten klagen über mehr als 200 verschiedene Symptome. *Ärzteblatt* 15.07.2021. https://www.aerzteblatt.de/nachrichten/125635/Long-COVID-Patienten-klagen-ueber-mehr-als-200-verschiedene-Symptome. Zugegriffen: 19. Juli 2021.

Bankenverband. (2018). o.V. Geldköpfe Teil 1: Der erste Mensch auf der Münze. https://bankenverband.de/blog/geldkopfe-teil-1-der-erste-mensch-auf-einer-munze/. Zugegriffen: 21. März 2019.

Bayerisches Münzkontor. (2019). o.V. Die „Mark" vor 1945. *Bayerisches Münzkontor.* https://www.muenzkontor.de/muenzkunde-numismatik/die-deutsche-mark-vor-1945. Zugegriffen: 22. März 2019.

Biegger, S. (2022). 30 Milliarden-Aufbaufonds. Flutopfer hoffen auf schnelle Hilfe. *Tagesschau* 07.09.2021. https://www.tagesschau.de/wirtschaft/unternehmen/wiederaufbaufonds-fluthilfe-101.html. Zugegriffen: 10. März 2022.

Bohmeyer, M., & Cornelsen, C. (2019). Bedingungsloses Grundeinkommen. 1000 Euro mehr im Monat – Auch für Managersöhne und Sozialamtbetrüger. *Die Zeit* 23.01.2019. https://www.zeit.de/arbeit/2019-01/bedingungsloses-grundeinkommen-michael-bohmeyer-buchauszug/komplettansicht. Zugegriffen: 18. März 2019.

Bräutigam, T. (2013). Knappe Rohstoffe. Wann bauen wir das letzte Windrad? https://www.wiwo.de/technologie/green/knappe-rohstoffe-wann-bauen-wir-das-letzte-windrad/13547618.html. Zugegriffen: 13. März 2019.

Bundeszentrale für politische Bildung. (2018). Entwicklung des grenzüberschreitenden Warenhandels. http://www.bpb.de/nachschlagen/zahlen-und-fakten/globalisierung/52543/entwicklung-des-warenhandels. Zugegriffen: 15. März 2019.

Bundeszentrale für politische Bildung bpb. (2016). Weltbruttoinlandsprodukt. Stand: 12.06.2016. http://www.bpb.de/nachschlagen/zahlen-und-fakten/globalisierung/52655/welt-bruttoinlandsprodukt. Zugegriffen: 1. Apr. 2019.

Diekmann, F. (2018). Superreiche: 45 Deutsche besitzen so viel wie die ärmere Hälfte der Bevölkerung. *Spiegel.* http://www.spiegel.de/wirtschaft/soziales/vermoegen-45-superreiche-besitzen-so-viel-wie-die-halbe-deutsche-bevoelkerung-a-1189111.html. Zugegriffen: 23. Jan. 2018.

Dönhoff, M. G. (1997). *Zivilisiert den Kapitalismus. Grenzen der Freiheit.* DVA.

Dullien, S. (2021). Weltwirtschaft: Nach Corona kommt die Deglobalisierung. *Hans Böckler Stiftung.* https://www.boeckler.de/data/impuls_2021_02_S2-3.pdf. Zugegriffen: 28. Juni 2021.

Eckert, D. (2018). Automatisierung. Diese Jobs sind besonders von Robotern bedroht. *Die Welt* 16.02.2018. https://www.welt.de/wirtschaft/article173642209/Jobverlust-Diese-Jobs-werden-als-erstes-durch-Roboter-ersetzt.html. Zugegriffen: 18. März 2019.

Eltis, W. (1989). David Ricardo. In J. Starbatty (Hrsg.), *Klassiker des ökonomischen Denkens* (Bd. 2, S. 188–207). Beck.

Erhard, L. (1964). Wohlstand für alle. 8. Auflage, bearbeitet von Wolfram Langer. https://www.ludwig-erhard.de/wp-content/uploads/wohlstand_fuer_alle1.pdf. Zugegriffen: 17. Juni 2018.

Ettel, A., & Zschäpitz, H. (2015). Zufriedenheit und Gehalt – Die Wahrheit über Glück. https://www.welt.de/wirtschaft/article147904505/Zufriedenheit-und-Gehalt-Die-Wahrheit-ueber-Glueck.html. Zugegriffen: 13. März 2019.

Europäischer Rat. (2022). Restriktive Maßnahmen der EU als Reaktion auf die Krise in der Ukraine. *Europäischer Rat* https://www.consilium.europa.eu/de/policies/sanctions/restrictive-measures-ukraine-crisis/. Zugegriffen: 10. März 2022.

Europäisches Parlament. (2018). Plastikmüll und Recycling in der EU: Zahlen und Fakten. http://www.Europarl.Europa.eu/news/de/headlines/society/20181212STO21610/plastikmull-und-recycling-in-der-eu-zahlen-und-fakten. Zugegriffen: 8. März 2019.

Faigle, P. (2010). Reichtumsstudie: 60.000 Euro reichen für ein schönes Leben. https://www.zeit.de/wirtschaft/2010-09/studie-reichtum-glueck. Zugegriffen: 13. März 2019.

Feldenkirchen, M. (2015). Vereinigte Oligarchen von Amerika. *Spiegel* 29.08.2015. http://www.spiegel.de/spiegel/print/d-138379369.html. Zugegriffen: 14. März 2019.

Flämig, H. (2018). *Luft- und Klimabelastung durch Güterverkehr.* Forschungsinformations- system (FIS) Mobilität und Verkehr. https://www.forschungsinformationssystem.de/servlet/is/39787/. Zugegriffen: 18. März 2019.

Fratzscher, M. (2022). *Geld oder Leben. Wie unser irrationales Verhältnis zum Geld die Gesellschaft spaltet.* Berlin.

Fricke, T. (2018). Reich und arm. Wie der Immobilienboom das Land spaltet. *Spiegel* 29.09.2018. http://www.spiegel.de/wirtschaft/service/immobilien-wie-der-boom-die-spaltung-der-gesellschaft-vertieft-a-1230495.html. Zugegriffen: 15. März 2019.

Gabriel, M., & Scobel, G. (2021). *Zwischen Gut und Böse. Philosophie der radikalen Mitte.* Edition Körber.

Giesen, C., & Hägler, M. (2017). E-Mobilität: China führt Quote für E-Autos ein. https://www.sueddeutsche.de/wirtschaft/e-mobilitaet-china-fuehrt-quote-fuer-e-autos-ein-1.3687137. Zugegriffen: 13. März 2019.

Habekuß, F. (2019). Artensterben. Wie geht es den Arten? https://www.zeit.de/2019/03/artensterben-oekosystem-umwelt-schutz-zerstoerung. Zugegriffen: 13. März 2019.

Haidacher, B. (2015). *Bargeldmetaphern im Französischen. Pragmatik, Sprachkultur und Metaphorik.* Frank & Timme.

Hank, R., & von Petersdorff, W. (2013). Gewinne privatisieren, Verluste sozialisieren. *FAZ* 22.12.2013. https://www.faz.net/aktuell/wirtschaft/wirtschaftspolitik/gewinne-privatisieren-verluste-sozialisieren-wie-wir-lernten-die-banken-zu-hassen-12722023.html. Zugegriffen: 18. März 2019.

Harvard. (2019). *HarvardX.* Free online courses from Harvard University. https://www.edx.org/school/harvardx. Zugegriffen: 18. März 2019.

Hasse, E. S. (2012). Brotzeit. Uschi Glas engagiert sich für Schulkinder. *Welt* 07.05.2012. https://www.welt.de/regionales/hamburg/article106269940/Uschi-Glas-engagiert-sich-fuer-Schulkinder.html. Zugegriffen: 21. März 2019.

6 The Most Pressing Issues of Tomorrow's Economy

Herrmann, U. (2016). *Kein Kapitalismus ist auch keine Lösung. Die Krise der heutigen Ökonomie oder was wir von Smith, Marx und Keynes lernen können* (3. Aufl.). Westend.

Honey. C. (2016). Überfischung. Wir essen die Weltmeere leer. *Die Zeit* 19.01.2016. https://www.zeit.de/wissen/umwelt/2016-01/ueberfischung-bedrohung-arten-fehler-angaben. Zugegriffen: 15. März 2019.

Hurtz, S. (2017). Sind Smartphones doch etwa ein Problem? *SZ* 25.10.2017. https://www.sueddeutsche.de/digital/dokureihe-homo-digitalis-sind-smartphones-vielleicht-doch-ein-problem-1.3723358. Zugegriffen: 18. März 2019.

IAB. (2021). Wie stellen sich Arbeitnehmer das Arbeiten nach der Pandemie vor? *Techniker Krankenkasse* zitiert aus der Studie des Instituts für Arbeitsmarkt- und Berufsforschung (IAB). https://www.tk.de/firmenkunden/service/fachthemen/coronavirus-arbeitgeber/homeoffice-nach-corona-2104308. Zugegriffen: 27. Juni 2021.

Kaufmann, S. (2017). Millionärssteuer. So viel zahlen Menschen mit hohem Einkommen. https://www.berliner-zeitung.de/wirtschaft/millionaerssteuer-soviel-steuern-zahlen-menschen-mit-hohem-einkommen-27875330. Zugegriffen: 3. März 2019.

Kennedy, J. F. (1961). Antrittsrede vom 20.01.1961, Deutsche Fassung. https://www.jfklibrary.org/learn/about-jfk/historic-speeches/inaugural-address. Zugegriffen: 29. Mai 2019.

Knauer, R. (2015). 25 Jahre FCKW-Verbot. Es bleibt ein Loch ohne Boden. *Spektrum der Wissenschaft* https://www.spektrum.de/news/25-jahre-fckw-verbot-wie-steht-es-um-das-ozonloch/1352353. Zugegriffen: 21. März 2019.

Kohlenberg, K., & Uchatius, W. (2008). Finanzkrise. Wo ist das Geld geblieben? *Die Zeit* 27.02.2008. https://www.zeit.de/2008/49/DOS-Wo-steckt-das-Geld. Zugegriffen: 19. März 2019.

Krieger, A. (2016). Plastikmüll im Meer. Zahlen und Fakten nach Meeresregionen. http://anjakrieger.com/2016/06/02/plastikmuell-meer-zahlen-region-vergleich/#5. Zugegriffen: 18. März 2019.

Küng, H. (2010). *Anständig wirtschaften – Warum Ökonomie Moral braucht.* Piper.

Lange, K. (2018). Wie Digitalisierung die Arbeitswelt verändert. Wer Karriere macht und wer um seinen Job bangen muss. Interview Lange K mit Penning S. *Manager Magazin* 26.10.2018. http://www.manager-magazin.de/unternehmen/artikel/karriere-und-jobverlust-digitaler-wandel-veraendert-arbeitswelt-a-1127180.html. Zugegriffen: 18. März 2019.

Lee, F. (2017). Klimaschutz in China. „Kohlefreie Zone" in Peking. *Die Zeit* 17.10.2017. https://www.zeit.de/wirtschaft/2017-10/klimaschutz-klimawandel-china-regierung-smog-emissionen. Zugegriffen: 21. März 2019.

Lütge, C., & Esfeld, M. (2021). *Und die Freiheit? Wie die Corona-Politik und der Missbrauch der Wissenschaft unsere offene Gesellschaft bedrohen.* Riva.

Lütge, C., & Uhl, M. (2017). *Wirtschaftsethik.* Vahlen.

Mankiw, G. N., & Taylor, M. P. (2012). *Grundzüge der Volkswirtschaftslehre* (5., überarb. u. erweit. Aufl.). Schäffer-Poeschel.

Marx, K. (2009). *Das Kapital – Kritik der politischen Ökonomie* (Ungekürzte Ausgabe nach der zweiten Auflage von 1872 mit einem Geleitwort von Karl Korsch aus dem Jahre 1932, unveränderter Nachdruck). Anaconda.

McKinsey. (2015). Competing for the connected customer—perspectives on the opportunities created by car connectivity and automation. https://www.mckinsey.com/~/media/mckinsey/industries/automotive%20and%20assembly/our%20insights/how%20carmakers%20can%20compete%20for%20the%20connected%20consumer/competing_for_the_connected_customer.ashx.. Zugegriffen: 14. Okt. 2019.

Meadows, D. (1972). *Die Grenzen des Wachstums. Bericht des Club of Rome zur Lage der Menschheit.* Deutsche Verlagsanstalt.

Merkel, W. W. (2013). Fracking: Zu viele Risiken, zu wenig Wissen. *Welt* 11.07.2013. https://www.welt.de/wissenschaft/article117938329/Fracking-zu-viele-Risiken-zu-wenig-Wissen.html. Zugegriffen: 15. März 2019.

Merz, S. L. (2015). Industrie 4.0 ist keine Theorie mehr. Die vierte industrielle Revolution kommt in der Wirklichkeit an. *Computerwoche* 21.12.2015. https://www.computerwoche.de/a/die-vierte-industrielle-revolution-kommt-in-der-wirklichkeit-an,3096002. Zugegriffen: 18. März 2019.

Müller, C. (2015). *Nachhaltige Ökonomie. Ziele, Herausforderungen und Lösungswege*. De Gruyter Oldenbourg.

Oberhuber, N. (2015). Glyphosat: Gift für mehr Wachstum. *Die Zeit* 06.08.2015. https://www.zeit.de/wirtschaft/2015-08/glyphosat-unkrautvernichter-krebs-landwirtschaft-ertraege-monsanto/komplettansicht. Zugegriffen: 15. März 2019.

Oxfam. (2017). 8 Männer besitzen so viel wie die ärmere Hälfte der Weltbevölkerung. https://www.oxfam.de/ueber-uns/aktuelles/2017-01-16-8-maenner-besitzen-so-viel-aermere-haelfte-weltbevoelkerung. Zugegriffen: 14. März 2019.

Oxfam. (2018). Bericht zur sozialen Ungleichheit: 82 Prozent des weltweiten Vermögenswachstums geht ans reichste Prozent der Bevölkerung. https://www.oxfam.de/presse/pressemitteilungen/2018-01-22-82-prozent-weltweiten-vermoegenswachstums-geht-ans-reichste. Zugegriffen: 14. März 2019.

Paech, N. (2012). *Befreiung vom Überfluss. Auf dem Weg in die Postwachstumsökonomie*. Oekom.

Paech, N. (2019). Grundzüge einer Postwachstumsökonomie. http://www.Postwachstumsoekonomie.de/material/grundzuege/. Zugegriffen: 15. März 2019.

Pietsch, D. (2017). *Grenzen des ökonomischen Denkens – Wo bleibt der Mensch in der Wirtschaft?* Eul/Lohmar.

Pietsch, D. (2020). *Prinzipien moderner Ökonomie. Ökologisch, ethisch, digital*. Springer.

Pietsch, D. (2021). *Die Ökonomie und das Nichts. Warum Wirtschaft ohne Moral wertlos ist*. Springer.

Pietsch, D. (2022). *Unsere Wirtschaft ethisch überdenken. Eine Aufforderung*. Springer (in Vorbereitung).

Precht, R. D. (2016). *Tiere denken. Vom Recht der Tiere und den Grenzen des Menschen*. Goldmann.

Precht, R. D. (2018). *Jäger, Hirten, Kritiker: Eine Utopie für die digitale Gesellschaft*. Goldmann.

Precht, R. D. (2022). *Freiheit für alle. Das Ende der Arbeit wie wir sie kannten.* Goldmann.

Radtke, R. (2022). Todesfälle mit Coronavirus (COVID-19) nach Ländern 2022. https://de.statista.com/statistik/daten/studie/1100818/umfrage/todesfaelle-aufgrund-des-coronavirus-2019-ncov-nach-laendern/. Zugegriffen: 10. März 2022.

Rau, K. (2021). Arbeitswelt nach Corona. „Hybrides Arbeiten ist sicherlich die anstrengendste Form", Interview mit der Arbeitsforscherin Barbara Stöttinger. *Wirtschaftswoche* 27.05.2021. https://www.wiwo.de/erfolg/beruf/arbeitswelt-nach-corona-hybrides-arbeiten-ist-sicherlich-die-anstrengendste-form/27212258.html. Zugegriffen: 18. Okt. 2021.

Reuter, H. (2014). Amazonas Regenwald: Pro Stunde werden 526 Fußballfelder abgeholzt. *Die Welt* 07.11.2014. https://www.welt.de/wissenschaft/umwelt/article134117363/Pro-Stunde-wurden-526-Fussballfelder-abgeholzt.html. Zugegriffen: 15. März 2019.

Rövekamp, M. (2016). Digitalisierung bis Demografie. Wie sich die Arbeitswelt wandelt. *Der Tagesspiegel* https://www.tagesspiegel.de/wirtschaft/digitalisierung-bis-demografie-wie-sich-die-arbeitswelt-wandelt/14898360.html. Zugegriffen: 18. März 2019.

Schipper, L. (2015). Was eigentlich ist das Internet der Dinge? *FAZ* 17.03.2015. https://www.faz.net/aktuell/wirtschaft/cebit/cebit-was-eigentlich-ist-das-internet-der-dinge-13483592.html?printPagedArticle=true#pageIndex_0. Zugegriffen: 18. März 2019.

Schömann-Finck, C. (2011). Kurz erklärt. Was sind eigentlich Leerverkäufe? *Focus Money* https://www.focus.de/finanzen/boerse/kurz-erklaert-was-sind-eigentlich-leerverkaeufe_aid:505874.html. Zugegriffen: 21. März 2019.

Schröder, U. (2022). Russland-Ukraine-Krieg/Chancen und Gefahren von Sanktionen gegen Putin. *Deutschlandfunk* 10.03.2022. https://www.deutschlandfunk.de/sanktionen-gegen-putin-russland-ukraine-krieg-100.html. Zugegriffen: 10. März 2022.

Schultz, S. (2013). So rechnet Apple seine Steuerlast klein. *Spiegel* 21.05.2013. http://www.spiegel.de/wirtschaft/unternehmen/apples-steuertricks-in-der-uebersicht-a-901015.html. Zugegriffen: 15. März 2019.

Senzel, H. (2022). Jahrhundert-Hochwasser bedroht Sydney. *Tagesschau* 03.03.2022. https://www.tagesschau.de/ausland/ozeanien/flut-australien-103.html. Zugegriffen: 10. März 2022.

Spiegel Online (o. V.). (2018). Mieten sollen erneut kräftig steigen 26.12.2018. https://www.spiegel.de/wirtschaft/service/deutschland-mieten-sollen-2019-um-bis-zu-fuenf-prozent-steigen-a-1245410.html. Zugegriffen: 29. Mai 2019.

Spiegel Online. (11.06.2021). G7 Staaten wollen ärmeren Ländern eine Milliarde Impfdosen bereitstellen. *Spiegel* 11.06.2021. https://www.spiegel.de/ausland/corona-g7-staaten-wollen-aermeren-laendern-eine-milliarde-impfdosen-bereitstellen-a-23f47dd0-2acb-4836-940c-a4f83a72b9a5. Zugegriffen: 20. Juni 2021.

Statistisches Bundesamt. (2021). Die Folgen der Corona-Pandemie in 10 Zahlen, Pressemitteilung Nr. N 023 vom 31.März 2021. *Statistisches Bundesamt.* https://www.destatis.de/DE/Presse/Pressemitteilungen/2021/03/PD21_N023_p001.html. Zugegriffen: 20. Juni 2021.

Steinhilber, J. (2021). Wie sich die Globalisierung nach Corona verändern muss. Zeit für einen grundlegenden Wandel. *Neue Gesellschaft.* Frankfurter Hefte Ausgabe 04/2021. https://www.frankfurter-hefte.de/artikel/zeit-fuer-einen-grundlegenden-wandel-3173/. Zugegriffen: 28. Juni 2021.

Ter Haseborg, V. (2021). Lieferketten: Globalisierungs-Killer Corona? Von wegen! *Wirtschaftswoche* 04.06.2021. https://www.wiwo.de/politik/konjunktur/lieferketten-globalisierungs-killer-corona-von-wegen/27254224.html. Zugegriffen: 28. Juni 2021.

Tierschutzbund. (2019). Kosmetikpositivliste. https://www.tierschutzbund.de/information/service/publikationen/kosmetik-positivliste/. Zugegriffen: 15. März 2019.

Umweltbundesamt. (2018a). EU-Plastikstrategie: Guter Absatz, aber zu unkonkret. *Umweltbundesamt* https://www.umweltbundesamt.de/themen/eu-plastikstrategie-guter-ansatz-aber-zu-unkonkret. Zugegriffen: 18. März 2019.

Umweltbundesamt. (2018b). Biozide. *Umweltbundesamt.* https://www.umweltbundesamt.de/themen/chemikalien/biozide. Zugegriffen: 18. März 2019.

Umweltbundesamt. (2019). Verpackungen. *Umweltbundesamt* 28.12.2018. https://www.umweltbundesamt.de/themen/abfall-ressourcen/produktverantwortung-in-der-abfallwirtschaft/verpackungen#textpart-1. Zugegriffen: 18. März 2019.

Unmüßig, B. (2022). Corona-Pandemie, Impfstoffverteilung und globale Gerechtigkeit. *Heinrich Böll Stiftung* 10.02.2022. https://www.boell.de/de/2022/02/10/corona-pandemie-impfstoffverteilung-und-globale-gerechtigkeit-eine-zwischenbilanz. Zugegriffen: 10. März 2022.

Vaupel, M., & Kaul, V. (2016). *Die Geschichte(n) des Geldes. Von der Kaurischnecke zum Goldstandard – So entwickelte sich das Finanzsystem.* Börsenmedien AG.

Wallacher, J. (2007). Impulse der ökonomischen Glücksforschung für die Wirtschaftsethik. https://www.hfph.de/hochschule/lehrende/prof-dr-dr-johannes-wallacher/artikel/wallacher-personalfuehrung.pdf. Zugegriffen: 13. März 2019.

Weimann, J., Knabe, A., & Schöb, R. (2011). *Measuring happiness – The economics of well-being.* Boston: The MIT Press. Dtsch.: (2011). *Geld macht doch glücklich: Wo die ökonomische Glücksforschung irrt.* Stuttgart: Schäffer-Poeschel.

White, J. (2022). SAP erlaubt Mitarbeitern Homeoffice zu jeder Zeit. *Manager Magazin* 02.06.2021. SAP-Vorständin Julia White im Gespräch mit Reuters. https://www.manager-magazin.de/unternehmen/tech/sap-mitarbeiter-koennen-homeoffice-machen-wann-sie-wollen-a-1283fedc-dcdf-4dae-95ee-a8bc1704f101. Zugegriffen: 10. Marz 2022.

Zukunftsinstitut: Megatrends Neo-Ökologie. (2019). https://www.zukunftsinstitut.de/artikel/mtglossar/neo-oekologie-glossar/. Zugegriffen: 8. Mai 2019.

Acknowledgements

A book usually has many mothers and fathers, but only one author. I would like to take this opportunity to thank all those people without whom this book would not have been possible. I would like to highlight in particular Dr. Isabella Hanser and her team from Springer Verlag - and especially Lisa Wötzel - who have supervised me and accompanied me with patience and constant motivation on the way to publication.

Over the years, numerous intellectual pioneers have repeatedly supported and motivated me on my way to becoming an author. Three are mentioned as representatives: firstly, my academic teacher, Professor emeritus Dr. Manfred Perlitz, who laid the foundations of my scientific and professional career and still accompanies me in many questions of life, and secondly, Dr. Markus Seidler and Dr. Patrick Strunkmann-Meister, who repeatedly motivated me to write down my ideas and thoughts on economics.

Finally, I would like to thank the most important people in my life: my parents as well as my wife and my son for their constant emotional and motivating support and their firm belief in me. I dedicate this book to my son and his generation of economists.

Munich, October 2019

References

Ärzteblatt. (2021). Long COVID: Patienten klagen über mehr als 200 verschiedene Symptome. *Ärzteblatt* 15.07.2021. https://www.aerzteblatt.de/nachrichten/125635/Long-COVID-Patienten-klagen-ueber-mehr-als-200-verschiedene-Symptome. Zugegriffen: 19. Juli 2021.

Aquin, T. (1985). *Summe der Theologie* (3 Bände). In Bernhard, J. von (Hrsg.). Kröner.

Aquin, T. (2012). *Summa Theologiae*. http://www.unifr.ch/bkv/summa/inhalt1.htm. Zugegriffen: 6. Juni 2019.

Aristoteles. (1995a). *Philosophische Schriften in sechs Bänden*. Übersetzt von Rolfes E. Felix Meiner. Meiner.

Aristoteles. (1995b). *Philosophische Schriften in sechs Bänden* (Politik, Bd. 4). Übersetzt von Rolfes E. Felix Meiner. Meiner.

Aristoteles. (2007). *Nikomachische Ethik* (2. Aufl.). Tusculum.

Atkinson, A. B. (2015). *Inequality – what can be done?* Harvard University Press.

Bankenverband. (2018). o. V. *Geldköpfe Teil 1: Der erste Mensch auf der Münze.* https://bankenverband.de/blog/

geldkopfe-teil-1-der-erste-mensch-auf-einer-munze/. Zugegriffen: 21. März 2019.

Bayerisches Münzkontor. (2019). o. V. Die „Mark" vor 1945. *Bayerisches Münzkontor.* https://www.muenzkontor.de/muenzkunde-numismatik/die-deutsche-mark-vor-1945. Zugegriffen: 22. März 2019.

Bentham, J. (1776). A fragment on government. In von J. H. Burns & H. L. A. Hart (Hrsg.), *A comment on the commentaries and a fragment on government* (S. 391–551). (The collected works of Jeremy Bentham) London 1977.

Beutter, F. (1989). Thomas von Aquin. In J. Starbatty (Hrsg.), *Klassiker des ökonomischen Denkens* (2 Bände, S. 56–75). Beck.

Biegger, S. (2022). 30 Milliarden-Aufbaufonds. Flutopfer hoffen auf schnelle Hilfe. *Tagesschau* 07.09.2021. https://www.tagesschau.de/wirtschaft/unternehmen/wiederaufbaufonds-fluthilfe-101.html. Zugegriffen: 10. März 2022.

Bick, A. (2012). *Die Steinzeit.* (2., Korr. u. ak. Aufl.) Theiss in Wissenschaftliche Buchgesellschaft (WBG).

Bofinger, P. (2015). Adam Smith. Der Segen des Egoismus. In L. Nienhaus (Hrsg.), *Die Weltverbesserer – 66 große Denker, die unser Leben verändern* (S. 31–34). Hanser.

Böhm, S. (1996). Die Verfassung der Freiheit. In N. Piper (Hrsg.), *Die großen Ökonomen. Leben und Werk der wirtschaftswissenschaftlichen Vordenker* (2., überarb. Aufl., S. 105–111). Schäffer-Poeschel.

Böhm, S. (2009a). Joseph A. Schumpeter. In H. D. Kurz (Hrsg.), *Klassiker des ökonomischen Denkens* (Bd. 2, S. 137–160). Beck.

Böhm, S. (2009b). Friedrich August von Hayek. In H. D. Kurz (Hrsg.), *Klassiker des ökonomischen Denkens* (Bd. 2, S. 228–249). Beck.

Bohmeyer, M., & Cornelsen, C. (2019). Bedingungsloses Grundeinkommen. 1000 Euro mehr im Monat – auch für Managersöhne und Sozialamtbetrüger. *Die Zeit* 23.01.2019. https://www.zeit.de/arbeit/2019-01/bedingungsloses-grundeinkommen-michael-bohmeyer-buchauszug/komplettansicht. Zugegriffen: 18. März 2019.

Born, K. E. (1989). Jean Baptiste Colbert. In J. Starbatty (Hrsg.), *Klassiker des ökonomischen Denkens* (2 Bände, S. 96–113).Beck.

Bortis, H. (o. J.). *Anfänge der Wirtschaft und Wirtschaft der Antike*. https://www.unifr.ch/withe/assets/files/Bachelor/ Wirtschaftsgeschichte/Anfaenge_der_Wirtschaft_Wige.pdf. Zugegriffen: 19. März 2019.

Braunberger, G. (2008). Ordoliberalismus. Das verwaiste Erbe der Freiburger Schule. *FAZ* 19.06.2008. https://www.faz. net/aktuell/ordoliberalismus-das-verwaiste-erbe-der-freiburg- er-schule-1912163-p2.html. Zugegriffen: 20. März 2019.

Braunberger, G. (2015). Friedrich List. Der Feuerkopf der Globalisierung. In L. Nienhaus (Hrsg.), *Die Weltverbesserer – 66 große Denker, die unser Leben verändern* (S. 23–26). Hanser.

Braunberger, G. (2015a). Joseph Schumpeter, Vergesst mir die Banken nicht. In L. Nienhaus (Hrsg.), *Die Weltverbesserer – 66 große Denker, die unser Leben verändern* (S. 249–253). Hanser.

Braunberger, G. (2015b). Walter Eucken. Der wahre Neoliberale. In L. Nienhaus (Hrsg.), *Die Weltverbesserer – 66 große Denker, die unser Leben verändern* (S. 63–67). Hanser.

Bräutigam, T. (2013). *Knappe Rohstoffe. Wann bauen wir das letzte Windrad?*https://www.wiwo.de/technologie/green/knappe-ro- hstoffe-wann-bauen-wir-das-letzte-windrad/13547618.html. *Zugegriffen: 13. März 2019.*

Brodersen, K. (Hrsg.). (2006). *Aristoteles – 77 Tricks zur Steigerung der Staatseinnahmen, Oikonomika II*. Reclam.

Brost, M. (1999). Immer alles im Lot. Jean-Baptiste Say: Traité d'Économie Politique. *Die Zeit* 27.05.1999. https://www. zeit.de/1999/22/199922.biblio-serie_3_s.xml. Zugegriffen: 14. März 2019.

Bundeszentrale für politische Bildung. (2018). *Entwicklung des grenzüberschreitenden Warenhandels*. http://www.bpb. de/nachschlagen/zahlen-und-fakten/globalisierung/52543/ entwicklung-des-warenhandels. Zugegriffen: 15. März 2019.

Bundeszentrale für politische Bildung bpb. (2016). *Weltbruttoinlandsprodukt*. 12.06.2016. http://www.bpb.

de/nachschlagen/zahlen-und-fakten/globalisierung/52655/welt-bruttoinlandsprodukt. Zugegriffen: 1. Apr. 2019.

Caspari, V. (2009). John Maynard Keynes. In H. D. Kurz (Hrsg.), *Klassiker des ökonomischen Denkens* (Bd. 2, S. 161–186). Beck.

Daniels, A. (1996). Zölle fürs Vaterland. In N. Piper (Hrsg.), *Die großen Ökonomen. Leben und Werk der wirtschaftswissenschaftlichen Vordenker* (2., überarb. Aufl., S. 127–132). Schäffer-Poeschel.

Dettling, W. (1996). Wie modern ist die Antike? In N. Piper (Hrsg.), *Die großen Ökonomen. Leben und Werk der wirtschaftswissenschaftlichen Vordenker* (2., überarb. Aufl., S. 3–7). Schäffer-Poeschel.

de Marchi, M. (1989). John Stuart Mill. In J. Starbatty (Hrsg.), *Klassiker des ökonomischen Denkens* (2 Bände, S. 266–290). Beck.

Diekmann, F. (2018). Superreiche: 45 Deutsche besitzen so viel wie die ärmere Hälfte der Bevölkerung. *Spiegel.* http://www.spiegel.de/wirtschaft/soziales/vermoegen-45-superreiche-besitzen-so-viel-wie-die-halbe-deutsche-bevoelkerung-a-1189111.html. Zugegriffen: 23. Jan. 2018.

Dönhoff, M. G. (1997). *Zivilisiert den Kapitalismus. Grenzen der Freiheit.* DVA.

Dullien, S. (2021). Weltwirtschaft: Nach Corona kommt die Deglobalisierung. *Hans Böckler Stiftung.* https://www.boeckler.de/data/impuls_2021_02_S2-3.pdf. Zugegriffen: 28. Juni 2021.

Eckert, D. (2018). Automatisierung. Diese Jobs sind besonders von Robotern bedroht. *Die Welt* 16.02.2018. https://www.welt.de/wirtschaft/article173642209/Jobverlust-Diese-Jobs-werden-als-erstes-durch-Roboter-ersetzt.html. Zugegriffen: 18. März 2019.

Eisermann, G. (1989). Vilfredo Pareto. In J. Starbatty (Hrsg.), *Klassiker des ökonomischen Denkens* (Bd. 2, S. 158–174). Beck.

Eltis, W. (1989). David Ricardo. In J. Starbatty (Hrsg.), *Klassiker des ökonomischen Denkens* (2 Bände, S. 188–207). Beck.

Erhard, L. (1964). *8. Aufl., bearbeitet von Wolfram Langer.* https://www.ludwig-erhard.de/wp-content/uploads/wohlstand_fuer_alle1.pdf. Zugegriffen: 17. Juni 2018.

Eschbacher, V. (2017). Warum Republikaner Obamacare verabscheuen. *Tiroler Tageszeitung* 24.02.2017. https://www.tt.com/politik/weltpolitik/12664194/warum-republikaner-obamacare-verabscheuen. Zugegriffen: 29. Mai 2019.

Ettel, A., & Zschäpitz, H. (2015). *Zufriedenheit und Gehalt – Die Wahrheit über Glück.* https://www.welt.de/wirtschaft/article147904505/Zufriedenheit-und-Gehalt-Die-Wahrheit-ueber-Glueck.html. Zugegriffen: 13. März 2019.

Europäisches Parlament. (2018). *Plastikmüll und Recycling in der EU: Zahlen und Fakten.* http://www.europarl.europa.eu/news/de/headlines/society/20181212STO21610/plastikmull-und-recycling-in-der-eu-zahlen-und-fakten. Zugegriffen: 08. Mai 2019.

Europäischer Rat. (2022). Restriktive Maßnahmen der EU als Reaktion auf die Krise in der Ukraine. *Europäischer Rat*https://www.consilium.europa.eu/de/policies/sanctions/restrictive-measures-ukraine-crisis/. *Zugegriffen: 10. März 2022.*

Faigle, P. (2010). *Reichtumsstudie: 60.000 Euro reichen für ein schönes Leben.* https://www.zeit.de/wirtschaft/2010-09/studie-reichtum-glueck. Zugegriffen: 13. März 2019.

Feldenkirchen, M. (2015). Vereinigte Oligarchen von Amerika. *Spiegel* 29.08.2015. http://www.spiegel.de/spiegel/print/d-138379369.html. Zugegriffen: 14. März 2019.

Felderer, B. (1989). Léon Walras. In J. Starbatty (Hrsg.), *Klassiker des ökonomischen Denkens* (Bd. 2, S. 59–75). Beck.

Festinger, L. (2001). *A theory of cognitive dissonance* (Combined Academic Publ. Zuerst veröffentlicht 1957). Stanford University Press.

Fischer, M. (2011). Der Freihändler. *Wirtschaftswoche* 04.12.2011. https://www.wiwo.de/politik/konjunktur/david-ricardo-der-freihaendler/5886714.html. Zugegriffen: 14. März 2019.

Flämig, H. (2018). *Luft- und Klimabelastung durch Güterverkehr.* Forschungsinformations- system (FIS) Mobilität und Verkehr. https://www.forschungsinformationssystem.de/servlet/is/39787/. Zugegriffen: 18. März 2019.

Flashar, H. (2013). *Aristoteles – Lehrer des Abendlandes.* Beck.

Fratzscher, M. (2022). *Geld oder Leben. Wie unser irrationales Verhältnis zum Geld die Gesellschaft spaltet.* Berlin.

Frenkel, R. (1996). Gelächter im Gottesdienst. In N. Piper (Hrsg.), *Die großen Ökonomen. Leben und Werk der wirtschaftswissenschaftlichen Vordenker* (2., überarb. Aufl., S. 218–222). Schäffer-Poeschel.

Fricke, T. (2018). Reich und arm. Wie der Immobilienboom das Land spaltet. *Spiegel* 29.09.2018. http://www.spiegel.de/wirtschaft/service/immobilien-wie-der-boom-die-spaltung-der-gesellschaft-vertieft-a-1230495.html. Zugegriffen: 15. März 2019.

Friedman, M. (1953). *Essays in positive economics.* https://pdfs.semanticscholar.org/4af4/acabcbae145c9d21bca3cfb-34fdbb55282a0.pdf. Zugegriffen: 23. Juni 2018.

Friedman, M. (2016). *Kapitalismus und Freiheit* (11. Aufl. mit einem Geleitwort von Horst Siebert). Piper.

Gabriel, M., & Scobel, G. (2021). *Zwischen Gut und Böse. Philosophie der radikalen Mitte.* Edition Körber.

Gaertner, W. (2009). Amartya Sen. In H. D. Kurz (Hrsg.), *Klassiker des ökonomischen Denkens* (Bd. 2, S. 354–372). Beck.

Gerken, L. (Hrsg.). (2000). *Walter Eucken und sein Werk. Rückblick auf den Vordenker der Sozialen Marktwirtschaft* (Untersuchungen zur Ordnungstheorie und Ordnungspolitik (Walter Eucken Institut), Bd. 41). Mohr Siebeck.

Giesen, C., & Hägler, M. (2017). *E-Mobilität: China führt Quote für E-Autos ein.* https://www.sueddeutsche.de/wirtschaft/e-mobilitaet-china-fuehrt-quote-fuer-e-autos-ein-1.3687137. Zugegriffen: 13. März 2019.

Gilibert, G. (1989). François Quesnay. In J. Starbatty (Hrsg.), *Klassiker des ökonomischen Denkens* (2 Bände, S. 114–133). Beck.

Graß, R.-D. (1996). Marx der Bourgeoisie. In N. Piper (Hrsg.), *Die großen Ökonomen. Leben und Werk der wirtschaftswissenschaftlichen Vordenker* (2., überarb. Aufl., S. 69–74). Schäffer-Poeschel.

Habekuß, F. (2019). *Artensterben. Wie geht es den Arten?* https://www.zeit.de/2019/03/artensterben-oekosystem-umweltschutz-zerstoerung. *Zugegriffen: 13. März 2019.*

Haidacher, B. (2015). *Bargeldmetaphern im Französischen. Pragmatik, Sprachkultur und Metaphorik.* Frank& Timme.
Hank, R., & Petersdorff, von W. (2013). Gewinne privatisieren, Verluste sozialisieren. *FAZ* 22.12.2013. https://www.faz.net/aktuell/wirtschaft/wirtschaftspolitik/gewinne-privatisieren-verluste-sozialisieren-wie-wir-lernten-die-banken-zu-hassen-12722023.html. Zugegriffen: 18. März 2019.
Harvard. (2019). *HarvardX.* Free online courses from Harvard University. https://www.edx.org/school/harvardx. Zugegriffen: 18. März 2019.
Hasse, E. S. (2012). Brotzeit. Uschi Glas engagiert sich für Schulkinder. *Welt* 07.05.2012. https://www.welt.de/regionales/hamburg/article106269940/Uschi-Glas-engagiert-sich-fuer-Schulkinder.html. Zugegriffen: 21. März 2019.
Häuser, K. (1989). Friedrich List. In J. Starbatty (Hrsg.), *Klassiker des ökonomischen Denkens* (2 Bände, S. 225–244). Beck.
Hayek, F. A. (2007). *The road to serfdom text and documents. Nachdruck der Originalversion von 1944.* The University of Chicago Press.
Hennings, K.-H. (1989). Eugen von Böhm-Bawerk. In J. Starbatty (Hrsg.), *Klassiker des ökonomischen Denkens* (Bd. 2, S. 175–190). Beck.
Herrmann, U. (2016). *Kein Kapitalismus ist auch keine Lösung. Die Krise der heutigen Ökonomie oder was wir von Smith, Marx und Keynes lernen können* (3. Aufl.). Westend.
Heuser, U. J. (1996). Geld, Freiheit, Ideologie. In N. Piper (Hrsg.), *Die großen Ökonomen. Leben und Werk der wirtschaftswissenschaftlichen Vordenker* (2., überarb. Aufl., S. 274–280). Schäffer-Poeschel.
Heuser, U. J. (2012). Schreck der Ökonomen. *Die Zeit* 16.05.2012. https://www.zeit.de/2012/21/L-P-Kahneman/komplettansicht. Zugegriffen: 20. März 2019.
Heuser, U. J. (2018). Ökonomie: Was wissen Sie über Wirtschaft? *Die Zeit* 31.01.2018. https://www.zeit.de/2018/06/oekonomie-wirtschaft-grundwissen. Zugegriffen: 14. März 2019.
Höffe, O. (2015). Platon. Griechenlands bester Ökonom. In L. Nienhaus (Hrsg.), *Die Weltverbesserer – 66 große Denker, die unser Leben verändern* (S. 129–131). Hanser.

Hoffmann, J. (1992). Alles pendelt sich ein. *Die Zeit* Nr. 49/1992 vom 27.11.1992. https://www.zeit.de/1992/49/alles-pendelt-sich-ein. Zugegriffen: 14. März 2019.

Hoffmann, T. S. (2009). *Wirtschaftsphilosophie – Ansätze und Perspektiven von der Antike bis heute*. Marix.

Holderied, T. (2010). Ich weiß nicht, was ich ohne Obamacare tun soll. *jetzt* 06.05.2017. https://www.jetzt.de/usa/junge-amerikaner-sagen-ihre-meinung-zu-obamacare. Zugegriffen: 14. März 2019.

Honey. C. (2016). Überfischung. Wir essen die Weltmeere leer. *Die Zeit* 19.01.2016. https://www.zeit.de/wissen/umwelt/2016-01/ueberfischung-bedrohung-arten-fehler-angaben. Zugegriffen: 15. März 2019.

Horn, K. (2015a). Carl Menger. Die Preise richten sich nicht nach den Kosten. In L. Nienhaus (Hrsg.), *Die Weltverbesserer – 66 große Denker, die unser Leben verändern* (S. 199–202). Hanser.

Horn, K. (2015b). Friedrich August von Hayek. Wider die Anmaßung von Wissen. In L. Nienhaus (Hrsg.), *Die Weltverbesserer – 66 große Denker, die unser Leben verändern* (S. 57–59). Hanser.

Hülser, K. H. (Hrsg.). (1991a). *Platon. Sämtliche Werke griechisch und deutsch* (10 Bände). Insel.

Hülser, K. H. (Hrsg.). (1991b). *Platon. Sämtliche Werke griechisch und deutsch* (Bd. 10). Insel.

Hurtz, S. (2017). Sind Smartphones doch etwa ein Problem? *SZ* 25.10.2017. https://www.sueddeutsche.de/digital/dokureihe-homo-digitalis-sind-smartphones-vielleicht-doch-ein-problem-1.3723358. Zugegriffen: 18. März 2019.

IAB. (2021). Wie stellen sich Arbeitnehmer das Arbeiten nach der Pandemie vor? *Techniker Krankenkasse* zitiert aus der Studie des Instituts für Arbeitsmarkt- und Berufsforschung (IAB). https://www.tk.de/firmenkunden/service/fachthemen/coronavirus-arbeitgeber/homeoffice-nach-corona-2104308. Zugegriffen: 27. Juni 2021.

Janssen, H. (2009). Walter Eucken. In H. D. Kurz (Hrsg.), *Klassiker des ökonomischen Denkens* (Bd. 2, S. 187–204). Beck.

Kahneman, D. (2012). *Schnelles Denken, langsames Denken*. Penguin.

Kaier, E. (Hrsg.). (1974). *Grundzüge der Geschichte: Band 1 Von der Urgeschichte bis zum Ende der Völkerwanderungszeit* (Moritz Diesterweg 12. Aufl.). Moritz Diesterweg, cop.

Karier, T. (2010). *Intellectual capital – Forty years of the nobel prize in economics*. Cambridge University Press.

Kaufmann, S. (2017). *Millionärssteuer. So viel zahlen Menschen mit hohem Einkommen*. https://www.berliner-zeitung.de/wirtschaft/millionaerssteuer-so-viel-steuern-zahlen-menschen-mit-hohem-einkommen-27875330. Zugegriffen: 3. Mai 2019.

Kennedy, J. F. (1961). *Antrittsrede vom 20.01.1961, Deutsche Fassung.* https://www.jfklibrary.org/learn/about-jfk/historic-speeches/inaugural-address. Zugegriffen: 29. Mai 2019.

Keynes, J. M. (2016). *The economic consequences of the peace*. Introduction by Former Chair of the Federal Reserve Paul Volcker. Skyhorse Publishing/Anodos Books, Whithorn, Reissue 2016 (originally published 1919).

Keynes, J. M. (2017). *Allgemeine Theorie der Beschäftigung, des Zinses und des Geldes* (Neuübersetzung von Nicola Liebert). Duncker & Humblot.

Kirk, G. S., Raven, J. E., & Schofield, J. (2001). *Die vorsokratischen Philosophen. Einführung, Texte und Kommentare*. Metzler.

Klier, A. (2009). *Amartya Kumar Sen & Martha Craven Nussbaum. Jedem nach seinen Befähigungen*. https://www.alexander-klier.net/wp-content/uploads/2012/06/Artikel-Bef%C3%A4higungen.pdf. Zugegriffen: 20. März 2019.

Knauer, R. (2015). 25 Jahre FCKW-Verbot. Es bleibt ein Loch ohne Boden. *Spektrum der Wissenschaft*. https://www.spektrum.de/news/25-jahre-fckw-verbot-wie-steht-es-um-das-ozonloch/1352353. Zugegriffen: 21. März 2019.

Kohlenberg, K., & Uchatius, W. (2008). Finanzkrise. Wo ist das Geld geblieben? *Die Zeit* 27.02.2008. https://www.zeit.de/2008/49/DOS-Wo-steckt-das-Geld. Zugegriffen: 19. März 2019.

Köhler, B. (2006). Serie Ökonomen: Amartya Sen: Das Gewissen der Ökonomie. *Bilanz* 14.03.2006. https://www.bilanz.

ch/unternehmen/serie-oekonomen-amartya-sen-das-gewissen-der-oekonomie#. Zugegriffen: 20. März 2019.

Krelle, W. (1989). Jean-Baptiste Say. In J. Starbatty (Hrsg.), *Klassiker des ökonomischen Denkens* (2 Bände, S. 172–187). Beck.

Krieger, A. (2016). *Plastikmüll im Meer. Zahlen und Fakten nach Meeresregionen.* http://anjakrieger.com/2016/06/02/plastikmuell-meer-zahlen-region-vergleich/#5. Zugegriffen: 18. März 2019.

Küng, H. (2010). *Anständig wirtschaften – Warum Ökonomie Moral braucht.* Piper.

Kurz, H. D. (1996a). Das System der natürlichen Freiheit. In N. Piper (Hrsg.), *Die großen Ökonomen. Leben und Werk der wirtschaftswissenschaftlichen Vordenker* (2., überarb. Aufl., S. 29–36). Schäffer-Poeschel.

Kurz, H. D. (1996b). Geiz der Natur. In N. Piper (Hrsg.), *Die großen Ökonomen. Leben und Werk der wirtschaftswissenschaftlichen Vordenker* (2., überarb. Aufl., S. 37–43). Schäffer-Poeschel.

Kurz, H. D. (Hrsg.). (2009). *Klassiker des ökonomischen Denkens* (Bd. 2). Beck.

Kurz, H. D. (2015). Karl Marx. Die Entzauberung des Kapitalismus. In L. Nienhaus (Hrsg.), *Die Weltverbesserer – 66 große Denker, die unser Leben verändern* (S. 78–81). Hanser.

Lange, K. (2018). Wie Digitalisierung die Arbeitswelt verändert. Wer Karriere macht und wer um seinen Job bangen muss. Interview Lange K mit Penning S. *Manager Magazin* 26.10.2018. http://www.manager-magazin.de/unternehmen/artikel/karriere-und-jobverlust-digitaler-wandel-veraendert-arbeitswelt-a-1127180.html. Zugegriffen: 18. März 2019.

Lee, F. (2017). Klimaschutz in China. „Kohlefreie Zone" in Peking. *Die Zeit* 17.10.2017. https://www.zeit.de/wirtschaft/2017-10/klimaschutz-klimawandel-china-regierung-smog-emissionen. Zugegriffen: 21. März 2019.

Lenel, H. O. (1989). Walter Eucken. In J. Starbatty (Hrsg.), *Klassiker des ökonomischen Denkens* (Bd. 2, S. 292–311). Beck.

References

Leube, K. R. (1996). Das Ich und der Wert. In N. Piper (Hrsg.), *Die großen Ökonomen. Leben und Werk der wirtschaftswissenschaftlichen Vordenker* (2., überarb. Aufl., S. 91–96). Schäffer-Poeschel.

Lingen, M. (2019). *Alfred Müller-Armack*. Internetseite der Konrad-Adenauer-Stiftung. https://www.kas.de/web/geschichte-der-cdu/personen/biogramm-detail/-/content/alfred-mueller-armack-v1. Zugegriffen: 20. März 2019.

Lütge, C., & Esfeld, M. (2021). *Und die Freiheit? Wie die Corona-Politik und der Missbrauch der Wissenschaft unsere offene Gesellschaft bedrohen*. Riva.

Lütge, C., & Uhl, M. (2017). *Wirtschaftsethik*. Vahlen.

Mankiw, G. N., & Taylor, M. P. (2012). *Grundzüge der Volkswirtschaftslehre* (5., Überarb. u. erweit. Aufl.). Schäffer-Poeschel.

Marx, K. (2009). *Das Kapital – Kritik der politischen Ökonomie* (Ungekürzte Ausgabe nach der zweiten Auflage von 1872 mit einem Geleitwort von Karl Korsch aus dem Jahre 1932, unveränderter Nachdruck). Anaconda.

Marx, K., & Engels, F. (1983). *Manifest der Kommunistischen Partei*. Nachdruck Reclam.

März, E. (1989). Joseph Alois Schumpeter. In J. Starbatty (Hrsg.), *Klassiker des ökonomischen Denkens* (Bd. 1, S. 251–272). Beck.

McKinsey. (2015). *McKinsey connectivity and autonomous driving consumer survey 2015*. McKinsey.

Meadows, D. (1972). *Die Grenzen des Wachstums. Bericht des Club of Rome zur Lage der Menschheit*. Deutsche Verlagsanstalt.

Merkel, W. W. (2013). Fracking: zu viele Risiken, zu wenig Wissen. *Welt* 11.07.2013. https://www.welt.de/wissenschaft/article117938329/Fracking-zu-viele-Risiken-zu-wenig-Wissen.html. Zugegriffen: 15. März 2019.

Merz, S. L. (2015). Industrie 4.0 ist keine Theorie mehr. Die vierte industrielle Revolution kommt in der Wirklichkeit an. *Computerwoche* 21.12.2015. https://www.computerwoche.de/a/die-vierte-industrielle-revolution-kommt-in-der-wirklichkeit-an,3096002. Zugegriffen: 18. März 2019.

Mierzejewski, A. C. (2005). *Ludwig Erhard. Der Wegbereiter der Sozialen Marktwirtschaft. Biografie.* Siedler.
Mill, J. S. (2004). *Principles of political economy* (Great mind series). Prometheus Books.
Müller, C. (2015). *Nachhaltige Ökonomie. Ziele, Herausforderungen und Lösungswege.* de Gruyter Oldenbourg.
Müller-Armack, A. (1990). *Wirtschaftslenkung und Marktwirtschaft* (Sonderausgabe). Kastell.
Nienhaus, L. (2009). *Die Blindgänger: Warum die Ökonomen auch künftige Krisen nicht erkennen werden.* Campus.
Nienhaus, L. (Hrsg.). (2015). *Die Weltverbesserer – 66 große Denker, die unser Leben verändern.* Hanser.
Oberhuber, N. (2015). Glyphosat: Gift für mehr Wachstum. *Die Zeit* 06.08.2015. https://www.zeit.de/wirtschaft/2015-08/glyphosat-unkrautvernichter-krebs-landwirtschaft-ertraege-monsanto/komplettansicht. Zugegriffen: 15. März 2019.
Oltmanns, T. (1996a). Ökonomie gegen die Armut. In N. Piper (Hrsg.), *Die großen Ökonomen. Leben und Werk der wirtschaftswissenschaftlichen Vordenker* (2., überarb. Aufl., S. 75–81). Schäffer-Poeschel.
Oltmanns, T. (1996b). Die Weisheit des Auktionators. In N. Piper (Hrsg.), *Die großen Ökonomen. Leben und Werk der wirtschaftswissenschaftlichen Vordenker* (2., überarb. Aufl., S. 63–68). Schäffer-Poeschel.
Oswalt, W. (1996). Die Ordnung der Freiheit. In N. Piper (Hrsg.), *Die großen Ökonomen. Leben und Werk der wirtschaftswissenschaftlichen Vordenker* (2., überarb. Aufl., S. 195–207). Schäffer-Poeschel.
Ott, A. E. (1989). Karl Marx. In J. Starbatty (Hrsg.), *Klassiker des ökonomischen Denkens* (Bd. 2, S. 7–35). Beck.
Oxfam. (2017). *8 Männer besitzen so viel wie die ärmere Hälfte der Weltbevölkerung.* https://www.oxfam.de/ueber-uns/aktuelles/2017-01-16-8-maenner-besitzen-so-viel-aermere-haelfte-weltbevoelkerung. Zugegriffen: 14. März 2019.
Oxfam. (2018). *Bericht zur sozialen Ungleichheit: 82 Prozent des weltweiten Vermögenswachstums geht ans reichste Prozent der*

Bevölkerung. https://www.oxfam.de/presse/pressemitteilungen/2018-01-22-82-prozent-weltweiten-vermoegenswachstums-geht-ans-reichste. Zugegriffen: 14. März 2019.
Paech, N. (2012). *Befreiung vom Überfluss. Auf dem Weg in die Postwachstumsökonomie.* Oekom.
Paech, N. (2019). *Grundzüge einer Postwachstumsökonomie.* http://www.Postwachstumsoekonomie.de/material/grundzuege/. Zugegriffen: 15. März 2019.
Pietsch, D. (2014). *Mensch und Welt – Versuch einer Gesamtbetrachtung.* Eul/Lohmar.
Pietsch, D. (2017). *Grenzen des ökonomischen Denkens – Wo bleibt der Mensch in der Wirtschaft?* Eul/Lohmar.
Pietsch, D. (2020). *Prinzipien moderner Ökonomie. Ökologisch, ethisch, digital.* Springer.
Pietsch, D. (2021). *Die Ökonomie und das Nichts. Warum Wirtschaft ohne Moral wertlos ist.* Springer.
Pietsch, D. (2022). *Unsere Wirtschaft ethisch überdenken. Eine Aufforderung.* Springer.
Piketty, T. (2014a). *Das Kapital im 21. Jahrhundert.* Beck.
Piketty, T. (2014b). *Capital in the twenty-first century.* Boston: Harvard University Press. Deutsche Ausgabe. *Das Kapital im 21. Jahrhundert.* Beck.
Piper, N. (1996a). Der Unternehmer als Pionier. In*Die großen Ökonomen. Leben und Werk der wirtschaftswissenschaftlichen Vordenker* (2., überarb. Aufl., S. 97–104). Schäffer-Poeschel.
Piper, N. (Hrsg.). (1996b). *Die großen Ökonomen. Leben und Werk der wirtschaftswissenschaftlichen Vordenker* (2., überarb. Aufl.). Schäffer-Poeschel.
Platon (1991a). Theaitetos. Sämtliche Werke IV. In K. H. Hülser (Hrsg.), *Sämtliche Werke griechisch und deutsch* (Bd. 10). Insel.
Platon (1991b). Politeia. Sämtliche Werke V. In K. H. Hülser (Hrsg.), *Sämtliche Werke griechisch und deutsch* (Bd. 10). Insel.
Platon (1991c). Nomoi. Sämtliche Werke IX. In K. H. Hülser (Hrsg.), *Sämtliche Werke griechisch und deutsch* (Bd. 10). Insel.
Plickert, P. (2008). Joseph Stiglitz. Kassandra der Finanzkrise. *FAZ* 06.10.2008. https://www.faz.net/aktuell/beruf-chance/

mein-weg/joseph-stiglitz-kassandra-der-finanzkrise-1714311. html?printPagedArticle=true#pageIndex_0. Zugegriffen: 20. März 2019.

Plickert, P. (2015). Ludwig von Mises. Der letzte liberale Ritter. In L. Nienhaus (Hrsg.), *Die Weltverbesserer – 66 große Denker, die unser Leben verändern* (S. 38–41). Hanser.

Precht, R. D. (2016). *Tiere denken. Vom Recht der Tiere und den Grenzen des Menschen.* Goldmann.

Precht, R. D. (2018). *Jäger, Hirten, Kritiker: Eine Utopie für die digitale Gesellschaft.* Goldmann.

Precht, R. D. (2022). *Freiheit für alle. Das Ende der Arbeit wie wir sie kannten.* Goldmann.

Radtke, R. (2022). Todesfälle mit Coronavirus (COVID-19) nach Ländern 2022. https://de.statista.com/statistik/daten/studie/1100818/umfrage/todesfaelle-aufgrund-des-coronavirus-2019-ncov-nach-laendern/. Zugegriffen: 10. März 2022.

Rau, K. (2021). Arbeitswelt nach Corona. „Hybrides Arbeiten ist sicherlich die anstrengendste Form", Interview mit der Arbeitsforscherin Barbara Stöttinger. *Wirtschaftswoche* 27.05.2021. https://www.wiwo.de/erfolg/beruf/arbeitswelt-nach-corona-hybrides-arbeiten-ist-sicherlich-die-anstrengendste-form/27212258.html. Zugegriffen: 18. Okt. 2021.

Recktenwald, H. C. (1989). Adam Smith. In J. Starbatty (Hrsg.), *Klassiker des ökonomischen Denkens* (2 Bände, S. 134–155). Beck.

Reuter, H. (2014). Amazonas Regenwald: Pro Stunde werden 526 Fußballfelder abgeholzt. *Die Welt* 07.11.2014. https://www.welt.de/wissenschaft/umwelt/article134117363/Pro-Stunde-wurden-526-Fussballfelder-abgeholzt.html. Zugegriffen: 15. März 2019.

Rieter, H. (1989). Alfred Marshall. In J. Starbatty (Hrsg.), *Klassiker des ökonomischen Denkens* (Bd. 2, S. 135–157). Beck.

Rosenbach, M. (Hrsg.). (2011). *Seneca. Philosophische Schriften lateinisch und deutsch* (2. Aufl., Bd. 5). Wissenschaftliche Buchgesellschaft.

Rövekamp, M. (2016). Digitalisierung bis Demografie. Wie sich die Arbeitswelt wandelt. *Der Tagesspiegel.* https://

www.tagesspiegel.de/wirtschaft/digitalisierung-bis-demografie-wie-sich-die-arbeitswelt-wandelt/14898360.html. Zugegriffen: 18. März 2019.

Sander, O. (1996). Die Zeit gehört Gott. In N. Piper (Hrsg.), *Die großen Ökonomen. Leben und Werk der wirtschaftswissenschaftlichen Vordenker* (2., überarb. Aufl., S. 8–13). Schäffer-Poeschel.

Schefold, B. (1989). Platon und Aristoteles. In J. Starbatty (Hrsg.), *Klassiker des ökonomischen Denkens* (2 Bände, S. 19–55). Beck.

Scherf, H. (1989). John Maynard Keynes. In J. Starbatty (Hrsg.), Thomas Morus. In J. Starbatty (Hrsg.), *Klassiker des ökonomischen Denkens* (2. Bd., S. 273–291). Beck.

Schipper, L. (2015a). John Stuart Mill. Das Glück im Kapitalismus. In L. Nienhaus (Hrsg.), *Die Weltverbesserer – 66 große Denker, die unser Leben verändern* (S. 106–109). Hanser.

Schipper, L. (2015b). Thorstein Veblen. Spott auf die feinen Leute. In L. Nienhaus (Hrsg.), *Die Weltverbesserer – 66 große Denker, die unser Leben verändern* (S. 176–180). Hanser.

Schipper, L. (2015c). Amartya Sen. Anwalt der Armen. In L. Nienhaus (Hrsg.), *Die Weltverbesserer – 66 große Denker, die unser Leben verändern* (S. 150–153). Hanser.

Schipper, L. (2015e) Was eigentlich ist das Internet der Dinge? *FAZ* 17.03.2015. https://www.faz.net/aktuell/wirtschaft/cebit/cebit-was-eigentlich-ist-das-internet-der-dinge-13483592.html?printPagedArticle=true#pageIndex_0. Zugegriffen: 18. März 2019.

Schmidt, R. H. (2001). Nobelpreis. Rütteln an den Grundfesten. *Die Zeit* 18.10.2001. https://www.zeit.de/2001/43/200143_nobelpreis.xml/komplettansicht. Zugegriffen: 20. März 2019.

Schmitt, U. (2013). „Obamacare" ist Teufelswerk – und absoluter Renner. *Die Welt* 06.10.2013. https://www.welt.de/politik/ausland/article120662017/Obamacare-ist-Teufelswerk-und-absoluter-Renner.html. Zugegriffen: 29. Mai 2019.

Schömann-Finck, C. (2011). Kurz erklärt. Was sind eigentlich Leerverkäufe? *Focus Money*. https://www.focus.de/finanzen/boerse/kurz-erklaert-was-sind-eigentlich-leerverkaeufe_aid:505874.html. Zugegriffen: 21. März 2019.

Schröder, U. (2022). Russland-Ukraine-Krieg/Chancen und Gefahren von Sanktionen gegen Putin. *Deutschlandfunk* 10.03.2022. https://www.deutschlandfunk.de/sanktionen-gegen-putin-russland-ukraine-krieg-100.html. Zugegriffen: 10. März 2022.

Schultz, S. (2013). So rechnet Apple seine Steuerlast klein. *Spiegel* 21. Mai 2013. http://www.spiegel.de/wirtschaft/unternehmen/apples-steuertricks-in-der-uebersicht-a-901015.html. Zugegriffen: 15. März 2019.

Schwarz, G. (2015). Milton Friedman. Konsequent liberal. In L. Nienhaus (Hrsg.), *Die Weltverbesserer – 66 große Denker, die unser Leben verändern* (S. 209–212). Hanser.

Sen, A. (2000). Ökonomie für den Menschen – Wege zu Gerechtigkeit und Solidarität in der Marktwirtschaft. Hanser (Titel der Originalausgabe (1999) Development as freedom. New York: Oxford University Press).

Senzel, H. (2022). Jahrhundert-Hochwasser bedroht Sydney. *Tagesschau* 03.03.2022. https://www.tagesschau.de/ausland/ozeanien/flut-australien-103.html. Zugegriffen: 10. März 2022.

Siedenbiedel, C. (2013). Ökonom Gary Becker: Gegensätze ziehen sich an. *FAZ* 01.08.2013. https://www.faz.net/aktuell/wirtschaft/menschen-wirtschaft/oekonom-gary-becker-gegensaetze-ziehen-sich-an-12308018.html. Zugegriffen: 14. März 2019.

Smith, A. (2009). *Wohlstand der Nationen*. Nach der Übersetzung von Max Stirner, herausgegeben von Heinrich Schmidt. Anaconda.

Smith, A. (2010). *Theorie der ethischen Gefühle* (Philosophische Bibliothek Felix Meiner Band 605, übersetzt von Eckstein, W. und herausgegeben von Brandt, H.D.). Felix Meiner.

Spahn, H.-P. (2009). Milton Friedman. In H. D. Kurz (Hrsg.), *Klassiker des ökonomischen Denkens* (Bd. 2, S. 282–300). Beck.

References

Spiegel Online (o. V.) (2018). *Mieten sollen erneut kräftig steigen* 26.12.2018. https://www.spiegel.de/wirtschaft/service/deutschland-mieten-sollen-2019-um-bis-zu-fuenf-prozent-steigen-a-1245410.html. Zugegriffen: 29. Mai 2019.

Spiegel Online. (11.06.2021). G7 Staaten wollen ärmeren Ländern eine Milliarde Impfdosen bereitstellen. *Spiegel* 11.06.2021. https://www.spiegel.de/ausland/corona-g7-staaten-wollen-aermeren-laendern-eine-milliarde-impfdosen-bereitstellen-a-23f47dd0-2acb-4836-940c-a4f83a72b9a5. Zugegriffen: 20. Juni 2021.

Starbatty, J. (Hrsg.). (1989). *Klassiker des ökonomischen Denkens* (2 Bände). Beck.

Starbatty, J. (1996). Weltgeschichte mit Heilsplan. In N. Piper (Hrsg.), *Die großen Ökonomen. Leben und Werk der wirtschaftswissenschaftlichen Vordenker* (2., überarb. Aufl., S. 211–217). Schäffer-Poeschel.

Statistisches Bundesamt. (2021). Die Folgen der Corona-Pandemie in 10 Zahlen, Pressemitteilung Nr. N 023 vom 31.März 2021. *Statistisches Bundesamt.*https://www.destatis.de/DE/Presse/Pressemitteilungen/2021/03/PD21_N023_p001.html. *Zugegriffen: 20. Juni 2021.*

Stehle, A. (2014). Jedes Angebot schafft sich seine Nachfrage. *Wirtschaftswoche* 06.02.2014. https://www.wiwo.de/politik/konjunktur/geistesblitze-der-oekonomie-xiv-jedes-angebot-schafft-sich-seine-nachfrage/9412150.html. Zugegriffen: 29. Mai 2019.

Steinhilber, J. (2021). Wie sich die Globalisierung nach Corona verändern muss. Zeit für einen grundlegenden Wandel. *Neue Gesellschaft*. Frankfurter Hefte Ausgabe 04/2021. https://www.frankfurter-hefte.de/artikel/zeit-fuer-einen-grundlegenden-wandel-3173/. Zugegriffen: 28. Juni 2021.

Steinmann, G. (1989). Thomas Robert Malthus. In J. Starbatty (Hrsg.), *Klassiker des ökonomischen Denkens* (2 Bände, S. 156–171). Beck.

Stiglitz, J. E. (2002). *Globalization and its discontents*. Norton.

Stiglitz, J. E. (2015). *The Great Divide – unequal societies and what we can do about them*. Norton.

Straubhaar. (2017) Dieser Nobelpreisträger brach mit allen Heiligtümern. *Die Welt* 10.10.2017. https://www.welt.de/wirtschaft/article169490204/Dieser-Nobelpreistraeger-brach-mit-allen-Heiligtuemern.html. Zugegriffen: 20. März 2019.

Streissler, E. (1989). Carl Menger. In J. Starbatty (Hrsg.), *Klassiker des ökonomischen Denkens* (Bd. 2, S. 119–134). Beck.

Streminger, G. (2017). *Adam Smith. Wohlstand und Moral – Eine Biographie.* Beck.

Ter Haseborg, V. (2021). Lieferketten: Globalisierungs-Killer Corona? Von wegen! *Wirtschaftswoche* 04.06.2021. https://www.wiwo.de/politik/konjunktur/lieferketten-globalisierungs-killer-corona-von-wegen/27254224.html. Zugegriffen: 28. Juni 2021.

Thornton, P. (2015). *Die großen Ökonomen. 10 Vordenker deren Werk unser Leben verändert hat.* Börsenbuch.

Tierschutzbund. (2019). *Kosmetikpositivliste.* https://www.tierschutzbund.de/information/service/publikationen/kosmetik-positivliste/. Zugegriffen: 15. März 2019.

Umweltbundesamt. (2018a). EU-Plastikstrategie: Guter Absatz aber zu unkonkret. *Umweltbundesamt.* https://www.umweltbundesamt.de/themen/eu-plastikstrategie-guter-ansatz-aber-zu-unkonkret. Zugegriffen: 18. März 2019.

Umweltbundesamt. (2018b). Biozide. *Umweltbundesamt.* https://www.umweltbundesamt.de/themen/chemikalien/biozide. Zugegriffen: 18. März 2019.

Umweltbundesamt. (2019). Verpackungen. *Umweltbundesamt* 28.12.2018. https://www.umweltbundesamt.de/themen/abfall-ressourcen/produktverantwortung-in-der-abfallwirtschaft/verpackungen#textpart-1. Zugegriffen: 18. März 2019.

Unmüßig, B. (2022). Corona-Pandemie, Impfstoffverteilung und globale Gerechtigkeit. *Heinrich Böll Stiftung* 10.02.2022. https://www.boell.de/de/2022/02/10/corona-pandemie-impfstoffverteilung-und-globale-gerechtigkeit-eine-zwischenbilanz. Zugegriffen: 10. März 2022.

Vaupel, M., & Kaul, V. (2016). *Die Geschichte(n) des Geldes. Von der Kaurischnecke zum Goldstandard – So entwickelte sich das Finanzsystem.* Börsenmedien AG.

Veblen, T. (2007). *Theorie der feinen Leute: Eine ökonomische Untersuchung der Institutionen*. Fischer Taschenbuch.

von Oertzen, P. (1991). Karl Marx. In W. Euchner (Hrsg.), *Klassiker des Sozialismus* (Bd. 1, S. 139–156). Beck.

von Petersdorff, W. (2015). Thomas Malthus. Der traurige Pastor. In L. Nienhaus (Hrsg.), *Die Weltverbesserer – 66 große Denker, die unser Leben verändern* (S. 115–118). Hanser.

von Weizsäcker, C. C. (2015). John Maynard Keynes. In L. Nienhaus (Hrsg.), *Die Weltverbesserer – 66 große Denker, die unser Leben verändern* (S. 16–19). Hanser.

Wagener, H.-J. (2009). Vilfredo Pareto. In H. D. Kurz (Hrsg.), *Klassiker des ökonomischen Denkens* (Bd. 2, S. 26–47). Beck.

Wallacher, J. (2007). *Impulse der ökonomischen Glücksforschung für die Wirtschaftsethik*. https://www.hfph.de/hochschule/lehrende/prof-dr-dr-johannes-wallacher/artikel/wallacher-personalfuehrung.pdf. Zugegriffen: 13. März 2019.

Weimann, J., Knabe, A., & Schöb, R. (2011). *Measuring happiness – The economics of well-being*. The MIT Press. Auf Deutsch erschienen (2011)*Geld macht doch glücklich: Wo die ökonomische Glücksforschung irrt*. Schäffer-Poeschel.

Weischedel, W. (2005). *Die philosophische Hintertreppe. Die großen Philosophen im Alltag und Denken* (Ungekürzte Ausgabe). Verlagsgesellschaft.

White, J. (2022). SAP erlaubt Mitarbeitern Homeoffice zu jeder Zeit. *Manager Magazin* 02.06.2021. SAP-Vorständin Julia White im Gespräch mit Reuters. https://www.manager-magazin.de/unternehmen/tech/sap-mitarbeiter-koennen-homeoffice-machen-wann-sie-wollen-a-1283fedc-dcdf-4dae-95ee-a8bc1704f101. Zugegriffen: 10. Marz 2022.

Zank, W. (1993). Reiche Bauern, reiches Land. *Die Zeit* Nr. 8/1993. https://www.zeit.de/1993/08. Zugegriffen: 19. Febr. 1993.

Zank, W. (1996a). Reiche Bauern, reiches Land. In N. Piper (Hrsg.), *Die großen Ökonomen. Leben und Werk der wirtschaftswissenschaftlichen Vordenker* (2., überarb. Aufl., S. 20–25). Schäffer-Poeschel.

Zank, W. (1996b). Der Staat als Hebel. In N. Piper (Hrsg.), *Die großen Ökonomen. Leben und Werk der wirtschaftswissenschaftlichen Vordenker* (2., überarb. Aufl., S. 157–162). Schäffer-Poeschel.

Zank, W. (1996c). Lob der Enthaltsamkeit. In N. Piper (Hrsg.), *Die großen Ökonomen. Leben und Werk der wirtschaftswissenschaftlichen Vordenker* (2., überarb. Aufl., S. 44–49). Schäffer-Poeschel.

Zank, W. (1996d). Freiheit und Sozialismus. In N. Piper (Hrsg.), *Die großen Ökonomen. Leben und Werk der wirtschaftswissenschaftlichen Vordenker* (2., überarb. Aufl., S. 55–56). Schäffer-Poeschel.

Zukunftsinstitut: Megatrends Neo-Ökologie. (2019). https://www.zukunftsinstitut.de/artikel/mtglossar/neo-oekologie-glossar/. Zugegriffen: 8. Mai 2019.

GPSR Compliance
The European Union's (EU) General Product Safety Regulation (GPSR) is a set of rules that requires consumer products to be safe and our obligations to ensure this.

If you have any concerns about our products, you can contact us on

ProductSafety@springernature.com

In case Publisher is established outside the EU, the EU authorized representative is:

Springer Nature Customer Service Center GmbH
Europaplatz 3
69115 Heidelberg, Germany

www.ingramcontent.com/pod-product-compliance
Lightning Source LLC
LaVergne TN
LVHW040730250326
834688LV00031B/234